Praise for
Lincoln's Emancipation Proclamation

"This impressive work is a splendid history of the genesis, issuance and aftermath of Lincoln's epoch-making Emancipation Proclamation . . . The political and legal reasoning behind Lincoln's series of hugely difficult decisions has never been presented so well before nor in such authoritative detail . . . It's hard to imagine that this book will soon be surpassed as the definitive work on the subject."

—*Publishers Weekly* (starred)

"Authoritative and scholarly storytelling, bursting with quotes from contemporaries and period newspapers . . . rich and compelling . . . Guelzo has begun a conversation that is long overdue. And he has done so with a book that immediately takes its place not only as the newest study of emancipation, but far and away, the very best."

—Harold Holzer, *Civil War Book Review*

"Though it was doubtless the most important document of Abraham Lincoln's presidency the Emancipation Proclamation remains a profoundly misunderstood and underappreciated work. Hopefully, that will now change, thanks to Professor Allen C. Guelzo's incisive history of the document . . . Guelzo destroys many of the popular myths concerning the Proclamation . . . and he shows convincingly how a war that had begun to preserve the Union gradually devolved into a conflict about slavery."

—*New York Post*

"The book is a tour de force, making it impossible for anyone to take seriously the simplistic views of Lincoln and the Proclamation that all too often dominate the historical debate today . . . *Lincoln's Emancipation Proclamation* is the definitive treatment of emancipation. Allen Guelzo deserves our immense gratitude for returning this critical document to its place of honor in the history of the American Republic."

—Mackubin Thomas Owens, *National Review*

"By setting the Proclamation in its exceedingly dicey context, Guelzo shows how tempting it is to read a false tidiness into political acts that in their time and place were perilously contingent, more gamble than sure thing."

—*The Washington Post*

"New research, new perspectives, new questions and new answers to old questions about this complex and endlessly fascinating man [Abraham Lincoln] continue to inspire books that are a stimulation of the mind, if not also of the flesh . . . The complex story of how the war to preserve the Union evolved into a war to give that Union 'a new birth of freedom' has been told many times—but never so well as Allen Guelzo tells it in *Lincoln's Emancipation Proclamation*." —James M. McPherson, *The Nation*

"*Lincoln's Emancipation Proclamation* restores in its fullness to our memory and understanding an unrivalled act of American statesmanship. In accomplishing this, Guelzo demonstrates the rare discernment—I do not hesitate to say wisdom—required of the serious historian . . . There is no more fitting praise for this book than to say that it is worthy of its subject."

—Peter Schramm, *The Claremont Review of Books*

"Guelzo compellingly defends President Lincoln's actions . . . His book will appeal most to those who like to steep themselves in the history of that time. But the author, with his careful use of sources, has served all of us. His book is a gentle reminder that, to understand what those in the past were up to, we need to put aside our ways of thinking and attempt to view the world through their eyes." —*News & Record* (Greensboro, NC)

"A fluent study of a transformative document in American history . . . Guelzo does a fine job of linking the legal complexities hidden within the document to other contemporary legal issues, such as Lincoln's suspension of the writ of habeas corpus . . . a valuable contribution to Civil War–era history." —*Kirkus Reviews*

"Most if not all of the preceding works [on the Emancipation Proclamation] will now pale with the publication of *Lincoln's Emancipation Proclamation*, by this highly respected Lincoln scholar . . . With this volume, decades of misunderstanding about Lincoln's most controversial action now give way to exactly what Lincoln's proclamation was, for then and for all times." —*Richmond Times-Dispatch*

"Guelzo makes a compelling case for Lincoln as the Great Emancipator and for the Proclamation as a great document in the American tradition of freedom of equality." —*Philadelphia Inquirer*

"A book of great import to anyone who wants to recover the central meaning of the Civil War and America and needs to understand the contingencies of freedom; for all libraries." —*Library Journal*

ALSO BY ALLEN C. GUELZO

Abraham Lincoln: Redeemer President

Edwards in Our Time:
Jonathan Edwards and the Shaping of American Religion
(with Sang Hyun Lee)

Holland's Life of Abraham Lincoln
(editor)

The Crisis of the American Republic:
A New History of the Civil War and Reconstruction

For the Union of Evangelical Christendom:
The Irony of the Reformed Episcopalians, 1873–1930

Manning Ferguson Force, *From Fort Henry to Corinth*
(editor)

Edwards on the Will:
A Century of American Philosophical Debate, 1750–1850

LINCOLN'S EMANCIPATION PROCLAMATION

The End of Slavery in America

Allen C. Guelzo

Simon & Schuster Paperbacks

New York London Toronto Sydney

SIMON & SCHUSTER PAPERBACKS
Rockefeller Center
1230 Avenue of the Americas
New York, NY 10020

First Simon & Schuster paperback edition 2005

SIMON & SCHUSTER PAPERBACKS and colophon are registered trademarks
of Simon & Schuster, Inc.

For information about special discounts for bulk purchases,
please contact Simon & Schuster Special Sales:
1-800-456-6798 or business@simonandschuster.com

Designed by Elliott Beard

Manufactured in the United States of America

10 9 8 7 6 5 4 3 2

The Library of Congress has cataloged the hardcover edition as follows:

Guelzo, Allen C.
    Lincoln's Emancipation Proclamation : the end of slavery in
America / Allen C. Guelzo.
        p.   cm.
    Includes bibliographical references.
    1. United States. President (1861–1865 : Lincoln).
Emancipation Proclamation.   2. Lincoln, Abraham, 1809–1865.
3. Slaves–Emancipation—United States.   I. Title.
E453.G9   2004
973.7'14—dc22   2003063310

ISBN 0-7432-2182-6

      0-7432-6297-2 (Pbk)

But what is a slave? A slave is a man robbed of his soul, he and his race, until the end of posterity; a man doomed from father to son to think with the brains and will through the volition of another; a man divested of the first sacred right of man; to wit, individuality; a being changed from his nature; in a word an artificial monster, a moral eunuch, undeserving of the deprivation. The church castrates the child to make him sing well, but you . . . castrate him that he may pick your cotton. This is the only difference.

EUGENE PELLETAN, *An Address to King Cotton*, 1863

Let it then be understood, as a great principle of political economy, that no people can be free who themselves do not constitute an essential part of the ruling element of the country in which they live. . . . The liberty of no man is secure, who controls not his own political destiny.

MARTIN R. DELANY, "The Political Destiny of the Colored Race on the American Continent," 1854

How to present unwelcome truth in a way that leads a substantial number of men and women to change how they act, how they vote, and what they uphold as law is a task worthy of a great statesman in a democracy.

JAMES R. STONER, "The Genteel Abolitionist," 2003

Those of us engaged in this racial struggle in America are like knights on horseback—the Negroes on a white horse and the white folks on a black. Sometimes the race is terrific. But the feel of the wind in your hair as you ride toward democracy is really something! And the air smells so good!

LANGSTON HUGHES, "The Fun of Being Black," 1943

When the fundamental principles of republics, nay, of all governments, are assailed with presumptuous rashness, and . . . the securities of constitutions are assailed and questioned, does our literature come out, and unmask the deceit, and vindicate the truth, or does it lie by, and with indolent ease sleep over the evils, or silently evade its duty by hoping for the best, or softly whisper regrets, lest it should rouse opposition, or encounter obloquy?

JOSEPH STORY, *Address to the Harvard Alumni Society*, August 23, 1842

FOR JOHN AND MARY ANN LEWIS

ACKNOWLEDGMENTS

IT HARDLY SEEMS FAIR that the intellectual debts I have piled up can be paid in so free and easy a currency as mere acknowledgments. But there are some debts which are never meant to be repaid, at least not in the kind of currency we give to cashiers and tellers, and these few words are simply the public avowal of those kinds of debts.

First and foremost are the debts owed to people, and principal among these are the ones owed to Michael Burlingame, the foremost Lincolnian of our generation. Michael's encouragement of this project has come in many different forms—the sharing of accommodations for a week in Springfield, photocopies of letters and documents on the Emancipation Proclamation from his overflowing files, advance texts of his edition of William O. Stoddard's newspaper dispatches, and a reading of the hesitant first pieces of the manuscript. But debts are also owed to John Sellers of the Library of Congress, who not only opened access to papers and collections but unstintingly shared transcriptions of his own editorial work on the Horatio Nelson Taft diaries and pointed out manuscript resources in other Washington-area archives I would otherwise have missed. The debt list must also include Dr. Thomas F. Schwartz of the Illinois Historic Preservation Agency and Kim Bauer of the Illinois State Historical Library, neither of whom seemed to know what the word *no* meant when I begged for copies of important materials from the various Lincoln holdings in Springfield. And then three of my students in the Templeton Honors College at Eastern University—Joshua R. Meservey, Jonathan D. Price, and Domenick Paul Rowe—happily peeled off time from summer and Christmas vacations to copy citations and, in Joshua's case, ransack the Hannibal Hamlin Papers at the University of Maine for me. A particular word of thanks goes to Harold Holzer of the Metropolitan Museum for a copy of Charles Eberstadt's *Lincoln's Emancipation Proclamation;* to Dr. H. Dean Trulear for drawing my attention to George D. Kelsey's Emancipation Day address, "Negro Americans, What Now?" in 1940; and to my nephew, Justin Hotchkiss of Boston University, for retrieving a copy of Kelsey's manuscript from the George Kelsey Papers at Drew University.

And then there are the institutions that have played more than a small role in the making of this book. Dr. James G. Basker and his staff at the Gilder-Lehrman Institute were a highly valuable resource, not only for the materials in the Gilder-Lehrman Collection but for their constant interest in and encouragement of this work. It is unusual that an administrator (or, in my case, a semi-administrator, as head of the Templeton Honors College at Eastern University as well as the Grace F. Kea Professor of American History) is allowed sabbatical leave, but Eastern's president, Dr. David Black, generously endorsed my request for leave for the academic year 2002–2003. Equal thanks go to Dr. Robert P. George and the James Madison Fellows Program at Princeton, not only for a Madison Fellowship for that year but for the delightful company at Princeton of James Stoner, Hadley Arkes, Dennis Patterson, David Dalin, Frank Beckwith, Micah Watson, Michael and Seana Sugrue, Judi Rivkin, and James McPherson, and for access to the substantial holdings of the Firestone Library of materials relating to the Emancipation Proclamation.

The Firestone Library, the Library of Congress, and the Illinois State Historical Library were only the largest of the many library and manuscript collections used for this book. In addition, I have enjoyed the most astounding helpfulness from Sean Monahan (Hawthorne-Longfellow Library at Bowdoin College), Sara Hartwell (Rauner Special Collections

Library at Dartmouth College), Jennifer Colby (Washburne Norlands Library, Livermore Falls, Maine), Mary-Jo Kline (Sterling Memorial Library Manuscripts and Archives, Yale University), Alissa Rosenberg (Minnesota Historical Society Library), Melissa Mead (Rare Books and Special Collections, Rush Rees Library, University of Rochester), Tanya Chebotarev (Rare Book and Manuscript Library at Columbia University), Robyn Train and James A. Mundy (Union League of Philadelphia), Michael Musick and Budge Weidman (National Archives), and the staffs of the State Historical Society of Wisconsin, the Bentley Historical Library at the University of Michigan, the Manuscripts and Archives Division of the New York Public Library, the New-York Historical Society, and the Houghton Library at Harvard University. My longtime affiliation with the McNeil Center for Early American Studies at the University of Pennsylvania opened access to the Van Pelt Library at Penn, for which I am particularly grateful to the center's director, Dr. Daniel K. Richter.

The availability of materials on the Internet and in CD-ROM or DVD format has played much more of a role in this book than one might expect from a researcher whose technology skills are but little advanced over hunt-and-peck. The emancipation materials posted on the University of Maryland's *Free at Last: A Documentary History of Slavery, Freedom, and the Civil War* (www.inform.umd.edu/EdRes/Colleges/ ARHU/Depts/History/Freedman) and the mammoth resources contained in the *Making of America* websites maintained by Cornell University and the University of Michigan (www.cdl.library.edu/cgi) were a scholarly cornucopia. But just as important were the transcriptions of the Abraham Lincoln Papers at the Library of Congress undertaken by the Lincoln Studies Center at Knox College (Douglas L. Wilson and Rodney O. Davis, directors) and posted on the Library of Congress website (www. memory.loc.gov/ammem/alhtml/almss). Digitized images of the *Congressional Globe*, the *Statutes at Large*, and other collections of Congressional documents are also available through the Library of Congress website, and blessings should descend upon the head of the unknown officer who first proposed that posting. Other digitized resources have come my way from the Lincoln Legal Papers Project, whose omnitalented director, Dr. Daniel W. Stowell, is now embarking on what I feel sure will be the most remarkable of all Lincoln editorial achievements, *The Papers of Abraham Lincoln.*

Parts of this book have already been floating in the scholarly ether, thanks to the generous invitations to me from a variety of organizations and individuals to offer some advance insights into it:

- "Lincoln and the Abolitionists," in the *Wilson Quarterly* (Autumn 2000)
- "Re-Examining the Racial Record of Abraham Lincoln," in the *Journal of Blacks in Higher Education* (Autumn 2000)
- "Defending Emancipation: Abraham Lincoln and the Conkling Letter, August, 1863," in *Civil War History* (December 2002)
- "Understanding Emancipation: Lincoln's Proclamation and the End of Slavery in America," versions of which were presented to the annual Lincoln Symposium at Knox College (September 21, 2002), the Seminar on Slavery and Emancipation at the Loudoun County Museum (January 8, 2003), and the annual Lincoln Symposium of the Lincoln Institute of Washington, D.C. (March 22, 2003) and forthcoming in the *Journal of Illinois History*
- "How Abe Lincoln Lost the Black Vote: The Lincoln Image in the African-American Mind," originally presented to the Abraham Lincoln Association's annual Lincoln symposium in Springfield on February 12, 2002, and forthcoming in *The Journal of the Abraham Lincoln Association*
- "Was Lincoln a Racist?" presented to the annual Lincoln Symposium at the Union League of Philadelphia (March 20, 2002) and as the Alphaeus Mason Lecture at Princeton University (February 14, 2003)
- "Courtroom Denials: Historical Problems and Pitfalls in Reparations Litigation, from Lincoln to the Present," originally presented to the conference organized by Manning Marable and the African-American Studies Department at Columbia, *Forty Acres and a Mule: The Case for Black Reparations* (November 9, 2002) and

scheduled to appear in *Souls: A Critical Journal of Black Politics, Culture and Society;* and

- "Providence and Prudence: Abraham Lincoln's Search for a Moral Politics," presented to the conference on *Lincoln and American Democracy* at the University of Chicago (May 10, 2003) and to be included in an as-yet-untitled volume of essays from the University of Chicago Press.

In a somewhat lighter vein, I've dwelt on aspects of this project in articles and op-eds on emancipation and slave reparations in the *Los Angeles Times* (June 11, 2001), the *Wall Street Journal* (November 22, 2002), and the *Washington Post* (January 1, 2003), and on National Public Radio on September 22, 2002, and February 10, 2003.

Much closer to home, some final words of thanks must go to my editor at Simon & Schuster, Alice Mayhew, and her associate, Emily Takoudes, as well as to my always-enthusiastic agent at Writer's House, Michele G. Rubin. Medals for patience are certainly owed to Gerri Wissinger, my administrative assistant at the Templeton Honors College, and to Ellen Mergner, who oversees interlibrary loans for Eastern University's Warner Library and who never flinched at any of the monstrous ILL requests I made of her.

Anyone persistent enough to have followed all of these acknowledgments to the end will, I hope, realize how dependent a single writer is on the goodwill of so many other people and institutions. I will take this opportunity to make a recommendation: No single source has proven more interesting or offered more unexpected revelations than the newspapers of the Civil War era, and especially those of Washington: John W. Forney's *Morning Chronicle*, Simon Hanscom's *National Republican*, the *Evening Star*, and the venerable *National Intelligencer*. Many of these survive only in microform versions in single repositories, such as the Library of Congress or the Boston Public Library, and are difficult to access by interlibrary loan or even by inspection on-site. Any ambitious digitizer of Civil War–related resources could hardly do a greater deed than to undertake the scanning and digitizing of these newspapers, beginning with the Washington papers, so as to offer them in CD-ROM or DVD format.

Alongside me at all times has been my wife, Debra, whose faithfulness and patience with this project were always a shelter from weariness, discouragement, and the heat of the day; Jerusha, Alexandra, and Jonathan looked on as always in bemusement, but in at least two cases, they showed more-than-remarkable indulgence by actually coming to events to hear me speak about the Proclamation. To them all belong my love and thankfulness; in their love, I find life, liberty, and emancipation of my own.

Allen C. Guelzo
THE VILLAS, CAPE MAY, NEW JERSEY
*July 25, 2003, thirty-three years after
Kerkrade, the Netherlands*

CONTENTS

INTRODUCTION

*T*HE EMANCIPATION PROCLAMATION is surely the unhappiest of all of Abraham Lincoln's great presidential papers. Taken at face value, the Emancipation Proclamation was the most revolutionary pronouncement ever signed by an American president, striking the legal shackles from four million black slaves and setting the nation's face toward the total abolition of slavery within three more years. Today, however, the Proclamation is probably best known for what it did *not* do, beginning with its apparent failure to rise to the level of eloquence Lincoln achieved in the Gettysburg Address or the Second Inaugural. Even in the 1860s, Karl Marx, the author of a few proclamations of his own, found that the language of the Proclamation, with its ponderous *whereas*es and *therefore*s, reminded him of "ordinary summonses sent by one lawyer to another on the opposing side." When the Lincoln Memorial was dedicated in 1922, quotations from the Second Inaugural and the Gettysburg Address flanked the great Daniel Chester French statue of the seated Lincoln, but there was no matching quotation from the Proclamation, only a vague, elliptical representation in Jules Guerin's mural, *Emancipation of a Race*, which was mostly lost to sight near the ceiling of one of the memorial's side chambers.[1]

But the unkindest cut at the Proclamation came from the hands of

Columbia University historian Richard Hofstadter, in his essay on Lincoln in *The American Political Tradition and the Men Who Made It* (1948). A onetime member of the circle of American Marxist intellectuals around *Partisan Review*, Hofstadter repudiated the traditional Progressive view of American political history as a struggle between the legacies of the liberal Thomas Jefferson and the conservative Alexander Hamilton. Instead, Hofstadter viewed American politics as a single, consistent, and deeply cynical story of how capitalism had corrupted Jeffersonians and Hamiltonians alike and turned the United States into "a democracy of cupidity rather than a democracy of fraternity." But he reserved his angriest words for Lincoln and for the Emancipation Proclamation. Lincoln's opposition to slavery, in Hofstadter's reckoning, was kindled only by the threat it posed to free white labor and the development of industrial capitalism. Lincoln "was, as always, thinking primarily of the free white worker" and was "never much troubled about the Negro." No one, then, should be fooled by the Proclamation. Its motives were entirely other than had been advertised, and that fact explained its stylistic flaccidity. "Had the political strategy of the moment called for a momentous human document of the stature of the Declaration of Independence, Lincoln could have risen to the occasion." Instead, what he composed on New Year's Day, 1863, "had all the moral grandeur of a bill of lading."* It accomplished nothing because it was intended to accomplish nothing "beyond its propaganda value."[2]

---

* Hofstadter could not have realized this, but a bill of lading was a surprisingly important commercial document in the antebellum economy. "There is no one instrument or contract used in commercial transactions made to subserve so many various, useful, and important purposes, as the Bill of Lading," wrote P.C. Wright in *DeBow's Review* in July 1846. "Yet it appears . . . that there is no one so little understood, as to its legal effect, when applied to some of the purposes to which it is peculiarly adapted. . . . A Bill of Lading is defined to be an instrument signed by the master of a ship, or by someone authorized to act in his behalf, whereby he acknowledges the receipt of merchandise on board his vessel, and Engages . . . to deliver the same at the port of destination in safety. . . ." If this was what the Emancipation Proclamation was supposed to do, then Hofstadter was offering Lincoln more of a compliment that he intended.

The influence of Hofstadter's easily repeatable quip about "the moral grandeur of a bill of lading" has had long innings, and even the most favorably disposed of modern Lincoln biographers have found themselves forced to concede that the Proclamation "lacked the memorable rhetoric of his most notable utterances." [3] And perhaps for that reason, no serious study of the Proclamation has appeared since John Hope Franklin's brief *The Emancipation Proclamation* in 1963, written for its centennial. (That centennial itself was a disappointing affair, capped by President John F. Kennedy's refusal to give the principal address at ceremonies at the Lincoln Memorial on September 22, 1963, for fear of suffering deeper losses of Southern Democrats in his reelection bid the next year.) As the Proclamation's negative symbolic power has risen, efforts to interpret the text have diminished, and examination of the Proclamation's contents has subsided into offhand guesswork and angry prejudice. The Proclamation has become a document (as Garry Wills once described the Declaration of Independence) "dark with unexamined lights." As with Jefferson's Declaration, we have lost in the cultural eddies of the last hundred and forty years the assumptions that would make the Emancipation Proclamation readable. [4]

Recapturing at least some of those assumptions will begin, I think, with recognizing in Abraham Lincoln our last Enlightenment politician. The contours of Lincoln's mind—his allegiance to "reason, cold, calculating, unimpassioned reason"; his aversion to the politics of passion; the distance he maintained from organized religion; his affection for Shakespeare, Paine, and Robert Burns; and his unquestioning belief in universal natural rights—were all shaped by the hand of the Enlightenment. But the most important among the Enlightenment's political virtues for Lincoln, and for his Proclamation, was prudence.

Prudence carries with it today the connotation of "prude"—a person of exaggerated caution, bland temperance, hesitation, a lack of imagination and will, fearfulness, and a bad case of mincing steps. This view would have surprised the classical philosophers, who thought of prudence as one of the four cardinal virtues and who linked it to shrewdness, exceptionally good judgment, and the gift of *coup d'oeil*—the "coup of the eye"—which could take in the whole of a situation at once and know almost automatically how to proceed. Among political scientists, it has more specific meanings, but those meanings are usually just as repellent—of cunning, *realpolitik*, and in some quarters, an unhealthy preoccupation with the neo-classicism of Leo Strauss. (So let me say, for the benefit of the hunters of subtexts, that I can cheerfully confess to never having read Leo Strauss, nor, for that matter, to possessing much aptitude for the peculiar dialect spoken by my political science friends.) It is an ironic rather than a tragic attitude, in which the calculus of costs is critical rather than crucial or incidental. It prefers incremental progress to categorical solutions and fosters that progress through the offering of motives rather than expecting to change dispositions. Yet, unlike mere moderation, it has a sense of purposeful motion and declines to be paralyzed by a preoccupation with process, even while it remains aware that there is no goal so easily attained or so fully attained that it rationalizes dispensing with process altogether. Montesquieu found the origins of political greatness in "prudence, wisdom, perseverance," since prudence would "guard the passions of individuals for the sake of order and guard the guardians for the sake of freedom." In the new American republic, James Madison argued (in the forty-third of the *Federalist Papers*) for ratification of the 1787 Constitution on the grounds of "the rights of humanity," the "considerations of a common interest," and on "prudence." So also for Lincoln: The practice of politics involved the rule of prudence, and "obeying the dictates of prudence" was as important for Lincoln as obeying "the obligations of law." He hoped, as president, that "it will appear that we have practiced prudence," and in 1861, he promised that the management of the Civil War would be "done consistently with the prudence . . . which ought always to regulate the public service" and without allowing the war to degenerate "into a violent and remorseless revolutionary struggle."[5]

It is this politics of prudence which opens up for us a way to understand Lincoln's strategy in "the mighty experiment" of emancipation. The most salient feature to emerge from the sixteen months between his inauguration and the first presentation of the Proclamation to his cabinet on July 22, 1862, is the consistency with which Lincoln's face was set toward the goal of emancipation from the day he first took the presidential oath. Lincoln was not exaggerating when he claimed in 1858 that he "hated" slavery:

> I hate it because of the monstrous injustice of slavery itself. I hate it because it deprives our republican example of its just influence in the world—enables the enemies of free institutions, with plausibility, to taunt us as hypocrites—causes the real friends of freedom to doubt our sincerity, and especially because it forces so many really good men amongst ourselves into an open war with the very fundamental principles of civil liberty—criticising the Declaration of Independence, and insisting that there is no right principle of action but self-interest.

But in Lincoln's case, prudence demanded that he balance the integrity of *ends* (the elimination of slavery) with the integrity of *means* (his oath to uphold the Constitution and his near-religious reverence for the rule of law). Lincoln understood emancipation not as the satisfaction of a "spirit" overriding the law, nor as the moment of fusion between the Constitution and absolute moral theory, but as a goal to be achieved through prudential means, so that worthwhile consequences might result. He could not be persuaded that emancipation required the headlong abandonment of everything save the single absolute of abolition, or that purity of intention was all that mattered, or that the exercise of the will rather than the reason was the best ethical foot forward.[6]

Far too often, Lincoln's apologists hope to give the lie to Hofstadter's scalding attack by pulling apart means and ends, either apologizing for the former or explaining away the latter, a sure sign that they have no better grasp on the politics of prudence than Hofstadter. Most often, this pulling apart happens whenever we are tempted to plead that Lincoln was either a man in *progress* or a man of *patience*. That is, Lincoln was (as Horace Greeley put it) "a growing man," growing in this case from a stance of moral indifference and ignorance about emancipation at the time of his election in 1860, toward deep conviction about African-

American freedom by the time of the Emancipation Proclamation less than two years later. Or else that Lincoln already had all the racial goodwill necessary for emancipation but had to wait until the right moment in the war or the right moment in the growth of Northern acceptance of the idea of emancipation. These are both generous sentiments, but I am not sure that generosity is quite what is needed for understanding Lincoln's proclamation. Rather than needing to develop *progress,* I believe that Abraham Lincoln understood from the first that his administration was the beginning of the end of slavery and that he would not leave office without some form of legislative emancipation policy in place. By his design, the burden would have to rest mainly on the state legislatures, largely because Lincoln mistrusted the federal judiciary and expected that any emancipation initiatives which came directly from his hand would be struck down in the courts. This mistrust is also what lies behind another curiosity: Lincoln's rebuffs to the covert emancipations that Congress constructed under the cover of the two Confiscation Acts (of August 1861 and July 1862), the "contraband" theory confected by the ingenious Benjamin Butler, and the two martial-law emancipation proclamations attempted by John Charles Frémont and David Hunter. Lincoln ignored the Confiscation Acts, showed no interest in Butler's "contraband" theory, and actually revoked the martial-law proclamations—not because he was indifferent to emancipation, but because he was convinced (and with good reason) that none of these methods would survive challenges in federal court.

But why, if he was attuned so scrupulously to the use of the right legal means for emancipation, did Lincoln turn in the summer of 1862 and issue an Emancipation Proclamation—which was, for all practical purposes, the very sort of martial-law dictum he had twice before canceled? The answer can be summed up in one word: time. It seems clear to me that Lincoln recognized by July 1862 that he could not wait for the legislative option—and not because he had patiently waited to discern public opinion and found the North readier than the state legislatures to move ahead. If anything, Northern public opinion remained loudly and frantically hostile to the prospect of emancipation, much less emancipation by presidential decree. Instead of exhibiting *patience,* Lincoln felt stymied by the unanticipated stubbornness with which even Unionist slaveholders refused to cooperate with the mildest legislative emancipation policy he could devise, and threatened by generals who were politically committed to a negotiated peace. (We usually underrate the menace posed by the generals, largely because, in the end, it did not materialize, but on at least some level, Lincoln feared that emancipation risked triggering a military coup d'etat by General George McClellan and the Army of the Potomac.) Thus Lincoln's Proclamation was one of the biggest political gambles in American history.

But gambles are not necessarily inconsistent with prudence, and Lincoln's gamble may be considered a prudent one for the role that providence came to play in it. For a man with such a vague religious profile, Lincoln nevertheless understood that a significant part of the politics of prudence involved a deference to providence—whether one defined *providence* as the work of an active and interventionist God or merely the forces of history, economics, or ideas.

Lincoln was raised in an environment saturated with notions of providential determinism, beginning with his upbringing among the "hardshell" Separate Baptists. As he did with so much else in his upbringing, Lincoln lost what little faith he might have had, and he acquired more notoriety than was good for an ambitious young politico in Illinois as an "infidel." It was an Enlightenment infidelity, a rationalistic deism stoked in equal parts by the smile of Voltaire and the arguments of Tom Paine. But even then, Lincoln's unbelief had this much still in common with the Calvinism he had forsaken—both subscribed alike to the notion that all events were determined by forces beyond human power.

This is not the most optimistic way of looking at the world, but it can lend a certain confidence to one's plans if the direction in which determinism is pointing also happens to be the upward path you are following. Lincoln, like so many other secular determinists shaped by the Enlightenment's delight with the idea of a mechanically predictable universe—Thomas Henry Buckle, Karl Marx, Adolphe Quetelet, Pierre Laplace—thought that progress, improvement, and invention were written into the script of human affairs beyond the power of human effacement. And that meant, from Lincoln's vantage point, that an institution as hateful and retrograde as slavery had to be as inalterably doomed as superstition and tyranny. Whatever the occasional wrong moves—the economic surge of the cotton South, the overthrow of the safeguards against slavery's expansion by the Kansas-Nebraska Act, even the Civil War itself—the fundamental direction of events was inevitable and required only a certain amount of machinery-tending to put things back on the rails.

The carnage, the stalemate, and the incomprehensible rebel victories of the War's first year conspired to strip Lincoln of his optimism in the natural, pleasant ascent of progress, but not of his fundamental belief in providence. Instead, the war saw him veer away from a providence defined by indifference and the iron law of cause and effect, and back toward the providence of a mysterious and self-concealing God whose will for the human future did not necessarily move according to the sweet and logical processes of progress. And in the case of emancipation, Lincoln came to see the Proclamation as the only alternative God had left to emancipation being swept off the table entirely.

All the same, Lincoln never intended the Proclamation to be a substitute for a long-term legislative solution, and in fact, that hope for a legislative solution eventually bore fruit as the Thirteenth Amendment. The Proclamation was an emergency measure, a substitute for the permanent plan that would really rid the country of slavery, but a substitute as sincere and profound as the timbers that shore up an endangered mine shaft and prevent it from collapsing entirely.

UNDERSTANDING PRUDENCE as the key to Lincoln's political behavior gives us the "big picture" behind the Emancipation Proclamation. It does not speak automatically to four very specific questions about the Emancipation Proclamation that I am asked nearly everywhere I go. First and most frequent is the Hofstadter question: *Why is the language of the Proclamation so bland and legalistic?* The answer, I think, really should be obvious, and it was not because Lincoln wrote the Proclamation grudgingly and of necessity. Very simply: The Proclamation is a legal document, and legal documents cannot afford very much in the way of flourishes. They have work to do. In this instance, we are dealing with a document with a very great deal of it to do, and one which had to be composed with the understanding that every syllable was liable to the most concentrated legal parsing by the federal court system. If it falls short of the eloquence of the Gettysburg Address, I only have to point out that the Gettysburg Address was not a document anyone could take into court, and at least in legal terms, it was not intended to accomplish anything. In other words, Lincoln could afford eloquence at Gettysburg; he could not in the Proclamation.

The second question is linked to the Hofstadter question, if only because Hofstadter believed, wrongly, that a linkage between the two existed: *Did the Proclamation actually do anything?* Because the Proclamation limited emancipation only to the states or parts of states still in rebellion and did not include the slaves in the four loyal slave states—Delaware, Maryland, Kentucky, and Missouri—it has been easy to lampoon the Proclamation as a puff of political air. But laws are not the less laws merely because circumstances render them inoperative at a given time or place. I should be ashamed to offer myself as an example, but I do so only because it will force Lincoln's critics to examine their own terms: Every day that I traveled between Paoli and Princeton, I took liberties with the speed limit which the Commonwealth of Pennsylvania and the State of New Jersey forbid. (Judging from the abandon with which other drivers flew past me, most of my readers, it is safe to say, are doubtless implicated in similar offenses.) The guardians of the turnpike might have lacked the energy, the technology, or even the power to enforce the legislated speed limits, but they certainly possessed the perfect and unimpaired authority to do so, as I would have discovered if ever once they had gotten me to stop. The same is true with Lincoln and the Proclamation. Lincoln may not have had the *power* available to him to free every slave in the Confederacy, but he certainly had the *authority,* and in law, the authority is as good as the power. The proof is in the pudding: No slave declared free by the Proclamation was ever returned to slavery once he or she had made it to the safety of Union-held territory.

This raises a related question: *Did the slaves free themselves?* In 1979, Leon Litwack laid the foundations for an alternative view of

emancipation when he urged historians to regard emancipation not as
an event beginning and ending with Lincoln but as a process in which
pressure was exerted on Lincoln and Congress by the slaves themselves.
By running away, by labor sabotage, and by volunteering to serve the
Union armies, the slaves forced Lincoln's hand toward emancipation.
But looked at in the larger context of nineteenth-century American
race relations, the "self-emancipation" thesis asks for too great a suspension of disbelief. Without the legal freedom conferred first by the
Emancipation Proclamation, no runaway would have remained "self-
emancipated" for very long. The files on the first year and a half of the
war bulge with accounts of thwarted slaveowners with court papers in
their hands and sheriffs at their sides, stalking through the camps of
Union regiments in pursuit of slave runaways as though a barbecue
rather than a war was in progress. Without the Proclamation, the Confederacy even in defeat would have retained legal title to its slaves, and
there is little in the oppressive patterns of coercion Southerners employed before the Civil War or afterward in Reconstruction to suggest
that they would not have been willing to reclaim as many of their self-
emancipated runaways as they could; and if the record of the federal
courts in the post–Civil War decades is any proof, the courts would
probably have helped them.

In the same skeptical spirit, a fourth question is frequently aimed at
the intentions behind the Proclamation: *Did Lincoln issue the Proclamation only to ward off European intervention or inflate Union morale?* To
this, I can only say that if intervention and morale were Lincoln's
primary concerns, then an Emancipation Proclamation was probably
the worst method, and at the worst time, with which to have met them.
Abroad, there was as much danger that an Emancipation Proclamation
would trigger foreign intervention as there was that the Proclamation
would discourage it. At home, Pennsylvania politician Alexander McClure
warned Lincoln that "political defeat would be inevitable in the great
States of the Union in the elections soon to follow if he issued the
Emancipation Proclamation." Significantly, Lincoln agreed "as to the
political effect of the proclamation." He knew that the Proclamation,
for all that he hoped it would forestall the generals and put the Union

cause unreservedly on the side of the angels, might just as easily convince them to accelerate plans for an intervention or put Lincoln's administration on the side of the losers. To his surprise, McClure found that this made no dent in Lincoln's determination. Those who have sung in Richard Hofstadter's choir need, as McClure needed, to take a new measure of that determination.[7]

BUT IT IS NOT simply the complexities of Lincoln's mental habits or the difficulty involved in piecing together the circumstances and chronology of Lincoln's decision to emancipate which make the Proclamation so difficult for us to grasp. A good deal of our befuddlement is wrapped up in the way that our notions of political ethics have changed since Lincoln's day. Even as Lincoln emerged onto the national political scene in the 1850s, the politics of prudence that had guided Enlightenment political theory was being devalued in favor of a Romantic politics of ethical absolutism. One source of that absolutism lay close to home for Americans in the radical perfectionism of evangelical Protestant revivalism; another was the influence of Immanuel Kant, mediated through English and American Romantics such as Emerson, Samuel Taylor Coleridge, Frederick Augustus Rauch, and James Marsh, the "Vermont Transcendentalist." What the American Romantics particularly admired in Kant was his attempt to locate a source for ethical judgments within men (instead of imposed externally, through divine revelation or natural law), in a "categorical imperative" that yields absolute and universal answers to ethical dilemmas. "We do not need science and philosophy to know what we should do to be honest and good, yea, even wise and virtuous," argued Kant in his *Fundamental Principles of the Metaphysic of Morals.* What we need to do is obey the imperative. Kant's hope was to be able to isolate moral decisions from the flux of circumstance, culture, and individual experience, and thus escape the threat of moral relativism. He was, in other words, looking for a way out of the mechanistic universe, where ethics is simply a pretty name we give to justify whatever decisions circumstances force upon us. Kant sought to base the right or wrong of things solely on the principle that moved the will to choose one thing over another. Purifying the will trumps the claims of all other values, and willing purely is all that is necessary to overcome injustice. As much as Kant believed in universal rational criteria for ethical behavior, those criteria spoke in (as Isaiah Berlin put it) "the language of inner voices." [8]

It is the convergence of American evangelical absolutism and the ethic of the imperative that, more than anything else, erects a translucent shield between our habits of mind and Lincoln's, passing enough light to make us think we see but not enough to allow us to understand. This is not to say that Lincoln, as a man of the Enlightenment, possessed a superior morality or always did well and right. Nor does it mean that Lincoln was untinged by certain elements of Romanticism himself or that he conforms in precise anticipation to all our American anxieties about race and reconciliation at the beginning of the twenty-first century. It would be special pleading to claim that Lincoln was in the end the most perfect friend black Americans have ever had. But it would also be the cheapest and most ignorant of skepticisms to deny that he was the most significant. And if the Emancipation Proclamation was not, as Richard Hofstadter so mordantly complained half a century ago, the most eloquent of Lincoln's writings, it was unquestionably the most epochal. It may have had little more "moral grandeur" than a "bill of lading," but Lincoln's Emancipation Proclamation was still a bill that itemized the destinies of four millions of human beings, bound in the way of danger for the port of American freedom.

One

FOUR WAYS
TO FREEDOM

T ABOUT "11½ o'clock" on the night of March 11, 1861, a small "canoe" cautiously bobbed up beside the granite wharf of Fort Sumter, a three-story brick pentagon that squatted on a man-made spit of rubble in the middle of the harbor of Charleston, South Carolina. The sentry at the stone gate called for the officer of the watch, Captain John Gray Foster, a New Hampshire engineer, to deal with their mysterious late-night visitor. But when Foster came down to the wharf to investigate, what he found shivering before him was "a negro boy," a fugitive slave. In all but one detail, the runaway's story was the same one Foster had heard time and time again: His master had beaten him within an inch of his life for some vague offense, and he had taken his leave. The one detail that was new was paddling out to Sumter, rather than hightailing it for the swamps or the forests as generations of runaway slaves had done before. The "boy" had

heard that the federal government, or at least its representatives in the
solitary company of United States artillerymen in Fort Sumter, were
now going to free the slaves, and he had paddled out in a stolen canoe to
get their protection.[1]

Foster was relieved that his visitor was not more "unusual." The garrison inside Fort Sumter had been on their guard against surprise attack
ever since December, when the surrounding circle of Charleston harbor
began to teem with men and with guns pointed directly at Sumter. It
was not that Charleston had a grievance with Foster and the artillerymen who defended Sumter; Charleston's complaint, and the complaint
of the entire slaveholding South, was against the government that
Sumter and its flag represented. Five months before, Abraham Lincoln
of Illinois, the nominee of the six-year-old antislavery Republican
party, had been elected president of the United States on a platform that
pledged to restrain the growth of black slavery in the American Union
to the fifteen states where it was then legal. Although Lincoln repeated
that he was interested only in preventing the further spread of slavery
into the federally administered territories of the West, this promise was
read by unappeased slaveowners as a threat to the survival of slavery itself in their states. Not only did the economic health of slavery depend
on continued expansion; the political influence of white slaveowners in
the federal government depended on organizing new slave states in the
Western territories whose representatives in Congress would always ensure enough of a balance between slave and free states to safeguard
slavery from Congressional interference. Even more, slavery was the
principal means that a culture in the old South relied upon to secure
white racial supremacy.

Lincoln's election was the first sign in the eyes of anxious Southerners that slavery's national political power was slipping and liable to slip
further. "Mr. Lincoln has said that there will be no cessation of agitation
until the North sees that a policy is inaugurated which will place slavery
'where the public mind will rest in the belief that it is IN THE COURSE
OF ULTIMATE EXTINCTION!' " raved J. Randolph Tucker in the
March 1861 issue of the *Southern Literary Messenger.* "That the leading object of the mass of the [Republican] party, as a near or ultimate

purpose, is the emancipation of the slaves, no man who has marked the power of the fanatical element in the organization and the growth of it can doubt." *DeBow's Review* agreed: "If African slavery in the Southern States be the evil their political combination affirms it to be, the requisitions of an inexorable logic must lead them to emancipation." Not just emancipation, either, but "forcible emancipation is *certain*, if we remain in the union."[2]

Southerners, who had dominated the American presidency from its beginnings, knew all too well that a president could use the power of executive patronage to stack the western territories with antislavery officials (who would make sure the territories were organized without protections for slavery), plant antislavery federal postmasters, judges, and marshals throughout the slave states, and commission antislavery officers for the military who would turn every federal fort into a refuge for runaways. Could the slave South expect to grow, or even survive, when Lincoln "wields the offices and patronage of the Government to cement and strengthen the anti-slavery sentiment which brought his party into existence?" asked Georgian Howell Cobb. "Can it prevent the use of that patronage for the purpose of organizing in the South" a band of turncoats "to be the allies of this party in its insidious warfare upon our family firesides and altars?"

South Carolina, the most defiant and fiery of the slave states, saw no reason simply to wait for this to happen. On December 20, 1860, a special state convention moved to secede from the federal Union and declared "the dissolution of the union between the State of South Carolina and other States under the name of the United States of America."[3] South Carolina was followed over the next six weeks by the slave states of the lower South—Mississippi, Florida, Alabama, Georgia, Louisiana, and Texas—and then by the upper South states of Arkansas, Virginia, North Carolina, and Tennessee. In February, the seceders formed a new union of their own, the Confederate States of America, and demanded that the United States government turn over all the property, military as well as civil, that it owned on what was now Confederate soil.

The more loudly Southerners repeated their dire prophecies of federally imposed emancipation, the more widely their slaves, in an entirely different accent, believed them. Slaves had only to listen at the keyhole, catch a glimpse of a newspaper, or keep their ears open in the railroad station, and they would quickly hear, despite white precautions, that Lincoln's election meant freedom. The New York journalist James R. Gilmore learned very early that "the blacks, though pretending ignorance, are fully acquainted with the questions at issue in the pending contest," and from the day of Lincoln's election in November 1860, wildfire stories had been spreading among Georgia slaves that they "were to be free on the day of Lincoln's election." In Missouri, Louis Hughes remembered "the slaves whispering to each other: 'We will be free.' " Outside Nashville, young John McCline's father would meet at night with other slaves to "talk over the events and progress of the Lincoln campaign." They were sure that "he was against slavery and would use every means in his power to crush it." Even privileged slaves like Robert Smalls, who worked as the pilot of the small Charleston steamboat *Planter*, gathered the *Planter*'s small crew of slave boatmen after hours and warned them, "This, boys, is the dawn of freedom for our race."[4]

Behind the slaveowners' rage at Lincoln lurked the dread not only that Lincoln meant emancipation but that emancipation meant insurrection and race war on the model of the Nat Turner slave revolt in 1831 or the massacres of white planters by their former slaves in San Domingue in 1791. Lincoln's election followed by little more than a year the attempt of the conscience-tortured abolitionist, John Brown, to begin a slave uprising by seizing the weapons stored at the federal arsenal at Harpers Ferry, Virginia. No matter that the raid failed, that Brown was swiftly tried and hanged, or that Lincoln publicly condemned Brown. "When abolition comes by decree of the North," predicted Georgia supreme court justice Henry L. Benning, "very soon a war between the whites and the blacks will spontaneously break out everywhere." The kind of apocalypse Benning prophesied touched every racial and sexual anxiety of the white South. The race war would be fought "in every town, in every village, in every neighborhood, in every road." The North would take advantage of this turmoil to intervene in favor of the blacks, and the result would be the extermination or exile of the whites—"so

far as the men are concerned; and as for the women, they will call
upon the mountains to fall upon them." One planter in Maury
County, Tennessee, convinced himself in February 1861 that "a servile
rebellion . . . is more to be feared now than [it] was in the days of the
Revolution against the mother country," when the British recruited and
armed runaway slaves to fight their former American masters. In South
Carolina, Henry William Ravenal was surprised to find so "much alarm
among the people of servile insurrection" and wrote for the *Charleston
Mercury* on "the necessity of vigilance on the part of our people against
the secret plottings & machinations of the fanatic abolitionists, who will
surely come among us in friendly guise to tamper with our negroes." In
Texas, fires in Dallas, Denton, and Pilot Point sent fearful whites in pursuit of slave rebels who planned "to burn the houses and kill as many of
the women and children as they could while the men were gone."
Within a month, as many as fifty blacks and whites had been executed
by home guards and vigilante mobs.[5]

Yet where was the evidence of these plots? Fort Sumter might have
represented freedom to the fugitive who stood that night before Captain
Foster, but to Foster, it was simply an unpleasant tour of duty. The federal Constitution he had sworn to uphold when he graduated from West
Point and was commissioned in the Corps of Engineers in 1846 gave
Foster no authority to deal with crimes under state laws, and especially
crimes like running away from slavery. If anything, the one federal
statute touching on slavery—the Fugitive Slave Law of 1793 and its up-
dated version from 1850—actually required him to turn over runaways
to state authority. And so, without comment, Foster told the "negro boy"
on the jetty he could not stay, and "he was at once sent back." The next
day, a party of "four negroes (runaways)" turned up at the gates of Fort
Pickens, in Pensacola harbor, hoping for sanctuary. The commandant,
Lieutenant Adam Slemmer, had icily refused all demands by secession
authorities in Florida to surrender the federal property under his command. But at the same time, Slemmer would do nothing to touch the
property of Floridians under the laws of that state, which of course included the "four negroes." The runaways were convinced "that we were
placed here to protect them and grant them their freedom," Slemmer

reported. But "I did what I could to teach them the contrary," and that afternoon he took them back to Pensacola and turned them over to the city marshal. That night, four more runaways showed up at Fort Pickens, and the next morning, Slemmer made the same trip.

The unhappy fugitives could not have known this, but Slemmer and Foster were actually fairly representative, not only of the military's attitude toward slavery, but also of the general political mind of the North. The number of outright abolitionists was few and was colored an angry red by the associations its leaders—William Lloyd Garrison, Wendell Phillips, Abby Kelley, Sarah and Angelina Grimke, Theodore Dwight Weld, Charles Grandison Finney—had acquired with "quack economics, quack politics, quack law, quack learning" and an unrelenting absolutism that stooped to ask for no sympathy that was not a mirror of their own purposes. "As to the governments of this world, whatever their titles or forms, we shall endeavor to prove that, in their essential elements, and as at present administered, they are all anti-Christ," Garrison declared, at once alienating all but the tiniest sliver of the American people, who understood themselves to be the real government of the United States. But in case any Americans had dodged this missile, Wendell Phillips decided to increase the volume of explosive: "The Constitution and government of this country is worth nothing, except it is or can be made capable of grappling with the great question of slavery. . . . The best use of good laws is to teach men to trample bad laws under their feet." As a result, "not one-tenth of the citizens of" the Northern states "were in favor of immediate and unconditional emancipation," remembered Maine congressman James G. Blaine.[6]

The insult that the unblinking self-righteousness of the abolitionists offered to Northerners was compounded by the injury Northern merchants were likely to suffer if emancipation disrupted the Northern economy. The Democratic mayors of both Boston and New York, Joseph M. Wightman and Fernando Wood, were deeply sympathetic to the South, and so were "many prominent citizens," the Beacon Hill and Beekman Hill blue bloods who were described by an irritated John Murray Forbes as " 'club men' who live by wine, cards, tobacco and billiards." Alexander McClure disgustedly admitted that Philadelphia, although a

Northern city in a free state, was also "the great emporium of Southern commerce" and that Philadelphia's merchants were interested in emancipation in an inverse ratio to "the fearful problem of sacrificing millions of dollars due from their Southern customers." In Ohio, Jacob Dolson Cox (the son-in-law of the abolition revivalist Charles Grandison Finney) was warned by Democratic state leader David Tod that any attempt by Lincoln and the Republicans to use the secession crisis as an excuse to emancipate slaves "would find the two hundred thousand Ohio Democrats in front of us," blocking the way across the Ohio River.

Even Northerners who considered themselves antislavery might feel perfectly satisfied simply opposing any further extension of slavery into the West, favoring the colonization of freed slaves somewhere outside the United States (with west Africa as the dumping ground of choice), with schemes of gradual emancipation, or even with no action at all, so long as blacks got no nearer than they already were. "We look upon slavery as a curse," wrote one antislavery Delaware Unionist, "but we also look upon freedom possessed by a negro, except in a very few cases, as a greater curse." And, as in the South, even antislavery opinions sat alongside an undercurrent of white apprehension that emancipation meant race war, the unavoidable slaughter of white and black when black became free. "It is not for us," warned Philadelphian J. L. Baker, to hasten emancipation "by revolution and servile insurrection, to put torches and pikes into the hands of such a population to be used against the whites, in re-enacting all the horrors of a St. Domingo massacre." [7]

Fear of "servile insurrection" and revulsion at the possibility of emancipation was even greater in the national capital, only thirty miles downriver from Harper's Ferry and the specter of John Brown. Washington was still "an overgrown village" when Abraham Lincoln took the oath of office on March 4, 1861, "as unattractive, straggling, sodden a town, wandering up and down the left bank of the yellow Potomac, as the fancy can sketch." [8] Surrounded as it was on one side by secessionist Virginia and on three others by near-secessionist Maryland, Washington was "in all social and industrial aspects a Southern town" and fully as hostile to the preachers of emancipation as New Orleans or Mobile. Slavery was legal in the District of Columbia (although not the slave trade) and Washington

society—"if it may be so-called," snorted Ohio senator John Sherman—
"looked upon 'Abolition' with dread and disgust."

Moncure Conway, who first came to Washington in 1854, found "the
few anti-Slavery men then in Congress" being "utterly ignored by
Washington society" and defensively gathered around Massachusetts
senator Charles Sumner "into a little Massachusetts of their own."
William O. Stoddard, who came to work for the Lincoln White House
after Lincoln's inauguration, remembered the capital "as 'secesh' to the
backbone" and that almost every street had certain windows through
which pianos dinged out "Dixie" and "The Bonnie Blue Flag." Even
Benjamin B. French, the Commissioner of Public Buildings and one of
the few old Washington hands who considered himself "an ultra Union
man," was "utterly opposed to any intermeddling with Southern rights"
and advocated "concession & Conciliation" as the best policy for the new
Lincoln administration.[9]

The Thirty-sixth Congress was limping in just that spirit through
its final lame-duck session when Lincoln arrived for his inauguration,
and it continued sitting right up to March 4, 1861, deliberating over
compromises that would lure the South back into the Union. In the
House of Representatives, a Committee of Thirty-three was authorized
on December 4, 1860, to prepare compromise measures; after considering almost thirty possible actions, the committee nervously reported
back on January 14 with recommendations for, among other things, a
constitutional amendment to forbid Congress "to abolish or interfere,
within any State, with the domestic institutions thereof." The Senate's
own compromise committee, the Committee of Thirteen, took its lead
from Kentucky senator John J. Crittenden, who proposed a roster of six
new amendments that prevented the abolition of slavery by Congress,
not only in the states but anywhere "under its exclusive jurisdiction,"
which included the territories, all federal property, and the District of
Columbia.[10]

All of these compromise proposals came to ruin on the rocks of
Republican opposition in Congress, which drew strength from the
knowledge that the next Congress, riding in on Lincoln's coattails,
would be a Republican show. "I will never agree to put into the Consti-

tution of the country a clause establishing or making perpetual slavery anywhere," announced Illinois Republican senator Lyman Trumbull. But this resistance did not mean that the Republicans actually intended to disestablish or unmake slavery where it was. Trumbull might have no desire to see slavery coated with permanence by a constitutional amendment, but at the same time he assured the Senate that he would not take the iron flail of emancipation after it, much less make war for emancipation. Many Republicans "so recoiled from the thought of sectional strife that for the sake of peace they were ready to forgo their demand for the Congressional prohibition of slavery in the Territories." Massachusetts Republican George Boutwell assured Southerners just before the election that "whenever the Republican party comes into power, the moderate and conservative and upright minds of the South will see that we contemplate no injury to them." Wisconsin Republican senator J. R. Doolittle was advised not to press too hard on the secessionists. "For my own part I hold that slavery while it is debasing to our own [race] has been to the African necessarily beneficial," one of his constituents wrote. "[I] don't defend it on abstract grounds . . . but I regard it as a State necessity, & to be treated as such where it is & removed in ages hence if ever."

This attitude would be as prevalent within the inner circles of Lincoln's cabinet as it was on the floors of the Senate and the House. Salmon P. Chase, whom Lincoln had tapped for secretary of the treasury, had established a lengthy and selfless record in his native Ohio as an antislavery governor and the "attorney general for fugitives." Still, even Salmon Chase acknowledged that the Constitution tied his hands. "There in the Slave States are fellow citizens, who verily believe otherwise than I do, and who insist on its fulfillment and complain of bad faith in its nonfulfillment: and . . . I am not at liberty to substitute my convictions for theirs." Chase reminded August Belmont years later that "I never favored interference by Congress with slavery in the states" and had hoped only "to bring about a union of all Democrats on the ground of the limitation of slavery to the States in which it then existed."[11]

Similarly, William Henry Seward, whom Lincoln intended to nominate as secretary of state, had made his name in New York state politics as an eloquent and formidable opponent of slavery. He achieved national notoriety in the Senate in 1858 when, as a Republican senator from New York, he predicted that slavery and freedom were locked in an "irrepress-ible conflict," something that Southerners angrily read as a prediction of war on slavery. Yet Seward was no ideologue. From the moment Lincoln nominated him for the State Department, the abolitionists "began to mistrust Mr. Seward, who no longer seemed to them the hero of principle they had so long idolized." One of his fellow cabinet members, Gideon Welles, the secretary of the navy, pegged him accurately as "neither an Abolitionist nor a Free-Soiler." [12] If there was a plot afoot to use the new presidency as a cover to leverage the nation toward slave emancipation, the evidence for it was exceedingly thin on the ground.

IT WAS NOT Seward, Chase, or Congress who set off the stampede to secession, but the relatively unknown Lincoln, although even there, Lincoln had sent more than enough signals about moderation on the slavery issue to make the *New Orleans Bee* regard his nomination for the presidency as "a masterstroke of political craft." Nor was Lincoln merely talking for effect when he reiterated that he had "no purpose, directly or indirectly, to interfere with the institution of slavery in the States where it exists."

The Constitution and constitutional law had erected a firewall be-tween federal and state spheres of sovereignty, and in an era before the Fourteenth Amendment, it was the states, not the federal government, that determined what the range of civil rights in any state might be. The Constitution left it to the states to determine women's legal standing and voting rights (Lincoln had once advocated women's suffrage in Illinois), whether communities ought to be taxed to provide free public educa-tion, whether banks should be allowed to incorporate, what were the exact terms of citizenship, and, in this case, whether blacks could be en-slaved. "I confess I hate to see the poor creatures hunted down, and caught, and carried back to their stripes and unrewarded toils," Lincoln wrote to Joshua Speed, a slaveholder and probably his closest friend, in 1855. But "I also acknowledge your rights and my obligations, under the constitution, in regard to your slaves," even though "the great body of

the Northern people" have to "crucify their feelings, in order to maintain their loyalty to the constitution and the Union." In his great debates
with Stephen A. Douglas during his run in 1858 for Illinois's Senate seat,
Lincoln affirmed that "I have neither assailed, nor wrestled with any
part of the constitution. . . . The legal right of Congress to interfere with
the institution in these states, I have constantly denied." And as late as
1864, he still could not "see how any of us now can deny and contradict
all we have always said, that Congress has no constitutional power over
slavery in the states." [13]

Lincoln was being perfectly transparent when he declared, "If slavery
is not wrong, nothing is wrong." But when he spoke against slavery, he was
speaking against the institution, and not necessarily for its black victims.
Slavery, for Lincoln, was any relationship of economic restraint, or any
systematic effort to box ambitious and enterprising people like himself
into a "fixed condition of labor, for his whole life." But he was not enough
moved by American slavery's singular injustice to its African captives to
call for their immediate emancipation. Lincoln was serving his second
term as an Illinois state legislator when the state legislature resolved in
January 1837 that "property in slaves, is sacred to the slave-holding states
by the Federal Constitution." Lincoln and Whig judge Daniel Stone
protested that "the institution of slavery is founded on both injustice and
bad policy." But Lincoln's protest bent obligingly in the other direction far
enough to add that "the promulgation of abolition doctrines tends rather
to increase than to abate its evils."

A Springfield neighbor, John E. Roll, heard Lincoln reply to the
question of whether he was an abolitionist with the comment, "I am
mighty near one." But being "near one" was precisely the point. If to be
opposed to slavery was to be "near" abolitionism, then almost the entire
population of the Northern free states was "near" abolitionism too. And
even when Lincoln would talk about emancipation, it was not on the
abolitionists' terms. He told Missouri lawyer James Taussig in 1863 that
"the Union men in Missouri who are in favor of gradual emancipation
represented his views better than those who are in favor of immediate
emancipation." Lincoln's own plan for emancipation would deal effectively with the disease while also prudently ensuring that the medicine

did not choke the patient to death. It would "have the three main features—gradual—compensation—and the vote of the people." And, if practicable, it might have a fourth, colonization. Lincoln endorsed the idea of freed blacks colonizing in Africa as early as his days as a storekeeper, postmaster, and surveyor in New Salem, Illinois. In later years, he was involved with the Illinois chapter of the American Colonization Society, and in 1854, he explained that "my first impulse would be to free all the slaves, and send them to Liberia,—to their own native land." (He did, however, immediately concede that "whatever of high hope . . . there may be in this, in the long run, its sudden execution is impossible.")[14]

As a lawyer in Springfield, Lincoln had no involvement with Springfield's small free African-American community, apart from his role in a handful of cases—thirty-four out of the more than five thousand cases that he participated in during his professional life—and even there, no pattern of particular interest in immediate abolition emerges. In at least two of these cases, in 1845 and 1847, Lincoln successfully defended whites who had been accused of harboring fugitive slaves, and in 1841, in *Bailey v. Cromwell*, he even obtained freedom for a slave woman, Nance. At the same time, though, Nance's freedom was actually a by-product of the real issue in the suit, a promissory note. In 1841, Lincoln arranged a settlement in *Kane v. May and Eastham* that involved transferring ownership of a slave girl to Kane, and from 1850 until 1862, Lincoln and his wife, Mary Todd Lincoln, were embroiled in litigation in Kentucky over the settlement of the estate of Mary's father, litigation that netted the Lincolns a share in the proceeds of selling the Todd family slaves. The most startling case of all occurred in 1847, when Lincoln agreed to represent a Kentucky slaveowner, Robert Matson, in Matson's effort to reenslave a runaway mother and her children.[15] Slavery was, in Lincoln's judgment, detestable and on its way to the grave, and he would not be unhappy to help it get there. But in the meantime, as it was dying the death that progress, democracy, and the Founding Fathers had all decreed for it, slavery was still legal. And slaveowners like Matson had rights, even in free Illinois, which during this passing phase had to be respected.

All the same, white Southerners (and blacks, too, as it turned out) were not entirely wrong in sensing a profound danger to slavery in the election of Lincoln. He had come out of political limbo in 1854 as an enemy to the expansion of slavery made possible by the Kansas-Nebraska Act, and in 1858, he had challenged Stephen A. Douglas (the author of the Kansas-Nebraska bill) for the Senate with the alarming declaration that "a house divided against itself cannot stand."

> I believe this government cannot endure, permanently half *slave* and half *free*. . . . It will become *all* one thing, or *all* the other. Either the *opponents* of slavery, will arrest the further spread of it, and place it where the public mind shall rest in the belief that it is in the course of ultimate extinction; or its *advocates* will push it forward, till it shall become alike lawful in *all* the States, *old* as well as *new*—*North* as well as *South*.

Lincoln only meant by this that Kansas-Nebraska, by letting down the bar to slavery in the territories, was inviting a collision between slavery and freedom, not that he was advocating such a collision. But it sounded as though he were, and unsettled Southerners quoted the statement as proof "of the objects of the Republicans." Also, Southerners patient enough to leaf through back issues of the *Congressional Globe* would find that Lincoln, during his lone term in Congress as an Illinois representative, 1847 to 1849, proposed a bill to emancipate the slaves of the District of Columbia. His bill, true to his ideal of emancipation, asked for a District referendum on slavery. But if the referendum was favorable to abolition, Lincoln wanted the president empowered to issue a proclamation that provided for gradual emancipation and the legal abolition of slavery, and for compensation to slaveowners "from the treasury of the United States the full value of his or her slave." A board of commissioners would be assembled "for determining the value of such slaves as their owners may desire to emancipate under this section." Lincoln's bill never actually made it onto the Congressional calendar, but his role in it earned at least the accolade of the *New York Tribune* that he was "a strong but judicious enemy to Slavery." [16]

People who had known Lincoln long and well were convinced that his face was set toward emancipation from the day of his nomination for the presidency. After Kansas-Nebraska, Lincoln was determined that there must be no further extension of slavery, no more fearful back-tracking to Southern demands, and no more clever manipulations of the law to purchase a few more years of life for the Slave Power. He took his election to the presidency as a vindication of this policy, and a sign that enough national rage and resistance had accumulated against slavery that the hour to begin the dismantling of the Slave Power had arrived. Emancipation, wrote Illinois congressman Isaac Arnold in 1866, was Lincoln's "deepest, strongest desire of the soul," and from the time of his election he "hoped and expected to be the *Liberator* of the slaves." Joshua Speed told William Henry Herndon, Lincoln's longtime law partner, that "my own opinion of the history of the emancipation proclamation is, that Mr. Lincoln foresaw the necessity for it—long before he issued it." George Boutwell, the Massachusetts abolitionist, believed that Lincoln "was personally the enemy of slavery, and he ardently desired its abolition." Joseph Gillespie was convinced that Lincoln "had it in his mind for a long time to war upon slavery until its destruction was effected." Leonard Swett, who had worked with Lincoln through the 1850s on the old Eighth Judicial Circuit and who now became an unofficial political courier for Lincoln, remembered that Lincoln "kept a kind of account book of how things were progressing . . . and whenever I would get nervous and think things were going wrong, he would get out his estimates and show how everything on the great scale of action . . . was going exactly—as he expected." Emancipation, for Lincoln, was never a question of the end but of how to construct the means in such a way that the end was not put into jeopardy.[17]

One reason that Lincoln could represent Robert Matson in Illinois and plan for emancipation in Washington was his conviction that, given enough time and a restraint on expansion, slavery would exhaust itself and die out on its own, without risking the disruption of the Union. Matson could be defended because he was within the law; slaves could be emancipated because that too was within the expectation of the Constitution, and the law curved ineluctably toward emancipation. "You may examine the debates under the Constitution and in the first session of Congress and you will not find a single man saying that Slavery is a good thing," Lincoln wrote in 1859. "The reason is this. The Framers of the Organic Law believed that the Constitution would *outlast* Slavery and they did not want a word there to tell future generations that Slavery had ever been legalized in America." If slavery were isolated in the states where the Constitution left it legal, it would asphyxiate through its own tendency to chew up the very soils it used. He "was quite sure it would not outlive the century." [18]

But emancipation agendas built around Lincoln's favorite "three main features"—gradualism, compensation, "and the vote of the people"—earned him no sympathy from either the Southern white supremacists or the abolitionists. "Who is this huckster in politics?" Wendell Phillips exclaimed after Lincoln's election. "Who is this county court advocate?"

> Here is Mr. Lincoln. . . . He says in regard to such a point, for instance as the abolition of slavery in the District of Columbia, that he has never studied the subject; that he has no distinctive ideas about it. . . . But so far as he has considered it, he should be, perhaps, in favor of gradual abolition, when the slave-holders of the district asked for it! Of course he would. I doubt if there is a man throughout the whole South who would not go as far as that. . . . That is the amount of his anti-slavery, if you choose to call it such, which according to the Chicago thermometer, the Northern states are capable of bearing. The ice is so thin that Mr. Lincoln, standing six feet and four inches, cannot afford to carry any principles with him onto it!

This was not a good way to persuade Abraham Lincoln. He told Pennsylvania congressman William D. Kelley that he loathed "the self-righteousness of the Abolitionists," and he spoke about them to antislavery activist Eli Thayer "in terms of contempt and derision." John Eaton, who helped educate newly freed slaves, remembered Lincoln exclaiming (of a "well-known abolitionist and orator," probably Phillips), "I don't see why God lets him live!"

If Lincoln's differences with the abolitionists could be put on paper in the form of a comparative table, the two columns would go on for quite a way. Where the abolitionists built their argument on the demand of evangelical religion for repentance, Lincoln preferred gradualism and compensation for emancipated slaves. Where they preached from passion and choice, he worked from reason and prudence; where they called for immediatism without regard for consequences, it was precisely the economic consequences of slavery and its extension which kindled Lincoln's opposition in the 1850s. And where they brushed aside the Constitution, Lincoln would proceed against slavery no farther than the Constitution allowed. It was, on those terms, easier to push the thought of emancipation into the future. "God will settle it, and settle it right," Lincoln told Robert Browne in 1854, "but for the present it is our duty to wait." [19]

BUT LINCOLN was not going to be allowed to wait. He carefully wrote out his inaugural address before leaving Springfield, and on March 4, standing on a temporary platform erected on the East Portico of the Capitol, Lincoln said little to gladden the hearts of the abolitionists. "Apprehension seems to exist among the people of the Southern states, that by the accession of a Republican Administration, their property, and their peace, and personal security, are to be endangered," Lincoln declared (in a "voice . . . not very strong or full-toned" but still strong enough to carry "out over the acres of people before him with surprising distinctness"). "There has never been any reasonable cause for such apprehension," he assured them. "All the protection which, consistently with the Constitution and the laws, can be given, will be cheerfully given to all the States." It was true, of course, that "one section of our country believes slavery is right, and ought to be extended, while the other believes it wrong, and ought not to be extended," but "this is the only substantial dispute," and that certainly afforded no grounds for a response as violent "as the destruction of our national fabric." He even gave a nod in the direction of the compromise committees in Congress. "Many worthy, and patriotic citizens are desirous of having the national constitution amended," and Lincoln, while he would "make no recommendation of amendments," also did not see it as the president's task to stand in the way of "a fair opportunity being afforded the people to act upon it." Nor was he even opposed to the Crittenden compromises. "We are not enemies, but friends. We must not be enemies." Let reason rule, and "the chorus of the Union" would once again "swell . . . when again touched . . . by the better angels of our nature." [20]

It was not angels but demons that the abolitionists saw in Lincoln's inaugural. "Mr. Lincoln opens his address by announcing his complete loyalty to slavery in the slave States," Frederick Douglass, the black abolitionist, groaned in *Douglass' Monthly*. "He stands upon the same moral level with [the slaveholders], and is in no respect better than they." But Douglass knew too little about Abraham Lincoln to recognize what Lincoln's friend, Leonard Swett, recognized as one of Lincoln's favorite lawyerly tactics for lulling opposing counsel into complacency: to give away, with what seemed incompetent generosity, all the unimportant points in a case, and then turn and hang the opposition on the one remaining point. "By giving away six points and carrying the seventh he carried his case, and the whole case hanging on the seventh, he traded away everything which would give him the least aid in carrying that." [21]

Just so in this inaugural address: The striking thing about it was what Lincoln did *not* say. He made concessions, but none concerned the points on which slaveholders most wanted concessions—the right to take slaves as property in all of the western territories, the abandonment of the federal forts in the South, a sectional veto on federal legislation, the right of secession. He endorsed the Fugitive Slave Law as a constitutional necessity, not a property right, and even introduced the dangerous question of whether the federal government was the appropriate agency for enforcing it. (Every Southerner knew that if the Fugitive Slave law was reduced to being a matter of state authority, the free states would refuse to adopt enabling statutes for the recapture of fugitives, and a flood of runaways would bolt toward federal installations across the South, where state authority did not apply.) Lincoln even said kind things about compromise amendments "to the effect that the federal government, shall never interfere with the domestic institutions of the State." But that left wide open the possibility that the federal government could still hold out incentives to the slave states, especially in the upper South, to emancipate the slaves by their own vote.

The inaugural address fell very short of being an abolitionist manifesto, and top-lofty abolitionist orators and newspapers were not discreet about informing him of this. But Lincoln knew that as president he had no authority to issue manifestos of any sort. "We reason as though Mr. Lincoln wielded a dictatorial, unrestricted power at the White House, accounting solely to the God of his conscience," Eugene Pelletan scolded the ultras. "But Mr. Lincoln simply presides over a republic where popular opinion rules, and he is surrounded by divers opinions upon the question of slavery." To Southern whites, however, Lincoln was offering nothing that they did not already have, while leaving his own hands suspiciously free. "At Montgomery," the temporary Confederate capital in Alabama, Henry William Ravenal found that "the tone of Lincolns inaugural was thought belligerent." The slave system had flourished for six decades because the federal government had been full of people who believed it was right or who were unwilling to challenge it. That day was now over, and simply by refusing to help, promote, and encourage it any longer, Lincoln was putting slavery in mortal jeopardy. To the abolitionist elect, Lincoln might seem "far from being up to the full measure of what ought to be thought and felt on the slavery question," but as Harriet Beecher Stowe shrewdly reminded readers of the radical New York paper *The Independent*, "in this case to arrest is to cure." [22]

Five weeks later, the Confederates surrounding the beleaguered garrison in Fort Sumter learned that, after considerable backing and filling, Lincoln had authorized a relief mission to resupply the fort. He pledged no effort to add reinforcements and promised to limit the supplies to nonmilitary necessities. But the impatient Confederates only saw that if Lincoln could sail even the most innocuous relief mission into Charleston without hindrance from the Confederacy, the Confederate government's claims to secession, sovereignty, and independence would have approximately the same standing as the Declaration of Independence would have had if the British Army had paraded through Philadelphia to the door of Independence Hall. At half-past four on the morning of April 12, 1861, the rebel artillery sent its shells flying toward Sumter.

FORTRESS MONROE sat squatly on the tip of Old Point Comfort, another brick-and-stone pentagon guarding the mouth of the James River and the waters of Hampton Roads from any approach by warships on the Chesapeake Bay. In May of 1861, it was the last stronghold of federal military authority left on the sacred soil of Confederate Virginia and the likeliest springboard for federal military operations up the James River peninsula. On May 23 (the same day Virginians voted by a three-to-one margin to ratify Virginia's secession from the Union), a reconnaissance party from the First Vermont Volunteers slipped over the causeway that linked Fortress Monroe to the mainland and drove off rebel pickets around the village of Hampton. The Hamptonites promptly fled inland, leaving behind their slaves, who now milled around happily with the Northern soldiers. That evening, three of these slaves talked their way through the Vermonters' picket lines, and the next morning, they were brought before Fortress Monroe's commandant, Major General Benjamin Franklin Butler.

Butler was no abolitionist. He was actually a Unionist Democrat from Massachusetts who had supported the nomination of Jefferson Davis as Democratic candidate for president in 1860. (Davis was now the provisional president of the Confederate States of America.) Only a month before, Butler had offered federal troops to Maryland governor Thomas Hicks to preempt any possibility of a slave insurrection. But in the course of that month, civil war had begun in earnest, and with that event Butler turned himself into slavery's first deadly enemy in uniform. A lawyer before the war, he now reasoned as a lawyer in war: Captain Foster and Lieutenant Slemmer had sent back the runaways at Sumter and Pickens, since in time of peace the Fugitive Slave Law was still binding on federal officers; however, the same rule might no longer apply in time of war, especially because, under questioning, it developed that the three runaways were the property of a rebel colonel from Hampton, Charles K. Mallory. More questioning revealed that they had bolted for Fortress Monroe because Mallory was planning to take them to South Carolina to work on Confederate "military operations" there. (The Confederacy had lost no time in issuing demands "to impress slaves and free negroes" to dig ditches, heave up fortifications, and perform camp duties so as to release more of the South's outnumbered white manpower for combat; free blacks who tried to plead their freedom as an exemption "were told that they would be sold and sent farther South if they did not go.")[23]

Under the terms of the Paris Convention of 1856 on maritime law, enemy and neutral property might be legally seized if that property was being used by the enemy to wage war. *Ergo,* property, in that case, became "contraband of war." If, as slaveowners had always insisted, slaves were indeed chattel property, and these three particular examples of property were about to be applied to the greater good of the rebel war effort, why might not Butler do his bit in weakening the rebellion by declaring the three men "contraband of war" and seizing them for the use of the United States?

This was a greater compliment to Butler's ingenuity than to his legal acumen: The Paris Convention, after all, had been addressing questions about cargoes of "warlike instruments, or materials by their own nature fit to be used in war," not runaway slaves covered by domestic statutes that directed the return of such property to its owners. But, as Butler was quick to point out, Virginia had proclaimed itself part of an entirely new nation. Hence, these slaves were covered, not by a domestic statute, but by international law, and that made them "contraband." This was, of course, a lawyer's joke: Goods and material can be "contraband," but not people, unless the sort of people in question are regarded as no different from goods and materials. But joke or not, the idea was an instant success (more important, said Isaac Arnold, "than a battle gained"). Northern whites who felt squeamish at the thought of "slaves declared freemen" had "no objection to their being declared contrabands." Two days later, there were eight more "contrabands" waiting for Butler; the next day, there were forty-seven. Butler wrote out receipts for them and sent the receipts to their masters.[24]

The Confederates were not amused. But Lincoln's new secretary of war, Simon Cameron, approved Butler's action, provided that Butler did not begin actually snatching slaves from their masters, and provided he put them to some sort of useful occupation at Fortress Monroe and kept "an account of the labor by them performed, of the value of it and of the expense of their maintenance." This plan quickly proved unworkable. By July, Butler had nine hundred contrabands on his hands and less and less work, room, and food for them. Similarly, it was no easy matter to distinguish between runaways who really were contraband—in other words, slaves who had been conscripted by the Confederates as military laborers—and runaways who were simply runaways.[25]

These problems not only multiplied, but spread to Maryland, which was a slave state but also still loyal to the Union. Legally, the Fugitive Slave Law still operated in Maryland, and Unionist slaveholders there fully expected that Butler's contraband rule had no reference to them. So when a slave belonging to Catharine Noland of Rockville (just outside Washington) was rumored to have found shelter in the camp of the First Ohio Volunteers, she sent her son, a Union sergeant, with a note from the adjutant general's office asking for the return of the slave. The problem was that these particular Ohio volunteers were "practicing a little of the abolition system" and refused to let Noland's son search their camp. Letters flew back and forth, and the colonel of the regiment hotly denied that Noland's slave had ever been there, and that was the end of it. Still, if loyal slaveholders were going to be treated by the army just as though they were rebels, or as though there were no Fugitive Slave Law, then everything the Confederates had ever said about Lincoln might be confirmed, and Marylanders might as well join the Confederates, if only to protect their investments in slaves. "The impunity with which these acts are daily perpetrated and the outrages practiced upon those seeking to recover their slaves, by the soldiers," warned Maryland congressman Charles Calvert, "are justly incensing our citizens against the Government for permitting such violations of our Constitutional rights."[26]

These "violations" were liable to have a stiff price tag for Abraham Lincoln. By the middle of May 1861, eleven slaveholding states, from Virginia to Texas, had seceded from the Union. To Lincoln's relief, the four slave states of the Border—Missouri, Kentucky, and Delaware, in

addition to Maryland—had not. But through the month of April it had
been touch and go in the Maryland legislature, while in Missouri a
miniature civil war had broken out between the secessionist governor
and the loyalists in the legislature and in St. Louis. Kentucky, with the
largest slave population in the Border, decided to "take no part in the
civil war, now being waged, except as mediators and friends to the belligerent" and on May 20 proclaimed a "position of strict neutrality."
One sharp jolt, one careless word, one idiot in newly made shoulder
straps practicing "a little of the abolition system," and the whole Border
might fall over into Confederate hands, and that would be the end of it
all, for Lincoln, the North, and the slaves. The Border states held the
wheat, corn, meat, and manufacturing that the cotton-bloated South
lacked; they accounted for more than a third of the white population of
the South; and they controlled the great inland rivers—the Ohio, the
Mississippi, the Potomac—that were the highways of the American
economy. Missouri, in fact, shared a lengthy river boundary with western Illinois that reached as far north as Iowa, and Maryland's three
boundaries with the District of Columbia meant that the moment secessionists gained control of the state house in Annapolis, Washington itself
would be encircled by rebels. "I think to lose Kentucky is nearly the
same as to lose the whole game," Lincoln wrote. "Kentucky gone, we can
not hold Missouri, nor, as I think, Maryland. These all against us, and
the job on our hands is too large for us. We would as well consent to separation at once, including the surrender of this capitol." So Lincoln
promised Kentucky senator Garrett Davis in the most soothing fashion
that he would do nothing to threaten "the institutions or property of any
state, but, on the contrary, would defend them to the full extent with
which the Constitution and laws of Congress have vested the president
with the power." He would respect Kentucky's oddball neutrality, and
"if Kentucky or her citizens . . . made no demonstration of force against
the United States, he would not molest her." But it was not a concession
he enjoyed making. "Professed Unionists," he grumbled that August,
gave him "more trouble than rebels." [27]

Some of the Border states' touchiness grew out of the way the
Thirty-seventh Congress was organized when it came together in special

session on July 4, 1861. Thanks to the November elections and the withdrawal of the seceding South's predominantly Democratic representatives, the Republicans were left with a substantial majority in both houses of Congress, 106 Republicans facing a humiliated minority of 42 Democrats and 28 Border-state Unionists in the House, 31 Republicans and only 17 Democrats and Unionists in the Senate. Of the Republican senators, slightly more than half could be classified as Radicals—a small cadre of abolitionists, and a larger penumbra of Republicans who believed that striking down slavery was the best way to strike down secession. The leadership of this group—Charles Sumner and Henry Wilson of Massachusetts, Zachariah Chandler of Michigan, Ben Wade of Ohio—occupied the center desks on the Republican side of the Senate chamber, with the rest of the Republican senators ranged around them, and they dominated the informal Republican caucus that met "almost every day" during Congressional sessions "so as to leave no chance for hesitation, or division, amongst themselves." Navy Secretary Gideon Welles, an old antislavery New Englander and former Democrat, feared "the acts of caucus" as "despotic, mandatory, and decisive." [28]

In practice, however, Congressional Republicans looked more like "a strange medley" than a controlling power. In the House, chairmanships of committees went to only three Radicals, James Ashley of Ohio (Territories), Owen Lovejoy of northern Illinois (Agriculture), and Thaddeus Stevens of Pennsylvania (Ways and Means). Even in the caucus, Minnesota Radical Morton Wilkinson admitted that "it was not always fair sailing." Nor were the Radicals always consistent in their radicalism. Thaddeus Stevens—"bitter, quick as electricity, with a sarcastic, blasting wit" and easily picked out of a crowd for his "short clubfooted leg" and "a long-haired wig"—was often seen as the incarnation of Radicalism. But Stevens had to agree in 1860 that there was no "desire or intention, on the part of the Republican party . . . to interfere with the institutions of our sister States." Lovejoy "at once went into an Achillean rage" whenever the subject of slavery came up. But even Lovejoy, whose brother had been murdered by a proslavery mob in 1837, admitted that "I have no power to enter the State of North Carolina"—or any other state, for that matter—"and abolish slavery there by an act of Congress." [29]

The Democrats in Congress might have made more of the Republicans' divisions if they had not been so badly demoralized themselves by the bitter self-destruction of the party in the 1860 election (which cost them control not only of the presidency and Congress but also of all but four Northern governorships and three Northern state legislatures). On top of this debacle came the untimely death of the North's greatest Democratic voice, Stephen A. Douglas, in June of 1861.[30] Douglas's role in Congress was gradually taken over by a new and comparatively inexperienced cadre of Midwestern Democrats—Samuel S. Cox and Clement Laird Vallandigham of Ohio, Daniel Voorhees of Indiana—whose attitude toward Lincoln was often as hostile as that of their quondam Southern brethren. Although "born and bred in a free state," Vallandigham "avowed himself a pro-slavery man." And not only proslavery, but a proslavery westerner who had no hesitation about putting the interests of the Ohio River valley ahead of the good of the Union. "I became and am a Western sectionalist," Vallandigham announced proudly. "I am as good a western fire-eater as the hottest salamander in this House." His "denunciations were the most extreme, and his expressions of contempt and ill-will were wholly unbridled." Along with the Border state Unionists in Congress, the Democrats relentlessly prophesied that any move to incorporate emancipation into the war would flood the Northern labor market with cheap black labor and crowd Northern farmhands and industrial workers out of their jobs. "We intend to have in our State, as far as possible, a white population," announced one Indiana Democrat, "and we do not intend to have our jails and penitentiaries filled with the free blacks."[31]

The central midwestern states of Ohio, Indiana, and Illinois held the strongest bloc of Democratic stand-fasts (together, they sent seventeen Democratic representatives to the House in 1860). They were also the states hit hardest when the Confederates closed commercial traffic on the Mississippi, and farmers with goods to ship to New Orleans, small factories with markets in the South, and banks with loans to Southerners downriver were economically flattened within weeks after Sumter. With the Midwest a hotbed of Democratic discontent, it would have been unwise for any Republicans to underestimate the power of the opposition. Despite the Democrats' poor showing in the 1860 elections, state elections in the spring of 1861 showed how quickly public opinion could shift, even in the midst of war. Democrats captured major urban elections in Cincinnati and Cleveland; in Rhode Island, the Democratic governor was reelected and two Republican congressman defeated; and in Kentucky and Maryland, antiwar Democrats captured every Congressional district but one in each state.[32]

A good deal of veto power therefore remained in the hands of the most intransigent of the Border state senators and representatives—in the Senate, Lazarus Powell, John Breckinridge, and Garrett Davis of Kentucky; James Bayard and Willard Saulsbury of Delaware; and Trusten Polk and Waldo Johnson of Missouri; and in the House, Charles Wickliffe, Robert Mallory, and John J. Crittenden of Kentucky (Crittenden had accepted reelection in 1860, but to the House rather than to the Senate). So, when the special session assembled in Washington on July 4, Republicans were ready to tread lightly around the Border staters, and the Border state delegations in both House and Senate were ready to play on that fear.

The next day, Lincoln sent a special message to Congress on the outbreak of the war, describing his actions since April in calling up the militia of the states, purchasing weapons and materials, and issuing a call to the states for state volunteer regiments. He was careful to avoid broad swipes at Southern infamy—the Border staters *were* Southerners—and he patiently defined the war as a question of whether a democracy built on the consent of the people has any chance of surviving if a political minority refuses to cooperate with the decisions of the majority. "This issue embraces . . . the question whether a constitutional republic, or a democracy—a government of the people, by the same people—can . . . maintain its territorial integrity, against its own domestic foes." This was certainly an important question, but it was also an abstract one. The durability of democracies was also not the question the ultras on either side had hoped he would plunge into, and it allowed Lincoln to pass them by without a single direct reference to slavery.

It did no good. Once both houses had organized themselves, Phillip Fouke of Illinois's Eighth District was on his feet to resolve that "while we hold in one hand the sword of justice . . . it becomes our solemn and Christian duty to offer with the other continuously to our deluded brethren the olive branch of peace." Three days later, a Senate resolution approving Lincoln's call for volunteers was attacked by Trusten Polk of Missouri as an outrage on the Constitution, and on July 10, Clement Vallandigham asked the House to blame the war not on the secessionists but on "the violent and long-continued denunciation of slavery and slaveholders." Vallandigham was followed by his fellow Ohioan, William Allen, who angrily appealed to the House to adopt a resolution pledging "that it is no part of the object of the present war against the rebellious States to interfere with the institution of slavery therein." [35]

Lincoln could ignore them for the time being because a military solution to the rebellion seemed within easy reach. On July 2, federal troops under the creaking Brigadier General Robert Patterson had splashed across the Potomac River into Virginia near Harper's Ferry, intending to occupy the Shenandoah Valley. On July 11, a scratch force of 2,000 Ohio militiamen under a former West Point engineer named George B. McClellan handily routed a small Confederate force at Rich Mountain, in western Virginia, giving the Union control of almost a quarter of Virginia's territory. On July 17, a force of 35,000 Union volunteers stumbled unsteadily out of Washington into northern Virginia, intending to evict the rebel government from its new capital at Richmond. Their commander, Major General Irvin McDowell, was unhappy about the prospects of his ill-trained, inexperienced, and riotously overconfident soldiers. But Lincoln brushed those doubts away. "You are green, it is true," he told McDowell at a meeting with his generals and cabinet, "but they are green also; you are green alike." If McDowell would just move on Richmond, the Confederates might be out of business before the special session of Congress ended.

But on July 21, McDowell's volunteers, regimental colors flying and bands jubilantly playing "Dixie," marched across a small stream near Manassas known as Bull Run and into a lethal confrontation with 30,000 Confederates. The rebels were, admittedly, just as green as Lincoln had supposed, and McDowell's plan—feint across the stream with one part of his army and then launch a clever flanking movement around the left of their positions that would collapse the Confederates in panic—came commendably close to working. But McDowell had not anticipated the last-minute appearance of Confederate reinforcements on his own flank. It was the federals who panicked and ran, and the army that was supposed to be marching on Richmond ended the day slumping dazedly back to Washington in the rain. The next day, a rabid Confederate sympathizer, William Owner, watched them pass through the capital, "sullen, dirty and broken down." Almost five hundred of McDowell's men were dead, and the rest were a demoralized mob.[34]

"The battle of Bull Run gave a rude shock to the theory under which the war had been prosecuted up to that time," recalled New York lawyer Montgomery Throop. Congress opened for business the next morning, whistling down their shock by resolving that "the reverses of the Army . . . have in no manner impaired the ultimate success of our arms" and minus several of its members who had gone out to watch the Bull Run battle for entertainment and who had not returned. (New York congressman Alfred Ely had actually been captured by the Confederates and would cool his heels in Richmond for the next six months.) Horace Greeley, whose *New York Tribune* had led the cheer for McDowell's expedition, now concluded that the rebels "cannot be beaten." He advised Lincoln to give up any notion of trying consequences again with the Confederates. "Do not fear to sacrifice yourself to your country," he wrote Lincoln, and "have Mr. Crittenden move any proposition that ought to be adopted."

John J. Crittenden, as it turned out, had exactly that in mind. Hoping to keep Northern shame over the Bull Run debacle from erupting into legislation, Crittenden stepped in to offer a resolution to the House on July 22. Surprisingly, the opening of the resolution firmly blamed "the present deplorable civil war" on "the disunionists of the southern States": That much made it clear that the Border states were more loyal to the Union than people like Vallandigham, who a week before had wanted to blame the war on the Radicals. However, behind the protest of loyalty, the real point of Crittenden's resolution was to remind Congress that events on the battlefield had no implications for slavery, which is why the balance of his resolution went on to state that "this war is not waged upon our part in any spirit of oppression, nor for any . . . purpose of overthrowing or interfering with the rights or established institutions of those States." The Crittenden Resolution, carefully crafted to keep slavery from becoming the target, passed by a whopping vote of 117 to 2. "To thorough-going anti-slavery men this seemed like an apology for the war," recalled the disgusted George Julian, a Radical Republican congressman from Indiana's Fifth District, "and a most ill-timed revival of the policy of conciliation." The Senate, however, was another matter. Charles Sumner frankly looked upon Bull Run as a blessing in disguise, feeling sure that it would galvanize antislavery fence-sitters into realizing that the rebels were in earnest and that the Union would have to take earnest measures against slavery to defeat them. "The battle and defeat," he predicted, would do "much for the slave." [35]

The mechanism for "earnest" dealing was actually already in hand. Along with Lincoln's address to the special session on July 4, Treasury Secretary Salmon Chase had sent a report to Congress that recommended, almost as an afterthought, that the government should seize "the property of those engaged in insurrection" and sell it to contribute funds to the war effort.[36] The confiscation (and destruction) of property in time of war were blackened but routine features of insurrection and civil war in Europe from time out of mind, although from the time of Hugo Grotius, the seventeenth-century Dutch "father" of the "law of nations," lawyers and judges had struggled to construct a netting of rules and laws that would restrain the most vicious wartime behavior. It was, however, difficult to find all-around agreement on what these codes should look like, and for the most part, the study of international law had to be patched together from surveys of treaties (especially the ambitious system of alliances fashioned at the Congress of Vienna in 1815), military and maritime tradition, and massy textbooks on legal theory. Not until the Paris Convention—the first great international effort at writing restraint into the making of war between nations—had the major European powers finally agreed to a series of written protocols that defined what would (and would not) be acceptable conduct between nations in conflict, just in time for Benjamin Butler to dip into those protocols for his novel definition of "contraband of war." [37]

Despite the obstacles in the way of defining it, comparatively few legal thinkers doubted that a "law of nations" existed and that governments could in some way be held accountable to it. In the United States, the authors of the federal Constitution authorized Congress "to define and punish" breaches of "the law of nations," put explicit limits on property seizures and the use of martial law on fellow citizens, and outlawed bills of attainder (which allowed legislatures to inflict the death penalty for treason without jury trials). Even the notion of treason itself was hedged in by the Constitution's forbidding Congress to "work Corruption of Blood"—to pass bills of "pains and penalties" that went beyond punishing traitors themselves and reached down to impoverish their families by permanently confiscating a convicted traitor's property.[38]

For those reasons, the Constitution made implementing Chase's confiscation recommendation less easy than it looked. During the War of 1812, the Supreme Court had held that the property of British subjects in the United States could not be taken without "some legislative act expressly authorizing its confiscation." So, the idea of seizing rebel property was referred to the Senate Judiciary Committee—where, as it turned out, Lyman Trumbull was one of the rare Radicals sitting as chair of a Congressional committee—for the necessary "legislative act." What Trumbull's committee came back with on July 15 was a confiscation bill that tried to evade the constitutional restriction on "pains and penalties" by declaring the property of anyone "aiding, abetting or promoting insurrection" open to seizure as "prize and capture," as though all such property resembled the capture of prizes at sea. And since the Constitution brought "all cases of admiralty and maritime jurisdiction" under the authority of the federal courts, such "prizes and captures" could be processed through a United States district court and the whole procedure could be handled *in rem* (without the presence of the property's owner).[39]

Trumbull did not press for immediate consideration of the bill, although on July 20 he did announce that he had an amendment that he wanted to add to it. The amendment made liable to "prize and capture" the claim of anyone "to be entitled to the service or labor of any other person" if they "shall employ such person in aiding or promoting any insurrection." In that case, the person's "claim" would fall into the same category as seized property, and the enslaved "person . . . shall be henceforth discharged therefrom." In effect, what Trumbull and his committee were asking was that slaves used by the Confederate military, like prizes captured on the high seas, be made liable to federal confiscation just like other forms of "property." This was, from the moment he proposed it, interpreted as a covert emancipation scheme, hidden behind the contention that the property of traitors in the act of waging war ought somehow to be forfeit. As with Butler's use of *contraband* at Fortress Monroe, Trumbull and the Judiciary Committee were trying to bring Confederate property under the category of international law, specifically, in this case, admiralty law (hence the vocabulary of "prize and capture"). In that way, the constitutional ban on attainder would have no application. In the time of war between nations, the confiscation of contraband or of any other property "which, in their actual condition are of immediate use for warlike purposes" was perfectly legal.[40]

Neither scheme served its goal very well. The first problem was that contraband and confiscation were stretching the law of nations and admiralty law to cover categories they had never included before, and the Border staters, nervously eyeing their own slaves, were not likely to buy it. American diplomat Henry Wheaton's *Elements of International Law*, for instance, exempted "private property on land . . . from confiscation" in time of war and categorically forbade applying the rules of prize in "maritime warfare" to "the operations of war by land."[41] The second problem was political. Confiscation of contraband and other property was regarded as justified in time of war, but only between belligerent nations. Only "when two powers are at war," wrote Henry Wager Halleck (a bookish West Pointer–turned-lawyer who compiled the other major American treatise on international law), do "they have a right to make prize of the ships, goods, and effects of each other upon the high seas." But Lincoln's contention from the start of the war was that the Confederacy was *not* a nation. The Constitution neither envisioned nor permitted secession by individual states; the attempted secession of the rebels and the formation of the Confederate government was, consequently, null and void, and anything that looked like conceding legitimate nationhood to the Confederates was anathema.

Lincoln had already been burned by making one concession like this in April, when he proclaimed a blockade of the Confederacy's ports "in pursuance of the laws of the United States and of the law of nations in such case provided." But according to the "law of nations" and the Paris Convention, he could only "close the ports" of the rebels; blockades, with all the rights of prize and capture, could only be imposed on *nations*. Still, blockade was what he needed to starve the Confederate war effort, and so a blockade of the entire Confederate coastline was proclaimed on April 19, 1861. Lincoln paid dearly for that concession; the British and the French promptly recognized the Confederacy as a legitimate belligerent, meaning that the Confederates would now be allowed to purchase arms and raise loans on British and French soil. He would not make another such concession to Confederate claims to nationhood if he could help it, no matter how useful Trumbull and Butler thought it might be to emancipation.[42]

On the other hand, suppose the war *was* only a domestic rebellion. Then, the Constitution draped the ban on attainder over the confiscation of slave contraband, and the Supreme Court was more than ready to move in at once with some form of injunction. Considering the domination of the Supreme Court by its chief justice, the venerable Roger B. Taney, an old-time Maryland Democrat and the author of the proslavery *Dred Scott* decision in 1857, neither contrabands nor confiscation was liable to survive a court challenge. Unless Butler or Trumbull had some other way of evading the constitutional prohibition of attainder, there was nothing in the law of either contraband or confiscation that necessarily dispossessed slaveholders of their title to their contraband or confiscated property. "The possession of real property by a belligerent," warned Henry W. Halleck, "gives him a right to its use and to its products, but not a completely valid and indefeasible title, with full power of alienation." Once the war was over, slaveowners had full right to claim the return of their slaves. Confiscation certainly did not emancipate such slaves, nor did it guarantee the contrabands freedom.[43]

Still, what Trumbull brought to the floor of the Senate on July 20 was only an amendment and not an original part of the Judiciary Committee's bill, and under ordinary circumstances, it probably would have been sent back to the committee for some more cutting and pruning and, upon reflection, a quiet nod in the direction of the wastebasket. But Bull Run intervened, and suddenly the Senate Radicals began looking for a weapon to beat the Confederacy with, and Trumbull's amendment seemed perfectly suited to their purpose. Border staters like Marylander James Pearce warned that Trumbull's amendment was a de facto "act of emancipation, however limited and qualified," and John Breckinridge of Kentucky described it as the first step on a slippery slope that would lead to "a general confiscation of all property, and a loosing of all bonds." But since something had to be done to strike at the rebels now that the army had failed, the amendment was passed thirty-three to six, without a single vote from the Border state senators in favor.[44]

On August 2, the House began its own debate on the confiscation act, a debate even hotter and longer than the Senate's. The Border state representatives again accused the bill's backers of slipping emancipation their way under the guise of a war measure. If "the use of a slave, by the authority of the owners, in any mode which will tend to aid or promote this insurrection, will entitle that slave to his freedom," protested Kentuckian Henry Burnett, "then that amounts to a wholesale emancipation of the slaves in the seceding or rebellious states." Ohioan John A. Bingham, chairman of the House Judiciary Committee, assured Burnett that "no just court in America" would ever construe Congressional confiscation "to the effect, that . . . this law amounts to an emancipation of their slaves." But that was exactly how John J. Crittenden saw confiscation playing out. From the beginning of the republic, Crittenden declared, "the Congress of the United States had no power to legislate upon the subject of slavery within the States." If, as their own president held, the Republicans thought secession was a legal impossibility, then the rebel states were still, in reality, part of the Union, and Congress still had no authority to touch slavery for any purpose or for any reason. "Does war change the powers of Congress in this respect?" Presumably not. Therefore, Crittenden continued, "Absence of all power of legislation in time of peace must be the absence of the same power at all times. You have no power, by your Constitution, to touch slavery at all."[45]

The House voted to return the confiscation bill to the ignominy of committee, but the next day Bingham was back from the Judiciary Committee with a revised bill. Calls for votes were lost in a flurry of shouting and arm waving. A motion to table the bill was put forward, which failed, and then another motion for postponement was argued over, which also failed. Finally, on still another vote of sixty to forty-eight, the bill passed.

Four days later, Lincoln signed it. "The President had some difficulty in consenting to approve the act of Congress," wrote Treasury Secretary Chase, and according to the *New York Times,* Lincoln "finally consented only upon the most urgent entreaties of prominent members of the Senate." It is not difficult to understand why he hesitated. For one thing, the timing could not have been worse. Lincoln could not see the wisdom in threatening to confiscate property from people who had just demonstrated that they would fight to hold on to it. "The Military situation was so discouraging" after Bull Run "that in the President's view it would have been wiser for Congress to refrain from enacting laws which, without success in the field, would be null and void." More important was Lincoln's skepticism about whether a confiscation plan, or even a contraband plan, would survive a constitutional test. He could understand the humanitarian appeal of the contraband plan, and John Hay, writing anonymously as Lincoln's mouthpiece for one of the Border state newspapers, promised that "all negroes, once lawfully confiscated from the possession of their rebel owners, shall become free men." The difficulty lay in the question of how confiscation could happen *lawfully.* Neither Butler's contraband policy nor the confiscation bill did more than make the slaves wards of the federal government; most likely, given the makeup of the federal judiciary, confiscation would be struck down as a violation of the ban on attainder and "corruption of blood." For that reason, Lincoln showed little energy in enforcing the bill. He gave no directions on enforcement to Attorney General Edward Bates, and Bates, an elderly Missouri Whig who had no use for any emancipation that did not immediately deport the blacks it emancipated, declined to issue a circular of instructions to federal attorneys. As if to confirm Lincoln's skepticism, the occasional federal district attorney who did try to initiate confiscation proceedings found it almost impossible to gather sufficient evidence. "It cannot be said," recalled James G. Blaine, a freshman congressman from Maine, "that the results flowing from the measure, either in restraining the action of Southern men or in securing to the National Treasury money derived from confiscated property, were at all in proportion to the importance ascribed to it in the discussions of both branches of Congress." [46]

This was not quite what the Radicals had hoped for. "I wish you would visit Washington at once to press upon the Presdt. the duty of Emancipation," an exasperated Charles Sumner wrote, as the first session of the Thirty-seventh Congress adjourned on August 6 and the momentum generated by Bull Run dissipated. "Somebody should see the Presdt. every day, & exhibit to him this supreme duty." Almost on cue, Zachariah Chandler wrote to his wife that "Trumbull, Wade & myself have been busy night & day since our arrival," often in the White House until midnight, trying to persuade Lincoln. The most Sumner and the others would see, however, was a circular issued to field officers by War Secretary Simon Cameron, detailing military policy toward fugitive slaves in vague and routine language. Beyond that, Cameron gave no more guidance to the army than Attorney General Bates gave to federal attorneys. Far from being the sound of jubilee, "the Confiscation Act of the 6th of August was," as George Julian remarked, "regarded as a child of the same sickly ancestry" as the Crittenden Resolution. [47]

JOHN CHARLES FRÉMONT was an American celebrity, and mostly in the worst sense of the word. Born illegitimate in Georgia and raised in Charleston, he joined the navy, wangled a transfer to the army's Topographical Corps, and in 1837 embarked on the first of five expeditions to map the great deserts and mountains west of the Mississippi and Missouri rivers. Handsome, daring, and blessed with subordinates willing to save him from the consequences of his not-infrequent dim-wittedness, he became a protégé of Thomas Hart Benton, the head of one of the first families of the Democratic Party. In 1841, he eloped with Benton's daughter, Jessie, and then managed to charm his outraged father-in-law into a reconciliation. The next year, he was back to exploring with the help of Kit Carson and in 1843 became the greatest sensation since Lewis and Clark by publishing his journal of the expedition. His third expedition in 1846 was overtaken by the outbreak of the Mexican War. But Frémont converted this threat into an opportunity by invading Mexican California, rallying the American settlers there to insurrection, and delivering Los Angeles to American occupation in 1847. He eventually settled in Monterey, where he made a fortune in the Gold Rush, and in 1850 served a shortened term as one of the new state of California's senators.

Something about Frémont did not quite add up in people's minds. He was publicly aloof, unbending, and unnaturally preoccupied with the political limelight but without the wisdom to keep himself in it. (In 1851, he was rebuffed by California voters when he tried to run for a full term as senator.) The suspicion grew that the power and the brains on display in Frémont's journals were really Jessie Benton Frémont's, since Jessie Frémont was eager to reflect her husband's political glory as she had her father's and quite determined to manufacture that glory if she had to. The formation of the new Republican Party in the mid-1850s came as the Frémonts' great opening. Although the Benton clan were Southerners, Democrats, and slaveholders, Thomas Hart Benton challenged the Democratic Party establishment over the extension of slavery into the territories. His son-in-law's opinions on most political issues were unknown, but Frémont allowed himself to be converted to the Republican cause, and by the spring of 1856, "Frémont the Pathfinder" was being touted as a reputable Republican presidential candidate.

This was not because Frémont possessed any recognizable political genius. He was "the merest baby in politics," snorted Horace Greeley. "He don't know the ABCs, and attributes importance to the most ridiculously insignificant matters and regards the most vital as of no account." [48] But he had Jessie, and Jessie Frémont was prepared to use every ounce of influence that came with being a Benton to obtain the prize for her husband. She appealed for support, as only a Benton could, to Francis Preston Blair, the head of the other great Democratic family of the

Age of Jackson, and Blair's son, Francis Preston Blair, Jr., who had also lost his Democratic faith over slavery and joined the Republicans. The Blairs and the Bentons went back a long way, and Elizabeth Blair Lee (Francis's sister) had developed a particularly strong tie with Jessie Frémont. Together, Francis Blair and Jessie Frémont were the chief engineers of Frémont's nomination as the Republican candidate for president in June 1856. But not even the accumulated political chits of the Blairs and Bentons together could get Frémont elected. James Buchanan won by 400,000 votes—not a bad showing for a first-time party in a national election, but not what the Frémonts and Blairs had wanted. When old Thomas Hart Benton died in 1858, it appeared that the Frémont star had sunk for good.

The secession crisis caught up with Frémont in Paris, where he was promoting more California mining ventures. He was back in New York by February 1861 and met Lincoln as Lincoln was en route to his inaugural. Lincoln considered him alternately for a seat in the cabinet and as minister to France. But given the great standing of the Bentons in Missouri and the aura of conquering fame that surrounded the Pathfinder, Frémont was instead commissioned as a major general and, after a personal meeting with Lincoln on July 2, was put in charge of the newly created Department of the West.[49]

Technically, Frémont was responsible for the entire sweep of the Great Plains, from the Mississippi to the Rockies. But his headquarters would be St. Louis, and his real job would be to keep slaveholding Missouri in the Union. It was to his advantage that St. Louis was an antislavery island in the shallow sea of Missouri slaveholding, especially because of its high concentration of immigrant German refugees whose failures in the European liberal revolutions of 1848 left them hostile to the aristocratic pretensions of the Slave Power in America. It was also to Frémont's advantage that Francis Preston Blair and his brother Montgomery had planted themselves in St. Louis in the 1840s, along with their cousin, Benjamin Gratz Brown. Like the Bentons, the Blairs were antislavery and had decisively parted company with the Democratic Party over Kansas-Nebraska. Although Montgomery Blair relocated to Washington in 1853 (where he would defend Dred Scott before Roger Taney and the Supreme Court), the Blair influence in Missouri remained substantial. With Montgomery Blair joining Lincoln's cabinet as postmaster general, nothing could have seemed more reasonable to Lincoln than to expect that the Blairs' political weight would be ranged against the interests of secession and, presumably, on the side of their friend, John Charles Frémont.

Lincoln had not plumbed the follies Frémont was capable of, nor had the Blairs. When Frémont arrived in St. Louis in late July 1861, he found that a good deal of the action seemed already to be over. The state's secessionist governor, Claiborne Jackson, had tried to commandeer the state militia and the federal arsenal in St. Louis. But the commandant of the arsenal garrison, Captain Nathaniel Lyon, struck first. Lyon surrounded and disarmed the militia's encampment and chased off Governor Jackson and his allies into the hinterland. A provisional Unionist state convention had assembled, a Unionist provisional governor had been chosen, and state-wide elections for a new legislature were scheduled for the fall of 1862. But on August 10, Lyon was killed in a savage fight with more Confederates than he had counted on at Wilson's Creek, and from that point on, everything seemed to spiral out of control. The Confederates managed to recruit 40,000 volunteers and began a campaign to recover southern Missouri, while Confederate guerrillas began harassing federal outposts, destroying rail lines, and burning Unionist settlements outside St. Louis.

Bedeviled by whispers of rebel plots within the city, Frémont declared martial law in St. Louis on August 14 and put enforcement into the particularly clumsy hands of his loutish quartermaster. When the new Unionist governor protested, Frémont brushed him aside and insulated himself from any further interruptions behind a bodyguard of German and Hungarian revolutionaries. "We have got instead of a General an Egotist," one Unionist complained to Montgomery Blair. "It is much easier to gain access to . . . the Courts of Europe . . . than to the August presence of our *Gen.*," although this aloofness did nothing to prevent the "going *on* at all times of the *California* speculators who surround him like summer pigs." Insult by insult, Frémont was alienating precisely the people Lincoln needed to placate in the Border states.[50]

Frémont struck again at his rebel tormentors on August 30, when he declared martial law once more, this time throughout the state. For good measure, he tacked onto his martial-law declaration a list of the crimes that had particularly irritated him, along with their punishments: court-martial and execution for armed guerrillas, "the extreme penalty of the law" for saboteurs, and "sudden and severe punishment" for those dabbling in "treasonable correspondence" or "fomenting tumults." In addition, in the spirit of the Confiscation Act, "the property, real and personal, of all persons . . . who shall take up arms against the United States, or who shall be directly proven to have taken an active part with their enemies in the field, is declared to be confiscated to the public use, and"—here was the red flag—"their slaves, if any they have, are hereby declared free men." This was an astounding proclamation, and for a number of reasons. The first was that Frémont was flinging his declaration of martial law out over the whole state, including parts of it in rebel hands where he had no hope of enforcing anything. The second was the threat of execution for guerrillas and saboteurs, since this might invite retaliation by the Confederates, retaliation that would poison rather than pacify Missouri's troubled politics.

But the biggest source of amazement was the confiscation provision. Frémont was proposing not just to confiscate the property actually used by the Confederate military, but to confiscate "for the public use" the "real and personal" property of anyone and everyone who could be shown to have taken the Confederate side in some way, including property as vast as a widow's farm (if her son happened to be off fighting for the Confederacy) or as mundane as a wife's piano (if her husband was an active Confederate sympathizer). Above all, the confiscations would include slaves, whether they had worked on rebel forts or dug rebel ditches or not. And slaves so confiscated were declared "free men." [51] Frémont had opened up a third way of striking at slavery, this time through the imposition of martial law.

American jurisprudence had never had an easy time defining martial law or the powers of military courts and tribunals, even during a war. Only two proclamations of martial law had occurred since the adoption of the Constitution, one by Andrew Jackson in New Orleans when the city was under British attack in 1815, and the other during the bizarre Dorr Rebellion in Rhode Island in 1842. "Martial law is a thing not mentioned by name, and scarcely as much as hinted at, in the Constitution and statutes of the United States," admitted Caleb Cushing, a former attorney general, in 1856. "I say, we are without law on the subject." The one thing the lawyers could agree upon was that the essence of martial law is the suspension of the writ of habeas corpus, the ancient common-law right of civil courts to demand that all other state authorities—including the military—hand over cases involving civilians to the civil courts' jurisdiction. In times of war, and especially insurrection, suspending the writ allowed governments and generals to strike swiftly and severely at saboteurs and spies without going through a tedious civil arrest and trial.[52]

But if it was useful, suspending the writ was also dangerous, and the federal Constitution sanctioned the writ's suspension only "in Cases of Rebellion or Invasion," and even then failed to specify exactly who had the authority to announce a suspension. Still, "Rebellion" was exactly what was happening, and Lincoln could not wait for Congress to approve suspension while Confederate sympathizers in Maryland were blowing up bridges and cutting telegraph wires north of Washington. So, relying on his designation by the Constitution as "Commander-in-Chief of the Army and Navy of the United States, and of the militia of the several States, when called into the actual Service of the United States," Lincoln suspended the writ of habeas corpus along the Baltimore-Philadelphia corridor on April 27 and then extended the suspension northward to include New York on July 2—the same day the president met for the last time with John Charles Frémont before sending him west.

Lincoln's suspension of habeas corpus set off a constitutional furor. On May 25, Union officers seized John Merryman, a Confederate sympathizer who was recruiting Marylanders for the Confederate Army, and imprisoned him at Fort McHenry in Baltimore. The next day, Chief Justice Taney issued a writ of habeas corpus to transfer Merryman to the Maryland civil courts—where anyone could have predicted that proslavery judges would have released Merryman on sight. The commandant at Fort McHenry refused to surrender Merryman, and on May 27, Taney issued an opinion, *ex parte Merryman*, which insisted that Merryman was entitled to release and denouncing Lincoln's suspension of the writ as unconstitutional. However, Taney had no means for compelling Lincoln to yield, while Lincoln, as "Commander-in-Chief of the Army and Navy," could conveniently ignore Taney's demand—at least, while the war was still on.[53] (Not until Congress passed the Habeas Corpus Act in 1863 was Lincoln actually free from the threat of postwar indictment and prosecution.)

Lincoln's example may have strengthened Frémont's assumption that the quickest solution to civil turmoil like that in Missouri was to reach for martial law. It seems never to have occurred to Frémont to ask why Lincoln had not suspended the writ and declared martial law throughout the Border states, the answer being that any more suspensions of civil law would have unleashed still more constitutional confrontation and magnified the argument of every Confederate agitator in the Border. (Only the week before, Lincoln had had to appease the anger of Kentucky's governor, Beriah Magoffin, over the presence of federal army recruiters on the supposedly "neutral" soil of Kentucky.) But nothing in Lincoln's use of "war powers" had reached so far as to decree emancipation, and nothing would so long as the Border states were in the delicate condition Missouri was in that summer. Nor were Lincoln's listening posts along the Border slow to remind the president of the wisdom of his caution or the casual destructiveness of Frémont's directive. "I have just seen Frémont's proclamation," wrote Joshua Speed from Cincinnati on September 1. "It will hurt us in K[entuck]y."

> The war should be waged upon high points and no state law be interfered with—our Constitution & laws both prohibit the emancipation of slaves among us—even in small numbers—If a military commander can turn them loose by the thousand by mere proclamation—It will be a most difficult matter to get our people to submit to it.

It was no argument to Speed that Frémont's decree applied only to Missouri: "You can not declare my neighbors negroes free—without affecting mine," Speed wrote to Salmon Chase the next day. A day later, writing again to Lincoln, Speed was even more feverish. "That foolish proclamation of Frémont . . . will crush out every vestage of a union party in the state." Lincoln might "as well attack the freedom of worship in the north or a right of a parent to teach his child to read— as to wage war in a slave state upon such a principle." [54]

Not only Speed, but every one of the administration's vital lines to the Border states was humming with horror. Joseph Holt, who had been secretary of war in the previous administration and was serving Lincoln now as the army's judge advocate general, spoke for his native Kentucky when he wrote Lincoln "of the alarm & condemnation with which the union loving citizens of Kentucky . . . have read this proclamation." Others wrote even more frantically, prophesying that "if this is not immediately disavowed, and annulled, Kentucky will be lost to the Union." A delegation of Louisville Unionists implored Speed to tell Lincoln that "there is not a day to lose in disavowing emancipation or Kentucky is gone over the mill dam." Garrett Davis warned Chase that "the proclamation fell amongst us with pretty much the effect of a bomb shell" and "caused me despondency for the first time for Ky." And Chase himself was inclined to agree. "My own conviction is that Genl F's position in regard to slaves is not the true one," argued the treasury secretary. Proclamations declaring the slaves of rebels free only opened up questions about "Who is a Rebel, & Who are the Slaves of rebels," something which "must be decided upon trial & proof & Gen. F. had no authority to institute courts for such proceedings." [55]

What haunted all of these protests was the terror that any step toward emancipation would open up the long-feared Pandora's box of slave rebellion. "We have brought before us, whenever the abolition of slavery is spoken of as a practical subject, visions of riot and revenge on the part of the slaves, and the massacre of the former masters and their households," complained a contributor to the *New Englander and Yale Review.* "We are told that the emancipation of the negroes would be like the letting loose of so many wild beasts to devastate and devour." And that was exactly what Lincoln heard now from the Border states. "All of us who live in the slave states whether Union or loyal have great fear of insurrection," wrote Joshua Speed. "Will not such a proclamation read by the slaves incline them to assert their freedom?" Indeed it would, he concluded, and two days later wrote Lincoln to predict even more fearfully, "Cruelty & crime would run riot in the land & the poor negroes would be almost exterminated" by enraged whites. None of Lincoln's listeners in the Border, lost in the assumption of white racial superiority, could even begin to contemplate the possibility that it might be themselves, not their slaves, who might be facing extermination.[56]

FRÉMONT REMAINED HAPPILY INDIFFERENT to the embarrassment he had caused Lincoln, and his obtuseness seemed only to increase as he began picking quarrels with the Blairs. Frémont had unpleasantly surprised Frank Blair when Blair, home from the special session of Congress, pressed Frémont on why the Pathfinder had ignored Nathaniel Lyon's plea for reinforcements, and he proceeded so routinely to ignore Blair's advice on how to handle Missouri Unionists that Blair began to wonder if Frémont saw himself in "some sort of rivalry with me." By the end of August, Frank Blair wrote his brother Montgomery in Washington that he was "beginning to lose my confidence in Frémont's capacity," and Montgomery Blair, in turn, gloomily advised Lincoln that, despite being "for many years warmly attached to Genl Frémont," he believed that the general should be dismissed. "The war men of St. Louis concur in representing the condition of affairs there to be such that I am constrained against my own prepossessions to unite with them in the conclusion that this step is required by public interests."[57]

Lincoln, on the other hand, needed no time to see what damage Frémont's proclamation would do. His chief of staff, John Nicolay, noticed that "this at once troubled the Prest." for the "exceedingly discouraging effect upon the Union men of Ky. who had been pretty successfully coaxed along by the Admn to keep their State loyal." On September 2, "upon consultation," Lincoln wrote confidentially to Frémont. With surprising gentleness, he did not rescind Frémont's proclamation or even order Frémont to withdraw it himself. He only ordered that Frémont not proceed to execute anyone "without first having my approbation or consent," lest he set off a round of reprisals and retaliations. And he asked

Frémont to "modify" his plan to emancipate the slaves of the disloyal so that it conformed to "the first and fourth sections" of the Confiscation Act—in other words, to confine any emancipations to slaves actually used in the Confederate war effort, and not to free the slaves of just anyone whom Frémont suspected of disloyalty. "This letter is written in a spirit of caution and not of censure." It was not emancipation he objected to but the way Frémont had chosen to go about it.[58]

Frémont, however, showed no more interest in listening to the President of the United States than to anyone else. "He evidently considered himself clothed with proconsular powers," commented an incensed Gideon Welles, Lincoln's secretary of the navy, as though "he was a representative of the Government in a civil capacity as well as a military commander." So on September 8 Frémont wrote back to Lincoln, telling him that he knew more about the situation in Missouri than Lincoln did and would not "modify" anything about emancipation unless Lincoln "will openly direct me to make the correction." He entrusted the letter to his wife, who left for Washington "by the night train" and placed her husband's defiant response in Lincoln's hands during an evening meeting at the White House on September 10. Lincoln was not in a good mood. "The General ought not to have done it," Lincoln told her. He "should never have dragged the Negro into the war." The next day, Lincoln wrote back to Frémont, issuing a direct order that the emancipation clause in Frémont's proclamation "be so modified, held, and construed as to conform to and not to transcend the provisions on the same subject contained in the act of Congress entitled 'An act to confiscate property used for insurrectionary purposes,' approved August 6, 1861."[59]

It is difficult to imagine what Frémont hoped to accomplish by this truculence. Montgomery Blair eventually concluded that Frémont planned, by surrounding himself "with a German Staff, by distributing his money patronage among them [and] by flattering them with the idea of their controlling the politics of the country," to build "a Western Confederacy" out of the ruins of the old Union, with himself as its "Chief." Far-fetched as this seems, it was not entirely unlike what Frémont had succeeded in doing in California in 1847, and Lincoln had received the distinct impression from his interview with Jessie Benton

Frémont that "if Gen Frémont should conclude to try conclusions with me he could set up for himself." But whether or not Frémont was dreaming dreams of personal empire, Lincoln had no intention of backing away from Frémont's unapologetic insubordination.

Even before Frémont's letter was delivered, Lincoln had made Frémont the subject of a cabinet discussion on September 9, and the next day he sent Montgomery Blair and Quartermaster General Montgomery Meigs (a Blair brother-in-law) to St. Louis to make a personal inspection of Frémont's conduct. Predictably, Montgomery Blair reported that Frémont "seems Stupified & almost unconscious, & is doing absolutely nothing" and recommended that Meigs be immediately put in Frémont's place. On the other hand, Lincoln did not want "to act precipitately." He sent a second mission to St. Louis in the form of Secretary of War Cameron and Adjutant General Lorenzo Thomas, with directions to replace Frémont with Major General David Hunter.

But Frémont, as he had once managed with Thomas Hart Benton, talked Cameron into giving him another chance. Not until General Thomas's highly critical report of the Missouri situation was published in the *New York Times* and the cabinet had given "the vexed question of the recall of Genl. Frémont" another discussion on October 22 did Lincoln finally send a dismissal to Frémont, hand-carried for the president privately by his old Illinois legal crony, Leonard Swett.[60]

From being pelted by Frémont's enemies, Lincoln went to enduring a hot wind of abuse from Frémont's admirers and from the abolitionists, who instantly made the Pathfinder their latest martyr. With Congress out of session, George Julian was "on the stump" in Indiana when the news of Frémont's proclamation was announced, and Julian "found the masses everywhere so wild with joy, that I could scarcely be heard for their shouts." Massachusetts governor John Andrew, speaking in New York City, hailed Frémont's proclamation as the beginning of war against treason in earnest, and if as a by-product of that earnestness, "other men beside those of my own peculiar complexion and blood shall taste the sweets of liberty, God be praised." Lincoln's order to "modify" the proclamation came as a "chilling influence" on all this exultation. John Locke Scripps, the editor of the *Chicago Tribune*, complained to

Lincoln that "the Northwest is, as near as such a thing is possible, a unit in support of Frémont's proclamation," while the "modification of the proclamation has everywhere been regarded as a backward step . . . far more fatal than a retreat from a battle-field." Joseph Medill agreed: "The President's letter to Gen Frémont has cast a funeral gloom" over Chicago. "It comes upon us like a killing June frost." Radical senators like Benjamin Wade savaged Lincoln's "modification" as the sort of "ethics" which "could only come of one, born of poor white trash, and educated in a slave state." Charles Sumner was particularly disappointed because, after binding Frémont, it seemed as if Lincoln had thrown away the one tool that would not break in his hand. "To me the Presdt's letter is full—too full of meaning," Sumner sighed to law professor Francis Lieber. "It means that Slavery shall only be touched by Act of Congress & not through Martial Law." To Jessie Benton Frémont, it meant something much more personal—that Abraham Lincoln was possessed of "a sly slimy nature."[61]

None of these attacks cut as close to the bone for Lincoln as the criticism offered by Illinois's junior Republican senator, Orville Hickman Browning, whose friendship with Lincoln went back over a quarter-century to when Lincoln was still a "friendless, uneducated, penniless" young man in New Salem, Illinois. Browning was neither an abolitionist like Sumner nor a nervous fidget like Joshua Speed. "I am not in the habit of becoming needlessly excited," Browning remarked, with a good deal of truth. But he found the "modification" disheartening. "It is in no spirit of fault-finding that I say I greatly regret the order modifying Genl Frémont's proclamation," Browning wrote on September 17. Not only did the proclamation have "the unqualified approval of every true friend of the Government within my knowledge," but Browning could find little fault with the "legality or propriety" of executing guerrillas, nor could he understand why "traitors who are warring upon the constitution and laws" have any protection under those laws for their slaves. Under the terms of Lincoln's "modification," Browning could easily imagine arresting and hanging "traitors," all the while carefully ensuring their title to their slaves. "Is a traitors negro more sacred than his life?"[62]

He was surprised, a week later, to get a "Private & confidential" response from Lincoln that bristled with irritation but contained Lincoln's most sustained exposition of what the Constitution and the war permitted him, as president, to do. Lincoln wanted Browning to understand that, "as far as he could understand the law," Frémont's proclamation had not been a legitimate exercise of martial law at all. It was "*purely political,* and not within the range of *military* law, or necessity." If Frémont wanted to declare martial law and emancipate slaves, he was perfectly within his rights to do so, but only "as long as the necessity lasts." A pasture seized for "an encampment, or a fortification" was fair game; but to say that it "shall no longer belong to the owner or his heirs forever . . . is purely political, without the savor of military law about it."

Similarly, Frémont could have seized slaves, "but when the need is past, it is not for him to fix their permanent future condition," much less to make them "free men." Like it or not, in a democracy, "that must be settled according to laws made by law-makers, and not by military proclamations." Anything else was simply "dictatorship," and even the best-intentioned dictatorship would mean the death of "any government of Constitution and laws." He also wanted Browning to understand what the practical consequences of Frémont's proclamation would have been. "No doubt the thing was popular in some quarters, and would have been more so if it had been a general declaration of emancipation." But in Kentucky, "the very arms we had furnished Kentucky would be turned against us." [63]

Browning remained unconvinced. On September 30, he wrote back to Lincoln with "my own views of the legal principles involved," most of which involved redefining secessionist "citizens" as "public enemies" and therefore outside the pale of law. After Frémont's dismissal, Browning wrote a conciliatory letter, but Lincoln chose not to reply. The president would always insist afterwards that, personally, he "thought well of Frémont," and in 1863 he told his secretary, John Hay, that "even now I think well of his impulses." It was not the proclamation or even the emancipation provision that led Lincoln to sack the Pathfinder, but his insubordination and mismanagement. "I do not say Congress might not with propriety pass a law" to legalize military emancipation "just such as General Frémont proclaimed." And, for that matter, "I do not say I might not, as a member of Congress, vote for it." But in terms of both principle and policy, he could not let Frémont's proclamation stand. As Lincoln explained to one of Sumner's admirers, Charles Edward Lester, "We didn't go into the war to put down slavery, but to put the flag back, and to act differently at this moment, would, I have no doubt, not only weaken our cause but smack of bad faith." And if there was one thing Abraham Lincoln, a man prickly over questions about his own lack of religion, dreaded above all others, it was the suggestion that he had ever acted in "bad faith." There was no excuse, even in time of civil war, for a president "expressly or impliedly," directly or through one of his generals, to "seize and exercise the permanent legislative functions of the government."[64]

Perhaps, in the long view, Frémont's recall was the fate reserved for "the pioneer in any movement." Lincoln mused that such pioneers are "not generally the best . . . to carry that movement to a successful issue." Moses, for one, "began the emancipation of the Jews, but didn't take Israel to the promised land after all." So with Frémont. "It looks as if the first reformer of a thing has to meet such a hard opposition and gets so battered and bespattered that afterward, when people find they have to accept his reform, they will accept it more easily from another man." Frémont's mistake was not resorting to martial law but the failure to apply it correctly. "The powder in this bombshell will keep dry," Lincoln told Lester, "and when the fuse is lit, I intend to have them touch it off themselves."[65]

THE COMMON DEFECT in all three of these devices for emancipating slaves—contraband, confiscation, and martial law—was their lack of permanence. Butler's inventive labeling of runaway slave workers as "contraband of war" said nothing about the legal status of the contrabands, much less about emancipating those who simply had secessionist masters. Trumbull's Confiscation Act was also limited to "property" actively used in serving the Confederacy, something which proved almost impossible to demonstrate in court. And confiscation neither guaranteed emancipation to those slaves who were confiscated, nor guaranteed that their masters would not be able to sue successfully in federal court to reenslave them on the grounds that the act was unconstitutional. The same was true of Frémont's military emancipation. Under martial law, Frémont could seize whatever property he liked for military purposes and even declare slaves free. But once the war emergency was over, the federal court dockets would fill up with appeals that either attacked such proclamations as unconstitutional or denied that specific cases really fell within the definitions of the proclamation. And none of the three methods, of course, did anything to slavery itself, which would remain perfectly legal no matter how many individual slaves were emancipated.

Which is why Lincoln scarcely ever mentioned contrabands, was skeptical about the Confiscation Act, and "modified" Frémont's proclamation: None of them had any promise that they would stick. And if any one of them failed to survive a court challenge, the prospect for all future emancipation would be set back just as Taney's decision in *Dred Scott* had set back the struggle to keep slavery out of the territories. And this was before any consideration of the possible political debris these schemes would shake out in the Border states or in Congress. In the wake of Bull Run, recalled James Blaine, "the military situation was so discouraging that in the president's view it would have been wiser for Congress to refrain from enacting laws which, without success in the field, would be rendered unnecessary." [66]

There was, however, a fourth way that possessed the double virtue of being unassailably constitutional (so that it would never run the risk of challenge in the federal courts) and politically unentangled with the war effort (so that racist Democrats in the North could not paralyze and divide support for the war by painting the war as a stalking horse for abolitionism). Despite the claims of Lincoln's critics, past and present, that his indifference to the first three schemes showed indifference to emancipation itself, his first proposal for this fourth way came as early as the fall of 1861. This fourth way—Lincoln's own preferred method since the 1850s—was to offer a federally financed compensation scheme to persuade the slave states themselves to abolish slavery by an act of their own legislatures. "Mr. Lincoln always contended that the cheapest way of getting rid of slavery," recalled Joseph Gillespie, "was for the nation to buy the slaves & set them free." This was not, to be sure, something Lincoln believed he could do unilaterally. Any permanent emancipation could only be achieved by action of the states themselves, wiping out their slave statutes voluntarily. But this did not mean that the federal government could not put motives to emancipate in their minds that would hasten the decision. It could offer financial incentives—"buying the slaves," so to speak, by providing subsidies to the slave states, "making the emancipation gradual and compensating the unwilling owners."

No doubt this way would be costly, but it would not be nearly so costly as civil war. "In the mere financial, or pecuniary view, any member of Congress, with the census-tables and Treasury-reports before him, can readily see for himself how very soon the current expenditures of this war would purchase, at fair valuation, all the slaves in any named State." It would also avoid the catastrophic economic results of an immediate emancipation, since sudden abolition would wipe out something like $6 billion in capital investment (in 1861 dollars, no less), disrupt the production of a cotton crop worth $198 million on the international markets, and lead to "the sudden . . . depreciation of real estate, the depreciation of stocks and securities as of banks and railways, dependent for their value upon the inland commerce in the products of slave-labor." Much as putting compensation into the hands of slaveholders looked to abolitionists like blood money, it meant in financial terms that slaveholders would have in hand the cash necessary for hiring their former slaves as free laborers and allow the Southern economy to move along without a breakdown.[67]

The government could further sweeten the proposition by allowing state emancipation plans to take their time and emancipate gradually, as most of the Northern states had done after the Revolution and as the British West Indies did in 1833. "In my judgment," Lincoln explained, "gradual, and not sudden emancipation, is better for all." It would allow slave states to "adopt some practical system by which the two races could gradually live themselves out of their old relation to each other, and both come out better prepared for the new." That meant that, at the very least, "education for young blacks should be included in the plan." And perhaps the plan could be structured so that during the transition to freedom, one could simply abandon the idea of someone being a *slave* and begin treating him as a free-labor contractor. "The power, or element, of 'contract' may be sufficient for this probationary period; and, by its simplicity, and flexibility, may be the better." Two things were certain, though: The first was that the transition should be short, so that the interim should not become some form of indefinite semislavery, stretching off into the dim future. "If the period from the initiation to the final end, should be comparatively short, and the act should prevent persons being sold, during that period, into more lasting slavery, the whole would be easier." Lincoln warned, "I do not wish to pledge the general government to the affirmative support of even temporary slavery, beyond what can be fairly claimed under the constitution." And it should begin as soon as possible. "It should begin at once, giving at least the new-born, a vested interest in freedom, which could not be taken away."[68]

The question, of course, was where to begin. Obviously, Lincoln would be getting no hearing for such a plan in what was now the Confederacy. Lincoln wrote George Robertson in 1855, "So far as peaceful, voluntary emancipation is concerned, the condition of the negro slave" in the lower slave states "is now as fixed, and hopeless of change for the better, as that of the lost souls of the finally impenitent." But Lincoln hoped that the still-loyal Border slave states might be more malleable. The slave populations there were smaller than further south, and, Lincoln believed, the people less wedded to the Slave Power. "Not that all the states tolerating slavery would very soon, if at all, initiate emancipation; but . . . the more Northern" might if sufficient motives were held out to them. And that gradual movement would have the added advantage not only of beginning the long process of legally extinguishing slavery but also of undercutting the remaining slave states in the Confederacy. They would see "that in no event, will the former ever join the latter, in their proposed confederacy," and that might deflate the rebellion at the same time.[69]

If Lincoln planned to make any such offer, he would need to move soon. The Thirty-seventh Congress would convene for its first regular session in December, and as Lincoln reviewed the progress of the war situation with John Nicolay in October, there was little in it anyone could find cheering. In his notes, Nicolay jotted a litany of gloom:

Chase says the new loan will be exhausted in 11 days. . . .

October here, and instead of having a force ready to descend the Mississippi, the probability is that the army of the West will be compelled to defend St. Louis. . . . Frémont ready to rebel. . . .

Cameron utterly ignorant and regardless of the course of things.

There was every possibility that a surly and disappointed Congress might decide to take matters into its own hands, with results no one could predict. So, sometime after Frémont's dismissal, Lincoln decided to try his own plan and asked Joseph Kennedy, the superintendent of the federal census, for a table of figures on the slave population of Delaware.[70]

As the smallest and most northerly of the slave states, Delaware counted fewer than 1,800 slaves in its three counties, and most of them were concentrated in Sussex County, which shared a substantial border with Maryland. No other state had so little to lose by willingly parting with slavery, and as recently as 1847, the minuscule Delaware legislature had come within a single vote of adopting a gradual emancipation plan. On the other hand, the simple fact that slavery had survived in Delaware was a testimony to the gigantic role played by racism in propping up slavery, even when all the economic incentives for it had evaporated. Slavery was no longer "a valuable source of prosperity" in Delaware, but ending it, prophesied one Delaware newspaper, would "elevate the Negro to an equality with the white man or rather . . . degrade the white man by obliterating the distinction between the races." Lincoln also had to be wary of the fact that Delaware had no organized Republican political presence he could call upon to act for him. Rather than embracing an antislavery party like the Republicans, Delaware's non-Democrats had cobbled together a Unionist political coalition known as the People's Party, which had managed to get its nominee for

Delaware's lone congressional seat, George Fisher, elected in 1860. Lincoln and the Republicans had actually been drubbed in Delaware in the 1860 election, and Delaware's senators, James Asheton Bayard and Willard Saulsbury, were two of the most truculent proslavery Democrats on Capitol Hill. The door was open, but not wide open.[71]

What helped to keep the wedge in the door was the slim majority the People's Party held in the state legislature, which was conveniently in special session while Congress was not. So, early in November, Lincoln invited George Fisher to a meeting in Washington to discuss making an offer of gradual and compensated emancipation to the Delaware legislature. Fisher might not have been a Republican, but he was antislavery and certainly willing to cooperate in introducing gradual emancipation to Delaware. Lincoln afterward sent Fisher drafts of two bills Fisher could submit to the Delaware legislature, specifying that Delaware would abolish slavery by 1893. All children born to Delaware slaves after the adoption of the bill and all Delaware slaves over the age of thirty-five would be immediately free; all others would become free at age thirty-five, although free children with slave mothers might still be subject to compulsory apprenticeship until age twenty-one for males and age eighteen for females. For this, Lincoln would pay the state of Delaware $719,200 in 6 percent United States bonds, doled out in thirty-one annual installments. And since every gradual emancipation scheme since the adoption of the Constitution had tended to pick up speed on its own, Lincoln additionally offered to compress the compensation into ten payments of $71,920 and abolish slavery in Delaware by 1872.[72]

By the time Congress was ready to reconvene for the new session in December, Lincoln was confident that Delaware would take his bait. Orville Hickman Browning, who arrived in Washington the day before the session opened, stopped by the White House and found Lincoln "very hopeful of ultimate success."

He suggested to me the policy of paying Delaware, Maryland, Kentucky & Missouri $500 a piece for all the negroes they had according to the census of 1860, provided they would adopt a

system of gradual emancipation which should work the extinction of slavery in twenty years, and said it would require only
about one third of what was necessary to support the war for one
year. . . . There was no disagreement in our views upon any
subject we discussed.

All of this depended not only on the Delaware legislature but on the
willingness of the new session of Congress to issue the necessary bonds.
But Lincoln was as confident of Congressional cooperation as he was of
Delaware's. And if gradual emancipation worked with Delaware, then
the other Border states would see how little risk there was in signing on
and how much they had to gain by cashing in their slaves before the continuing war unsettled slavery further. The Delaware "proposition"
could thus "be made use of as the initiative to hitch the whole thing to."
The rebels would see the handwriting on the wall, the Union would be
restored, and slavery would be on the short road to extinction. "If Congress will pass a law authorizing the issuance of bonds for the payment
of the emancipated Negroes in the border states," Lincoln cheerfully
assured his old judicial friend, David Davis, then "Delaware, Maryland,
Kentucky, and Missouri will accept the terms." By these means, "it
seemed to him that gradual emancipation and governmental compensation" would bring slavery "to an end." [73]

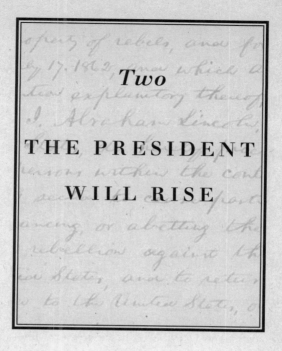

Two

THE PRESIDENT
WILL RISE

$\mathcal{T}$HE THIRTY-SEVENTH CONGRESS opened its first regular session at noon on Monday, December 2, 1861, with ceremonies in the Capitol that were almost perfunctory. The Senate "appointed [a] committee to inform [the] President of [its] organization & adjourned," while in the House "a light skirmishing party of buncombe resolutions" was "sent forward to clear the way for the approach of the heavy artillery of bills and enactments." The weather was delightfully mild, and "Penn Av^e is thronged from morning till late at night." But there was a distinct edginess in the atmosphere over the ill progress of the war. "Congress had hardly come together," wrote James Blaine, "when the change of opinion and action upon the Slavery question became apparent." There would be, promised Iowa congressman James W. Grimes, "more during the session than growling and showing our teeth." [1]

The fuel for this disgruntlement was provided by the disheartening inertia of the Union armies in the fall of that year. For a short while, the pain of the July disaster at Bull Run was eased by the cashiering of the losing general, Irvin McDowell, and his replacement by the victor of western Virginia, George Brinton McClellan. Unlike the slouchy and dark-humored McDowell, everything about McClellan promised action and victory. Graduating second in his class at West Point in 1846, McClellan was immediately posted as a staff officer in the Mexican War. He then served as an official observer of the Crimean War—a conflict which, as it turned out, taught him almost all the wrong lessons about how to conduct a war. Impatient with the slow eddies of promotion in the peacetime army, McClellan resigned his commission and established himself, with equal success, first as chief engineer of the Illinois Central Railroad and then, in 1860, as president of the Ohio & Mississippi Railroad. The fall of Sumter called him back into uniform as a major general of Ohio volunteers, and his quick but successful campaign in western Virginia placed upon his brow all the laurels the North had been hoping to distribute to victorious Yankee generals. Short but dapper, courtly, and sporting a French-style military goatee, McClellan carried himself with a confidence and authority that excited old Washingtonians who had never seen anything more in the military way than a militia muster. Out of the ashes of Bull Run, McClellan appeared as the Union phoenix, "pointed out by Providence," as Jacob Dolson Cox remembered, "as the ideal chieftain who could repair the misfortune and lead our armies to certain victory."[2]

For a while, this was exactly what seemed likely to happen. Congressman Albert Riddle recalled that "as by a potent magic, obedience, discipline, neatness, and the air military" were imposed on the defeated and disorganized volunteer regiments around Washington. McClellan breathed confidence back into the beaten volunteers and, with a certain Napoleonic flair, made them feel that they were soldiers. Not only soldiers, but an army, and in token of that, McClellan bestowed on these men the name they would carry through the rest of the war, the Army of the Potomac. In November, Lincoln appointed McClellan general-in-chief of all the federal armies, so that he could coordinate the entire war effort on land. New supply and training programs were put into place, a glittering staff (including two French imperial princes) was recruited, and, as one might expect from an engineer, a complete chain of fortifications was built around Washington—forty-eight forts and artillery lunettes in all, stocked with nearly five hundred pieces of artillery.[3]

The problem was that McClellan did no more than that. "The autumn passed away in grand reviews and showy parades, where the young General appeared with a numerous staff composed of wealthy young gentlemen," wrote an impatient Gideon Welles, but "as time wore on and no blow was struck or any decisive movement attempted, complaints became more numerous and envy and jealousy found opportunity to be heard." McClellan's political loyalties aroused still more suspicion that all was not right with the Young Napoleon. As a Democrat with ties to the major Democratic political moguls, McClellan labored to keep "the papers & the politicians" from dragging "the nigger question" into the war. "I am fighting to preserve the integrity of the Union & the power of the Govt—on no other issue." He would prove it, too, by issuing a series of directives to departmental commanders to take no part in harboring, employing, confiscating, or emancipating slaves. To Don Carlos Buell, a fellow Democrat who inherited command of all federal operations along the touchy Kentucky border, McClellan insisted that "we are fighting only to preserve the integrity of the Union." Buell should take every step to reassure Border state slaveholders that "their domestic institutions will in no manner be interfered with." There would be no more Frémont proclamations or Butler contrabands if McClellan could help it, and enforcement of the Confiscation Act was something the civil courts could worry about.[4]

McClellan's indifference surprised and then angered Radical Republicans in Congress who were eager to strike their own blow at slavery. Once the "buncombe" of the opening of the session had been dealt with, Thomas Eliot of Massachusetts was on his feet in the House of Representatives to propose a joint resolution that, only four months earlier, would have been walking on wind. It was true, Eliot announced, that "the war in which we are engaged . . . has for its object the suppression of . . . rebellion and the reestablishment of the rightful authority of the national Constitution and laws." But, he continued, "the maxim that the safety of the State is the highest law, subordinates rights of property and dominates over civil relations." Ensuring safety in this case meant authorizing "the president of the United States, as the commander-in-chief of our army, and the officers in command under him . . . to emancipate all persons held as slaves in any military district in a state of insurrection"—in effect, to use martial law to destroy slavery.[5]

The first to speak to Eliot's resolution was the Democratic abolitionist-hater Clement Vallandigham, who wanted the resolution tabled. But if he expected that this would be as easy to do in December as it had been in July, he was wrong. The tabling motion died on a vote of seventy to fifty-six. Immediately, Pennsylvania Republican James Campbell offered another resolution, calling on Congress to "confiscate the property, slaves included, of all rebels," whether or not those slaves had ever been employed, as the Confiscation Act specified, in the Confederate war effort. Campbell was followed by the irascible Thaddeus Stevens with the biggest bang of all. Stevens wanted Lincoln "to be requested to declare free, and to direct all our generals and officers in command to order the freedom, of all slaves who shall leave their masters, or who shall aid in quelling this rebellion." This meant emancipation on the grand scale—of any slave, owned by whomever or put to whatever purpose—with the war itself as justification. "It is the established law of nations that NECESSITY is the measure of violence in war," added Stevens's fellow Radical from Ohio John Bingham, "all else essential, however destructive of their lives and property, is justifiable—a right and a duty." [6]

These resolutions were the signal for an angry cascade of speeches, motions, and proposed legislation. Owen Lovejoy swung first at generals who either refused to shelter runaways or who were actually returning them to their masters. On December 4, Lovejoy read a proposed bill to the House that amended the formal military law of the army—the Articles of War—to forbid army participation in the capture of fugitives. The next day, Lyman Trumbull rose in the Senate to propose a new Confiscation Act. Unlike Sumner and Stevens, Trumbull had little enthusiasm for the martial-law solution to slavery. "So far from admitting the superiority of the military over the civil power in time of war . . . I hold that under our Constitution, the military is as much subject to the control of the civil power in war as in peace." Accordingly, Trumbull's new Confiscation Act would provide for two things the original act had not. First, it extended the reach of confiscation beyond just property used in the Confederate war effort to include the property of any Southerner in arms or in office against the Union. Second, it held the military responsible in the war zones for cooperating with the courts in confiscating rebel property, whether the generals particularly liked the idea or not. And if the generals did not, the Radicals had prepared a weapon with which to prod them, in the form of a new joint House-Senate investigating Committee on the Conduct of the War. "The Congress appointed a War Investigating Committee," wrote Adam Gurowski, a Polish expatriate buried deep in a minor State Department job, in his diary. "There is hope that the committee will quickly find out what a terrible mistake this McClellan is, and warn the nation of him." [7]

The new Joint Committee, as well as the resolutions to protect contrabands and runaways, along with Trumbull's Second Confiscation Act, were only the larger marks on the paper that winter. Charles Sumner, as the chairman of the Senate Foreign Relations Committee, carved out a niche for antislavery activity in diplomacy by promoting bills to extend recognition to the black republics of Haiti and Liberia and to strengthen the treaties with Britain for the suppression of the Atlantic slave trade. Others, like George Julian, called for legislation to repeal the Fugitive Slave Law or, like Isaac Arnold, introduced "a Bill to render freedom national" and overturn the *Dred Scott* decision by banning slavery in the territories. "Slavery, by inviting this war, has received its death-blow," exulted the Washington *Sunday Morning Chronicle*. "It is now only necessary that the government be administered in the spirit of freedom to do away with this great evil."

What is easy to miss in these repeated clamors for action in Congress is how very narrow the scope of the action was. No one seriously proposed laying hands on slavery in the Border states, much less abolishing the institution of slavery. Lyman Trumbull's Second Confiscation Act was doomed to seven months of debate, amendment, and referral to committee before it came to a vote, and even then, its sponsors were unsure whether it would do anything more than offer a mild expression of Congressional wishfulness. Trumbull made no attempt in the new act to answer the nagging questions about legal conflicts with the constitutional ban on attainder; if anything, it made those questions worse by licensing the military to confiscate property without jury trials. "The confiscation act was more useful as a declaration of policy than as an act to be enforced," acknowledged Senator John Sherman of Ohio. Even Trumbull admitted that "so far from striking at all the property of each and every citizen in the seceded States, it would not probably reach the property of one in ten of the rebels, and in no case would touch the property of a loyal citizen." [8] Even from the Radicals, emancipation called up more eloquence than action.

Congress had reason for its hesitations, since every one of these measures was vehemently opposed by antiadministration Democrats or watered down by moderate Republicans whose constituencies at home were less than enthusiastic about emancipating black slaves. William Pitt Fessenden of Maine, the outstanding Republican moderate in the Senate, found "the Republican senators . . . equally divided" over the Second Confiscation Act, "one half urging provisions so severe that the more moderate half regarded them as violation of the Constitution." Orville Hickman Browning, who also had little in common with the Radicals, was convinced that the federal courts would find it "unconstitutional, since it amounted to an attainder." And if not the courts, then the army would make confiscation inoperable. "The soldiers of our great Army," declared Indiana Democrat Daniel Voorhees, were appalled "at the evil machinations of abolitionists in and out of Congress. . . . They want no four millions of slaves set free." Neither did the Northern people at home, and there the hard racist bedrock of the opposition was reached. "We want no more poetry about striking off chains and bidding the oppressed go," snarled Ohio Democrat Samuel S. Cox. "Plain people want to know whether the chains will not be put upon white limbs." Blacks were "vicious, indolent, and improvident," and emancipation would do nothing but unleash a horde of "pestilent" black refugees on the North, taking "the bread and meat from the families of white laborers." Cox's reading of history, including the history of emancipation in the West Indies, convinced him that "it is as hard to make a servile people free as a free people slaves," and the only likely result "from this policy of emancipation" would be "a conflict of the races." It would be San Domingue and Nat Turner and John Brown all over again, this time in the North.[9]

In the face of such racial and legal hostility, the Radicals' weapons for laying hands on slavery were few. "I think all the Slaves ought to be declared free by law of Congress," wrote John Bingham apologetically on December 19, but already it was plain that "I cannot get such a bill through now." [10]

THE REPUBLICAN RADICALS lived with the frustration of being the edge of a wave that was never quite making it to shore. Much of that failure could be blamed on the opposition and on the fainthearts of their own party. But a good deal of their frustration was vented upon Lincoln. Few of them could understand why Lincoln refused to join with them by vigorously enforcing confiscation or lighting better fires under his generals. "Our duty as a nation," declared Ohio Radical James Ashley to a crowd in Toledo in November, "has seemed to me from the first so plain that I have been not a little amazed at the apparent hesitancy and want of policy on our part." Why didn't Lincoln lead? Partly, they concluded, because of fear for the Border states; partly because, except for Chase, the cabinet was full of unreliables like Montgomery Blair and William Henry Seward; and partly because Lincoln was a man of good intentions but little willpower. "Lincoln means well but has no force of character," Zachariah Chandler complained in November 1861. Wade agreed: "I begin to despair of ever putting down this rebellion through the instrumentality of this administration," he wrote Chandler. "You will not inspire Old Abe, Seward, Chase or Bates with courage decision or enterprise, with a galvanic battery." When Julia Ward Howe visited Lincoln at the White House with Massachusetts governor John Andrew and the Radical Unitarian minister James Freeman Clarke, Clarke told her going out that "we have seen it all in his face, hopeless honesty; that is all." [11]

This was an easy conclusion for the veteran editors and Congressional hangers-on to jump to. Political insiders knew that Lincoln had come into office with no executive experience whatsoever, and few imagined that he was anything more than a well-intentioned party hack. "Now Abraham was honest; but he was not wise in his generation," wrote a New York satirist. "And he was called Abraham the well meaning. And men pitied him." [12] Yet, as Leonard Swett had once warned people, underestimating Abraham Lincoln had been the undoing of many an Illinois lawyer, judge, and politician, and the same was true in Washington. David Turpie, a Democrat who arrived in Washington in early 1862 to fill one of Indiana's vacant Senate seats, discovered that beneath the appearance of awkwardness, Lincoln "closely observed even the most casual gesture or remark. . . . No one ever left his presence without feeling that he fully apprehended what action was required of him, and why it was requested." During one international imbroglio on the high seas, Lincoln told his attorney general, Edward Bates, that "I am not much of a prize lawyer." Yet he was quite capable at other moments of being a very knowledgeable analyst of international law. The English lawyer George Borrett was surprised when visiting Lincoln in 1864 to hear Lincoln steer the conversation, "unasked, into a forcibly drawn sketch of the Constitution of the United States," launching "into some shrewd remarks about . . . the legal systems" of Great Britain and America. [13]

So, although Zachariah Chandler preferred to describe Lincoln as "*timid,* vacillating, & inefficient" on the subject of emancipation, the simpler truth was that while Congress was debating confiscation and martial law, Lincoln was following his own path to emancipation in Delaware, a path that meant "compensated and voluntary emancipation, on the one hand, and colonization of the freedmen on the other." In his Annual Message to the new session of Congress, Lincoln argued (without tipping his hand about the Delaware plan) that the attrition of war and the threat contained in the First Confiscation Act made compensation just as likely a vehicle for emancipation as abolition. Rather than risk seeing their slaves run off to the Union army, slaveholders in the Border states might be quite happy to get cash for what they could no longer keep. At that moment, Lincoln urged, Congress should be willing to step in with some form of subsidy to the states—in effect, buying a state's slaves, with the slaves then to "be at once deemed free."

It is unlikely that a public announcement of the Delaware plan in the Annual Message would have satisfied Chandler and the other Radicals; they shared none of Lincoln's concern with balancing ends and means, and a premature disclosure in December of the Delaware plan might have jeopardized its adoption by the Delaware legislature. Still, Lincoln never denied that, in preserving the Union, "all indispensable means must be employed." The day after sending the Annual Message to Congress, Lincoln ordered McClellan to stop the arrests of fugitive slaves in the District by the Army of the Potomac, and if slaveowners or hired deputies tried to seize runaways from army encampments, the seizures "should be immediately followed by the military arrest of the parties making the seizure." [14]

In February, Lincoln signed the death warrant for Nathaniel Gordon, the last man to be hanged for smuggling slaves on the high seas. And whatever doubts Lincoln had about the constitutionality of the Confiscation Acts "except in a comparatively harmless form," he would stand by their results, even to the point of recognizing confiscated slaves as legally, and irrevocably, free. He had already confided to John Hay that "all negroes, once lawfully confiscated from the possession of their rebel owners, shall become free men." As Lincoln told Wendell Phillips, when the truculent abolitionist was finally invited to speak before Congress in the spring of 1862, "The Negro who has once touched the hem of the government's garment shall never again be a slave." The only thing he would not tolerate was any effort by the partisans of other emancipation theories, especially in the military, to upstage his own plan for compensated emancipation. [15]

Depending on how much impatience boiled in one's system, gradualism and compensation were radical enough on their terms. As badly as Charles Sumner wanted Lincoln to use the martial-law bludgeon, Lincoln was sure that the carrot of compensated emancipation put him only a short distance behind whatever the stick of martial law could achieve, and that his plan would achieve the goal with greater legal permanence. "The only difference between you and me," Lincoln told Sumner when he briefed Sumner on the Delaware plan on November 30, "is a difference of a month or six weeks in time." In fact, by mid-December, Lincoln was already crafting a newer and more expanded version of the Delaware compensation plan. Sumner excitedly wrote Richard Cobden, the great English liberal, that "*the Presdt now meditates an early Message to Congress* proposing to buy the slaves in the still loyal states of Mo.-Ky.-Md.- & Del. & then proclaim Emancipation with our advancing armies." Compensated emancipation would not only begin the legal process of exterminating slavery throughout the republic, but the Border "would then be fixed to the union, & we should deal exclusively with the Cotton States." [16]

When Sumner brought Moncure D. Conway and William Ellery Channing, the doyen of New England's Unitarian ministry, to a January meeting at the White House, Channing lost no time in suggesting that Lincoln consider "emancipation with compensation for the slaves." Lincoln just as quickly replied that "he had for some years been in favour of that plan" and hinted that something of that nature might be in the offing. "Perhaps," Lincoln allowed, "we may be better able to do something in that direction after a while than we are now." In February Lincoln asked Treasury Secretary Chase to draw up a draft plan, offering compensation in return for emancipation in any of the Border states and in any of the rebel states that "now reject the counsels of their misleaders . . . and again send Senators & Representatives to Congress." Sumner wrote Orestes Brownson on February 2, predicting that "the President will rise. . . . He has counselled with Chase & myself on a proposition of greater magnitude than was ever yet submitted to a deliberative assembly." [17]

THE ONE EMANCIPATION WEAPON Lincoln refused even to consider was martial-law emancipation. His reluctance had less to do with the Radicals than with Lincoln's own personal uneasiness around the military. He had never felt the kind of spread-eagle enthusiasm that tossing plumes and glittering epaulettes aroused in so many otherwise sober republican hearts. Soldiers—particularly professional ones—were synonymous in Lincoln's mind with "arbitrary rule," with Metternich, Wellington, and Napoleon III. He was convinced, and not without reason, that "most of the officers of the army" came "from among Democrats because most of the West Point men were Democrats." As Lincoln reminded John Seymour, the brother of New York Democratic politico Horatio Seymour, "antislavery men, being generally much akin to peace, had never interested themselves in military matters and in getting up companies, as Democrats had." [18] Long ago, he had predicted that the greatest danger to the republic would likely come from "an Alexander, a Caesar, or a Napoleon" who "thirsts and burns for distinction; and, if possible . . . will have it at the expense of emancipating slaves, or enslaving freemen." Twenty-three years later, he found in the example of John Charles Frémont just how easily the potent fumes of brass and gunmetal could make men dream of Napoleonic power, and George McClellan seemed to be fast becoming a similar case.

What caught Lincoln entirely off guard in December 1861 was finding rumors of military radicalism within his own cabinet. By custom, the seven cabinet secretaries were expected to supplement the president's Annual Message to Congress by submitting annual reports of their own, a practice that saved presidents the tedium of reviewing every detail of the administration's business for Congress and left cabinet secretaries some liberty to make specific requests and recommendations of their own. What it was *not* supposed to do was give secretaries the opportunity to run an entirely separate game, and that was very nearly what War Secretary Simon Cameron had accomplished.

Of all his cabinet choices, Lincoln had been least enthusiastic about Cameron. Sixty-two years old, blink-eyed and satchel-mouthed, Cameron was a veteran Pennsylvania wire-puller, shameless in his rapacity and corruption and even more shameless in his "mean ambition to occupy exalted stations, for which he was utterly and hopelessly incompetent." Within six months, charges of corruption—of no-bid contracts, sweetheart deals, and incompetence—were already flying at

Cameron's head, and days after the opening of the new session of Congress, demands for an investigation of the War Department were bouncing through the House of Representatives. Lifting a finger to the political wind, the war secretary attempted to ingratiate himself with the Radicals by suddenly discovering a zeal for emancipation by military decree that no one else had noticed in him during the previous twenty-four years of his political career.[19]

Cameron moved first to ally himself with Treasury Secretary Chase, and with Chase's help issued the letters that endorsed Benjamin Butler's contraband plan at Fortress Monroe. "We agreed very early that the necessity of arming" the confiscated slaves "was inevitable," Chase claimed, and Cameron hinted to Butler that he could employ them "under such organizations and in such occupations as circumstances may suggest or require." In mid-November, Cameron created a sensation by taking the platform at a review of a new regiment and endorsing "the arming of negro troops." When he wrote his report to Congress at the end of the month, he not only vigorously endorsed confiscation but announced that "it is clearly a right of the Government to arm slaves."

> It is vain and idle for the Government to carry on this war, or hope to maintain its existence against rebellious force, without employing all the rights and powers of war.... If it shall be found that the men who have been held by the rebels as slaves are capable of bearing arms and performing efficient military service, it is the right, and may become the duty, of this Government to arm and equip them, and employ their services against the rebels.[20]

As if this were not inflammatory enough on its own, Cameron proceeded to have the Government Printing Office run off a thousand copies of the report, some for Congress and some for the newspapers, without sending it over to Lincoln. The president might never have known what was going to hit him had not the superintendent of government printing, John Defrees, placed one of the printed copies before him on the evening of December 2 and asked if he knew what was in it, since it would probably be in "the leading papers . . . the succeeding morning."

Lincoln was aghast. He "glanced over the copy placed in his hands, and his eye rested upon the passage in question, which had reference to arming the slaves," and then his heart leapt. "This will never do!" Lincoln exclaimed. "Cameron must take no such responsibility. That is a question which belongs exclusively to me!" Pencil in hand, "he struck out the objectionable clause" and ordered Defrees to telegraph every newspaper editor who had received a copy to embargo the report. Surprisingly, he administered only a private rebuke to Cameron, warning the secretary that any notion of putting guns into the hands of slaves "would hurt him in Kentucky," and "for a time the incident seemed forgotten." But Lincoln immediately began looking for "some place to put Cameron to get him out of the War Department." On January 11, the day after the usual Friday cabinet meeting and "without consultation or notice," Lincoln informed Cameron that he was being nominated the following Monday as United States minister to Russia. In his place, that same Monday, Lincoln nominated another Pennsylvanian, a fierce, stumpy Democratic lawyer, Edwin McMaster Stanton.[21]

Despite the example made of Frémont and Cameron, urgings about some form of military solution to emancipation refused to fade out of Lincoln's ill-disposed hearing. At the beginning of November, the Union Navy scored one of the few successes of that dismal fall when it seized bases for coaling and supplying its blockade of Southern ports on Ship Island, at the mouth of the Mississippi, and at Port Royal, on the Sea Islands of South Carolina. The commander of the army garrison deposited on Ship Island, John W. Phelps, had commanded the First Vermont Volunteers under Benjamin Butler at Fortress Monroe the previous spring, and it was the irascible Phelps who had been in charge of the operations that triggered the first appearance of the contrabands at Butler's gate. Phelps now circulated a testy proclamation to "the Loyal Citizens" of southern Louisiana, informing them in the tones of a soapbox orator that "the Slave States" are "under the highest obligations of honor and morality to abolish slavery." Indeed, whether they

realized it or not, abolition would mark the moment when "our Southern brethren . . . would begin to emerge from a hateful delirium." This
was not the stuff calculated to induce Louisiana's rebels to lay down
their arms, or to soothe Lincoln's anxieties about provoking the Border.
But Phelps was miles away from Washington, and his proclamation
made no threats about actually doing anything; to Phelps's chagrin, it
was ignored.[22]

It was less easy to ignore what was going on in South Carolina. On
November 7, a federal flotilla steamed into the Port Royal Sound and easily beat down the fire of two Confederate forts, sending rebel soldiers and
civilian plantation owners alike scampering off the islands of the sound
"quite as though fire and sword awaited them had they remained." They
left behind their houses and cotton fields, and more remarkably, they left
their slaves, who came down to the wharves by the hundreds, "wild with
excitement," to greet the Yankee sailors and marines. The army soon
disembarked from its transports to occupy the islands, and their commander, General Thomas W. Sherman, hastened to assure the Sea Island
whites "that we have come amongst you with no feelings of personal animosity; no desire to harm your citizens, destroy your property, or interfere
with any of your lawful rights or your social and local institutions." But
there were no whites left to hear. Instead, Sherman found himself with an
uncomprehending audience of 11,000 Sea Island slaves. "They thronged
into the camps in great numbers, often coming into camp, carrying in little bundles, all their worldly possessions, having a simple faith that when
they reached 'Massa Linkum's soldiers' they would be free."[23]

Sherman did not have enough military work to employ so many
slaves as contraband laborers, nor did he have much way of sorting out
which slaves could be considered contraband and which merely runaways. (In fact, it was not entirely clear that any of the slaves had actually run away, in the literal sense of things; it was their masters who
had done the running.) But there was cotton in the abandoned fields,
and the cotton was worth no small fortune; contrabands, with a little
stretching of the definition, could as easily be put to work harvesting
cotton for the benefit of the Union as building fortifications. Both
Chase and Charles Sumner saw at once that this situation might pro-

vide a kind of laboratory in which liberated slaves could begin learning how to work for wages while simultaneously turning a tidy profit in confiscated cotton for the government. Soon in procession came Treasury agents to create a new free-labor experiment that turned the slaves into wage earners, and a band of fifty-three Northern missionaries to open schools for the contrabands, or fugitives, or whatever they were in the eyes of the law.

The army, all the way up to General Sherman, took a dim view of the agents and the missionaries. But in March, Sherman was replaced by an abolitionist commandant, Major General David Hunter. Expected to carry out fresh operations against both Savannah and Charleston, Hunter found that he had too few soldiers even to hold Port Royal if the Confederates made a determined effort to recapture it. His eye wandered to the cotton-pickers, among whom, he noticed, there were more than enough able-bodied men to make up several regiments. On April 25, Hunter declared martial law along the Carolina, Georgia, and Florida coast; on May 9, he announced that since "slavery and martial law in a free country are altogether incompatible; the persons . . . heretofore held as slaves, are therefore declared free." Two days later, Hunter conducted a roundup of five hundred blacks around Port Royal, organized them into squads and companies as the First South Carolina Volunteers, and issued them weapons.[24]

The missionaries wept to see their unwilling charges dragged off to Hunter's mustering-in, but among antislavery Radicals, the weeping was tears of joy. "Today's news is that General Hunter at Port Royal proclaims a general emancipation in South Carolina, Georgia, and Florida!!!" exulted George Templeton Strong in New York. The Border staters and Democrats in Congress and the North also wept, but for entirely different reasons. "If General Hunter's proclamation declaring the slaves of his department forever free is not disowned by the administration and himself disgraced," read one threatening letter to Lincoln, "I will place my whole property to the value of three millions in the hands of the rebels for the use of the traitor Jeff Davis." An old-time Maryland politico, Reverdy Johnson, implored Lincoln, "For heavens sake, at once, repudiate it, & recall the officer" or "it will serve the rebels, nicer than a dozen victories." In Congress, Charles Wickliffe—— the "fierce pro-slavery member of Congress from Kentucky"——demanded an explanation three weeks later from Secretary of War Stanton for Hunter's incendiary decision to put rifles into the hands of blacks. "To arm the negroes of the South," raged Wickliffe, was "without law and against law." Worse, it was a racial slur on the superiority of white men. "It is an admission that the power of the United States, the Army and Navy of twenty million white men, is not equal to subdue and overthrow the army of the rebellion." The result, prophesied the Kentuckian, would of course be "to excite the slaves of the rural districts to a servile war . . . of murder, conflagration, and rapine." [25]

Lincoln was irritated, too, although not for the same cause as Charles Wickliffe. Although Salmon Chase tried to soften the proclamation by explaining it to Lincoln "as a military measure to meet a military exigency," this was probably the worst justification he could offer. Lincoln was not appeased. As the commander in chief of a military he had no good reason to trust, he alone would make any determination of what the military exigencies of this war were, not his generals or his cabinet or the Congress either. Lincoln scribbled a terse, one-sentence reply to Chase: "No commanding general shall do such a thing, upon *my* responsibility, without consulting me."

Two days later, on May 19, Lincoln issued his own proclamation, without consulting Chase. This was no "modification" but an outright cancellation. Unlike Frémont, Hunter had issued his proclamation with no qualifications whatsoever—nothing about needing to prove that the new black draftees were taken from masters who "have taken an active part in the rebellion," nothing about respecting "the ordinary tribunals" of civil law—and so Lincoln jerked Hunter back even more sharply than he had Frémont. Hunter's emancipation proclamation was "altogether void," and for the benefit of any other district commandant, Lincoln warned that "no commander, or person," had the authority "to make proclamations declaring the slaves of any State free." [26]

Lincoln's irritation at Hunter was that of a strategist blindsided by a rival strategy, not (like Wickliffe's) the howling of a no-compromise white supremacist. "Although the President repudiated his order," John

Hay assured a confidante, "he regards him none the less kindly." Curiously, he did not order Hunter to disband his black regiment, and he added to his "cancellation" the warning that he still reserved to himself, "as Commander-in-Chief of the Army and Navy," the power to "declare the Slaves of any state or states, free" whenever matters came to the point he had described in the Annual Message, when "it shall have become a necessity indispensable to the maintenance of the government." He did not want to reach for the military weapon, and he was not ready to surrender the hope of compensated emancipation, not yet.

MOST NORTHERN WHITES saw emancipation—when they were interested in it at all—as an emancipation for themselves, a means of ridding the republic of a moral embarrassment or eliminating an economic rival to free white labor. Even Lincoln had said, during the political turmoil of the 1850s, that one reason slavery needed to be contained was to preserve the western territories as "the happy home of teeming millions of free, white, prosperous people, and no slave amongst them. . . . We want them for the homes of free white people. This they cannot be, to any considerable extent, if slavery shall be planted within them." Even among abolitionists, the arrival of nationwide emancipation was expected to be followed by the removal of the freed slaves to some other place. "The difference of race between the white and the negro," predicted the impeccably antislavery New Englander James Russell Lowell, "will ever keep them apart, and forbid their amalgamation." [27]

This absurd indifference to the wishes or wants of the people who had most at stake led to another oddity of emancipation, the less-than-enthusiastic response of blacks themselves. At the beginning of the war blacks were discouraged by white officialdom from seeing any part for themselves in it. Jacob Dodson, a free black Washingtonian who had served in three of Frémont's western pathfinding expeditions, wanted in April 1861 to present Simon Cameron with "three hundred reliable colored free citizens" to defend the capital, but Cameron was not talking about black soldiers just yet, and he hurriedly waved Dodson away. "This Department has no intention at present to call into the service of the Government any colored soldiers." When black New Yorkers attempted to hold a recruitment meeting in Manhattan two weeks after the fall of Fort Sumter, the police broke it up lest the meeting "lead to some unpleasantness . . . as well as exasperate the South." A company of students at Ohio's black Wilberforce College offered themselves as a unit to Governor William Dennison, but they were rejected without a second thought. Blacks might very well hold themselves "in joyful readiness to bare our bosoms in battle in defense of the Union" (as a rally of "colored citizens" in Cleveland promised), but the answer John Mercer Langston received from Governor Dennison was typical of white Northern feeling: "This is a white man's government; that white men are able to defend and protect it, and that to enlist a negro soldier would be to drive every white man out of the service." [28]

None of these rebuffs came as a surprise to Northern blacks, who were all too familiar with the hollowness of Northern whites' pretensions to compassion. In truth, Northern whites "hate the Negro with a perfect if not a supreme hatred." And it was a hatred that was sullenly returned by many blacks. "The whites have always been an unjust, jealous, unmerciful, avaricious and bloodthirsty set of beings, always seeking after power and authority," declared the black abolitionist David Walker in his celebrated *Appeal to the Coloured Citizens of the World.* Hosea Easton, Hartford's foremost black minister, described whites as "a race of savages" whose history was "a continual scene of bloodshed and robbery." Henry Highland Garnet, minister to New York City's Shiloh Presbyterian Church, alternated between proclamations of human universality as "Children of one father" and suspicions that both whites and Indians were morally inferior to blacks. Martin Delany promoted a crude Afrocentrism that claimed "the Christian doctrine of three persons in one—Father, Son and Holy Ghost" as the discovery of "the wise men of Egypt and Ethiopia," and in 1851, Delany came close to boasting that blacks had survived in slavery where Indians had not because blacks were "a long-lived, hardy race," while the Indians were "wholly unaccustomed to labor" and sank "under the insupportable weight . . . of oppression and toil" placed upon them by whites. Even within the community of color, suspicion and self-contempt were rampant. "The nearer the negro or mulatto approaches to the white, the more he seems to feel his superiority over those of a darker hue," complained William Wells Brown. In 1855, Owen Lovejoy presented the Illinois legislature with an anticolonization petition "from the colored people of the State," opposing colonization "unless separate colonies be assigned to those of different shades of color." Their "objection" was "that blacks and mulattoes cannot live harmoniously together." No one in Civil War America, it turns out, had a monopoly on racial self-interest.[29]

So long as Lincoln coddled the Border states and suppressed every move by his generals to hitch emancipation to military decree, many Northern blacks felt a mounting inclination to wash their hands of an affair in which they were clearly unwanted. "To offer ourselves now," wrote the editor of the *Christian Recorder*, the newspaper of the African Methodist Episcopal Church, "is to abandon *self-respect* and invite insult." The African-American newspaper *Pine and Palm* warned that blacks who wanted to fight for the Union were only confirming the authority of the antiblack statutes in all the states of that Union. "If the colored people, under all the social and legal disabilities by which they are environed, are ever ready to defend the government that despoils them of their rights, it may be concluded that it is quite safe to oppress them." The *Weekly Anglo-African* urged blacks to have nothing to do with the war until the state and federal governments were willing to treat blacks as something other than "pariahs and outcasts." Before "you hand us bullets, give us ballots." They would wait to be persuaded that Lincoln meant emancipation.[30]

Waiting, however, was a luxury that the four million African-Americans still in slavery found incomprehensible. As federal troops set up occupation across the Border states, the Carolina coast, and the middle Mississippi valley, the arrival of the armies set off wild celebrations among slaves. "Wherever the national army advances into the insurrectionary region," Secretary of State Seward wrote to Charles Francis Adams, the American minister in London, "African bondsmen . . . come out to meet it and to offer their services." Lining the fence palings of plantations, standing in tattered groups along the roadside, black slaves watching the federal soldiers march past neither knew nor cared about the sincerity of their motives, the technicalities of gradualism or compensation, or the politics of confiscation. "Women dropped on their knees, seized with spasmodic religion, while men would pray and sing irrespective of what others were doing . . . crying excitedly: 'Glory Hallelujah! Massa Linkum's comin',' " remembered one federal artilleryman marching into the Louisiana countryside. A New Hampshire regiment "passed a farm of three thousand acres, with a large brick house" in Kentucky, and though "the owner did not come out to greet us, for he was a rebel," the "colored people . . . came out in full force to welcome us with 'God bless Mass'r Lincun's men!' They were as happy as they could be, and said, ' 'pears like we neber so glad before.' " [31]

Even the rumor of war was enough to soften and loosen the underpinnings of slavery. Fresh whispers of slave insurrections rose like the smell of decay in the mangrove swamps. "The question that is constantly asked," wrote one Mississippi officer to the state's governor, is "what is to become of my wife & children when left in a land swarming with negroes without a single white man on many plantations to restrain their licentiousness by a little wholesome fear?" Some slaveowners turned to appeasement to ensure order. "Strange what a difference there was on the place," recalled John McCline. "The overseer went about giving directions in the most kindly manner. Mistress, too, had put away her raw hide, and there was no cutting and slashing every one she met, as formerly." Others only redoubled their cruelty. Annie Row's elderly "Marster Charley" turned violent and "cuss everything and every body and us watch out and keep out of his way." Two of his sons enlisted in the Confederate army, and when one was killed, "Marster Charley" went berserk, "takes de gun offen de rack and starts for de field whar de niggers am a-workin'. My sister and I sees that and we'uns starts runnin' and screamin', 'cause we'uns has brothers and sisters in de field." Those whites with land or relatives further south gathered their slaves and moveables and fled deeper into the interior, away from the armies and the threat of freedom. "Their masters," one Iowa volunteer wrote dryly in his diary, "though they talk loudly about the happiness and contentment of their slaves, keep shoving them farther south as our army advances." [32]

Other blacks took the opportunity "Mass'r Lincun's soldiers" seemed to offer and ran away to join the swelling number of contrabands. This attempt involved bigger risks than most slaves expected. The legal niceties of the First Confiscation Act meant that many runaways would flee for Union camps or ships only to be turned away if they could not prove they had been put to Confederate service. The federal gunboat *Seneca* was boarded off Jacksonville, Florida, by "three slaves belonging to a Mr. Byar," but when their master appeared, obviously "too old to serve" and with proof that his two sons in the Confederate army were "not minors" and enlisted on their own, the *Seneca*'s commander "remanded the men to him." On land, runaways might be recaptured if Union officers allowed masters or slave catchers with "loyal" credentials to hunt through regimental encampments. Sergeant Samuel McIlvaine of the Tenth Indiana had enlisted to deny "the right of any portion of the people of the United States to sever, or rive in twain, and destroy this government, which stands out to the rest of the world as the polestar, the beacon light of liberty & freedom to the human race." He lifted no finger when the regiment's commander allowed "three or four slave hunters" to drag away two blacks who "had mixed with the Negro cooks and waiters and were thus endeavoring to effect their escape to the North." They "had counted on being protected in the regiment," but McIlvaine and his compatriots, who were so concerned about being a beacon light of liberty and freedom, allowed them to be disarmed and taken "without molestation on our part." [33]

But as the war took its toll of patience as well as lives, federal officers increasingly treated rampaging slaveowners as annoyances to be shooed off rather than as property owners to be respected. The men in the ranks, increasingly irked by Southern arrogance, silently allowed the runaways to pass through their lines or be absorbed into various forms of menial service. Jacob Dolson Cox gave "stringent orders" to his Ohio volunteers not to allow runaways into their camps, but if the fugitives managed to get in, "I declined to order the troops to arrest and return them." McClellan could issue general orders as he liked; Cox found it "impossible to come to any agreement in regard to the fugitive slaves who took refuge in our camps. The soldiers and many of the officers would encourage the negroes to assert their freedom, and would resist attempts to recapture them." When a rebel slaveowner showed up at the picket line of the Eighth Michigan outside Annapolis to reclaim a runaway, the men "pounced on him . . . & unless he had been protected, I think he would have lost his life in this Negro Hunt." [34]

The decision by white soldiers to intervene on behalf of black strangers was so widespread that it becomes easy to miss how utterly extraordinary these interventions were, especially since they were happening in the face of commanders' direct contrary orders. Overwhelming pity certainly played a role. Chaplain John Eaton was appalled by the great landmass of suffering that gathered around the Union camps, "men, women, and children in every stage of disease or decrepitude, often nearly naked, with flesh torn by the terrible experiences of their escapes." They presented themselves as raw humanity, not as property or even as black. "I had thought before that God had made the Negro for a slave for the whites," Elisha Stockwell of the Fourteenth Wisconsin recalled, but after seeing a slaveowner abuse two female slaves, "my views on slavery took a change." John McCline, who had no illusions about the good-heartedness of white people, was surprised to find that the federal soldiers "were very kind and friendly toward us, giving us many good and useful things, such as clothing, blankets, etc."

At the same time, the goodwill of Union soldiers might turn out to have no better cause than the opportunities the fugitives presented for hewing wood and hauling water. "All who agreed to follow the army and be of such use to it as saw fit to put us," McCline remembered, "would be useful, and would doubtless, find employment as cooks, or servants for officers, and should get wages." One Connecticut volunteer welcomed the "great numbers of negroes" who "left their owners' plantations" near Bayou LaFourche in 1862, since they "were only too happy to carry our soldiers' knapsacks, and this satisfaction was quite mutual," despite the fact that many of these chores were precisely what blacks had run away from. The humorist Robert Henry Newell pictured a Union officer addressing a runaway: "You have come to the right shop for freedom. You are from henceforth a freeman and a brother-in-law. . . . Go and black my boots." [35]

For the elderly and sick, however, manual labor like digging and carrying was impossible, and "in hundreds and thousands" the fugitives clotted the roadways of the Border states and lost themselves aimlessly in the mazes of Baltimore, Knoxville, and dozens of other stonily unwelcoming places. "The tocsin of freedom sounded and knocked at the door and we walked out like free men," wrote a black Alabama carpenter. But what had they walked into? Army encampments in the Border states and the occupied Confederacy were islands in a sea of legalized slaveholding, and fugitives on the roads could easily be arrested and sold all over again. The railroads out of Baltimore refused to carry fugitives northward for fear of being sued by slaveowners for conveying stolen property; along the Ohio River, town fathers on the northern banks stationed guards at the river ferries to prevent runaways from crossing into free Ohio. And that said nothing for what white mobs might do. One abolitionist officer told Charles Sumner that the easiest way to spirit runaways through Baltimore was "to tie the Negroes into a chain-gang, and, lash in hand, make a show of driving them through the city; 'in which case,' he declared, 'all Baltimore will be on its knees to you.' " [36]

As in so many other cases in time of war, policy played catch-up to circumstances. Around army encampments "thousands of negroes were living in the most awful condition . . . in deep ravines and in the remote woodland." In the early spring of 1862, with fugitives and contrabands flooding into the Union-held coastal strip around Hatteras Sound, General Ambrose Burnside tried to sort out the growing number of black runaways on his hands by appointing New Yorker Vincent Colyer as "superintendent of the poor" for his military district, giving him the job of organizing and feeding his directionless population of ex-slaves. In the Mississippi River valley, fugitives and the dependents of those working for the army were shuffled into "contraband retreats," and Chaplain Eaton was appointed to take charge of them as "superintendent of the freedmen." Eaton was intelligent and well-intentioned, but he had no better idea of what to do for the fugitives than his counterparts at Port Royal, and he ended up adopting much of Port Royal's system. From Eaton's camps, "squads of colored men and women under the protection of soldiers began to go out into the deserted fields of the Confederate planters and gather the crops of corn and cotton." Others were put to work laying out streets and building barracks and, in the case of the contraband camp at Corinth, Mississippi, a school, a church, a commissary, and a hospital. Still others were hired out for wages, with deductions made by the camp superintendents for government-issued clothing and food.[37]

By the end of 1862, Eaton had more than 13,000 contrabands and fugitives in schools run by contraband camps, and by the end of the war he was supervising camps in Memphis, Vicksburg, Natchez, Helena, Vidalia, Little Rock, Pine Bluff, President's Island, and (most significantly of all) Davis Bend, the Mississippi plantation once owned by Confederate president Jefferson Davis. Around Hatteras Sound, contraband camps sprang up at Beaufort, New Bern, and Roanoke Island, with more than 10,000 blacks living in them, and another 2,000 Virginia contrabands were herded together in squalor on Craney Island, six miles from Union-occupied Norfolk. Many of the camps were poorly run, and the hiring-out system paid fraudulently low wages. But there, at least, blacks found a measure of safety, supplies of clothing, and occasionally volunteer teachers for reading and writing. By the end of the war, something close to a hundred of these camps had been established throughout the Border states and the onetime Confederacy.[38]

The map of freedom had led these former slaves into a very different landscape than either white or black had dreamt, a legal no-man's-land in which they were not yet citizens but no longer property, unwanted and excluded but certainly no longer shackled. Breaking the bonds of that conundrum would prove even harder than breaking free of enslavement. "Slaves in the possession of the government of these United States can be nothing else but men," pleaded Henry Ward Beecher in November 1861. "You may call them 'contraband,'—you may with dexterity call them ingenious or evasive names." But "there are to-day thousands and thousands of emancipated men in the possession of this government, and it is bound to treat them in some sort, if not as citizens, yet as men." [39]

AS BEECHER SAW, the pretense that the fugitives and contrabands were merely an incident of war and that no long-term repercussions lay

in wait was headed for a hard collision with reality. That reality made itself felt most obviously in Washington. For a city whose population was
almost three-quarters Southern-born, slavery had a surprisingly low
profile in the capital. Congress had refused to enact slave code legislation
of its own for the District and had merely declared that the slave laws of
Maryland and Virginia (the states from which the hundred square miles
of the District had been carved) would remain in force, leaving the application of the technicalities to the Washington city council. Although
Washington's blacks counted for nearly 20 percent of the District's permanent population, only about one in five were enslaved. In every year
since 1800, the slave population of the District had grown relatively
smaller and smaller.[40]

Anyone, though, who mistook this regime for leniency missed how
oppressive life could be for blacks in Washington. Most free blacks were
day laborers, nine out of ten owning no house or lot, and among the few
who did, more than half owned property worth less than five hundred
dollars, a little more than the average yearly income of manual laborers.
They crowded into wooden tenements on an island formed by the Ana-
costia and Potomac rivers, on east Capitol Hill, Meridian Hill, and in
Georgetown. Since 1812, free blacks had been required to register with
the city and show freedom papers in order to live within the District;
since 1821, they also had had to post a bond of twenty dollars and find a
white Washingtonian to sign a sponsorship pledge. By 1860, any free
black who moved into the District had to put up a five-hundred-dollar
bond and find two white people to act as sponsors. Even then, free blacks
were expected to keep their freedom papers with them at all times, ready
for inspection on demand. The slave trade might have been extinct,
but fugitive-hunting was not, and any white man who could expose a
runaway or even trap free blacks without their papers could make a
convenient profit out of reward money.[41]

Yet the District of Columbia was also the one place in the Union
where Congress had undisputed sovereignty to deal directly with slavery.
As early as 1805, antislavery legislators had wished to abolish slavery in
the capital, first because of the embarrassment the presence of slavery in
the capital of a free republic created, and second because it was actually

the place where they could do it. The first full-dress call on the floor of the House for District emancipation came in February 1835, when New Yorker John Dickson demanded that "slavery and the slave trade in and through the District of Columbia may be abolished, with their appalling train of evils." The emancipation bill Lincoln had proposed as a congressman in 1849 was only one in a continuing line of such proposals, and the Compromise of 1850 had leaned far enough in that direction to abolish the slave *trade* in the District. But keeping slavery itself legal in the District was a symbolic issue for Southerners too, and Southern numbers in Congress smothered every motion that threatened District slavery for fifty-five years.[42]

With the outbreak of the war, a climate of Dickensian farce settled over slavery in Washington. Slavery remained legal, but Washington was the capital of a nation at war with a slave confederacy, and from the first shots at Sumter, it arose in the minds of every slave within walking or riding distance as the Promised Land. "Without newspapers or telegraph," slaves in northern Virginia and surrounding Maryland embraced as an article of faith "that to reach that point was to be no longer a slave." They came "in pairs, and again in squads, big and little, old and young, carrying all their worldly possessions, rolled up in bundles." A reporter for the Washington *Daily National Republican* "passed at least one hundred who were making their way to Washington," some from as far as "twenty miles west of Manassas." In the process, they encountered the curtain of lines and fortifications George McClellan was building around the capital, and a good many ended up, mostly for want of forethought, in the District jail (known to drunk and sober alike as "the Blue Jug"), until their masters could appear before a District court and reclaim them.[43]

This was an embarrassment for Congress and an embarrassment for Lincoln, since the marshal of the District, who was responsible for arresting the fugitives, was appointed by the president and happened to be Ward Hill Lamon, one of the president's oddest but closest friends from Illinois. Lamon had already annoyed several members of Congress by padding expense accounts and, outside the District, passing himself off as a brigadier general. But he roiled the waters still more when he began displaying an unusual zeal for arresting fugitives, an agitation fueled by rumors that Lamon and his officers were reaping tidy profits from capture fees. By December of 1861, 218 people had been crammed into a jail designed for 50, and the miserable conditions of the prison were an open secret in Washington.

For the Radicals, however, embarrassments were always moral opportunities. At the beginning of the December session, Henry Wilson of Massachusetts rose in the Senate to read into the record a damning report from "an officer of the government," one E. J. Allen (actually the celebrated detective Allan Pinkerton), who had found sixty blacks who had run away from "disloyal masters" languishing in the Blue Jug. The Senate erupted. "When the northern States find out that they are supporting here in jail the slaves of rebels who are fighting against us—that we are keeping at the public expense their slaves for them, until the war is over," New Hampshire's John P. Hale gasped, "it will have a tendency to enlighten some minds." When members of Congress came down to the Blue Jug to investigate for themselves, Lamon tarred himself further by ordering them shut out. "Resolutions were passed in Congress declaring the marshal guilty of contempt of that body for having presumed to issue what it deemed a contemptuous restriction of its rights, and a committee was appointed to wait upon the President to demand the instant dismissal of that insolent officer," Lamon remembered bitterly. But until they could show where Lamon had actually violated any statute, Lincoln "informed them that he would neither accept the resignation nor dismiss me from office." [44]

This was, though, just the point Wilson wanted to hammer home: Until slavery was wiped off the books of the District, neither the problem nor the fugitives were going to go away. On December 16, 1861, Wilson introduced a bill in the Senate to abolish slavery in the District (or, in an effort to follow the Constitution's avoidance of the word *slave*, a bill "for the release of certain persons held to service or labor in the District of Columbia"). The bill was duly printed and distributed and referred to the Senate's Committee on District Affairs, where Radical chieftain Ben Wade (who had been agitating for District emancipation since the 1830s) and Lot Morrill of Maine were members and James

Grimes of Iowa was chairman. Wilson's bill contained seven sections, but the key provisions were the immediate emancipation of all slaves "within the District of Columbia," the abolition of slavery as a legal institution, and the creation of a board of commissioners to award compensation, up to one million dollars, to "all persons holding claims to service or labor against persons discharged therefrom by this act." Lot Morrill undertook the management of the bill on the floor of the Senate, and, once the District Committee had vetted it, had it calendared for debate in March.[45]

Morrill opened the ball on March 12, bringing in Wilson's bill with seven amendments he and the District Committee had crafted. Four of the amendments were mere wordsmithing; the fifth forbade slaveowners from bringing slaves into the District after the passage of the act in order to obtain government compensation for them; the sixth prevented emancipated slaves from being bundled out of the District to be sold or kept in slavery elsewhere; and the last killed slavery's legal standing by repealing the Maryland slave statutes in force in the District since 1801.

It took no more than a few minutes of desultory discussion before debate became more intense than "in any other session of the American Congress on record." Garrett Davis of Kentucky stood up to propose an eighth amendment, a poison pill to guarantee that even the District Committee would back off from the bill: "And be it further enacted, That all persons liberated under this act shall be colonized out of the limits of the United States." Did this mean, demanded Wisconsin senator James R. Doolittle, that Davis was talking about forced deportation, "whether they are willing to be colonized or not?" It certainly did, Davis replied. While "many of the more intelligent colored men" of the District "thronged to the galleries of the Senate, and listened," Davis announced that blacks never "will consent to be colonized, when liberated" because freed slaves had only one notion of freedom, and that was "freedom from work." They would become "criminals; they will become paupers. They will be engaged in petty crime and misdemeanors." That result, in turn, would drive "the loyal people of the slave states" into support of the Confederates, since none of them would stand by the example set in the District and wait to have "their slaves liberated and to remain domiciled among them." The only solution, whether the problem was black "indolence" or white exasperation, was forced colonization. And Davis was confident that the difficulties and costs of relocating a quarter of the District's population *somewhere* would make even the most excited abolitionist stammer into silence.[46]

It almost worked. When Davis's amendment finally came to a vote on March 24, the Senate deadlocked, nineteen *ayes* to nineteen *nays,* and Vice-President Hannibal Hamlin, in his role as presiding officer of the Senate, had to break the tie—and keep Wilson's bill alive—by voting "in the negative." Davis, who saw defeat being dragged from the jaws of victory, uncoiled a long and defiant speech, telling the Senate that, as far as he was concerned, no emancipation legislation could have any legal standing whatsoever. Slaves were property. "My right to my land and my right to my slave are of the same origin and nature. They are identically the same . . . and there is no constitutional right on the part of the . . . Congress of the United States . . . to abolish slavery in the States, in the District of Columbia, or anywhere else." Pass whatever bill you like, Davis rasped, then "submit it fairly and honestly to the decision of the courts," and see what happens then.[47]

The failure of Davis's compulsory colonization amendment made it "very likely that the bill will pass" whenever a full vote was finally called. But the going was still uphill, and Wilson was forced to accept a compromise amendment that created a fund for colonization, although the amendment specified that colonization was strictly voluntary on the part of the freed slaves. Wilson had to speak in defense of his bill on March 25, followed on March 31 by Charles Sumner, who wanted Garrett Davis to understand that "in the eye of the Constitution, every human being within its sphere, whether Caucasian, Indian, or African, from the President to the slave, is a *person,*" and not property.[48]

The critical moment came when moderate Republicans Fessenden and Browning rose to endorse District emancipation. "The object and purpose of this war was not to affect slavery in the States, but to uphold the Constitution and the laws of the land," Fessenden announced on April 1. "But, sir, I did not say, nor did the party to which I belong ever say, that it pledged itself to do nothing that indirectly might affect the institution of slavery." Did Garrett Davis "suppose we came into power to sit still and be silent on this subject?" Davis made one lengthy, last-ditch speech on the rights of property in slaves "as it has been expounded by the Supreme Court" on April 2. But the next day, an exhausted Lot Morrill finally got the vote he wanted, and the District emancipation bill passed, twenty-nine to fourteen. It was the first time in the history of the Republic that Congress had taken a direct step against slavery.[49]

It was almost anticlimactic when the House took up the District emancipation bill on April 10. Despite a grueling six-hour session on April 11 and an impassioned plea from the elderly John Crittenden against the bill, it passed the House that afternoon, ninety-two to thirty-eight. It was one day shy of the first anniversary of the attack on Fort Sumter. "The *Event* here has been the passage of the Bill by the House abolishing Slavery in the District of Columbia," wrote longtime Washingtonian Horatio Nelson Taft in his diary. Five days later, Lincoln signed the emancipation bill into law. "Only the damndest of 'damned abolitionists' dreamed of such a thing a year ago," George Templeton Strong noted with satisfaction in his diary.[50]

The finished bill bore some interesting resemblances to the one Lincoln had tried to introduce into the House of Representatives in 1849, and it is tempting to wonder how much of a hand Lincoln had in its passage. "I have never doubted the constitutional authority of congress to abolish slavery in this District," Lincoln wrote in a comment he attached to the bill, "and I have ever desired to see the national capital freed from the institution in some satisfactory way." His early protest against slavery in the Illinois legislature in 1837 had been coupled with an assertion that "the Congress of the United States has the power, under the Constitution, to abolish slavery in the District of Columbia." And it was one of the burdens Stephen Douglas had sought to fasten onto Lincoln in the senatorial debates of 1858 that Lincoln "stands to-day pledged to the abolition of slavery in the District of Columbia." It was a burden Lincoln also accepted: "I confess I would be exceedingly glad to see Congress abolish slavery in the District of Columbia."[51]

Still, Lincoln's first hope for emancipation was Delaware, not the

District. He assured Virginian John Gilmer in December 1860—just after his election—that "I have no thought of recommending the abolition of slavery in the District of Columbia." There was no point to it, he explained. With the Southern majority still dominating Congress, "if I were to make such a recommendation, it is quite clear Congress would not follow it." He warned Seward a month before his inauguration that he would approve measures dealing with "fugitive slaves, District of Columbia, slave trade among the slave states" only if "what is done be comely, and not altogether outrageous." And for Lincoln, *comely* meant (as he explained to Horace Greeley) gradualism, compensation, and some form of popular vote, either in the legislature or by referendum. "I am a little uneasy about the abolishment of slavery in this District, not but I would be glad to see it abolished, but as to the time and manner of doing it." His real preference was to have "some one or more of the border-states . . . move first." Lincoln had told one Illinois judge, Henry Blodgett, that emancipation in the District "will be very little toward getting rid of slavery in the states," since it could always be said that his administration had forced the result. For that reason, "I do not talk to members of congress on the subject, except when they ask me." [52]

One other root of Lincoln's hands-off attitude can be traced to the bill's declaration of immediate rather than gradual emancipation. When Orville Hickman Browning carried the finished bill to him at the White House for his signature on the evening of April 14, Lincoln dallied over it until the early morning of the sixteenth. "There has never been, in my mind, any question upon the subject, except the one of expediency," Lincoln explained. But he was troubled by a bill that had the good intention of wiping out slavery at once but that also, at one slice, cut loose elderly blacks who could not support themselves, did nothing for slave orphans whose parents had been sold away who knows where, and could beggar a widow whose only income came from hiring out the slaves left by her husband. He told Browning "that old Gov Wickliffe [Charles Wickliffe, the proslavery Kentucky representative] had two family servants with him who were sickly, and who would not be benefitted by freedom, and wanted time to remove them, but could not get them out of the City until Wednesday, and that the Gov had come frankly to him and asked for time." But none of this sympathy was shared by the District's slaves, and Charles Sumner chided Lincoln for making himself—for two days, at least—the "largest slave-holder in the country." Any real sympathy, Sumner told Massachusetts governor John Andrew, would have seen that "during all this time poor slaves were in concealment" to avoid being sold out of the District by their masters, "waiting for the day of freedom to come out from their hiding places." [53]

Yet it was still emancipation, and Lincoln was "gratified that the two principles of compensation, and colonization, are both recognized, and practically applied in the act." So sign it he did, and the bill went back to Capitol Hill at one o'clock on the sixteenth. Blacks in the District celebrated with a citywide convention. The *Weekly Anglo-African* rejoiced that "whatever betide the nation, its physical heart is freed from the presence of slavery. . . . We can point to our Capitol and say to all nations, 'IT IS FREE!'" Frederick Douglass had his first genuinely good news of the war, so good that "I trust I am not dreaming but the events taking place seem like a dream." It was "that first great step towards that righteousness which exalts a nation." Henry Ward Beecher exulted on April 13, "It is worth living for a lifetime to see the capital of our government redeemed from the stigma and shame of being a slave mart. . . . We have found by experience that though Abraham Lincoln is sure, he is slow; and that though he is slow, he is sure!" But the bill also received its share of ugly dissent. "The old citizens, especially those who have been slaveholders, are bitter and heartless toward all the colored race," wrote Lois Bryan Adams, who moved to Washington to work in the Treasury department. Some vengeful ex-slaveowners had no qualms about stranding the sick or feeble on the streets. "Since the abolition bill has freed the negroes," raged William Owner, "already our alms house is crowded with them to overflowing. . . . They are made up of all the old crippled & diseased negroes who would have been taken care of by their masters." [54]

Owner had a point, if not quite the point he intended to make, for the District emancipation bill uncovered as many problems as it solved. Blacks were still frozen out of the District's schools, out of the legal system, even out of seats on Washington's new streetcar system, and piece by piece Congress had to adopt more legislation to remove these encumbrances. For one thing, the District emancipation bill declared the District's slaves "discharged and freed of and from all claim to such service or labor." But did this make them *free* or merely free them from the particular "service or labor" they were formerly held to? And who was a District slave? Not the contrabands, who had fled Confederate service for the District and were covered by the First Confiscation Act, but who were not exactly free either. Jacob Collamer, the shrewd old Vermont senator, pointed out that a slave freed in the District could very easily be reenslaved if he wandered over the boundary into Maryland, and the bill had to be amended to direct the keeping of a register of freed slaves and the issue of certificates of freedom. And none of these changes had the slightest effect on the plight of the District's mounting population of fugitive slaves, whose masters mostly lived in Maryland or Virginia and who therefore were not touched by the District legislation.[55]

The problem of the fugitives forced its way into the headlines once General McClellan moved the Army of the Potomac out on campaign in the spring of 1862 and command of the Washington garrison fell, on Lincoln's order, to James S. Wadsworth. A former New York lawyer and antislavery Democratic politico of considerable wealth, Wadsworth had turned Republican in 1856, and increasingly Radical thereafter. He immediately plunged into the legal quagmire of the District's fugitives by "taking measures to inform himself as to the loyalty of a master of a fugitive brought before him," and if he could satisfy himself that "the master was of secession sympathies," Wadsworth would invoke the Confiscation Act and issue the fugitive with a "military protection" to prevent arrest by Lamon's District police force. This action trenched straight across Lamon's pomposity, so in May, Lamon's officers boldly arrested a mulatto, Althea Lynch, as a fugitive and locked her in the Blue Jug until the District commissioners could examine her, despite her possession of one of Wadsworth's "protections."[56]

What the District police did not know was that Althea Lynch was also employed as General Wadsworth's cook, and Wadsworth, when he learned about the arrest, demanded that Lynch be released. Lamon being out of town, the warden of the prison refused. Wadsworth sent another demand, this time threatening force. He was again refused. That evening a squad of soldiers under Wadsworth's aide, Lieutenant John Kress, came down to the District jail, arrested the warden and the deputy marshal of the District, and released not only Lynch but every other fugitive there. When Lamon returned to Washington later that evening, he immediately called out the city police and, at two in the morning, recaptured the prison from the two soldiers left to guard it, and threw them into the Blue Jug's cells. Finally, by the end of the next day, Lamon and Wadsworth agreed to release the prisoners each had taken, and Lamon had the satisfaction of obtaining an opinion from Attorney General Bates that "in the present state of things in the District of Columbia the civil authority outranked the military; and he gave the further opinion that the military governor's conduct had been misguided and unauthorized, however philanthropic might have been his purposes and intentions." [57]

The controversy made for great political theater, but it accomplished little for the daily lives of the fugitives and contrabands, who lived in a legal twilight world between slavery and freedom. A makeshift contraband camp was erected beside the Old Capitol Prison in February, but the numbers of the contrabands and the complaints about them increased so rapidly that in May, Wadsworth shuffled the duty of overseeing them to a civilian superintendent, Danforth B. Nichols, a Northern white Methodist minister and the Washington representative of the American Missionary Society. The steadily swelling collection of contrabands was moved by Nichols to a collection of confiscated rowhouses on east Capitol Hill called "Duff Green's Row" after their former owner, the Kentucky secessionist Duff Green. By July, overcrowding and disease forced Nichols to begin searching for a new site. "In addition to the numerous nigs in Greens row," wrote naysaying William Owner, "several hundreds are quartered in the Navy Yard, the above buildings being large as they are were able to hold all the stolen Negroes." Nichols finally settled the contrabands into an unused wooden barracks at Twelfth and Vermont streets, in northwest Washington, that Nichols christened "Camp Barker." [58]

By the end of 1863, Camp Barker had processed over 5,000 contrabands, and the camp had to be moved yet again, this time with deliberate irony, to Arlington, the estate along the Potomac River which had been confiscated from none less than General Robert E. Lee of the Confederacy. There, the "Freedmen's Village" was opened. To support the contrabands, Nichols placed former slaves in jobs around Washington, and Wadsworth employed still others as fortification laborers at forty cents a day. The camp could shelter them for a while, but "Mr. Nichols at once urges them to seek a house for themselves and suitable employment, the object being to impress on their minds that they are expected to look to their own exertions for sustenance." Other antislavery whites began speaking at mixed-race gatherings and raising money to fund black schools and hospitals. When Frederick Douglass spoke at Washington's Bethel Church in 1864, fully one quarter of his audience was white.[59]

Freedmen's Village quickly became a magnet for "the charitable and the curious, and particularly . . . grim old Abolitionists, of both sexes, from the North." William O. Stoddard, one of Lincoln's White House staffers, paid a visit and found the village to be "a pretty wide reach of land fenced in, with a tight barrier of six-foot pine boards to keep out . . . any attempt on the part of the Fugitive Slave Law to play wolf with the sheep of this fold." The accommodations were little more than sheds, and Walt Whitman, who also visited the village, tried to "use" the residents "kindly, give them something, etc.," but found that it was difficult to put up with the squalor for long. "There's a limit to one's sinews & endurance & sympathies." But the relentless tide of fugitives squeezed even the village out of its pine stockade and forced the establishment of a second contraband camp, Camp Springdale, on the Arlington grounds. Camp Rucker in Falls Church, Camp Wadsworth in Langley, and Camp Collins on the District side of the Chain Bridge soon followed. By the end of the war, over 11,000 fugitives had passed through the District's contraband camps, most of them to uncertain futures in the North.[60]

Much of the uncertainty about that future grew out of the realization that, for all the hubbub about fugitives and contrabands in Washington and elsewhere, nothing had happened that actually freed any of them. In the end, there was no security for freedom apart from the raw, difficult work of erasing, state by state, the rust-red statutes that kept slavery lawful. The District emancipation bill pointed in the right direction, and Lincoln was confident that sooner rather than later, compensated emancipation would prove the way forward. "Should the experiment inaugurated by this measure of deliverance be crowned by wholesome consequences," editorialized John W. Forney's *Sunday Morning Chronicle,* "all the Border States will gradually accept the proposition of the President, and prepare for emancipation with compensation and colonization." What Lincoln had not counted on was the truculence of the Border staters and the unreliability of his own generals.[61]

LINCOLN HAD LONG ASSUMED that his Kentucky birth, his Border-state in-laws, the Todds, and his long years among the Southerners who had migrated to southern Indiana and southern Illinois gave him a special insight into the mind of the upper South. The *Chicago Tribune*'s Charles Ray, who had published one of the first calls for a Lincoln presidential nomination in his editorial columns, assured the skeptical New Englander Edward Pierce that Lincoln "is a Southern man by birth and education." Being "a Kentuckian, as he is" made Lincoln imagine that he was sufficiently "familiar with Slavery and its evils" to know better than others how it should be dealt with. This weakly founded confidence allowed Lincoln to persuade himself that the loyalty and Unionism of the citizens of the Border would, in the long run, overrule the temptations of the rebels to join the Confederacy and convince them that their investment in slavery was a bad bargain they would be well rid of. It made perfect sense to Lincoln to treat the Border states as a suspicious jury: avoid riling them, appeal to their fundamental good sense, and in the meanwhile quietly offer them reasons why they should finally turn in a favorable verdict.[62]

The most important part of that verdict would be an agreement to begin the process of emancipation. "If I can get this plan started in Delaware I have no fear but that all the other border states will accept it," Lincoln predicted to Delaware's representative, George Fisher. What he did not reckon with was the possibility that the Border states might see none of the connection Lincoln saw between loyal Unionism and disgust with slavery. Fisher confidently caucused with friends in the Delaware legislature, quietly circulated a petition favoring the emancipation bill with enough names to impress the waverers, and soothed the fearful with assurances "that we could have a large sum of money to compensate the slave holders for all losses that they might sustain by the loss of their slaves." But Fisher was surprised to find, over and over again, that even Unionists "who look upon slavery as a curse" were so deeply dyed by racial hatred that "we also look upon freedom possessed by a negro, except in a very few cases, as a greater curse."

Fisher struggled on, publishing the text of his "Act for the Gradual Emancipation of Slaves in the State of Delaware" in the newspapers at the beginning of February 1862 and squeaking it through the Delaware Senate by a five-to-four vote, despite a Democratic majority. But in the Delaware House, a straw poll showed Fisher that the bill would fail by a single vote. Hoping to fight another day, Fisher had the bill withdrawn. "No man in his senses," the Democratic newsheets in Delaware crowed, "supposes that the Government intends to give Delaware $900,000" to buy out slavery. "If it ever buys the slaves Delawareans will be saddled with the cost." [63]

The vigor with which Delaware threw compensated emancipation back in Fisher's—and Lincoln's—faces should have warned the president about underestimating how fanatically resistant the Border states might be to translating Unionism into emancipation. And not only the Border states. Vermont senator Jacob Collamer urged one meeting of Vermonters to support compensated emancipation since a complete buyout of all the South's slaves would cost each Vermonter only three hundred dollars. One "old leader" was so melted by Collamer's plea that he "waxed eloquent over the fact that the North shared the responsibility for slavery" and "declared himself willing to pay his share." Two days later, he looked up Collamer and explained, a little crestfallen, "Me and wife and the boys figure that our share would be just about all we've got; so I guess you might as well let that damned Negro question alone." [64]

Instead, Lincoln preferred to treat the Delaware refusal as a temporary setback which could be remedied by the next session of the legislature.

Three weeks after Fisher's bill died for want of support in the Delaware House, Lincoln sent to Congress a proposed joint resolution that not only restated most of the terms of the Delaware plan, but extended its offer of compensated emancipation to all of the Border states. "I recommend," Lincoln wrote to Congress on March 6, 1862, just as the debate over District emancipation was preparing to heat up,

> *Resolved* that the United States ought to co-operate with any state which may adopt gradual abolishment of slavery, giving to such state pecuniary aid, to be used by such state in it's discretion, to compensate for the inconveniences public and private, produced by such change of system.[65]

He offered no suggestions for the amounts of this "pecuniary aid," and he tried to soften the blow by pointing out the practical good effects of "gradual abolishment" on the war. So long as the Border states remained slave states, the Confederates would continue to fight on, in the hope of eventually dragging the Border states into the Confederacy with them. "To deprive them of this hope, substantially ends the rebellion, and the initiation of emancipation completely deprives them of it as to all the States initiating it." Of course, this approach involved giving the Border states what amounted to a blank check on the United States Treasury for whatever it would cost them "by such initiation." But "any member of Congress, with the census tables and Treasury reports before him, can readily see for himself how very soon the current expenditures of this war would purchase, at fair valuation, all the slaves in any named State." Simply adopting this resolution would, admittedly, do nothing to guarantee that any of the Border states would rise to the bait. But Lincoln could not believe, even after the failure of the Delaware proposal, "that it would not soon lead to important practical results."[66]

In what was starting to become a pattern for Lincoln, there is only the barest hint that he bothered to discuss the resolution beforehand with anyone. It is possible that Lincoln may have read the resolution to a specially called evening meeting at the White House on March 5, although no notes of that meeting survive. Charles Sumner claimed two months later that Lincoln read him the resolution and its accompanying explanation "from his own manuscript" on the morning of March 6. But for all practical purposes, the proposal was shaped without inviting comment or correction from anyone. Lincoln's invitation to Sumner did not include consulting with him about the nature or wording of the resolution, and apart from crinkling his brow at the oddness of the word *abolishment*, Sumner did "not suggest an alteration." [67]

The most immediate result, however, was a mixture of appalled silence and fustian outrage. "Since I sent in my message, about the usual amount of calling by the Border State Congressmen has taken place," Lincoln remarked to Montgomery Blair on March 9, "and although they have all been very friendly not one of them has yet said a word to me about it." Concluding that "the import of the message had been misunderstood" as some kind of ultimatum, Lincoln had Blair recruit as many of the members of the Border state Congressional delegations as possible and bring them to the White House the next day to hear him repeat his offer more loudly. In the first place, he explained, they should understand that "he did not pretend to disguise his Anti-slavery feeling; that he thought it was wrong and should continue to think so." On the other hand, both state law and the Constitution forbade him or Congress from issuing a mandate against slavery. He knew as well as any of them "that Emancipation was a subject exclusively under the control of the States, and must be adopted or rejected by each for itself," and he did not "claim nor had this Government any right to coerce them for that purpose." Still, the fact was that the continued existence of slavery in the Border states "strengthened the hopes of the Confederates that at some day the Border States would unite with them, and thus tend to prolong the War." In the name of the Union alone, "more would be accomplished towards shortening the War" through an agreement to begin a gradual emancipation along the Border "than could be hoped from the greatest victory achieved by Union armies." [68]

To Lincoln's dismay, the replies that tumbled from the mouths of the Border state congressmen were composed entirely of reasons why their states could never agree to his proposal. There was no need for Missouri to "initiate" a gradual emancipation plan, announced Missouri

representative John Noell, because "natural causes were there in operation which would, at no distant day, extinguish it." Marylanders were
ready "to give it up if provision was made to meet the loss," added John
Crisfield of Maryland, "but they did not like to be coerced into Emancipation, either by the Direct action of the Government, or by indirection."
Was it constitutional? Charles Wickliffe asked. Shouldn't there be a national referendum first? queried Missouri representative William Hall.
The atmosphere became so strained that old John J. Crittenden had to
bring the meeting to an end by pouring out the oil of assurance that
"whatever might be our final action, we all thought him solely moved by
a high patriotism and sincere devotion to the happiness and glory of his
Country."

This was, naturally, what people ought to say in the presence of the
President of the United States. But when debate on the resolution began
in Congress, all such restraint disappeared. Willard Saulsbury of
Delaware denounced the resolution "as the most extraordinary resolution that was ever introduced into an American Congress; extraordinary
in its origin" and "mischievous in its tendency." And Charles Wickliffe
could not resist the opportunity to ask, yet again, in "what clause of the
Constitution" Lincoln "finds the power in Congress to appropriate the
treasure of the United States to buy negroes, or to set them free." As
much as the resolution struck the skeptical abolitionist Moncure Conway
as "like shooting a gun a little at a time," nevertheless it "shocked the
border States." [69]

But the most violent words spouted from the lips of Northern Democrats, who could only imagine black emancipation in the Border meaning black emigration to the North. "Millions for the Union, but not one
cent for abolition," screeched New Jersey representative Nehemiah
Perry. The slightest breath of emancipation, he prophesied, would "ani-
mate, nerve, and strengthen" the rebels and demoralize Union soldiers,
who "will rise and tell you that they never trusted their lives to your care
to be thus sacrificed for the liberation of the 'almighty nigger.' " Northern whites wanted neither emancipation nor the bill to pay for it.
William Richardson of Illinois announced that his "people were not
prepared to enter upon the proposed work of purchasing the slaves of

other people, and turning them loose in their midst." Daniel Voorhees of
Indiana wanted "any Border slave State man here" to understand that
"for the people whom I represent on this floor," there was nothing they
wanted to do less than "become the purchasers" of Border-state slaves.

The violence of this opposition astounded old-line abolitionists like
Thaddeus Stevens, who thought the resolution "about the most diluted,
milk-and-water-gruel proposition that was ever given to the American
nation." But, as the *Daily National Republican* editorialized on March
10, "The great, transcendent fact is, that for the first time in two generations we have the recommendation from the presidential chair of the
abolition of slavery and of measures by Congress to invite and assist it."
We are no longer talking as we did in 1860, merely of keeping slavery
from expanding into the territories; "the work of abolishing it where it
now exists is proclaimed and recommended." The opposition in Congress
knew all too well what Lincoln's proposal implied. Emancipation was
now "the chief practical question for the consideration of the nation." [70]

With the issue of emancipation finally out in the open, Lincoln was
relieved when the House passed the resolution on March 11 by a vote of
eighty-nine to thirty-one. After little more than a week of debate, the
Senate did likewise on April 2 by a vote of thirty-two to ten. A week
later, Lincoln signed the joint resolution and sent it out to the Border
states for their action. "The Proposition of the Presidt. is an epoch,"
exulted Charles Sumner, "& I hope it will commence the end." [71]

Lincoln seems to have felt no particular urgency about the response.
"The view of Emancipation taken by the President may be called a Dis-
solving View," smirked *Vanity Fair*. "While the Abolitionists have been
excoriating their knotty knuckles, year after year, in frantic efforts to
scrub off the Great Black Spot, out comes President LINCOLN with a little vial of Benzine, and offers to do the job handsomely and completely,
and without barking anybody's knuckles, if Congress will only furnish
the necessary Soap." Lincoln told Horace Greeley at the end of March
that "if some one or other of the border-states would move fast, I should
greatly prefer it," but his main concern was that emancipation be presented with as little apparent arm-twisting as possible. "We should urge
it *persuasively*, not *menacingly*, upon the South." It was less important

to him that emancipation be put on a timetable than that it be framed in a way that would avoid a challenge in the federal courts, and that, as he repeated to Greeley, always meant the same three "main features— gradual—compensation—and vote of the people." He assured Carl Schurz that "he was not altogether without hope that the proposition he had presented to the southern states in his message of March 6th would find favorable consideration." [72]

Lincoln could take such a relaxed attitude toward Border-state emancipation principally because the military situation was finally starting to look as though he was going to get the time needed for implementing gradual emancipation. After the disastrous summer of 1861 and its bleak fall and winter, the early spring of 1862 suddenly flowered into Union victories. In the West, the Confederates unwisely decided to take the risk of violating Kentucky's "neutrality" and seized the key post at Columbus, where the Ohio River joined the Mississippi. This action tipped the Kentucky legislature into the hands of Unionists and permitted Union troops and Union recruiters to flood into the state. In a clumsy fight at Logan's Cross Roads in eastern Kentucky, Union general George H. Thomas hit two Confederate infantry brigades with a bayonet charge and sent them fleeing, to the disgust of their commander, "to Knoxville, Nashville, and other places in Tennessee." [73]

This was only the first ripple of a wave of good news from the West. In February, a combined force of troops and gunboats under a stumpy former Regular Army officer named Ulysses Simpson Grant floated itself down the Tennessee River into western Tennessee, where it handily bagged the Confederate troops guarding the river at Fort Henry. Hardly pausing for breath, Grant then marched overland and surrounded the Confederate garrison at Fort Donelson, which guarded Tennessee's other river highway, the Cumberland. After a brief and futile resistance, Donelson surrendered to him on February 16. Early in March, the reorganized Union forces in Missouri swept the state clear of Confederates, chasing them into Arkansas and decisively beating them in a two-day pitched battle at Pea Ridge. At the beginning of April, another combined army-and-navy operation under General John Pope forced the surrender of the Confederate post at Island No. 10 in the Mississippi River, which pried open the river to federal gunboats as far south as Vicksburg, Mississippi. And only three weeks later, a federal flotilla under Flag Officer David Farragut entered the mouth of the Mississippi River, blasted its way past two Confederate forts and an assortment of woefully outclassed rebel gunboats, and captured New Orleans. The great river highway of the Mississippi valley had been secured at both ends in little more than two months. A jubilant John Hay wrote, "With the capture of New Orleans and the opening of the Mississippi, the Southern mind will certainly reach the conviction that they can be overcome, and if you please, subjugated." [74]

There was even good military news in the East, despite the reluctance of George McClellan and the Army of the Potomac to show much of the aggressiveness of Grant, Pope, or Thomas. Resentful of prodding and superabundantly confident in his own military skill, McClellan resisted most of the Radicals' pressure "to worry the administration into a battle," and though Lincoln "defended McClellan's deliberateness," he also warned him that he could not ignore these demands forever while McClellan drilled and marched and reviewed. The warnings went unheeded, and McClellan went on stocking the upper command echelons of the Army of the Potomac with "his clique, and friends" who could not resist the temptation to play what the veteran soldier of fortune Phil Kearny called "a game of politics, rather than of War." Worse, McClellan now actually began slighting Lincoln publicly. On the evening of November 13, Lincoln, Seward, and John Hay waited for McClellan in the parlor of his headquarters at Fifteenth and H streets (a block away from the White House), only to have McClellan breeze in past the parlor doors, head upstairs, and go to bed. This gave Lincoln his first inkling that the problem with McClellan might be not too little action but too much of the wrong kind. As Hay put it, "this unparalleled insolence of epaulettes" raised a small cloud of apprehension about "the threatened supremacy of the military authorities." By January, Lincoln was receiving so little information on the state of military affairs that Attorney General Bates could only shake his venerable head: "It now appears that the Genl. in chief has been very reticent—kept his plans absolutely to himself, so that the strange and dangerous fact exists, that the Sec of War and the Prest. are ignorant of the condition of the army and its intended operations!"[75]

   McClellan told himself he had more than enough reasons to justify this secretiveness. For one thing, he was sure that Lincoln was loose-lipped. "If I tell him my plans," McClellan told Quartermaster General Montgomery Meigs, "they will be in the New York Herald tomorrow morning. He can't keep a secret." Given Lincoln's own penchant for secretiveness and McClellan's for talk, this complaint made little sense. But it rationalized in McClellan's mind the deeper reason for his military secrecy: his mounting contempt for the entire Republican administration. When Lincoln summoned McClellan to a cabinet meeting at the White House on January 13 to lay his strategic cards on the table, McClellan stonily replied "that no general commanding an army would willingly submit his plans to the judgment of such an assembly, in which some were incompetent to form a valuable opinion, and others incapable of keeping a secret." Secretary of War Stanton, McClellan wrote his wife, "is without exception the vilest man I ever knew or heard of." Navy Secretary Welles "is an old woman," Attorney General Bates "an old fool." He was certain that he had "but few friends in Congress," and he regarded Lincoln as "the *original gorilla.*" It was "perfectly sickening to deal with such people," especially since by comparison with his own incomparable talents, "every day brings with it only additional proofs of their hypocrisy, knavery & folly."[76]

   It amazed John Hay that Lincoln tolerated such insolence. McClellan "was treated by Lincoln with a long-suffering forbearance without any parallel in history." But the truth was that Lincoln felt he had no choice. When Ben Wade pressed Lincoln to fire McClellan, Lincoln replied, "If I relieve McClellan, whom shall I put in command?" *Anybody,* Wade replied, since *anybody* would be an improvement on McClellan. "Wade," Lincoln said, "*anybody* will do for you, but not for me. I must have *somebody.*" He briefly considered "taking the field himself" but gave it up. No one could deny that McClellan had turned the rabble of volunteers who survived Bull Run into the smartly turned-out Army of the Potomac, and there were so few professional officers with that level of competence that Lincoln could ill afford to cashier McClellan simply for possessing an overfull ego.[77]

But there were increasing signs that McClellan suffered from something worse than petty vanity. There was a growing assembly of rumor that any effort to remove McClellan would send ripples of mutiny through the Army of the Potomac, the army he had built and which adored him as no other American general had been adored since Washington. "I think there is scarcely a man in this whole army who would not give his life for me & willingly do whatever I ask," McClellan wrote, and this was one conviction he had good evidence for. That loyalty, laid side by side with his scarcely concealed hobnobbing with prominent Northern Democrats and his refusal to use the Army of the Potomac to enforce the First Confiscation Act, convinced suspicious Republicans that McClellan was drilling the Army of the Potomac "into an anti-Republican engine." "You know McClellan as well as I do," one of McClellan's generals wrote confidentially to Treasury Secretary Chase, "& I will not describe him further than to say that Jeff Davis has not a greater repugnance to, nor less confidence in, Republicans than has McClellan."[78]

Was it likely that his influence might "make the army dangerous in elections"? McClellan had already said privately that he was willing "to become Dictator" if the Senate should, like its ancient Roman model, call on him to deliver the country, and his letters were sprinkled with oblique allusions to "the course I had determined to pursue in such a contingency." And whether he had any particular goal in mind or not, McClellan had little skill in disguising his fascination with a political action. "There is rapidly increasing, and spreading from Washington over the country, a clear, but as yet cautiously undefined, unformulated understanding that there is a struggle going on," wrote White House secretary William Stoddard, a struggle "between the Constitutional supremacy of the civil authority, represented by the President, and the war-created strength of the military commander." Lincoln professed full confidence in McClellan's loyalty to the government, but he could not help hearing a steady file of congressmen—including Orville Hickman Browning—warn him that McClellan's "loyalty is beginning to be questioned in some quarters." Even within the Army of the Potomac, the ferocious but disgruntled Phil Kearny believed that McClellan was "a political fool, and a military traitor" who was "juggling, even with the enemy." [79]

Unnerving as the McClellan threat might seem, Lincoln was no more willing to allow McClellan to grab control of the government than he had been willing to allow Seward or the Radicals. By January, Lincoln's tolerance of McClellan had frayed to the point where the president irritably informed McClellan's chief of staff, Randolph Marcy (who also happened to be McClellan's father-in-law), that "the general impression is daily gaining ground that the Gen. does not intend to do anything. By a failure like this we lose all the prestige we gained by the capture of Ft. Donelson." In mid-January, Lincoln deliberately alarmed McClellan by inviting two proadministration generals to the White House for consultations on military affairs, remarking to them that "if General McClellan did not want to use the army, he would like to borrow it, provided he could see how it could be made to do something." On January 27 Lincoln publicly issued a General War Order, announcing over McClellan's head that "a general movement of the Land and Naval forces of the United States" would begin, with or without McClellan's blessing, on February 22. Taken off guard by the president's sudden display of impatience, McClellan finally submitted a reassuringly audacious plan to invade Virginia and seize Richmond. But "from that time," wrote John Hay in his diary, Lincoln "stopped going to McClellan's and sent for the General to come to him." [80]

The plan McClellan submitted on February 3 was not exactly what Lincoln had in mind. McClellan dismissed any notion of crossing the Potomac and staging a knock-down rematch of the Bull Run battle with the rebel army encamped at Manassas Junction. Instead, the general intended to use the federal navy's control of the Chesapeake Bay to slip the entire Army of the Potomac out of its Washington encampments by sea, land them just below Richmond at Urbanna or Fortress Monroe on the James River Peninsula, and be in a position to drive straight through the Confederate capital's back door before the Confederates at Manassas knew that he was there. This initially struck Lincoln as little more than the usual McClellan reluctance to get directly to grips with the rebels, and Lincoln directly ordered him to cross the Potomac and at least feel out the strength of the Confederate entrenchments around Manassas. McClellan did so, and found to his embarrassment that they were completely empty. Four days later, Lincoln relieved him of his overall position as General-in-Chief and confined the Little Napoleon's authority to the Army of the Potomac.

Still McClellan pressed for his Peninsula plan, and still Lincoln resisted. He was particularly uneasy about McClellan's demand to take virtually every last man in the Army of the Potomac on the campaign, leaving Washington with little more in the way of protection than the heavy artillery in its ring of forts. In the end Lincoln yielded, provided that McClellan left 30,000 men in Washington and northern Virginia to safeguard the capital, so on March 17, McClellan's *grande armée* clambered onto an armada of transports for the voyage to Fortress Monroe and the James River Peninsula. Finally, the last and greatest piece of the Union's war machine was in motion, and even though it took McClellan six weeks of siege operations to take the Confederate fortifications at Yorktown, and another three weeks for him to move his 70,000 men up to the outskirts of Richmond, victory now seemed to be within the Union's grasp.

Then, almost as quickly as it had been woven, the entire military and political fabric of Lincoln's hopes parted. In the West, Ulysses Grant pursued the beaten Confederates up the Tennessee River and pitched camp on the west side of the Tennessee at Shiloh Church. There, on April 6, the supposedly defeated rebels turned and surprised Grant in a savage two-day battle that cost 23,000 killed, wounded, and missing from both sides and that came within an ace of wrecking Grant's army and the national reputation he had won at Fort Donelson. Stunned into immobility, Grant's army was blended with a second federal force under the West's own version of George McClellan, Don Carlos Buell, and to Grant's frustration, all federal campaigning in the West slowed to the point of lethargy. Farragut's squadron twice tried to force its way up the Mississippi, only to receive a battering from the Confederate guns emplaced on the high bluffs at Vicksburg and to retire downriver with more wounds than it had given. "Everywhere we seem to have been struck

with paralysis," wrote the Radical journalist Whitelaw Reid, "everywhere the rebels seem to have been galvanized into unnatural energy."[81]

Meanwhile, on the Peninsula, the Army of the Potomac struggled
slowly through a succession of rain-swollen swamps and marshes below
Richmond, to the flooded banks of the Chickahominy River, where on
May 31, the Confederates pounced heavily on two isolated federal infantry corps at Fair Oaks. The Southerners lost 6,000 men in one futile
attack after another, but their reckless bravery unhinged McClellan,
who despairingly concluded that he was facing 200,000 rebels. He
pleaded piteously with Stanton and Lincoln to strip the Washington de-
fenses of every last man they could find and send them to his rescue.[82]

He pleaded in vain. A small rebel army under "Stonewall" Jackson
chose this moment to tear a strip up the Shenandoah Valley all the way
to Harpers Ferry, so the reinforcements McClellan craved went off to
deal with Jackson, meeting just the need Lincoln had anticipated. Jackson led them a wizardly chase down and around the valley, then swung
back toward Richmond at the end of June to join forces with the main
rebel army under Robert E. Lee. Together, Lee and Jackson dealt a stag-
gering series of blows to McClellan's inert army in what became known
as the Seven Days' Battle, and on June 26, McClellan began a baffled retreat back down the Peninsula. He had never actually faced more than
50,000 rebels, but in his own imagination he had endured a "terrible
contest," had been "attacked by greatly superior numbers in all directions," and had been "needlessly sacrificed" by the evil machinations
of abolitionists who saw him as the only obstacle to full control of the
government.

McClellan had no doubt who was to blame. When he paused on
June 28 to telegraph a report to Stanton, his sense of injury mounted to
a ferocious climax in the last sentence: "If I save this Army now I tell
you plainly that I owe no thanks to you or any other persons in Washington—you have done your best to sacrifice this Army." (The closing
was so outrageously insubordinate that the head of the War Department's telegraph office refused to add the offending sentence to the
copy he forwarded to the secretary and the president.) Lincoln was
taken completely off guard by McClellan's announcement of disaster.

"Save your Army at all events," the president telegraphed back the same day, and he promised, "Will send re-inforcements as fast as we can." [83]

A far greater disappointment was materializing for Lincoln in the Border states. Since March, none of the Border-state legislatures had moved a finger toward embracing the compensated emancipation resolution. In Kentucky and Delaware, the most obvious reason for inaction was that the legislatures would not be in session again until later in the year. But even with that excuse, it quickly became clear that, whatever Lincoln might have thought about the vulnerability of slavery in the Border, the Border states wanted to hear nothing about emancipation, compensated or otherwise. On the day George Fisher voted in favor of the District emancipation bill in Congress, he candidly admitted that Delaware would probably punish him in the fall elections for endorsing emancipation. A "Grand Union Demonstration" in Georgetown, Delaware, that July carefully omitted any reference to emancipation from its platform, a fact that a Democratic demonstration the next month gleefully highlighted: "Whereas, the Black Republican . . . meeting on July 22 failed to declare itself on . . . emancipation, RESOLVED, That we declare . . . our unalterable and uncompromising opposition to the proposition of the President of the United States for the abolition of slavery in the Border States, with pretended compensation to their owners or upon any other terms or conditions whatsoever." In Maryland, Unionists politely thanked Lincoln for "proferring co-operation with those states which desired the emancipation of slavery" but immediately turned to protesting the refusal of army officers in the District to return their fugitive slaves. "Before the adoption of that scheme, if it were even practicable, the slaves will have all escaped from the limits of Maryland." In Missouri, a state convention was in session to rewrite the state constitution, and Missouri Unionists seized the opportunity to propose a compensated emancipation amendment that would have gradually emancipated all Missouri slaves within twenty-five years. It failed by a vote of fifty-nine to eighteen, "refusing a single moment's debate." [84]

The chilly response of the Border states nettled Lincoln. When he revoked David Hunter's emancipation decree on May 19, he tacked onto his proclamation a sharp reminder to the Border states that it was their foot-dragging which provoked officers like Frémont and Hunter to reach for martial-law solutions—which in turn undermined support for legislative emancipation. "On the sixth day of March last," Lincoln reminded them, "I recommended to Congress the adoption of a joint resolution" that "now stands an authentic, definite, and solemn proposal of the nation to the States and people most immediately interested." If those states and their legislatures would not listen, perhaps the people would, and it was "to the people of those states I now earnestly appeal." What was wrong with compensated emancipation? They were being offered federal money for a commodity which, if the Maryland Unionists' complaint meant anything, they were having some difficulty keeping anyway. "You can not if you would, be blind to the signs of the times," and the times were full of tidings about runaways, fugitives, contrabands, and emancipation in the national capital. Compensated emancipation made no humiliating moral judgment about Border-state slaveowners and asked for no vengeful "rending or wrecking" of Border-state society. Unlike the solutions of the abolitionists, "it acts not the pharisee." On the contrary: It levied an obligation for compensating the Border-state slaveowners on the whole country, "casting no reproaches upon any." *Will you not embrace it?* Lincoln asked. *May the vast future not have to lament that you have neglected it.*[85]

And yet, even in the throes of his disappointment with the Border staters, the game was far from lost. All he needed from the Border staters was a beginning—not even a beginning, really; even the promise to begin would do—and time would take care of the rest. And if he had to wait for 1863 or for the next Congress, that would work, too, since once begun, not a single nineteenth-century emancipation scheme had ever rolled backwards. If anything, they had accelerated, and the provision of compensation would actually give the federal government a lever, the threat of recalling its funding, against any state legislature that developed second thoughts. Compensated emancipation required only time, and with the string of victories the Union armies were winning in the spring of 1862, it seemed quite reasonable to suppose that time was what Lincoln would have. The war would be over, perhaps by the end of 1862, and he would be president at least until 1864, and between this moment

and then, there would be quite enough time to make sure that the political dominoes tipped against each other and toward emancipation in the
Border and then in the pacified South.

But time was what George B. McClellan snatched away from him.
Three days after hastily promising McClellan that reinforcements would
be on their way to the Peninsula, a calmer Lincoln began to question the
wisdom of jumping to McClellan's panicked tune. He consulted again
with Stanton and Orville Hickman Browning and agreed to request the
governors of the Northern states (including Kentucky) to raise 300,000
fresh troops for the war. But as for sending anything more to McClellan,
"the idea . . . is simply absurd." Instead, Lincoln would send himself to
the Peninsula to gain his own perspective on McClellan's supposed
predicament. So, early on the morning of July 7, he slipped out of Washington on the steam sloop *Ariel* for McClellan's Peninsula headquarters
at Harrison's Landing.[86]

"The object of the presidential visit was to see the condition of the
army, and learn what change of plans, if any, were deemed necessary by
Gen. McClellan," reported the *Sunday Morning Chronicle*, and on the
surface, that seemed to be all that was going on. McClellan turned out
the Army of the Potomac for a grand review, Lincoln inspected the entrenchments thrown up around the Harrison's Landing encampment,
interviewed senior officers, and gave encouraging little speeches from
place to place until nine o'clock in the evening. He even clambered up on
the ramparts surrounding the encampment "in view of the rebel pickets" to have a look for himself at the enemy. But away from the rows
upon rows of spotlessly polished buttons, starched gaiters, and gilt
epaulettes, Lincoln had genuine cause for concern, not about the army,
but about McClellan. As soon as the *Ariel* came alongside the wharf at
Harrison's Landing, McClellan came on board and greeted Lincoln with
a letter which, when Lincoln read it, could only have sent cold chills
down the presidential spine.[87]

"I earnestly desire," McClellan's letter began, "in view of possible
contingencies, to lay before your Excellency, for your private consideration, my general views concerning the existing state of the rebellion." It
was a little unusual for generals to be lecturing presidents, although

McClellan had written to Lincoln two weeks before to ask whether he would welcome "by letter or telegram my views as to the present state of military affairs throughout the whole country." But as the president read on, it became clear that the "contingencies" McClellan had in mind were not the military ones a general could be expected to share with his commander in chief. McClellan wanted to talk politics. "The time has come when the Government must determine upon a civil and military policy, covering the whole ground of our national trouble." Lincoln could have been forgiven for wondering if the general had noticed that the president had been doing that for the past year, but McClellan's complaint turned out to be not about a lack of policy but about precisely the policies Lincoln had been following.[88]

In the first place, Lincoln needed to recognize that "this rebellion has assumed the character of a War." What this meant, in the vocabulary of international law, was that the rebellion had ceased to be the insurrection Lincoln always claimed it was and had become a legitimate struggle between two belligerent nations and ought to be recognized as such. Or at least we should not be "looking to the subjugation of any state, in any event." In the second place, the Confiscation Act of the previous August (and Trumbull's new Second Confiscation Act, which was coming toward a vote even as Lincoln was sitting in McClellan's tent) should be ignored. "All private property and unarmed persons should be strictly protected" and "all private property taken for military use should be paid or receipted for." And in case Lincoln missed the full connotations of *private property*, McClellan added, "Military power should not be allowed to interfere with the relations of servitude, either by supporting or impairing the authority of the master." Lastly, emancipation was out of the question. The government was perfectly entitled to seize slaves as laborers or employ any contrabands who might put themselves in the army's way, and this might somehow result in "working manumission," but only if the owners were compensated and—since it was manumission he was talking about, not emancipation—only with the consent of the owner.[89]

This was not the first time the American military and its civilian directors had chafed against each other: Winfield Scott had had a vitriolic go-round with Jefferson Davis when the latter was secretary of war in the 1850s. But this unsolicited bill of advice was, and still is, the most astounding letter ever addressed by a senior American general to a civilian commander in chief, astounding in the innocent frankness with which a soldier proposed to dictate the management of public affairs to the President of the United States, astounding in its willingness to make veiled threats. Unless Lincoln took McClellan's recommendations as the new policy guide, "the effort" to raise fresh troops "will be almost hopeless"; worse, "a declaration of radical views, especially upon slavery, will rapidly disintegrate our present Armies."

Coming from the mouths of proslavery congressmen in the heat of Capitol debate, those words were simply huffs and puffs; coming from the commander of the Army of the Potomac, they were something else entirely. But in the spirit of what McClellan must have supposed was helpfulness, he added, "In carrying out any system of policy which you may form, you will require a Commander-in-Chief of the Army." He, of course, did not "ask that place for myself," although no one who read McClellan's letter for a century and more afterwards had any doubt that McClellan was really nominating himself; he may have thought he was asking merely for reinstatement to his former—and still vacant—place as general-in-chief. But the Constitution vested the title and powers of *commander in chief* in the president, so that any appropriation of that highly charged vocabulary by another was as clear and direct a challenge as if Lincoln had been slapped in the face.[90]

All the whispers about McClellan's "putting his sword across the government's policy," about "his sympathies with the South" and his "incapacity and want of loyalty," now came home to roost. McClellan's own temperamental reluctance to act makes it difficult to fathom whether he had actually intended to menace Lincoln with the possibility of a military coup or was merely so far gone in his contempt for Lincoln that he believed that Lincoln would appreciate his suggestions. He certainly enjoyed the lack of enthusiasm the soldiers of the Army of the Potomac had shown for Lincoln. "I *had to order* the men to cheer & they did it very feebly." And he took no steps to dampen the rising murmurs from his own lieutenants for some sort of military intervention in Washington.

George Julian warned Congress that "officers high in command in the army of the Potomac" were plotting "to march upon the capital and disperse Congress as Cromwell did the Long Parliament." Quartermaster General Montgomery Meigs was appalled to hear "mutterings of a march on Washington to 'clear out those fellows' " among "officers of rank" at Harrison's Landing. McClellan's own judge advocate general, Cincinnati lawyer Thomas Key, was told "that a plan to countermarch to Washington and intimidate the President" into peace talks with the Confederates "had been seriously discussed." But McClellan wavered between petulant threats to resign and return to civilian life and careless hints about "taking my rather large military family to Washn to seek an explanation of their course." He wrote his wife on July 11 that "I have commenced receiving letters from the North urging me to march on Washington & assume the Govt!!" A month later he hinted at the possibility of a "coup," after which "everything will be changed in this country so far as we are concerned & my enemies will be at my feet." But he did nothing.[91]

Lincoln, however, returned to Washington on July 10, "grieved with what he had witnessed." He told Orville Hickman Browning that he was certain that "McClellan would not fight," and by the next day the rumors had begun to fly that "the Gov't is in a quandary about army affairs," with "the everlasting Nigger" as the "chief component of the difficulties." Worse, McClellan's ultimatum destroyed the illusion that time was on Lincoln's side, that gradual emancipation could be tended slowly and calmly while the war went on to its glorious conclusion. He now feared that if he acted at once to cashier McClellan, "his dismissal would provoke popular indignation"—not to mention that of the Army of the Potomac—"and shake the faith of the people in the final success of the war." If he were to begin the gradual emancipation of the Border-state slaves, it would have to happen under the cloud of a possible reaction by McClellan or the army, and that meant that something would need to happen at once rather than gradually. With Congress on the verge of adjournment, Lincoln "resolved to make one more earnest effort with the delegations from the border States, to initiate a policy of voluntary emancipation by those States." Two days later, he had twenty-nine of the Border-state representatives and senators in the White House to listen to his appeal.[92]

"If you all had voted for the resolution in the gradual emancipation message of last March," Lincoln told them bluntly, "the war would now be substantially ended," and, he might have added, George McClellan would not have an army at his disposal. "Discarding *punctillio*, and maxims adapted to more manageable times," he asked, "can you do better in any possible event?" Yes, you could, if you lit whatever fires were necessary under your home legislatures for compensated emancipation. "How much better for you, and for your people, to take the step which, at once, shortens the war, and secures substantial compensation for that which is sure to be wholly lost in any other event." He was not demanding that they abolish slavery at once; at this point, he was not even asking for them to begin gradually to "emancipate at once." What would suffice would be a simple decision "to emancipate gradually." But that decision would indeed have to come "at once." Before Congress adjourned, they must "consider and discuss it among yourselves" and "at the least, commend it to the consideration of your states and people." The truth was that "our common country is in great peril, demanding the loftiest views, and boldest actions to bring it speedy relief."

And if they refused? There was always one option open to Lincoln, an option he had up until now been convinced would be constitutionally pointless to reach for, but which the situation might now leave him without any alternative but to use. "An instance of it is known to you," he said ominously: the Hunter emancipation in May. "Gen. Hunter is an honest man," Lincoln warned them, and "I valued him none the less for his agreeing with me in the general wish that all men everywhere, could be free." Hunter had done the right thing in the wrong way, but "in repudiating it, I gave dissatisfaction, if not offence, to many whose support the country can not afford to lose." He was now under pressure to pick up Hunter's weapon himself, something the Border staters could save him from if they would make their decision *now*. "By conceding what I now ask, you can relieve me, and much more, can relieve the country in this important point." And to make the decision easier, two days later Lincoln submitted to the House "the draft of a Bill to compensate any

State which may abolish slavery within it's limits," committing the federal government to compensation by statute and not just resolution.[93]

"Oh," Lincoln groaned to his two Illinois allies in the House of Representatives, Isaac Arnold and Owen Lovejoy, the day after the meeting, "if the border States would accept my proposition! Then . . . you, Lovejoy, and Arnold, and all of us, would not have lived in vain! The labor of your life, Lovejoy, would be crowned with success—you would live to see the end of slavery." But it was all to no purpose. That evening the Border-state congressmen and senators caucused, reflected, and argued in "a stormy debate," and on July 14, twenty of them sent Lincoln a joint answer in which they not only folded their arms and refused his appeal but dragged the original March 6 resolution in for another beating and ended by reminding Lincoln to "confine yourself to your constitutional authority." The Border staters would do nothing to help him put compensated emancipation into action now. But so long as he was still commander in chief, there remained one way he could beat any opposition to the punch, and that was to use his military authority *for* emancipation before McClellan used his to stop it. It was not the way he liked, and he had within the past year cashiered one general and humiliated another for trying it on their own. And there was always the possibility that if he did reach for the emancipation lever, he might as easily provoke a reaction from McClellan as forestall one. But now, all other paths to freedom had been closed.

"The President himself has been . . . the bulwark of the institution he abhors, for a year," John Hay wrote on July 20. "But he will not conserve slavery much longer. When next he speaks in relation to this defiant and ungrateful villainy it will be with no uncertain sound." Two days later, Lincoln spoke.[94]

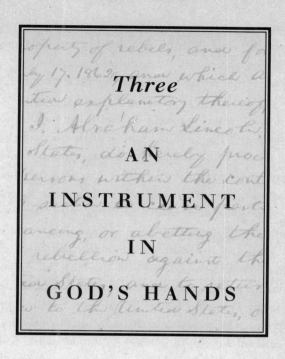

Three

AN INSTRUMENT IN GOD'S HANDS

EATH WAS Abraham Lincoln's silent neighbor. An infant brother, his mother, and an older sister all died before he was twenty, and his first love (some said his only real love) died from a fever before they could be married. He lost his second son, Eddie, to pulmonary tuberculosis in 1850, and then his third son, eleven-year-old Willie, the one who most resembled and delighted his father, died of typhoid fever in the White House in the grim February of 1862. Willie's "death was the most crushing affliction Mr. Lincoln had ever been called upon to pass through," remarked the portrait painter Francis Bicknell Carpenter (who took up residence in the White House for the first half of 1864), and for weeks afterward, Lincoln set aside Thursdays and closed himself off from the usual visitors "for the indulgence of his grief." His favorite poem, which he could recite by heart, was a dirgelike reminder of the brevity of life, and dreams of his own death would come to him on and off through his years in the White House.[1] So when the infant son of Lincoln's secretary of war, Edwin M. Stanton, died on July 10, 1862—a Thursday—from the complications of a vaccination, Lincoln's sympathies went out to a man who, like himself, buried his personal pain behind a glaze of silent remoteness.

Even as the death of Stanton's child called to mind his own roll of losses, however, Lincoln could not push slavery, emancipation, and the war out of view. On July 13, the morning of the Stanton funeral and the day after his last plea to the Border-state congressmen, Lincoln sent his carriage to pick up Secretary of State Seward and his daughter-in-law and Navy Secretary Welles; as this peculiar quartet bounced over the rutted streets to Stanton's rented house in Georgetown Heights, the president began to talk about emancipation. "He dwelt earnestly on the gravity, importance, and delicacy of . . . emancipating the slaves by proclamation." This was, as Welles wrote in his diary with impressive restraint, "a new departure for the President, for until this time . . . he had been prompt and emphatic in denouncing any interference by the General Government with the subject." Thunderstruck, Seward interrupted to say that "the subject involved consequences so vast and momentous, that he should wish to bestow on it mature reflection." But Lincoln "said he had given it much thought and had about come to the conclusion that it was a military necessity absolutely essential to the salvation of the Union, that we must free the slaves or be ourselves subdued." Since coming back from Harrison's Landing and appealing in vain to the Border staters, he now was convinced "that a change of policy in the conduct of the war was necessary." Welles shifted uneasily at the indecency of talking policy under the crepe of a funeral. But "during that ride, the subject [of emancipation] was the absorbing theme," and Lincoln kept coming back to it "two or three times on that ride." Only when they finally arrived at Stanton's door did Lincoln finally let it go, and only after telling the secretaries "to give the question special and deliberate attention."[2]

What stuck in Welles's mind were the words *military necessity* and *proclamation,* since it was not clear from Lincoln's comments just what he meant by them. They might, for all that Welles knew, refer to nothing more than some special endorsement of what was already coming to a vote in Congress as the close of the session loomed that week. After all, Lyman Trumbull's Second Confiscation Act had just emerged from a combined House-Senate conference committee on July 12, ready for a vote, and it contained a provision that required Lincoln to issue a "public warning and proclamation" that would put the act into execution sixty days after its passage. Or it might mean taking free blacks and escaped slaves—whether contrabands or simple fugitives—and doing by law what David Hunter had tried to do by decree, which was mustering them formally into federal service.

On July 8, the untiring Henry Wilson had introduced an amendment to the 1795 Militia Act which authorized the president "to receive into the service of the United States, for the purpose of constructing intrenchments, or performing camp service, or any other labor, or any military or naval service for which they may be found competent, persons of African descent." True enough, the army had been using blacks as laborers ever since the first three contrabands had shown up at Fortress Monroe, but always as civilians, not as formally enlisted soldiers of the United States Army. Even if Wilson intended nothing more than having blacks perform the same sorts of manual labor, the bill turned the entire situation upside down by proposing the formal mustering-in of blacks, laborers or otherwise. No sooner had it been read on the floor of the Senate than the dyspeptic Willard Saulsbury of Delaware was hysterically denouncing Wilson's "attempt . . . to elevate the miserable nigger, not only to political rights, but to put him in your Army." The bill reached even further in its thirteenth section, declaring free—not just confiscated, but *free*—any of these recruits whose masters were in arms against the Union. "This is a wholesale scheme for emancipation," spluttered Saulsbury, and so it was. The new Militia Act easily passed the Senate on July 15 and passed the House the next day; it too would await some form of enabling proclamation from Lincoln.[3]

On the other hand, *military necessity* conjured up the possibility that Lincoln was toying with something vastly different. There was, as Lincoln put it, one "last card" to play, and that was a vaguely defined category of presidential prerogatives known as the "war powers." The vagueness arose directly from the Constitution itself. Although the president was designated as "Commander-in-Chief of the Army and Navy of the United States, and of the militia of the several States, when called into the actual Service of the United States," nothing in that designation actually spelled out the precise duties that role obliged him to perform. For that reason, the most influential commentators preferred to err on the side of minimizing the president's war powers. Hamilton's essay in *The Federalist* on the presidency defined the "war powers" as little more than the functions of a military chief of staff, "as first general and admiral," and in the Mexican War case of *Fleming v. Page* in 1850, Lincoln's unrelenting judicial nemesis, Chief Justice Taney, had limited the powers of the president as commander in chief to "purely military" matters.[4]

At the same time, though, war had a way of making calm judicial opinion look ridiculous. In time of war, a president might need to fall back on war powers that allowed him to flex certain martial-law powers in civilian affairs but without invoking widespread military policing or the closure of the civil courts. Admittedly, the only body of opinion that described these "war powers" was a series of comments made by John Quincy Adams, the sixth president, on the floor of the House of Representatives in 1836, and again in 1841 and 1842, in which he goaded Southern congressmen with the premise that Congress had the "authority to interfere with the institution of slavery" in time of national emergency, including the power "to abolish it by treaties of peace." Other legal commentators hotly denied that any such war powers existed, no matter what prestige Adams enjoyed on the subject. But the notion refused to die. Immediately after Sumter, Charles Sumner was quick to urge Lincoln "that under the war power the right had come to him to emancipate the slaves." Sumner, who liked to think of himself as the inheritor of John Quincy Adams's mantle, believed that the use of the war powers was the one practical method for ending slavery. "Under the war power we can do what is . . . necessary for the purposes of the war, as justified by humanity, good sense and the consent of Christendom." If "there be in the hand of the war-power, as John Quincy Adams though there was, a right of emancipation, then let that be shown," urged Henry Ward Beecher, "and, in God's name, be employed!"[5]

Lincoln had actually resorted to something like those war powers at the beginning of the Civil War by suspending the writ of habeas corpus. The problem was that he had also gotten severely burned at the fingertips for doing so by Taney in *ex parte Merryman*. So, war powers or not, Lincoln ended up turning to Congress for approval after the fact. After that, it was a good question whether Lincoln could be persuaded to wheel the war powers out again for something as shattering as emancipation.[6]

One thing was certain: Lincoln had already shown that he had no more enthusiasm for the Second Confiscation Act than he had for the first. Seward counseled a veto, as did Orville Hickman Browning, who used the opportunity of carrying the bill to Lincoln's desk on the morning of July 14 to express "very freely my opinion that it was a violation of the Constitution and ought to be vetoed . . . whereas if approved it would form the basis upon which the democratic party would again rally, and reorganize an opposition to the administration." Instead, Lincoln asked Congress to hold off its adjournment, since "I may return [the Confiscation bill] with objections; and if I should, I wish Congress to have the oppertunity of obviating the objections, or of passing it into a law notwithstanding them." It did not take the Senate long to guess what Lincoln's objections were: The Second Confiscation Act "declares forfeiture, extending beyond the lives of the guilty parties; whereas the Constitution of the United States declares that 'no attainder of treason shall work corruption of blood, or forfeiture, except during the life of the person attainted.' " Lincoln spent most of July 15 "in his Library writing, with directions to deny him to everybody." But by the time Nicolay brought a memorandum from Lincoln up to Capitol Hill on the seventeenth, the "executive magnet had reached some members"—William Pitt Fessenden of Maine, in particular—and the wise heads in the Senate (over the resentful protests of Lyman Trumbull and Ben Wade, who bitterly criticized Lincoln's "back-kitchen way of doing this business") had already adopted a resolution restricting application of the bill to "act or acts" done after the passage of the act and disclaiming any "forfeiture of the real estate of the offender beyond his natural life." The same day, the Radicals published a manifesto in the Washington *Daily National Republican* defending the Second Confiscation Act and the Militia Act on the grounds of national "self-preservation." It was a good question whether the resolution had rendered the confiscation bill stillborn. At least Lincoln could now sign it in good constitutional faith, and an enabling proclamation would have to be written.[7]

Anyone in the business of second-guessing Lincoln might have assumed that this was what Lincoln wanted to talk about when he had Seward send out notices for a special Monday morning cabinet meeting on the twenty-first of July. Treasury Secretary Chase "found that the President had been profoundly concerned at the present aspect of affairs, and had determined to take some definitive steps in respect to military action and slavery." What he had drawn up were four "orders" to generals in the field. The first "contemplated authority to Commanders to subsist their troops in the hostile territory"—in other words, to "seize and use any property" the federal armies needed to "subsist" on Confederate territory as they marched across it. This authority would create a clean sweep for confiscation, since Lyman Trumbull's two Confiscation Acts authorized civil confiscation through the courts, while Lincoln's order would authorize confiscation by the armies without civil process. The second order was connected to the amending of the Militia Act to permit black recruitment, "that military and naval commanders shall employ as laborers . . . so many persons of African descent as can be advantageously used for military or naval purposes." Lincoln "was not prepared to decide the question" permanently, but for now, "he expressed himself as averse to arming negroes." The third order was little more than a footnote to the previous two: Officers in the field were to keep account of both seized property and "negroes employed" with "such degrees of certainty as would enable compensation to be made in proper cases," just in case subsequent court actions overturned the Confiscation Acts and forced the government to make restitution. There was "a good deal of discussion" of these orders; the first was "universally approved," the second "was approved entirely," and the third was agreed to by everyone except Chase, who "doubted the expediency of attempting to keep accounts for the benefit of the inhabitants of the rebel states."[8]

To Chase's satisfaction, Lincoln said nothing about returning blacks who enlisted as "laborers" to their masters, if the courts ever came to the point of so ordering. The point was omitted because Lincoln's solution to such a crisis was contained in the last order, providing "for the colonization of negroes in some tropical country." This was, by any reckoning, a poor reward for serving the Union cause. But it was easier for Lincoln to think about colonizing freed slaves than the alternative of having to return them to slavery if the war should come to some politically premature end. "I do not believe it would be physically possible, for the General government, to return persons, so circumstanced, to actual slavery," Lincoln wrote in his commentary on the Second Confiscation Act. "I believe there would be physical resistance to it, which could neither be turned aside by argument, nor driven away by force."[9] But that question was as yet so far over the horizon that, according to Chase, "the colonization project was not much discussed," and at the end of the day, Lincoln did no more than agree to continue the discussion into the regular cabinet meeting scheduled for the next day.[10]

That might have been that. The military confiscation order was bound to send tremors of disruption even deeper through Southern slavery, and the amending of the Militia Act committed the United States for the first time to declaring *free* at least some people who were now slaves. As Willard Saulsbury feared, the order definitely was an emancipation, even if limited to the relative handful of fugitives, runaways, and contrabands who could actually be enlisted into federal service. "These measures," predicted Salmon Chase confidently, "if all of them are adopted will decide everything." But Lincoln could not free himself from the fear that none of this would survive a mauling at the hands of Roger Taney; besides, like compensated emancipation, confiscation would require time to make itself felt, and time might prove to be in short supply.

Later that day, Lincoln signed another order, this time reminding overzealous federal commanders who had "for any proceeding or conduct" arrested the "subjects" of other nations—crews of British blockade runners, for instance—that whatever other punishments they felt like imposing, they could not extract a loyalty oath to the United States government from those "subjects" without causing diplomatic brouhahas. He left the White House before dark for the cool shade of the big rambling house at the Soldiers' Home, up the Seventh Street Pike, which the Lincolns were now using as a summer house, and from which the president enjoyed an unobstructed view from the front lawn down into the city. Across town, Hooley's Minstrels were opening their act at Grover's Theater, twenty-two white men in blackface strumming banjos and washboards, free men pretending to be slaves.[11]

TUESDAYS AND FRIDAYS were cabinet days, although Lincoln was far from diligent in observing this schedule. Unless a messenger from the State Department arrived with notice that a meeting was actually being held, the five secretaries and the attorney general stayed put behind their desks, and even when they received a summons, they sometimes ignored it if their pile of work was too pressing. Seeing that the cabinet had already devoted a special session on Monday to the confiscation and enlistment orders, the usual Tuesday summons met with something less than enthusiasm. Montgomery Blair, who was coming in from the Blair family estate in Silver Spring, almost skipped the meeting. But Lincoln was intent on continuing the previous day's agenda, and what was even more peculiar, he convened the meeting not in his own office as usual but in the oval second-floor library.[12]

It began blandly enough. "It was unanimously agreed that the Order in respect to Colonization should be dropped," Salmon Chase wrote in his diary afterward. Chase had noticed after the previous day's meeting that Lincoln had overlooked North Carolina in the list of rebel states where the military was authorized to "seize and use" property; he asked for an amendment to include "North Carolina . . . among the States named in the first order." Otherwise, the orders were adopted unanimously, and Stanton would send them out over the War Department telegraph as General Orders No. 154 that afternoon.[13]

Chase wanted one other amendment, this time to the second order (on black recruitment), which would permit the use of African-American volunteers not just for manual labor but for armed combat.

This request offered Lincoln the opening he wanted, because he actually had something far more dramatic to unveil. "I said to the cabinet that I had resolved . . . upon the adoption of the emancipation policy." The exact nature of that "emancipation policy" was contained in a handwritten "rough draft" on two sheets of lined paper; as Lincoln explained before reading it, he "proposed to issue a proclamation, on the basis of the Confiscation Bill" which would "emancipate, after a certain day, all slaves in the States which should then be in rebellion."

Gideon Welles, in an article written ten years later, recalled that Lincoln told everyone before reading his "Proclamation" that he wanted a "free discussion" among the cabinet members afterwards. But he also wished them to understand that the discussion would not be about whether or not he should issue this "order." All question of that "was settled in his own mind," and as much as "he desired to hear the views of his associates and receive any suggestions," still this was "his own scheme" and "the responsibility of the measure was his." He was frank to the point of bluntness: "I said to the Cabinet that I had resolved upon this step, and had not called them together to ask their advice, but to lay the subject-matter of a proclamation before them," Lincoln informed the painter Francis Carpenter, "suggestions as to which would be in order, after they had heard it read." [14]

Even with the previous week's advance warning that something was up, Welles and Seward were as surprised as any of the other cabinet secretaries. "Little was said by any one but the President," Welles recollected. When no one broke the silence, Lincoln plunged into the actual reading of the draft. For the first minute, it might have seemed that Lincoln was making a great fuss over nothing, because the draft began with what sounded like yet another "order." The Second Confiscation Act required the president to issue an enabling "proclamation" before the Act could be put into effect, and this opening sounded like little more than that:

In pursuance of the sixth section of the act of congress entitled "An act to suppress insurrection and to punish treason and rebellion, to seize and confiscate property of rebels, and for other purposes" Approved July 17, 1862, and which act, and the Joint Resolution explanatory thereof, are herewith published, I, Abraham Lincoln, President of the United States, do hereby proclaim to, and warn all persons within the contemplation of said sixth section to cease participating in, aiding, countenancing, or abetting the existing rebellion, or any rebellion against the government of the United States, and to return to their proper allegiance to the United States, on pain of the forfeitures and seizures, as within and by said sixth section provided.

The passage was important enough on its own terms, since it now meant officially that confiscation—military as well as civil—would become federal policy across the board. But the crippling truth about both Confiscation Acts, and even the military "order" of the day before, was that the sum total of blacks who actually gained legal freedom would be pitifully small. And it might be smaller still if, as Lincoln feared, the whole project was appealed to the federal courts after whatever close the war came to.

The next paragraph only seemed to get drearier, since it launched into yet another cap-in-hand offer of Lincoln's favorite scheme for federally compensated emancipation:

And I hereby make known that it is my purpose, upon the next meeting of congress, to again recommend the adoption of a practical measure for tendering pecuniary aid to the free choice or rejection, of any and all States which may then be recognizing and practically sustaining the authority of the United States, and which may then have voluntarily adopted, or thereafter may voluntarily adopt, gradual abolishment of slavery within such State or States.

Almost as if determined to rehearse backwards the entire political history of the last year, Lincoln promised (in words that recalled the Crittenden resolution of the previous summer) "that the object is to practically restore, thenceforward to be maintain[ed], the constitutional relation between the general government, and each, and all the states, wherein that relation is now suspended, or disturbed; and that, for this object, the war, as it has been, will be, prossecuted." What sense did this make now? If this was all Lincoln had in mind, the cabinet could just as well have stayed in their offices.[15]

But it was not. For with a turn of one of his long pages, Lincoln proceeded to transform confiscation into emancipation and Lyman Trumbull's bizarre application of the law of prize into an executive decree based on the war powers.

> And as a fit and necessary military measure for effecting this object, I, as Commander-in-Chief of the Army and Navy of the United States, do order and declare that on the first day of January in the year of Our Lord one thousand, eight hundred and sixtythree, all persons held as slaves within any state or states, wherein the constitutional authority of the United States shall not then be practically recognized, submitted to, and maintained, shall then, thenceforward, and forever, be free.

In this single sentence of eighty-five words, Lincoln tersely identified the legal rationale for emancipation, the schedule by which he would do it, the people who were legally affected by it, and the new legal condition those same people would enjoy. The authority underlying it would be the war powers the president held as *Commander-in-Chief of the Army and Navy of the United States*. Without actually laying aside the offer of compensated emancipation for those willing to take it, Lincoln would completely rewrite the title deeds of the South's four million slaves to make them, at one stroke, free. He would, to lay it out in detail, override the authority of state slave codes; override even the sanctity of property ownership and civil court process; make no promise of compensation unless the rebel states actually laid down their arms; and he would do it all because, as John Quincy Adams had proposed twenty years before, "when a country is invaded, and two hostile armies are set in martial array, the commanders of both armies have power to emancipate all the slaves in the invaded territory."[16]

Not all slaves everywhere, though: By confining emancipation to the *states, wherein the constitutional authority of the United States shall not then be practically recognized*—in other words, the Confederacy—Lincoln exempted the Border states, with their civil courts open and laws (including laws on slavery) untainted by rebellion. On that point Lincoln had little choice. Without rebellion, not even the war powers could legally justify Lincoln in emancipating the slaves of those states. Laying aside entirely the popular fury emancipation by decree would generate in the Border if he ever reached for slavery there, Lincoln knew that nothing would melt faster under the gaze of Roger Taney and his ilk than a war powers emancipation in states where there was no state of war. On the other hand, the states of the Confederacy—*any state or states, wherein the constitutional authority of the United States shall not then be practically recognized*—were manifestly another matter, and here Lincoln opened the scope of the Proclamation dramatically. Having removed themselves from the civil jurisdiction of the United States, the rebel states were a theater of armed insurrection, and under the rubric of the war powers, Lincoln should have full scope to declare any kind of emancipation he thought would help suppress the rebellion—not just of slaves used in Confederate war service or the slaves of disloyal masters but of all the slaves, without exception, in all rebellious areas. And not merely seized as contraband, or vaguely "free," but permanently *free*, "thenceforward, and forever."

The first man in the room to find his tongue was Edward Bates, the attorney general, who "expressed his very decided approval" for "its immediate promulgation." This was a surprise, since the taciturn and white-haired Bates, along with Montgomery Blair, were the two members of Lincoln's cabinet who had always been the least enthusiastic about wholesale emancipations. "He was, it was well known, opposed to slavery," Bates began, and it was for just that reason that he actually welcomed the Proclamation. But Bates had a condition to attach to his endorsement, and that was "deportation"—the forced expulsion of all African-Americans from the country—immediately following emancipation. Because he was "fully convinced that the two races could not live and thrive in social proximity," Bates had been an advocate of compulsory colonization "for many years," and if emancipation were to take place now, he "wished a system of deportation to accompany any scheme of emancipation." [17]

Just as surprising as Bates's endorsement was Salmon Chase's lukewarm reception of the proclamation. Much as it had "my cordial support," Chase thought the invocation of the war powers involved "a great danger." In the first place, there were the legal question marks that surrounded presidential war-powers authority. If the threat from the federal courts had been a question when Frémont and Hunter tried to emancipate slaves, why wasn't it a question now, when Lincoln was preparing to step out onto the same limb? Wouldn't matters be safer if Lincoln allowed "generals to organize and arm the slaves" in their own military districts by their own martial-law authority "and by directing the Commanders of Departments to proclaim emancipation within their Districts as soon as practicable"?

Why Chase believed this approach would make emancipation easier or more proof against legal intervention was not clear, until he explained his real anxiety. A "universal emancipation" decree would set off pandemonium across the Confederacy, resulting in "depredation and massacre"; small-scale emancipations, where federal troops were securely in command of affairs, would be like controlled explosions and would prevent the rebels from screaming for foreign intervention to prevent race war. "I am not myself afraid of the negroes," Chase wrote in a letter to Benjamin Butler a week later, but he knew that "many honest men" were. Emancipation en masse would set the stage for another San Domingue. Chase had to demur: "The measure goes beyond anything I have recommended." [18]

The others—Gideon Welles, Interior Secretary Caleb Blood Smith, Stanton—remained silent, and Montgomery Blair, who had arrived midway through the meeting, "deprecated the policy" because of the disastrous political fallout an emancipation proclamation would generate among Northern voters as the fall midterm elections approached. The proclamation would be denounced as the license for black refugees, now free, to flood the Northern labor markets, and the rage and fear this would generate in white Northerners, who were already dispirited by the summer's military defeats, would "cost the Administration the fall elections." But Blair had missed Lincoln's opening remarks; Lincoln was no longer entertaining recommendations about *whether* he should emancipate, or even about *how*, but only about the technicalities of doing so.

Finally, when it was clear that no one else would speak, William Henry Seward, swathed in his odd combination of self-importance and shrewd political insight, had a few observations of his own to make. For a politician who had once been seen as a Radical, prophesying in 1858 an "irrepressible conflict" between North and South, Seward had proven curiously uninterested in making war on slavery. He wrote to Charles Francis Adams, the American minister to Great Britain, in July 1861 that "demanding an edict of universal emancipation" would only play into the hands of the Confederacy and even "precipitate a servile war." It was his conviction that the war was going to grind slavery to pieces anyway and that Congress and the president needed only to let that grinding take its course. Emancipation began, Seward explained, the day Lincoln was elected, and it needed no further help—nor the taking of further risks—from Lincoln. "Slavery was killed years ago," Seward told Francis Carpenter. "Its death knell was tolled when Abraham Lincoln was elected President. The work of this Administration is the suppression of the Rebellion and the preservation of the Union." [19]

So, like Bates, Seward announced that "I approve of this proclamation," but also like Bates, he had a condition to offer—not about its terms but about its timing. "The depression of the public mind, consequent upon our repeated reverses, is so great that I fear the effect of so important a step," Seward explained (in what Stanton's notes described as "a long speech"). He did not mean by that the same thing Blair had meant. Seward feared the "effect" on foreign opinion, and the all-important possibility of intervention in the war by France or Britain. The proclamation might provoke "foreign nations" to "intervene to prevent the abolition of slavery for the sake of cotton" or to prevent disruptions in the supply of cotton. Or it might provoke an intervention to head off something far worse. "It may be viewed as the last measure of an exhausted government, a cry for help" to the slaves themselves from an administration that had discovered that it lacked the power to win the war.

This decree would, Seward said, playing on a biblical simile, look like "the government stretching forth its hands to Ethiopia, instead of Ethiopia stretching forth her hands to the government" or like a "last *shriek* on the retreat." As such, the European empires would read it as an incitement to "servile insurrection," and Seward was keenly aware that both the British (with their memories of the Sepoy Mutiny only five years old) and the French (with off-again, on-again colonial wars to wage in North Africa) were anxious that the American civil war not become a stage on which the world would see men of color rising up to slaughter whites. Would it not be better to "postpone" the proclamation "until you can give it to the country supported by military success"?[20]

Unlike Bates or Blair, Seward had the weight of diplomatic reasonableness behind his objection. "The wisdom of the view of the Secretary of State struck me with very great force," Lincoln later told Francis Carpenter. "It was an aspect of the case that, in all my thought upon the subject, I had entirely overlooked." And yet, even then, Lincoln was not entirely persuaded to pull back. As the meeting broke up, Lincoln took Stanton aside to discuss a call to the governors for 300,000 more recruits and mentioned, almost in passing, that "it was his intention on the following day to issue his Proclamation." But Seward was not finished. That evening, he brought Thurlow Weed to the White House to warn Lincoln that an emancipation proclamation "could not be enforced in the Rebel States—that it would add to the intensity of their hatred, and might occasion serious disaffection to the Union cause in the border States; that it would work no good and probably would do much harm, and that it was more prudent," as Seward had urged, "to wait on events."

The next morning, Lincoln had a blistering letter from Montgomery Blair on his desk, warning even more luridly that an emancipation proclamation would produce political disaster. At some point, Lincoln made up his mind to wait, to "publish the first three orders forthwith, and to leave the other"—on colonization—"for some further consideration." He would release only the first paragraph of the proclamation on July 25 as the enabling proclamation required by the Second

Confiscation Act. As he told Carpenter, "I put the draft of the proclamation aside . . . waiting for a victory." [21]

This was far from the conclusion Lincoln had hoped to come to, but it underscored just how little support for emancipation really existed, even among his allies. On July 21, Orville Hickman Browning bumped into Isaac Arnold on the pathway between the White House and the War Department and listened patiently as the fiery Chicagoan announced himself "eager for the President to issue a proclamation declaring all the slaves of rebels free." Browning thought this was beyond sanity. "I have always been in favor of seizing and appropriating all the slaves of rebels that we could lay our hands on, and make any valuable use of, but I have no faith in proclamations or laws unless we follow them by force and actually do the thing—and when done we dont need either the proclamation or law."

In May, Boston mayor Joseph Wightman had warned Lincoln in the most frigid terms not to mistake those "small sections or towns in the Commonwealth where the doctrine of emancipation and arming the slaves is regarded with favor" as representative over the larger opposition to emancipation that prevailed throughout the rest of Massachusetts, where "the mingling of questions in relation to Slavery with the crushing of the present rebellion, is viewed with the strongest terms of disapprobation." Bay Staters "*generally* have no sympathy with those who are agitating the question of emancipation at this time." This was not just talk. Charles Sumner was up for reelection to the Senate in the fall of 1862, and already an insurrection was brewing within the state Republican Party to dump Sumner in favor of a less volatile candidate. Some adroit political footwork at the party's state convention at Worcester on September 10 easily assured an endorsement for Sumner after all, but the dissidents, led by Harvard law professor Joel Parker, walked out and organized a People's Party, nominating as their candidate Charles Francis Adams.[22]

The vilest opposition to emancipation was rooted in the racist prejudices of the white North. "We may as well look this prejudice in the face as a disturbing element in the way of emancipation," acknowledged the *Weekly Anglo-African*. For those slow to notice, a toxic cloud of racial violence had boiled up that summer from white mobs. In Dayton, Ohio, Moncure Conway heard Clement Vallandigham curdle a crowd of white workingmen with accusations that "we abolitionists, having brought on the war, were now trying to bring a horde of negroes into Ohio to take the bread out of their mouths." A tobacco factory in Brooklyn that hired twenty-five blacks was burned to the ground; in New Albany, Indiana, and Cincinnati, labor riots broke out between white and black workers, and in Chicago, a white omnibus driver beat a black man who tried to board the bus. In Illinois, fresh restrictions on black voting and black immigration were endorsed by overflow majorities; in Lincoln's Springfield, a proposition to deny the "right of suffrage or office to negroes or mulattoes" was opposed by only 20 votes out of 2,500.

Even in Washington, blacks began organizing "in anticipation of a riot and mob by the laboring classes of whites." The bitter proslavery Washingtonian William Owner cackled in his diary, "The whites in the free States are getting a little taste of what they would inflict on the whites of the Slave States. At Cincinnati, Dayton and other places in Ohio, and at New Albany Ia. the negroes have attacked the whites killing several of them. The whites in their turn attacked the nigs drove them to the woods, burnt and otherwise destroyed their houses and moveables, and the end is not yet." If this was what emancipation provoked, what could be expected if Lincoln proposed to enlist blacks in the army? In Washington, the editors of the *Evening Star* were confident they knew: "The real object of attempting to attach them to the service by formal provision of law, is but to aid the scheme of forcing negro social and industrial equality upon the white laborers of the country." [23]

Lincoln himself remained uneasy with the additional step of "arming of negroes," but Chase had the distinct impression that he would not object if local department commanders "should, at their discretion, arm, for purely defensive purposes"—and not as Hunter had done—"slaves coming within their lines." Lincoln told General Ormsby Mitchell that black enlistment was worth experimenting with, if Mitchell thought he could take Vicksburg, use armed blacks to garrison the banks of the Mississippi River, and hold it "open below Memphis" so that white troops could be deployed elsewhere. But whether black

troops were defensive or otherwise, Lincoln "was very far from expressing the same dissatisfaction with [Hunter's] course that he would have
done four or five weeks ago." On August 4, the president declined the
offer of "two colored regiments from the State of Indiana" but turned a
blind eye when Edwin Stanton authorized the new department commander in the Carolinas, Brigadier General Rufus Saxton, "to arm, uniform, equip, and receive into the service of the United States such
number of volunteers of African descent as you may deem expedient,
not exceeding 50,000, and . . . detail officers to instruct them in military
drill, discipline, and duty, and to command them."

When Reverdy Johnson complained about the abrasive announce-
ments coming from General John W. Phelps, Benjamin Butler's abolitionist lieutenant who was now overseeing the military occupation of
New Orleans, Lincoln snapped back that any Louisianans who were
"annoyed by the presence of General Phelps" had only to recall that
Phelps was there because of them. And if they thought Phelps was bad,
they should consider what Lincoln might do next. "If they can conceive
of anything worse than General Phelps, within my power, would they
not better be looking out for it?" Wisdom should tell them that "the way
to avert all this is simply to take their place in the Union upon the old
terms." If they refused, they shouldn't be surprised if they "receive
harder blows than lighter ones." [24]

HOW LONG LINCOLN had been composing the July 22 "first draft" of
the Emancipation Proclamation is unclear. Stanton told Charles Sumner
as early as May 28 that "a decree of Emancipation would be issued
within two months," but Stanton gave no hint of what prompted this
prediction. One of Seward's diplomatic correspondents, Martin Ryerson, advised the secretary the same week that "although Hunter's
proclamation was at the time most ill-judged, yet I fear that before three
months some such measure will be imperatively demanded," although
again there was nothing in the letter to show that there was anything
but guesswork behind this statement.[25]

One voice, however, insists that the first draft of the Proclamation
was written as early as mid-June. Lincoln's vice-president, Hannibal

Hamlin, told an interviewer from the *Boston Herald* in 1879 that he "was the first person [Lincoln] ever showed the proclamation to. I saw it before he submitted it to the cabinet." Hamlin gave no date for this advance notice, but it raised eyebrows all the same, since Hamlin had never been particularly close to Lincoln and was never even invited to cabinet meetings. (Hamlin admitted that a vice-president was a political cipher, "a contingent somebody" whose only recognizable public role was to serve as presiding officer of the Senate. It was, in fact, worse even than that, since Lincoln ignored most of Hamlin's requests for patronage appointments, and in 1864, he allowed the Republicans to drop Hamlin from the Lincoln reelection ticket and substitute Andrew Johnson.) But Hamlin insisted that "we had intimate relations, and he often consulted me." According to Hamlin, Lincoln met him "one evening," asked what he was doing that night, and when Hamlin told the president that he was actually getting ready to leave town, Lincoln announced, "I want you to spend the evening with me at the Soldiers' Home." Hamlin met Lincoln at the White House for the president's customary evening carriage drive up to the Soldiers' Home, and "as soon as we had started, he drew from his pocket the rough draft of the proclamation, and read it over to me." [26]

Few have been inclined to accept Hamlin's claim, though Hamlin was persistent in making it in later years. He told Henry Clay Whitney the story about being accosted by Lincoln and taken out to the Soldiers' Home, although in that account, Lincoln did not produce the proclamation until "after tea" and then went on to ask Hamlin for "suggestions and corrections as he went along." Hamlin told Whitney that he had "made three suggestions, and Lincoln adopted two of them." Hamlin recounted the story not to gain fame for himself but to demonstrate that "the proclamation of emancipation was the proclamation of Abraham Lincoln," rather than the inspiration of Seward, Chase, or any other member of the cabinet. It remained for Hamlin's grandson, Charles Eugene Hamlin, to give the story its fullest form in 1899 and attach a date to it: June 18, 1862. "One day in the latter part of this session of Congress, [Hamlin] made up his mind to make a short visit at his home in Bangor." (Hamlin did in fact leave Washington on June 19, 1862, before the close of the Congressional session, so that he could begin campaigning for Republican candidates in the August Congressional elections in his home state of Maine.) This meeting with Lincoln played out in the same fashion, except that this time both men "rode horseback" to the Soldiers' Home, and the reading of the proclamation did not occur until "after supper" and behind the locked doors of the "library." [27]

Another, more likely, claimant to Lincoln's confidence was Owen Lovejoy, the abolitionist minister and congressman from northern Illinois who had tried to draft Lincoln for the Republican Party as early as 1854. Lovejoy died in 1864 without leaving any extended memoirs, but in a letter that February to William Lloyd Garrison, Lovejoy claimed to "have known something of the facts inside during [Lincoln's] administration," and he singled out the draft of the Emancipation Proclamation as one piece of evidence. "I had it from [Lincoln's] own lips: He had written the proclamation in the summer, as early as June, I think," Lovejoy noted, placing it roughly in the same month as Hamlin, "but [I] will not be certain as to the precise time." Gideon Welles was sure this consultation was more than merely the passing of an inside tip. "I have some reason to suppose that Owen Lovejoy, the avowed and leading Abolitionist in Congress, was confidentially consulted." In 1900, Robert H. Browne published the text of an interview he claimed to have had with Lovejoy, in which Lovejoy described in detail a meeting with Lincoln about the Proclamation. But Browne pegged the date as sometime at the end of August, well after the reading of the Proclamation's first draft in the cabinet. One other witness to a possible early version of the Proclamation was Indiana Republican congressman Schuyler Colfax, who long afterwards tried to persuade John Nicolay that in November 1863 Lincoln had shown him a "lost" draft of the Proclamation from July 1862, which "abolished Slavery at once on its promulgation." Orville Hickman Browning also listened to Lincoln read a "paper" on July 1 "embodying his views of the objects of the war, and the proper mode of conducting it in its relations to slavery. This, he told me, he had sketched hastily with the intention of laying it before the Cabinet." But far from this being any form of emancipation proclamation, Browning thought that Lincoln's "views coincided entirely with my own." [28]

ABRAHAM LINCOLN (1809–1865), sixteenth president of the United States. He had been a public critic and opponent of slavery since 1837, but was convinced that the best plan for emancipation had to incorporate some form of state legislative action, compensation to slaveholders, and a gradual rather than immediate schedule. In this photograph, taken by Alexander Gardner on August 9, 1863, Lincoln is holding a copy of the Washington *Daily Morning Chronicle*, published by newspaper entrepreneur John W. Forney as a pro-Lincoln news sheet.

SALMON PORTLAND CHASE (1808–1873), secretary of the treasury from 1861 to 1864. The most well-known advocate of immediate emancipation in Lincoln's cabinet, Chase had been a front-runner for the Republican presidential nomination in 1860, but was shunted aside by the Republican national convention as too radical. Lincoln appointed him chief justice of the Supreme Court in 1864.

MONTGOMERY BLAIR (1813–1883), postmaster general from 1861 to 1864. A member of the most prominent family in American politics, Blair was an anti-slavery Midwesterner and filed the brief in defense of Dred Scott in the notorious Supreme Court case of Dred Scott v. Sanford. Like Lincoln, he was committed to gradualism and strongly favored colonization of the freed slaves.

EDWARD BATES (1793–1869), attorney general from 1861 to 1864. Bates was a conservative anti-slavery Missourian. At the first reading of the Emancipation Proclamation on July 22, 1862, he spoke in favor of the document, but added that he hoped emancipation would be linked to compulsory deportation of the freed slaves. Lincoln once remarked that no members of his cabinet better reflected his own thinking on emancipation than Blair and Bates.

HANNIBAL HAMLIN (1809–1891), vice president of the United States. Hamlin was radical in his political sympathies and urged immediate emancipation on Lincoln. In 1879, Hamlin claimed that Lincoln had confidentially read a draft of the Proclamation to him as early as June 1862.

ROGER BROOKE TANEY (1777–1864), chief justice of the Supreme Court. His majority opinion in Dred Scott v. Sanford in 1857 extended constitutional sanction for slavery over all of the federal territories. He was bitterly opposed to Lincoln; much of Lincoln's emancipation strategy was crafted with a view to preventing a federal court appeal on which Taney could eventually rule.

ZACHARIAH CHANDLER (1813–1879),
senator from Michigan. A Radical
Republican and a member of the Joint
Committee on the Conduct of the War,
Chandler was, along with Benjamin
Wade and Charles Sumner, one of a trio
of Radical senators who hectored
Lincoln incessantly to emancipate the
slaves immediately on the basis of the
presidential "war powers."

ISAAC NEWTON ARNOLD
(1815–1885), Radical Republican
who represented Illinois' second
Congressional District (Chicago
and its bordering counties) in the
thirty-seventh Congress. Arnold
was Lincoln's principal defender
among the Radicals in Congress,
and his 1866 biography of
Lincoln argued that Lincoln had
been substantially more Radical
in his sympathies than
congressional Radicals had given
him credit for being.

"Contrabands" at Fortress Monroe, May 1861. This envelope mocks slaveholders vainly trying to prevent their slaves from escaping to the relative freedom of Fortress Monroe after Benjamin Butler, the commandant at the fort, declared runaways to be "contraband of war" and protected from recapture by their masters.

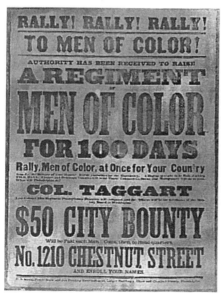

Recruitment poster for black troops. Despite Lincoln's initial fear that federal use of black soldiers would drive the Border slave states into joining the Confederacy, he agreed in July 1862 to allow the recruitment of blacks for noncombatant roles. Five months later, when Lincoln published the final Emancipation Proclamation, he authorized the enlistment of blacks as soldiers. Over the course of the Civil War, 180,000 blacks volunteered to serve.

MAJOR GENERAL GEORGE
BRINTON MCCLELLAN
(1826–1885), with his wife,
Mary Ellen. The
commander of the Union
armies and a Democrat, he
was unwilling to see
emancipation included
among the Civil War's
aims. The suspicions of
McClellan's disloyalty
helped convince Lincoln
that he could not wait for a
legislated end to slavery.

After Antietam and the issue of the Preliminary Emancipation Proclamation, Lincoln visited McClellan and the Army of the Potomac, partly to
test the general's loyalty. In this photograph, taken by Alexander Gardner
on October 3, 1862, at the headquarters of Major-General Fitz-John Porter,
near the Antietam battlefield, Lincoln and McClellan face each other, surrounded by members of McClellan's and Porter's staffs.

GIDEON WELLES (1802–1878), secretary of the navy. From Connecticut and originally a Jackson Democrat, Welles's opposition to slavery led him into the ranks of the Republicans in 1854. He was Lincoln's choice for a cabinet post as a gesture to New England, and to Welles's friends among the "War Democrats." In his diary, Welles left vivid accounts of the July 13, 1862, carriage ride during which Lincoln first announced to members of his cabinet that he "had about come to the conclusion that it was a military necessity" to "free the slaves," as well as detailed decriptions of Lincoln's presentation of the First Draft (on July 22nd) and the Preliminary Emancipation Proclamation (on September 22nd).

LIBRARY OF CONGRESS

NEW-YORK HISTORICAL SOCIETY

Adalbert Volck (1828–1912), a Baltimore dentist and Confederate sympathizer, executed a series of eight etchings during the war, lampooning the Union cause and Lincoln in particular. Lincoln is depicted here writing the Emancipation Proclamation while putting his foot on the Constitution and laws. The Devil holds Lincoln's inkwell.

Francis Bicknell Carpenter (1830–1900) was commissioned to paint a commemorative picture of "The First Reading of the Emancipation Proclamation" in 1864. Using the state dining room of the White House as a studio, Carpenter completed the fourteen-by-five-foot painting in July 1864. A lithograph version, prepared by A. H. Ritchie, sold in the thousands of copies. Carpenter carefully positioned the cabinet figures to indicate their political view of the Proclamation, Chase and Stanton to Lincoln's right as the chief advocates of emancipation, and Seward, Welles, Smith, Blair, and Bates ranged to the president's left in order of decreasing enthusiasm.

The most sensational claimant to an advance look at the Proclamation, however, has long been David Homer Bates, the manager of the War Department telegraph office. In 1907, Bates asserted that "until recently it has not been known, except by a few persons, that Lincoln wrote the first draft of the Emancipation Proclamation" while seated at a desk "in the cipher-room of the War Department telegraph office." According to Bates, "early one morning in June, 1862, shortly after McClellan's 'Seven Days' Fight,' " Lincoln appeared at the War Department telegraph office and asked Major Thomas T. Eckert, of the telegraph office staff, "for some paper, as he wanted to write something special." Since the White House had no telegraph connections of its own, Lincoln usually walked once a day across the "President's lawn" to the War Department's modest three-story headquarters, facing Seventeenth Street, and mounted the stairs to the second-floor telegraph suite next to Stanton's office. There he would read through the latest bulletins in the decryption file, chat with the operators at the bank of telegraph receivers Stanton had installed, and sometimes "spend hour after hour" with Stanton as news of great battles rattled into the office.[29]

On this occasion, though, Lincoln had something else in mind. The telegraph office, Bates claimed, was Lincoln's "haven of rest," the one place where he was "comparatively free from interruption" and could work without interference from "the pestering crowd of office seekers." It was, therefore, the one place he could compose an emancipation proclamation without having his concentration or privacy disturbed. "He would look out of the window a while and then put his pen to paper, but he did not write much at once," and when he rose to leave, he put his papers into Eckert's hands to be locked away in Eckert's desk until his next visit. "This he did nearly every day for several weeks," and not until Lincoln had finished the document did he tell Eckert "that he had been writing an order giving freedom to the slaves in the South."[30]

The common difficulty with crediting any of these stories is their distance from the event. Lovejoy's letter to Garrison about a "consultation" has the strength of being composed only eighteen months after the event and having the corroborating testimony of Welles's comment, but it is also the most vague, both in terms of time and substance. Robert

Browne's "interview" with Lovejoy was not published until thirty-six years after Lovejoy's death, and it spreads out to a length that makes a genuine word-for-word recollection dubious. Bates's story of the telegraph office only appeared with his book in 1907 and offered no supporting testimony from the staff of the telegraph office, most of whom were dead by then. Worse still, it stretches credulity to believe that Lincoln would have found any privacy for writing something as vital as an emancipation proclamation, much less a "haven of rest," in the noisy clatter of the War Department telegraph office, in the middle of a permanent crew of twelve civilian telegraph operators and the incessant coming-and-going of messengers, clerks, and War Department staff. Besides, neither of the two other War Department telegraphists who subsequently published accounts of their service, Thomas H. Sherman and William Bender Wilson, ever mentioned Lincoln using the telegraph office as a writing room, or claimed that Lincoln composed the Emancipation Proclamation there. And at least one informant on Lincoln's own White House staff, William O. Stoddard, testified that the draft of the proclamation was "waiting in one of the pigeonholes of the President's desk"—not in the War Department—"all through the hot oppressive days of this battle summer." [31]

An even greater difficulty with these accounts lies in the way other informants dated the writing of the July 22 draft. Francis Carpenter, whose principal assignment in 1864 was to paint a commemorative canvas of the reading of the first draft, always contended that Lincoln gave him "a detailed account of the history and issue of the great proclamation," and this "account" placed the writing of "the first draft of the Emancipation Proclamation . . . on board of the steam-boat returning from his 8th of July visit to the army at Harrison's Landing." Carpenter's claims have been treated with caution from the time his *Six Months at the White House with Abraham Lincoln* appeared in 1866, but there is little reason to doubt, as he told Theodore Munger, that Carpenter "heard the inside history of the Proclamation from [Lincoln's] own lips." Another informant whose "information was derived exclusively from Mr. L. himself" was the biographer Joseph Barrett, who also calendared the first draft of the proclamation "as early as July" and who agreed with Carpenter that it was probably written during the return from Harrison's Landing. Even Montgomery Blair believed that after "General McClellan's Harrison Landing letter, of July 7, 1862," Lincoln "no longer hesitated." [32]

The one slight dissent from this chronology came from Navy Secretary Welles. Welles believed that what Lincoln wrote on board the *Ariel* was most likely his last appeal to the Border-state congressmen and that the first draft was likely written on July 14, one day after the Stanton funeral and the same day that the majority report from the Border staters came back with its resounding refusal of cooperation. Welles, who was notoriously shaky about dating events (in articles for the *Galaxy* in 1872, he hesitantly suggested that the July 22 cabinet meeting had occurred on August 2), based his choice of July 14 on his unwillingness to "impute to [Lincoln] a disingenuous and a double part" in making a "proposition to the representatives of the border States" about compensated emancipation on July 12, having put the draft of a general emancipation proclamation in his desk pigeonhole on July 9. It never occurred to Welles that Lincoln did not necessarily see the two proposals as contradictions. Rather, as Lincoln told federal judge Thomas Duval, "he saw nothing inconsistent with the gradual emancipation of slavery and his proclamation." [33]

THE VARIETY of conflicting stories may have something to do with the uncharacteristic prodigality with which Lincoln leaked news of the Proclamation's existence. New York politico James A. Hamilton gave New York governor Edward Morgan a garbled version of the Proclamation's reading that described an emancipation proclamation presented to Lincoln "by several members of Congress and other gentlemen." Lincoln, as Hamilton heard, "approved of the policy thereby indicated, and declared that, with slight modifications, he would issue it," but "this purpose was frustrated by two members of his cabinet." Lincoln certainly read the first draft to James Speed, the brother of Joshua Speed, only to have Speed conclude that "it will do no good; probably much harm." The Washington *Evening Star* heard it "said in unusually well-informed circles" in early August "that direct and decisive action is to be taken in prosecution of the war." Southern Unionist Robert J. Walker brought the novelist and journalist James R. Gilmore to meet Lincoln on August 18, whispering to Gilmore that "I have good news for you, but it must be strictly confidential,—the Emancipation Proclamation is decided upon," news which Lincoln then authorized Gilmore to leak privately to Gilmore's boss at the *New York Tribune,* Horace Greeley. Leonard Swett told John Nicolay that Lincoln had hinted at having "written something" during a meeting at the White House on August 20, which "couldn't be anything else than the proclamation itself." Hiram Barney, the collector of the Port of New York and a key figure in New York Republican politics, also claimed fifteen years later that Lincoln had read him a draft of the Proclamation "in his own hand writing and in his pocket when we were together" in Washington on September 5. And if that was not enough, John Hay cryptically added to one of his anonymous editorials for the *Missouri Republican,* "Perhaps the time is coming when the President, so long forbearing, so long suffering with the South and the border, will give the word long waited for, which will breathe the life that is needed, the fire that seems extinguished, in the breasts of our men at arms." [34]

Even with these cues, the voices that demanded Lincoln throw hesitation to the winds and declare universal emancipation were few and weak, even among the abolitionist faithful. At an unusual Sunday afternoon cabinet meeting, Salmon Chase pitched into "the connection of the Slavery question with the rebellion . . . for the tenth or twentieth time," urging Lincoln to forget about proclamations and let an open invitation for the enlistment of slaves by the military be the means of pulling the props from under the Confederacy. A "Grand War Demonstration" rally on the White House grounds on August 6 adopted resolutions of flaming support for Lincoln and for "subjecting to confiscation the property of rebels," but not for emancipation. Nathaniel Eggleston wrote a lengthy article on "Emancipation" for the *New Englander and Yale Review,* hoping for "a proclamation of freedom to the enslaved," but agreeing with equal enthusiasm that "we should not shrink" from "securing emancipation by purchase or ransom." On August 22, the Massachusetts journalist and antislavery reformer Lydia Maria Child, risking what "may seem a violation of propriety for a woman," published a public letter to Lincoln, upbraiding him for allowing the Border-state slaveholders to pour so much sand into the wheels of progress against slavery. But even Child acknowledged "the extreme difficulties of your position." The "pro-slavery spirit of the land is a mighty giant," she lamented, and the best recommendation she could make "in the service of freedom" was for Lincoln to guarantee freedom to "the poor fugitives who toil for us" and to encourage more runaways "by making them feel *secure* of their freedom." [35]

Much more widely read than Child's letter was another public letter to Lincoln that appeared in the *New York Tribune* on August 20, from the pen of Horace Greeley. Lincoln had first met the garrulous and "dictatorial" editor in chief of the *Tribune* back in 1848, when Lincoln was serving his lone term in Congress and Greeley was just making the *Tribune* a citywide success. During the 1850s, Greeley built the *Tribune* into the nation's newspaper and made himself Radical Republicanism's journalist of record. But in 1858, like many other eastern Republicans, Greeley refused to support Lincoln's run for the Senate against Stephen Douglas, which wounded Lincoln deeply. Worse, Greeley made a colossal fool of himself and the *Tribune* in the summer of 1861 by braying "On to Richmond" in twenty-point headlines and getting as his answer the campaign that ended in ruin at Bull Run. Lincoln wanted to believe that Greeley had acted in "good faith," but he added, "he is wanting in common sense," not to mention predictability. "I infer," Lincoln dryly remarked to James Gilmore, "that you are not always able to keep Brother Greeley in the traces."

Still, in 1862, Greeley was nevertheless thought by Lincoln to be "a great man," and George Julian was sure that Lincoln had "the most profound personal respect for Mr. Greeley." Besides, Lincoln owed Greeley some important political debts that more than canceled out Greeley's indifference in 1858. Greeley's animosity toward the Seward faction in New York helped hold back a Seward presidential nomination in 1860, and Greeley had been loyally on hand to greet Lincoln when the president-elect arrived in Washington in February of 1861, despite plots and rumors of violence. Lincoln had not forgotten, either, that Greeley had handled the cancellations of Frémont's and Hunter's military emancipations with considerable restraint in the *Tribune*. In the pigeonholes above his desk, Lincoln kept one slot reserved exclusively for correspondence from Greeley. The editor had earned his soapbox, and he now used it to maximum effect.[56]

"I do not intrude to tell you," Greeley announced, "that a great portion of those who triumphed in your election . . . are sorely disappointed by the policy you seem to be pursuing with regard to the slaves of Rebels." That much, he supposed, was common opinion. What Greeley wanted to do was to "set succinctly and unmistakably before you . . . what we think we have a right to expect" from an antislavery Republican president in the midst of a civil war. That president should "EXECUTE THE LAWS"; he should especially "discharge . . . your official and imperative duty with regard to the emancipating provisions of the new Confiscation Act"; he should stop listening to "certain fossil politicians hailing from the Border Slave States"; he should make the army start fighting and stop arresting fugitives. Beyond that, Greeley's editorial (which he entitled "The Prayer of Twenty Millions," as if it were the single wish of the entire North) did little more than repeat itself. "I had not besought him," Greeley pointed out years later, "to proclaim general emancipation." (Greeley would not, in fact, receive news of James Gilmore's interview with Lincoln about the proclamation until the day after "The Prayer of Twenty Millions" went to press.)[37]

Greeley's letter was a sensation. Wendell Phillips thought it was "superb, terrific." Lincoln, by contrast, seemed to have no reaction at all, nor perhaps should he have, since "any President who had occupied the office previous to Mr. Lincoln, would have passed over such a letter in silence, however much it might have annoyed or pained him." A riposte from the White House would have been "an act wanting in dignity." None of the three diary-keepers in the cabinet mention the letter or any reaction from Lincoln to it, nor do Hay and Nicolay. But on August 23, an open letter by Lincoln to Greeley appeared in the editorial columns of Washington's most senior newspaper, the *Daily National Intelligencer*, the one paper in the capital that regularly carried the full texts of laws, resolutions, and notices, as well as news.[38] Two, evidently, could play the game of public letter.

Few of Lincoln's letters quite match the economy of expression, the passionless logical progress of his thinking, or the peculiar combination of firmness and generosity of this one of fewer than four hundred words. "I have just read yours of the 19th. addressed to myself through the New-York Tribune," he began without flourishes, and at once he threw the testimony of goodwill against Greeley. He would not bore Greeley by trying to "controvert" every *we complain, we require,* or *we think* in Greeley's letter, even if they contained "statements, or assumptions of fact, which I may know to be erroneous": Thus he deliciously planted the suggestion of error without exactly identifying it. He would not even try to chide Greeley for "an impatient and dictatorial tone," although that was certainly the first thing any who had read Greeley's letter would remember. To the contrary, in the spirit of common cause, "I waive it in deference to an old friend, whose heart I have always supposed to be right." Lincoln, not Greeley, now held the rhetorical high ground.

Greeley had unwittingly given Lincoln an opening when he began his letter with a criticism of the "policy you seem to be pursuing with regard to the Slaves of Rebels." This allowed Lincoln to turn his reply not to the "policy" but to the suggestion that he only *seemed* to have one, as though he had been cloaking it from public view for the past year. "As to the policy I 'seem to be pursuing' as you say, I have not meant to leave any one in doubt." Here it was: "I would save the Union." He would even "save it the shortest way" possible, or at least by whatever "shortest way" withstood scrutiny "under the Constitution." This was what he had pledged to do when he took the oath of office and what the Constitution and national safety demanded of him.

This reply maneuvered Greeley, and any other of Lincoln's critics, across a line which, since Lincoln occupied the side of *saving the Union,* could only mean that those on the other side were *not* interested in saving the Union. There were those, for instance, who were more in love with slavery than the Union, "those who would not save the Union, unless they could at the same time save slavery." And then there were those who put the destruction of slavery on a higher pedestal than *saving the Union*, "those who would not save the Union unless they could at the same time destroy slavery." What these partisans shared was a common indifference to the salvation of the Union, so that Greeley awoke to find that Lincoln had placed him hand in hand with Jefferson Davis. "I do not agree with them," Lincoln added, either one of them.

"My paramount object in this struggle is to save the Union," Lincoln repeated. But now the hinge of his argument turned, because there were more ways than one to accomplish the salvation of the Union. It might, for instance, be possible to "save the Union without freeing any slave." That was what the Border staters and last-ditch racists wanted, and if that worked, then he was constitutionally obligated to "do it." This was what Garrison and Phillips had accused him of trying to do all along, so there was no surprise there. But it was just as true that "if I could save [the Union] by freeing all the slaves," he would be just as obligated to do that, since his oath pledged him to save the Union without respect to method. The opposition in Congress had all along wanted a cast-iron promise that emancipation would never be on the table as a method for *saving the Union;* now Lincoln was reminding them that he had never made such a promise. Lastly, and here he tipped slightly the cards he planned to play in the Proclamation, "if I could save it by freeing some and leaving others alone I would also do that."

Laying out the available methods "to save the Union" in this fashion permitted Lincoln to sound so perfectly evenhanded that it has deceived more than a few in later times who forgot that evenhandedness was exactly what the "mighty giant" of the "proslavery spirit" raged against. To the defenders of slavery, there were no such things as *options*, only one everlasting, airtight rant for the survival of white supremacy. The moment Lincoln suggested that slavery was in *any* fashion negotiable— the moment he declared that "what I do about slavery, and the colored race, I do because I believe it helps to save the Union; and . . . I shall do less whenever I shall believe what I am doing hurts the cause, and I shall do more whenever I shall believe doing more will help the cause"—was the moment when all bets against emancipation were off. He was exactly what the slaveholder did not want: a president willing to listen to the other side, willing to consider that slaveholding might be an error and a lie. "I shall try to correct errors when shown to be errors; and I shall adopt new views so fast as they shall appear to be true views."

There was one last spike in the letter. "I have here stated my purpose according to my view of official duty," which was to say, what his oath, the Constitution, and the federal statute books required. He had said nothing up to this point about his own personal persuasion, and strictly speaking, he needn't have. But he did: "I intend no modification of my oft-expressed personal wish that all men every where could be free." [39] This was actually Lincoln's first statement, in any official presidential capacity, of an opinion on slavery. But coming as it did after a description of the various methods which lay logically before him, it was impossible not to read the statement as a subtle revelation of which way onlookers could expect his choice of method to fall. Massachusetts governor John Andrew smiled as he read the letter and remarked that "hope rises of a vigorous, large, bold and hopeful policy." As the president explained to Isaac Arnold and Owen Lovejoy after the letter appeared, his intention "in his letter to Mr. Greeley" was to make clear that "he would proclaim freedom to the slave just as soon as he felt assured he could do it effectively; that the people would stand by him, and that, by doing so, he could strengthen the Union cause." [40]

The newspapers picked up Lincoln's letter to Greeley like candy scattered on the floor. "So novel a thing as a newspaper correspondence between the President and an editor excites great attention," remarked Whitelaw Reid. In Washington, the *Daily Morning Chronicle* bugled its delight over Lincoln's "concise, expressive, and intelligent exposition," while the *Daily National Republican* hailed it as "decidedly *Lincolnic*." The *New York Times*, edited by Greeley's journalistic rival, Henry J. Raymond, reprinted Lincoln's letter and happily chided Greeley for trying "to substitute his conscience for Mr. Lincoln's in the present national perplexity." Lincoln's reply, by contrast, was all the evidence anyone needed "of abundant sanity in the White House."

One of Francis P. Blair's network of listeners reported that "the letter of the president to Horace Greeley meets with universal approbation. I have heard scores of Douglas Democrats declare that they would now support Lincoln for Dictator." Sydney Gay, the *Tribune*'s managing editor, who usually shouldered the task of softening Greeley's blows, wrote Lincoln that the letter "has infused new hope among us at the North," and Gay wanted the president to know that "the general impression is that as you are determined to save the Union tho' Slavery perish, you mean presently to announce that the destruction of Slavery is the price of our salvation."

Greeley, however, was unchastened. He congratulated himself that he had flushed Lincoln from cover and commented that, "As to Old Abe's letter, I consider it a sign of progress." The *Tribune* did not print Lincoln's reply. Instead, Greeley wrote a churlish response of his own in the *Tribune* on August 24, warning Lincoln to open his eyes to the necessity of "*recognizing, obeying,* and *enforcing the laws.*" [41]

The one thing that puzzled Greeley about Lincoln's reply was that it seemed to be no reply at all, at least not to his "Prayer of Twenty Millions." Greeley had wanted to know why Lincoln seemed so lackadaisical about applying the Confiscation Acts; Lincoln had said nothing whatsoever about the Confiscation Acts, but instead had given Greeley a lecture on his "paramount object" of saving the Union. "It is no answer to my 'Prayer,' " Greeley complained to James R. Gilmore. But Greeley soon enough guessed why. The reply had been drafted by Lincoln as part of a general statement about emancipation to be released in anticipation of the military "success" Seward had warned Lincoln to wait for; Greeley's letter had merely been the occasion for Lincoln to wheel it out, tack to the beginning a brief introduction about Greeley's "Prayer," and send it out for publication. Whitelaw Reid caught a rumor in Washington that "some days before Greeley's letter was published the President read to a friend a rough draft of what now appears in the form of a reply to Greeley and asked his advice about publishing it." Greeley himself accepted the explanation that Lincoln "had prepared it in advance, and took the occasion to get his views before the public." [42]

But why was Lincoln writing this in mid-August, only a month after Seward had persuaded him to wait until the Union Army had done something to make emancipation look triumphant instead of desperate?

What military "success" was so close that Lincoln felt that the time had come to send out signals, even oblique ones, about emancipation?

THE POST of general-in-chief had been vacant ever since March of 1862, when Lincoln had restricted McClellan to the command of the Army of the Potomac. McClellan's Harrison's Landing letter had made it abundantly clear that the Young Napoleon felt he deserved reinstatement. But when Lincoln returned to Washington from Harrison's Landing, one of his first decisions was to call not McClellan but Henry Wager Halleck to come east from the Department of Missouri as the new general-in-chief.

Lincoln knew Halleck largely by legal reputation, since Halleck was the author of the standard American textbook on international law. But Halleck had originally trained for the army, and the outbreak of the war in 1861 brought him back to the army with a major general's commission. In November, he took over Frémont's unhappy Department of Missouri, and from that point on, more victories had been won and more Confederate territory reclaimed in Halleck's department than in any other theater of the war. Never mind that it was not Halleck who had won the victories but Ulysses S. Grant at Forts Henry and Donelson and John Pope at Island No. 10; it was Halleck's department, and Halleck got the credit.

Bringing Halleck in as general-in-chief was not difficult. The trick would be removing McClellan from command of the Army of the Potomac, a task no one in Washington was eager to perform. But Halleck had a better idea: McClellan would be ordered to disengage his precious Army of the Potomac piece by piece from Harrison's Landing and send them back to northern Virginia. They would then be consolidated with the three army corps Lincoln had kept along the Potomac to protect the capital, and together they would become the "Army of Virginia"—and given a new field commander.[43] Lincoln might have turned to Grant, the victor of Henry and Donelson. But Grant still had hanging around his neck the near-disaster at Shiloh in April, and the Shiloh debacle had been further overshadowed by rumors that Grant had a drinking problem. So Lincoln turned to the other western possibility, John Pope.[44]

Few Union generals had more to commend them to Lincoln at that moment than John Pope. The son of old Judge Nathaniel Pope, who had presided over the Eighth Judicial Circuit in Illinois when Lincoln was first practicing law there, Pope had gotten into West Point on the recommendation of Ninian Edwards, Lincoln's brother-in-law; served through the Mexican War; married the daughter of a congressman; and was one of the four officers detailed as Lincoln's personal bodyguard on the harrowing trip from Springfield to Washington. Pope was aggressive, confident, and, unlike most West Pointers, politically reliable. Unhappily, that meant that two thirds of the personal assets he brought east turned out to be liabilities.

On July 14, Pope issued a routine taking-of-command order to the newly baptized Army of Virginia that set a new standard for Civil War bluster. "Let us understand each other," Pope began, in the style of a country schoolmaster facing a class of unruly boys. "I have come to you from the West, where we have always seen the backs of our enemies, from an army whose business it has been to seek the adversary and to beat him when he was found." This challenge was meant to sound energetic, but instead it sounded reckless; the situation was made worse when Pope followed this announcement with a series of orders authorizing the Army of Virginia to freely confiscate whatever rebel property it needed to "subsist." It gave "large numbers of our soldiers" the "idea that Gen. Pope's orders give them permission to help themselves to anything they can find, and consequently they have been roaming through the country, killing chickens, sheep, etc. quite extensively," in a manner horrifying to the sensibilities of George B. McClellan.[45]

Still tethered to Harrison's Landing, McClellan was beside himself. "I get no reinforcements & no information," he raged to New York Democrat Samuel Barlow. "I know nothing, absolutely nothing as to the plans and intentions of the Govt—but I have strong reason to believe that they literally have no plans, but are halting in a wretched state of indecision." He soon found out how wrong he was. He tried to offer Halleck the same advice he had offered Lincoln about "not making war upon the institution of slavery," but Halleck's only reply was to order McClellan to begin packing up the Army of the Potomac and sending it back to northern Virginia—and Pope. "If you or any one else had presented a better [plan]," Halleck said, "I certainly should have adopted it, but all of your plans require re-enforcements, which it is impossible to give you." By the time McClellan completed the evacuation of Harrison's Landing on August 23, he was a general without an army. He set up a pathetic little headquarters across the Potomac from Washington with nothing to command "except my staff" and "some one hundred men in my camp." All the rest had been "merged in Pope's army." Sulking over his humiliation, McClellan's kindest wish for John Pope was that "Pope will be thrashed during the coming week—& very badly whipped he will be & ought to be." [46]

That was not Lincoln's opinion. In the White House, John Pope was "the Coming Man . . . of the army"; the reply to Greeley, with its tiptoe intimations of emancipation, was written in the flush of confidence that a way had been found around the McClellan problem. Of course, if the McClellan problem *was* solved, that might eliminate the need for a proclamation altogether, since a cooperative commanding general like Pope could be relied on both to keep his own army in hand and to keep the rebel army on the run, allowing the president to go quietly back to his plans for wooing the Border states with compensated emancipation. It is, however, a measure of Lincoln's determination to go through with the proclamation that he kept posting signs of some impending change in the wind. And certainly the most underappreciated of those signs was an "audience" Lincoln gave on August 14 to a "Committee of colored men" at the White House to talk about colonization. [47]

Colonization disguised itself as benevolence to blacks when in fact what it really amounted to was protectionism for whites, which is why so many antislavery Northerners used it to sugarcoat emancipation. The Boston shipping magnate Robert Bennett Forbes put his view as plainly as his Republican sympathies permitted: "Should we take them to the Free States, and give them the privileges of citizenship, and keep them for laborers, to the exclusion of just so many whites, and tax the working community by lowering wages?" Obviously not, to Forbes, so the simplest solution was a crude precursor of apartheid. There were some, like William Seward, who took exception to this view ("I am always for bringing men and States *into* this Union," he said, "never for taking any *out*"), but most of them, including Garrison and Phillips, lived out on the edge of abolitionist radicalism. Even abolitionists like James Wadsworth thought that the best way forward after emancipation was "to organize the freedmen into self-sustaining and self-defending agricultural colonies, locating them on confiscated and on new, hitherto uncultivated lands." And it only confirmed the colonizationists in their own rectitude that slaveholders condemned their plan almost as violently as abolition.[48]

Republicans in the 1850s made no formal commitment to colonization, but Lincoln was sure that "a very large proportion of its members are for it, and that the chief plank in their platform—opposition to the spread of slavery"—simply assumed that colonization was a next step somewhere beyond the containment of slavery. It would be vital, argued Montgomery Blair, that Republicans deny any suggestion that they "seek to set negroes free among them to be their equals & consequently their rulers where they are numerous." How colonization was going to take place was something Lincoln never seriously addressed before 1861. "The enterprise is a difficult one," he admitted, but many other antislavery Northerners welcomed colonization as a kind of great white hope. After all, Lincoln's lifetime was witness to massive migrations of Europeans to North America, India, and Australia—not to mention an internal migration that Lincoln himself had lent a hand to as a militia captain, the forced relocation of woodland Indian tribes beyond the Mississippi. George Boutwell hoped that "South Carolina and Florida" might be "dedicated to the black population of this country," while Truman Smith, former Connecticut congressman and political powerbroker, advised Lincoln to establish "the freedmen of the States this side of the Mississippi" in colonies on "the west side of that river." Smith understood his motives as both "conservative and beneficient," since no "one in his senses" believed that the slaves "will remain free for an hour" once the Southerners were conquered and restored to the Union. For those more interested in keeping North America all white, "The island of Porto Rico, not two days' sail from our shores, could take them all," suggested Nathaniel Eggleston. "St. Domingo would be glad to take them, and then would have room for as many more." And of course, there were the examples of the Roman military colonies of antiquity and "the children of Israel" who "went out of Egyptian bondage in a body." If mass expatriations like these could work, why not the expatriation and colonization of freed slaves?[49]

But creating a practical black colonization plan would become necessary only if a large-scale emancipation was near enough to require it. In a perverse way, Lincoln's interest in colonization at this moment confirms the seriousness of his compensated emancipation plans in 1861, since his first Annual Message to Congress that December asked that "steps be taken for colonizing" emancipated slaves "at some place, or places, in a climate congenial to them," and to find further funding so that "the free colored people already in the United States could . . . be included in such colonization."

Even earlier, Lincoln had had fingers in the wind about possible colonial destinations. In March 1861, he directed the American minister to Guatemala to begin looking up possible colonization sites in Central America. In April, an entrepreneur and speculator named Ambrose Thompson wangled an introduction to Lincoln and presented himself as the head of the Chiriqui Improvement Company. The federal government had been dickering for some years over the purchase of a coaling station at Chiriqui, on the eastern shore of the isthmus of Panama. Thompson, who owned thousands of acres around Chiriqui, had in hand a four-page prospectus which extolled the virtues of Chiriqui—good natural harbor, coal mines ("the chief element and the strength of Naval Power") for the navy, "rich and beautiful vallies and plains"— and a paradisiacal location for a freedmen's colony that would ensure American dominance of the western Caribbean.

Thompson was only the first. Once the December Annual Message put Lincoln publicly on the side of colonization, and once Congress appropriated money for colonization in the District Emancipation bill and the Second Confiscation Act, other promoters for a "West India Company" and a "Port Royal Agricultural and Commercial Company" appeared with broad smiles and plans for the "ultimate removal" of blacks to "some of the strictly Troppical countries."[50]

Lincoln's willingness to lend an ear to the proposal of colonization has done more than almost anything else to erode his reputation as "the colored man's president." Colonization was a wordless abomination to the abolitionists and an insult to the North's free blacks. "We would respectfully suggest," erupted Frederick Douglass in 1849, "that it might be well to ascertain the number of free colored people who will be likely to need the assistance of government to help them out of this country," because it wouldn't be very many. "Our minds are made up to live here if we can, or die here if we must." Now the news of renewed plans for colonization provoked Robert Purvis, the wealthy black abolitionist, to ask in dismay, "With what law of economy, political or social, can you reconcile this project to banish from your shores the men that plough your fields, drive your teams, and help build your houses?" But economics, politics, and society had nothing to do with it, and in mid-August, Lincoln "sent word" to the leading black clergy of the District "that he had something to say to them of interest to themselves and to the country." Presidents did not, in anyone's memory, call black men to the White House to hear anything, much less matters of national interest. But on August 14, a committee of five—Edward M. Thomas (the president of the Anglo-African Institute for the Encouragement of Industry and Art), John F. Cook, John T. Costin, Cornelius Clark, and Benjamin McCoy—was ushered into the presidential office, with Lincoln "shaking hands very cordially with each one." [51]

Lincoln's message was straightforward: Colonization was an inevitability, and he needed volunteers to begin the work. "And why," he posed the rhetorical question, "should the people of your race be colonized, and where? Why should they leave this country?" Lincoln answered his own question with remarkable racial candor. "You and we are different races," and as every incident over two hundred and fifty years had proven, "your race are suffering, in my judgment, the greatest wrong inflicted on any people." But withdrawing that wrong—slavery—would only remedy part of that suffering, because "even when you cease to be slaves, you are yet far removed from being placed on an equality with the white race." This was simply a reality: "I do not propose to discuss this, but to present it as a fact with which we have to deal." Why *this* fact could not be dealt with in the same way that the fact of slavery was being dealt with, Lincoln did not stop to explain, nor did the committee dare to ask. The solution, as Lincoln saw it, was "for us both, therefore, to be separated." It would do the whites good and, for that matter, it would do blacks good, as well, to be out from under the white thumb. "I do not know how much attachment you may have toward our race," Lincoln said frankly. "It does not strike me that you have the greatest reason to love them."

But colonization had another advantage besides putting distance between the oppressor and the "systematically oppressed." If free blacks (who had little if anything to gain materially by colonization) would pledge themselves now to join a colonization project, it would convince white people who feared any form of emancipation without colonization that the fears were groundless. "You could give a start to white people," and thus "you would open a wide door for many to be made free." If "intelligent colored men, such as are before me, would move in this matter, much might be accomplished." This was asking a great deal in the way of sacrifice from the free black community, and it would, Lincoln admitted, only be natural for free blacks to take "(I speak in no unkind sense) an extremely selfish view of the case." But they needed—or rather, he needed them—to override that instinct and "for the sake of your race . . . sacrifice something of your present comfort for the purpose of being as grand in that respect as the white people." As a way of softening the "sacrifice," Lincoln hurried to assure them that his notion of colonization was not a traumatic resettlement across the Atlantic in Africa. "The place I am thinking about having for a colony is in Central America." He did not specify Chiriqui, but it was clear that Chiriqui was what he had in mind. "The particular place I have in view is to be a great highway from the Atlantic or Caribbean Sea to the Pacific Ocean" with "harbors among the finest in the world" and "very rich coal mines."

What Lincoln wanted from these men now was a promise, a commitment, some form of public testimonial "whether I can get a number of able-bodied men, with their wives and children, who are willing to go." Like an earlier Abraham, he would not be picky about numbers. "Could I get a hundred tolerably intelligent men, with their wives and children . . . ? Can I have fifty? If I could find twenty-five able-bodied men, with a mixture of women and children, good things in the family relation, I think I could make a successful commencement." [52]

The delegation looked at Lincoln silently, and then Edward Thomas promised that "they would hold a consultation and in a short time give an answer." This was all Lincoln needed. "Take your full time—no hurry at all," he said, and the meeting was over. Two days later, Thomas wrote Lincoln to thank him for making his case so persuasively but begged for more time to "confer with leading colored men in Phila New York and Boston." But the "leading colored men" gave Thomas no indication whatsoever that they had been convinced of anything by Lincoln. When Frederick Douglass read the newspaper accounts of the meeting, he rushed to cover Lincoln with denunciation. "In this address Mr. Lincoln assumes the language and arguments of an itinerant Colonization lecturer, showing all his inconsistencies, his pride of race and blood, his contempt for Negroes and his canting hypocrisy. How an honest man could creep into such a character as that implied by this address we are not required to show." Douglass was unimpressed by the "tone of frankness and benevolence" with which Lincoln acknowledged the unfairness of white racism. "To these colored people, without power and without influence, the President is direct, undisguised, and unhesitating. He says to the colored people: I don't like you, you must clear out of the country." [53]

And that, in large measure, has been the way Lincoln's colonization proposal has come down to us—as asking the once-oppressed to volunteer for expulsion and exile, so that their oppressors could breathe more freely. "To one who thinks of the Emancipator in terms of abolitionist stereotypes," remarked James Garfield Randall, the celebrated twentieth-century Lincoln biographer, with mocking mildness, "the words of his remarkable address to this group . . . will come as something of a surprise." [54] But as feeble as events proved colonization to be as an idea, there are two things in the interview that have been easy to miss. One is that, unlike Bates and Blair, Lincoln was asking for volunteers, not drafting conscripts; colonization, whether for good or ill, would remain voluntary, even if he could promise to sweeten the proposal by spending "some of the money" Congress had appropriated to fund colonization. The other is the linkage between colonization and emancipation. The conjunction of the Greeley letter, the reorganization of the army under Pope, and the colonization "lecture" point together toward an expectation that the emancipation moment might be just around the corner, perhaps to come with the next battle, somewhere south of Washington, on the road to Richmond. Hurrying a group of "colored men" to the White House to consider colonization made sense only if emancipation was itself hurrying toward hope.

As Lincoln quickly learned, it was not.

THE DISTANT "heavy firing" of artillery on the morning of August 29 was the first sign that something had gone disastrously wrong with John Pope. Two days before, 20,000 Confederate foot soldiers had descended like happy Visigoths on the Army of Virginia's supply base at Manassas Junction, just southwest of the old Bull Run battlefield, destroying trains, warehouses, and stores and pulling down the telegraph wires Lincoln relied on to know what was happening with the army. The Confederates then disappeared northward, and Pope, stung by embarrassment, pivoted the Army of Virginia and took off in hot pursuit, coming up in the process to the still-blackened battlefield around Bull Run where Irvin McDowell had come to grief a year before. There Pope found the Confederates who had torched Manassas Junction; he spent the entire day of the twenty-ninth pummeling them and fuming with impatience for the lead elements of the Army of the Potomac, who were just arriving on the scene from the Peninsula, to catch up and reinforce him. Pope did not know it, but the Confederates he was hoping to overwhelm at Bull Run were actually bait, dangled in front of him by Robert E. Lee, who slipped up behind Pope on the evening of August 29 and the next day dealt the "coming man" and the Army of Virginia a blow that nearly disintegrated them. The next day, Pope blearily pulled his battered mess of an army back toward Washington. "Well John, we are whipped again, I am afraid," Lincoln sighed to John Hay, and the next day the president wondered out loud to Hay whether "we may as well stop fighting." [55]

   The losses were ridiculously out of proportion to the forces involved—16,000 federals dead, wounded, or missing—as was the ease
with which the Confederates had sprung their trap. But the most sinis-
ter aspect of the second battle of Bull Run was the complaint that had
surfaced even before Pope had limped back to Washington: The battle
had been deliberately lost by McClellan's officers, who had either
failed to obey direct orders from Pope or who purposely dragged their
heels in coming to Pope's aid. "I think it my duty," Pope wrote to Halleck, "to call your attention to the unsoldierly and dangerous conduct
of many brigade and some division commanders of the forces sent
here from the Peninsula." Even among senior officers, "every word
and act and intention is discouraging." Pope's suspicion was that they
were obeying McClellan's orders to stay out of the battle. "These men
are mere tools or parasites," he added knowingly. "Its source is beyond
my reach, though its effects are very perceptible and very dangerous."
Whether from carelessness or arrogance, McClellan did nothing to dis-
pel the whisperings. With chilling indifference, he had concluded on
August 29 that it was best "to leave Pope to get out of his scrape & at
once use all our means to make the Capital perfectly safe," and he
spent most of the two days Pope was fighting for his life just thirty
miles away fussing over garrison details and promising to urge his old
corps commanders to hurry up.[56]

   Lincoln was indignant when the rumors of treachery on McClellan's part began trickling into the city along with the army's wounded.
Orville Hickman Browning picked up the story that two of McClellan's
faithful underlings in Pope's army had sent "a courier to Genl McClel-
land with a despatch signed by them saying 'hold on, dont send reinforcements, and we have Pope where we can ruin him,' and that the
despatch fell into the Presidents hands and he now had it." Lincoln later
told Browning that he knew of no such dispatch. But if there had been
one, Lincoln added with unusual bloodthirstiness, "the case would have
justified, in his opinion, a sentence of death." John Hay rode into Washington with Lincoln from the Soldiers' Home on September 1, and Lincoln "was very outspoken in regard to McClellan's present conduct. He
said it really seemed to him that McC wanted Pope defeated." There was

no way to prove any of this at the moment, but Lincoln still believed that "unquestionably he has acted badly toward Pope! He wanted him to fail."

Other parts of official Washington were even less restrained in their accusations. "It is treason, rank treason," bellowed Zachariah Chandler to Lyman Trumbull. "Your president is [as] unstable as water, if he has, as I suspect, been bullied by those traitor Generals. How long will it be before he will by them be set aside & a military dictator set up." Senator Henry Wilson became convinced that "there is a conspiracy on foot among certain generals for a revolution and the establishment of a provisional national government." As far away as New York, George Templeton Strong heard suggestions that McClellan would "come together" with Lee "and agree on some compromise or adjustment, turn out Lincoln and his 'Black Republicans' and use their respective armies to enforce their decision . . . and reestablish the Union and the Constitution." [57]

Suspicion of McClellan was so great that Treasury Secretary Chase hurriedly drew up "a protest, signed by himself and Stanton, denouncing the conduct of McClellan and demanding his immediate dismissal" from the army. "Chase frankly stated" to Gideon Welles "that he deliberately believed McClellan ought to be shot, and should, were he President." But on September 1, Lincoln did something even more surprising. The evening before, Halleck had sent "a dispatch" to McClellan at his diminished headquarters across the Potomac in Alexandria, "begging me to help him out of his scrape & take command here." McClellan, more full of himself than ever, rode into Washington the next morning "& had a pretty plain talk with him & Abe," and at the end, Lincoln returned command of the army to McClellan and ordered them to "fall back upon Washn." Almost at once "a rumor pervaded the town that McClellan was to resume his full command." When the cabinet assembled in Lincoln's office the next morning for the usual Tuesday meeting, the president was late, and Welles remembered that Stanton began speaking "in a suppressed voice, trembling with excitement," aghast at hearing that "McClellan had been ordered to take command of the forces in Washington." The others "expressed . . . general surprise," but before more could be said, Lincoln arrived, "and in answer to an inquiry from Mr. Chase, confirmed what Stanton had said."[58]

He had reinstated McClellan, the president explained, because McClellan "is a good engineer . . . [and] there is no better organizer," and "he can be trusted to act on the defensive." These were precisely the qualities that had turned the Peninsula campaign into a failure, but they were also the qualities the capital needed for its defense with a victorious rebel army only a day's march away. Lincoln neglected to mention one other reason for McClellan's reinstatement, the most obvious one of all: the question of what the army would do if McClellan was kept out of command.

As White House secretary William Stoddard put it, "A host of tongues and pens are busy with the assertion that the officers and men of the Army of the Potomac half-way refuse to serve under any other commander than McClellan." Whitelaw Reid had heard "military men" gabbling "for months" about "a Dictatorship as the end of all this distraction" and had dismissed it as mere talk; but now he was listening to "distinguished public men" and "Generals of the proslavery school" speak casually "of a possible coup d'etat." One of McClellan's senior generals was quoted in the *Daily National Intelligencer* threatening that if McClellan were not reinstated, "it would be a question between" the rebel "army and ours which should first get to Washington." As Lincoln explained afterward to Welles, despite the clear evidence that "there has been a design, a purpose in breaking down Pope . . . there is no remedy at present. McClellan has the army with him."[59]

Lincoln described the reinstatement of McClellan "in the face of . . . treasonable misconduct" the "greatest trial and most painful duty of his official life." But for McClellan it was vindication, and anyone who doubted McClellan's hold over the army had only to watch when McClellan rode out in the dusk of September 2 to meet Pope and the loose collection of mauled brigades and divisions straggling for miles behind him. "We were so glad to see him," recalled one New Yorker, "that we cheered him until we were hoarse." Another officer remembered the shouting that went up and down the line: "General McClellan is here!" The news "passed down the column" and the men "sent up such a hurrah as the Army of the Potomac had never heard before." Everywhere, McClellan was greeted with cheering of the "most wild and enthusiastic character."

Secretary Welles noted a more threatening edge to some of the cheering four days later, when "some twenty or thirty thousand" men tramped past his house on H Street, across from Lafayette Square, "for three hours." Welles thought this was strange, since normally the custom was for units marching through Washington to pass on the other side of Lafayette Square, on Pennsylvania Avenue, where they would give three cheers for the president as they passed the White House. This time, however, "there was a design in having them come up from Pennsylvania Avenue to H Street" because McClellan's headquarters was at the corner of H and Fifteenth. There "they cheered the General lustily, instead of passing by the White House and honoring the President." [60]

It had been two months since Lincoln had returned from Harrison's Landing, convinced that it was now or never with emancipation, and the situation was now, if anything, even bleaker than it had been then. What would come of it all, God only knew.

"I DON'T KNOW ANYTHING about Lincoln's Religion—don't think anybody Knew," Illinois judge David Davis told William Herndon years later. This was partly true, simply because Lincoln was "the most reticent—Secretive man I Ever Saw," and he was not given to self-revelation. But it was not entirely true, as Herndon himself knew. Lincoln's parents were strict Calvinist Baptists, and it was a revelation for Herndon to learn that in his youth, Lincoln had rejected it all and embraced a kind of Enlightenment deism. But it was a deism with a peculiar twist. The young Lincoln, like Melville and Hawthorne, found the all-powerful and all-controlling God of his parents simultaneously unbelievable and mesmerizing, and the combination made Lincoln both "a fatalist in philosophy and a skeptic in matters of religion," a kind of secularized Calvinist. When he came up to Springfield in 1837 to make his name as a lawyer, Lincoln quickly acquired a reputation for a cocky, let-me-show-you atheism. "Lincoln, when all were idle and nothing to do," recalled his friend James Matheny, "would talk about religion—

pick up the Bible—read a passage—and then Comment on it—show its falsity—and its follies on the grounds of REASON—would then show its own self made & self uttered Contradictions and would in the End— finally ridicule it and as it were Scoff at it." [61]

But "infidelity" did not get votes. Nor did it give Lincoln much solace when loss and disappointment—the deaths of his child and his father, his failed career as a congressman, and his futile pursuit of a federal office appointment—began battering him at the beginning of the 1850s. The Lincoln family began attending church, an Old School Presbyterian one where the Calvinism still glowed, and Lincoln paid regular pew rent and contributed occasional legal advice, although without making any motion toward actually joining. He made a qualified sort of peace with God, provided people understood that God was "a POWER that worked for righteousness" in the universe, not the Almighty of the Westminster Confession. Leonard Swett, who as a Presbyterian knew what he was talking about, thought that "if [Lincoln's] religion were to be judged by the line and rule of Church Creeds and unexceptionable language, he would fall far short of the standard." But if you allowed Lincoln to define matters by his own lights, then "he was full of natural religion; he believed in God as much as the most approved Church member." [62]

If there was any cardinal doctrine among Lincoln's beliefs, it was his confidence in the inevitability of progress. Isaac Cogdal, an old acquaintance from the New Salem days, remarked that "the great substantial groundworks of Religion" in Lincoln were his confidence "in the progress of man and of nations." His was a typically Enlightenment kind of optimism, coming from a man born at the end of the long Enlightenment era and steeped in the conviction that the American founding "contemplated the progressive improvement in the condition of all men everywhere." His earliest political causes in Illinois had been "improvement" projects, and in 1858, he wrote out a lengthy address on "Discoveries and Inventions" in which the basic argument was that "man is not the only animal who labors; but he is the only one who *improves* his workmanship." In every way that mattered, "improvement in condition—is the order of things in a society of equals." [63]

The voices of the Southern fire-eaters grated on this sensibility. Allowing slavery to expand rather than shrink to its death "would be to discard all the lights of current experience—to reject all progress—all improvement." But such truculence could never hold off the tide of the future for long. The war they caused would be a test of American mettle, a "people's contest," but the idea that it might fatally derail the American experiment was out of the question. Or at least it had been until now. "It had got to be midsummer, 1862," Lincoln told Francis Carpenter. "Things had gone from bad to worse, until I felt that we had reached the end of our rope," and after Pope's "disaster, at Bull Run . . . things looked darker than ever." Nothing had turned out as it was supposed to by the script of progress: The Confederates were victorious, McClellan was once more in the ascendant with an army that belonged more to him than to Lincoln as commander in chief, Great Britain and France would be happy to see a negotiated peace bring an end to the war and the Union, and the whole idea of emancipation was starting to drift away from him like the wraiths of battle smoke over Bull Run.[64]

From time to time, the thought preyed on Lincoln's mind that perhaps his confidence in the inevitability of progress was a gigantic mistake, that God was not a "POWER" after all but a personality who consciously moved all things by his own will. Lincoln had once posed the question to Orville Hickman Browning on a Sunday afternoon in the White House library, "Browning, suppose God is against us in our view on the subject in this country, and our method of dealing with it?" It was the first time that the devout Browning could recall that Lincoln showed any hint "that he was thinking deeply of what a higher power than man sought to bring about by the great events then transpiring." And it was not the last. In June, a delegation of Pennsylvania Quakers headed by Thomas Garrett, the famous "conductor" of fugitives on the Underground Railroad, waited on Lincoln to urge him to deal with slavery, but Lincoln, speaking off the cuff, turned his reply in a curiously theological direction. "The President responded . . . that he was deeply sensible of his need of Divine assistance" and that, echoing his ancestral Calvinism, "he had sometime thought that perhaps he might be an instrument in God's hands of accomplishing a great work." But events had disrupted that tidy assumption. "God's way of accomplishing the end . . . may be different from theirs." [65]

On the day he returned command of the army to McClellan, "wearied with all the considerations of law and expediency with which he had been struggling for two years," Lincoln locked himself away and, as he had always done as a lawyer in Springfield, began scribbling out notes to "bring some order into his thoughts." *The will of God prevails,* he wrote, a proposition no one could seriously doubt. The question was in whose favor that *will* was tending. People always claim that God is on their side, but logically, "God can not be for, and against the same thing at the same time." Suppose God, unlike forces or powers or universal progress, had a mind and a will that rose above an automatic attachment to this side or that. A living, thinking, reasoning, willing God, unlike a "POWER," would rise above predictability, rise perhaps to some other possibility that no one had anticipated. Given the course of "the present civil war," Lincoln had to concede that it *is quite possible that God's purpose is something different from the purpose of either party. . . . I am almost ready to say this is probably true.* After all, God, *by his mere quiet power, on the minds of the now contestants . . . could have either saved or destroyed the Union without a human contest. Yet the contest began.* The war itself was a clue that more was operating in the universe than mere necessity. "And having begun He could give the final victory to either side any day. Yet the contest proceeds." [66]

This was not a moment of blinding conversion, leading to clear and certain conviction. When yet another religious deputation, this time two Chicago clergymen and two prominent laymen who carried a mammoth petition for emancipation from a citywide "Christian War Meeting," waited on Lincoln on September 13, Lincoln brushed back their advice. "Religious men, who are equally certain that they represent the Divine will," had been haranguing him "for months" with declarations about the will of God. "I hope it is not irreverent for me to say that if it is probable that God would reveal his will to others, on a point so connected with my duty, it might be supposed he would reveal it directly to me." He would be more than happy to have it, but, he added with brusque pessimism, "these are not, however, the days of miracles, and I suppose it will be granted that I am not to expect a direct revelation." Did they want a proclamation? What good would that do? "I do not want to issue a document that the whole world will see must necessarily be inoperative, like the Pope's bull against the comet"—especially, he might have added, after General Pope's defeat by the Confederates. He did not dispute that "as commander-in-chief of the army and navy, in time of war . . . I have a right to take any measure which may best subdue the enemy." And he did not by any means foreclose on the possibility of "a proclamation of liberty to the slaves." But he was not going to act without knowing "the will of Providence in this matter," and "whatever shall appear to be God's will I will do." [67]

How Lincoln proposed to discern that will apart from "miracles," he did not explain, but in fact he was already asking for one.

ON THE FOURTH of September, Robert E. Lee and some 39,000 Confederate infantry splashed across the fords of the Potomac only twenty-five miles northwest of Washington, with the band of the Tenth Virginia blaring "Maryland, My Maryland" and its outriders carrying posters urging the slaveholding people of Maryland to rise in support of "the rights of which you have been despoiled." It was at this point that Lincoln decided, contrary to all his own experience, that if there was a God who twirled human destinies around the spindle of his will, it was time to test him, like Gideon of old. "When Lee came over the river," Lincoln told Massachusetts congressman George Boutwell, "I made a resolve that when McClellan drove him back—and I expected he would do it sometime or other—I would send the Proclamation after him." But it was more than a mere pale "resolve." *I made a solemn vow before God,* Lincoln later explained to Salmon Chase, *that if General Lee was driven back . . . I would crown the result by the declaration of freedom to the slaves.*[68]

And as if "the day of miracles" had suddenly elbowed its way back into the modern world, on September 13 two soldiers of the Twenty-seventh Indiana found a copy of Lee's campaign orders, with full details of the movements of the entire rebel army, in a field near Frederick, Maryland, where a courier had absentmindedly dropped it two days earlier. By noon, the lost orders were in the hands of George B. McClellan, who jubilantly informed Lincoln that "I have all the plans of the Rebels and will catch them in their own trap." The Army of the Potomac lurched into action. The next day, McClellan punched through a screen of rebel troops on South Mountain and plunged down toward Lee's startled and scattered divisions at Sharpsburg, Maryland, where the Antietam Creek flowed into the Potomac. Lee hurriedly pulled together whatever men he could force-march toward Sharpsburg. But on the morning of September 17, McClellan and the Army of the Potomac foamed toward them like an everlasting juggernaut. In an all-day battle of unprecedented ferocity, Lee was hammered almost to destruction, and he withdrew across the Potomac the following evening.[69]

McClellan jubilantly telegraphed his wife that he had won a complete victory, a judgment that turned out to be at least half wrong. Despite all the advantages of surprise, numbers, and position, McClellan hesitantly fed his infantry into the fight one piece at a time, instead of crushing Lee with a single collected blow. No doubt the rebels had been mangled as never before: By the time the sun set on September 17, Lee had suffered 2,700 killed and another 11,000 wounded or missing (compared to 2,010 federals dead and 10,000 wounded or missing). But mangled though they were, Lee's divisions managed to recross the Potomac into Virginia in reasonably good order, even without the benefit of any bands playing chirpy tunes about the Confederate liberation of Maryland. Lincoln could scarcely believe that McClellan, having backed Lee into a corner along the Antietam, could not bring himself to finish the rebels off. But complete or not, it was at least a victory. Seward had wanted a "success," and now he had it; Lincoln had made his vow, and now he would keep it.

Intermittently between September 5 and the battle at Antietam, Lincoln had "worked upon" the draft of the Proclamation "and got it pretty much prepared." Antietam was fought on a Wednesday, but Lee did not pull back over the river until Friday, and, Lincoln told Boutwell, "I could not find out till Saturday [September 20] whether we had really won a victory or not." Once the news was sure, so was the next step. "Mr. Lincoln says that he has promised God that he would issue the paper if

God would give us the victory over Lee's army," wrote William Stoddard, "and now all the later dispatches from the Antietam seem to call
upon him to keep his word." By then, Lincoln had closed up his office in
the White House and driven out to the Soldiers' Home, and so "it was
then too late to issue the Proclamation that week." But he drove back to
the White House on Sunday, locked himself in his office with the
Proclamation, and "dressed it over a little." And then, without fanfare,
at a called cabinet meeting "on Monday [September 22] I gave it to them
[the cabinet]." It was "my last card," Lincoln remarked to New York
lawyer Edwards Pierrepont, "and I will play it and may win the trick." [70]

This time, no one in the cabinet was surprised. When a visitor to the
White House told Secretary Chase on Sunday that the president, "being
very busy writing, could not see him," Chase immediately concluded,
"Possibly engaged on Proclamation." Hay knew enough about what
Lincoln was doing to describe, in his diary, Lincoln writing "the Proclamation on Sunday morning carefully," and indeed, the four pages of the
manuscript were obviously written straight through by Lincoln, without pauses or breaks. The cabinet meeting he called on Monday began
with Lincoln tersely reminding everyone that "for several weeks the
subject" of emancipation "has been suspended, but . . . never lost sight
of." The time had now come to issue the Proclamation. He lunged to the
climax: "When the rebel army was at Frederick, I determined, as soon as
it should be driven out of Maryland, to issue a Proclamation of Emancipation." No, he had done more than *determine.* "I said nothing to any
one; but I made the promise to myself, and (hesitating a little)—to my
Maker. The rebel army is now driven out, and I am going to fulfil that
promise."

No one who knew Lincoln could have ever predicted that he would
pop familiar references to the Ancient of Days into a cabinet discussion,
and Chase was so amazed that he asked Lincoln to repeat himself just to
be sure he had heard him aright. Much less could the members of the
cabinet have believed that Lincoln was going to commit them, and the
nation, to outright emancipation on the strength of a sign he had asked
from God, as though it were the Emperor Constantine or Oliver
Cromwell rather than Abraham Lincoln sitting at the head of the cabi-

net table. The idea of making policy on the basis of communications from the heavens was so foreign to Lincoln, not to mention old political warriors like Seward, Blair, Bates, Chase, and Welles, that Lincoln himself, "in a manner half-apologetic," conceded that "this might seem strange." But there was Lincoln saying it: "God had decided this question in favor of the slaves. He was satisfied it was right" and "was confirmed and strengthened in his action by the vow and the results." [71]

No one spoke, and so Lincoln picked up the four sheets of paper on which he had drafted the Proclamation and began reading it aloud to them. Like the first draft of July 22, this version of the proclamation opened cautiously and with full consciousness of the constitutional niceties he had to observe. *I, Abraham Lincoln, President of the United States of America, and Commander-in-chief of the Army and Navy thereof, do hereby proclaim and declare that hereafter, as heretofore, the war will be prossecuted for the object of practically restoring the constitutional relation between the United States, and each of the states, and the people thereof, in which states that relation is, or may be suspended, or disturbed.* Once again, he was careful to repeat his standing offer of compensation to *all slave-states, so called, the people whereof may not then be in rebellion against the United States, and which states, may then have voluntarily adopted, or thereafter may voluntarily adopt, immediate, or gradual abolishment of slavery within their respective limits.*

The tone in this version was noticeably different from that of the first draft. For one thing, it was entirely a military pronouncement, not a civil proclamation about an act of Congress attached gingerly to a war-powers proclamation. And once the preliminary legalities had been stated, this new proclamation dove directly to its real purpose: *That on the first day of January in the year of our Lord, one thousand eight hundred and sixty-three, all persons held as slaves within any state, or designated part of a state, the people whereof shall then be in rebellion against the United States shall be then, thenceforward, and forever free.* What was more, emancipation would not only proceed by military decree, it would become a military *act*, backed explicitly by federal bayonets. Almost as though he wanted to banish the suspicion that proclamations were nothing but "inoperative" words like papal bulls, Lincoln promised not only emancipation in name but by force, through the armed intervention of the federal armies and navy. *The executive government of the United States, including the military and naval authority thereof,* Lincoln ordered, *will recognize the freedom of such persons, and will do no act or acts to repress such persons, or any of them, in any efforts they may make for their actual freedom.*

Not even a war-powers proclamation, however, could trespass on the civil sovereignty of the law of slavery in the places where there was no war. Clearly, that meant the Border states, but for safety's sake, Lincoln also included any parts of the Confederate states under Union occupation, lest unhappy proslavery Unionists in western Tennessee or northern Virginia decide to invite Chief Justice Taney's courts to determine whether or not they deserved the rebel treatment. Montgomery Blair remembered Lincoln's explaining that "he had power to issue the proclamation only in virtue of his power to strike at the rebellion, and he could not include places within our own lines, because the reason upon which the power depended did not apply to them, and he could not include such places" simply because he himself "was opposed to slavery." [72] Lincoln therefore added with protective but tedious precision that *the executive will, on the first day of January aforesaid, by proclamation, designate the States, and parts of states . . . shall then be in rebellion against the United States,* with the designation resting on whether *that state, or the people thereof shall, on that day be, in good faith represented in the Congress of the United States.*

He added, for the benefit of McClellan and any of his other balky generals, a string of reminders from the past year's Congressional statutes that *all officers or persons in the military or naval service of the United States are prohibited from . . . returning fugitives,* that slaves caught up in the advance of the armies *shall be deemed captives of war, and shall be forever free of their servitude and not again held as slaves,* and that no one in the military, *under any pretence whatever,* had permission to set themselves up as the arbiter of which masters were loyal and which were rebels. The attorney general's office would see to that task whenever it got around to it, and in the meanwhile, confiscated "property" would remain securely in the hands of the army. [73]

Then Lincoln was done. Seward spoke up, saying as politely as he could that since Lincoln had obviously made up his mind about issuing the Proclamation, "nothing can be said further about that." But wouldn't the impact of the promise to *recognize the freedom of such persons* be greater if Lincoln expanded it to *recognize and maintain?* Chase was still dubious about the whole proposition of a presidential proclamation, but he thought Seward was right about the wording, and when Lincoln turned to the others for comment, there were no objections. It remained for Montgomery Blair to raise the only thoroughgoing dissent. "He did not concur in the expediency of the measure at this time, though he approved of the principle," and he was particularly uneasy at the effect it would have "on the Border States and on the Army." But if this was the only way to rid the nation of slavery, better "immediate Emancipation in the midst of Slave States, rather than submit to the perpetuation of the system." No one, curiously, questioned Lincoln's "authority on this subject." Even more curiously, no one thought long enough about Seward's proposed *recognize and maintain* to realize that this phrase might be the most shocking in the Proclamation.

The "efforts" which Seward and Lincoln were pledging the federal government to *recognize and maintain* included *any efforts* the slaves *may make for their actual freedom,* and that, quite conceivably, could include slave insurrection. (Assistant Secretary of War Charles Dana protested to Seward that this was the "bad egg in the pudding—& I fear may go far to make it less palatable than it deserves to be.") But if this implication worried Lincoln, he showed no signs of it. He grimly assured John W. Forney that "hereafter there will be no restriction in the employment of all men to put down this rebellion" and no more shilly-shallying about "the confiscation of rebel property" or "the cry of Negro equality and emancipation." Once the Proclamation took effect, Lincoln remarked to T. J. Barnett, "the character of the war will be changed. It will be one of subjugation and extermination." Emancipation "will be pushed after the 1st with all the power left in the federal arm," he added, and thereafter, he would shape "his policy" in a direction "more radical than ever." [74]

The president handed a copy to Seward to publish as a State Department circular the next day, and then called in Nicolay to have copies made, "one for the Senate and one for the House." Nicolay turned the copying job over to William Stoddard, who was so unnerved by the enormity of the document that he spoiled "a sheet or two of paper" trying to begin. But it was relief, not fear, that made Stoddard shaky. "They all seemed to feel a sort of new and exhilarated life," John Hay wrote two days later. "They breathed freer; the Prest. procn. had freed them as well as the slaves. They gleefully and merrily called each other and themselves abolitionists, and seemed to enjoy the novel sensation of appropriating that horrible name." [75]

Four

THE

MIGHTY ACT

THE PRELIMINARY Emancipation Proclamation was in the Washington papers the next day—the *National Republican* in the morning, the front page of the *Evening Star* and the *National Intelligencer* by six o'clock—and in every other urban, Northern daily newspaper worth reading. Vice-President Hannibal Hamlin wrote Lincoln to express his "undissembled and sincere thanks for your Emancipation proclamation. It will stand as the great act of the age." Washington lawyer Estwick Evans rushed a pamphlet into print, lauding the announcement as the beginning of "an EPOCH of an unheard-of magnitude." New York senator Ira Harris wrote Lincoln that "those who have been clamoring for a policy have got it—It is one upon which we can all stand and fight and win and save the Country." James Parton met Horace Greeley on Broadway "a day or two after the Proclamation was published" and saw that Greeley was "beaming with exultation, and he expressed in the strongest language his conviction that the ultimate triumph of the nation was certain." Another New Yorker, George Templeton Strong, thought the proclamation was "much discussed and generally approved." At the Northern railroad junction of Altoona, Pennsylvania, twelve of the Northern war governors were meeting, partly (it was rumored) to compose a joint demand for McClellan's dismissal, and on September 24 they voted to adjourn and visit Lincoln as a group to offer their congratulations for the Proclamation. In Lincoln's home state of Illinois, the Republican state convention in Springfield noisily endorsed the Proclamation, and Lincoln's old Illinois political friend, Jesse K. DuBois, was sure it had "the unanimous approbation of our Republican friends and all Loyal Democrats." [1]

It certainly pleased the Radicals in Congress, and some of them were delighted at what Lincoln was implying by the promise to *recognize and maintain* the slaves *in any efforts they may make for their actual freedom.* Thaddeus Stevens hoped that the slaves would be "incited to insurrection and give the rebels a taste of real civil war," while Stephen Pearl Andrews in the *Continental Monthly* urged that a "thousand mounted men" be recruited to raid deep into the South with news of the proclamation "with the authority to assemble and arm the slaves, retreating whenever assailed to the fastnesses of the mountains." For others, the Proclamation seemed like a breath of divine inspiration. Albert Gallatin Riddle described it as "the greatest human utterance" and compared it to "speaking a new world into being by Omnipotence." "At last the proclamation has come," Charles Sumner rejoiced. "The skies are brighter and the air is purer, now that slavery has been handed over to judgment." On the blustery evening of September 24, an emancipation parade led by the Marine Band thumped through the streets of Washington and stopped at the White House to demand a speech from Lincoln "with loud and enthusiastic cheers." [2]

But outside Radical and abolitionist circles, enthusiasm was in ominously shorter supply. Robert Bennett Forbes confessed to Charles Sumner, a fellow Boston Brahmin, that he was horrified at what he read as a plain enticement to "the slaves" that they "should be made free by killing or poisoning their masters and mistresses." A soldier in the

Eighty-first New York wrote that the Proclamation "creates quite a stir in our camp among the officers and men. Some are rejoicing over it, while others are threatening to abandon the service, declaring that they came to fight for the Union and to maintain the Constitution." Predictably, the editors' columns in the *Daily National Intelligencer* and *Evening Star* were chilly. "Where we expect no good we shall be only too happy to find that no harm has been done by the present declaration of the Executive," wrote the *National Intelligencer;* the *Evening Star* was more blunt, prophesying that the Proclamation would be "void of practical effect."[3] William Stoddard, whose pen had shaken while copying the Proclamation, gloomily recalled "how many editors and how many other penmen within these past few days"

> rose in anger to remind Lincoln that this is a war for the Union only, and they never gave him any authority to run it as an Abolition war. They never, never told him that he might set the negroes free, and, now that he has done so, or futilely pretended to do so, he is a more unconstitutional tyrant and a more odious dictator than ever he was before. They tell him, however, that his edict, his ukase, his decree, his firman, his venomous blow at the sacred liberty of white men to own black men is . . . a dead letter and a poison which will not work. They tell him many other things, and, among them, they tell him that the army will fight no more, and that the hosts of the Union will indignantly disband rather than be sacrificed upon the bloody altar of fanatical Abolitionism.[4]

The outright Lincoln haters only found in the Proclamation more reason for their hatred. William Owner grumbled into his diary that "the abolition papers or rather their editors are jubilant over the Proc. of ABE," but only for the "prospect that it will inaugurate a negro insurrection in the South. . . . The few independent papers at the north that oppose this edict look upon it as a broad hint to the nigs to cut their masters throats, and those of the women and children . . . and save the expense of prosecuting the war after Jany 1st 1863." Philadelphian Nathaniel Macon reminded Lincoln one more time that "slavery was a matter of domestic interest; and aside from the covenant pledging the surrender of fugitive slaves, the Federal government was clothed with no authority over it." In Illinois, Democratic newspapers in Chicago, Joliet, Quincy, Freeport, Jonesboro, Macomb, and Lincoln's hometown of Springfield bucked with hysterical denunciation. Lincoln and the Radicals "will go 'flaming' with the grand object of hugging niggers to their bosoms," jeered the *Macomb Eagle*. "Hoop de-dooden-do! The niggers are free!"

But even some of the people who had worked and prayed for the Proclamation were less than enthusiastic on its appearance. "Had it been issued at the beginning of the war when we were in high feather it might have done well," Illinois general William Ward Orme wrote to Leonard Swett, "but now . . . it looks really like a paper threat with no power behind it to enforce it." Henry Winter Davis, one of the Radical Republicans in the House, echoed Lincoln's worry that "in point of law, no court will hold it a valid title to freedom; that is my judgment as a lawyer." [5] Even Frederick Douglass admitted disappointment that the Proclamation was so modest in its demands and so legalistic in tone. "Had there been one expression of sound moral feeling against Slavery, one word of regret and shame that this accursed system had remained so long the disgrace and scandal of the Republic, one word of satisfaction in the hope of burying slavery and the rebellion in one common grave, a thrill of joy would have run round the world, but no such word was said, and no such joy was kindled." Massachusetts governor John Andrew, who learned about the Proclamation en route to the Altoona governors' meeting, wrote that "the proclamation of Emancipation" was a "mighty act," but it was wrapped in "a poor document . . . slow, somewhat halting, wrong in its delay till January." Some even suspected that Lincoln intended to execute no "mighty act" at all, and that once public opinion or Southern repentance registered itself, "the President will recoil from his Emancipation Proclamation." [6]

This bleak response annoyed Lincoln. When John Hay gingerly "spoke to him about the editorials in the leading papers," Lincoln impatiently replied that "he had studied the matter so long that he knew more about it than they did." Or at least he hoped he did. "When I issued that proclamation," Lincoln admitted to John McClintock, the Methodist newspaper editor and scholar, "I was in great doubt about it myself. I did not think the people had been quite educated up to it." Much as he thought "it was right," he was worried about bringing too much lightning down on his head. "Now we have got the harpoon fairly into the monster slavery," Lincoln remarked to Isaac Arnold, "we must take care that in his extremity, he does not shipwreck the Country."[7] And as with a harpooned whale, it was impossible to predict in what direction the monster was likely to bolt.

In the long weeks between the reading of the first draft of the Proclamation to the cabinet and the battle at Antietam, it had seemed that the unresponsiveness of the Border staters and the unreliability of McClellan and his army were the chief problems, problems that offered Lincoln no alternative but to seize the authority of the war powers and push emancipation into place with the trowel of a proclamation. But all through the summer, McClellan had remained inert, and when Lincoln was forced to recall McClellan to command, the general had proceeded to chase after the Confederates without a backward glance at Washington. After the lackluster response of Marylanders to Lee's so-called liberation of the state, the Border ceased to look like territory ripe and ready to join the Confederacy. Did Lincoln need the Proclamation after all?

But Lincoln had made his vow, and buried deep within the corners of his temperament was a fierce determination never to retract any commitment once made, including emancipation by proclamation. "He was always ready for every forward movement," recalled Massachusetts congressman George Boutwell, "and he could never be reconciled to a backward step, either in the field or the Cabinet." Lincoln assured Charles Sumner that "he is hard to be moved from any position which he has taken," so Sumner could stop worrying about the rumors of "recoil." Lincoln "could not stop the proclamation if he would, and would not if he could." He also reassured Boutwell that "no earthly power could have induced him to retract or qualify" the Proclamation's announcement. "My word is out to these people, and I can't take it back." All the same, no matter how gratifying McClellan's victory had been, or the failure of slaveowning Marylanders to rise, the results Lincoln saw in the week after issuing the preliminary Emancipation Proclamation gave him little joy. "It is six days old," Lincoln wrote in reply to Hannibal Hamlin on September 28, 1862, "and while commendation in newspapers and by distinguished individuals is all that a vain man could wish, the stocks have declined, and troops come forward more slowly than ever. This, looked soberly in the face, is not very satisfactory." The emancipation parade that demanded a speech from Lincoln on the twenty-fourth heard him explain that "what I did, I did after very full deliberation, and under a very heavy and a solemn sense of responsibility. . . . I can only trust in God I have made no mistake." [8]

The first place where that trust would be tested was in the Army of the Potomac, now encamped near Harpers Ferry while it licked its battle wounds. After Antietam, McClellan slowly cleared the north bank of the Potomac up to Harpers Ferry, announcing that "Maryland and Pennsylvania are now safe," as if this were the great object of the war. More than this McClellan would not do. As he explained lamely to Halleck on September 22, "the entire Army has been greatly exhausted by unavoidable overwork, hunger, & want of sleep & rest," and a movement across the river on Lee's track was out of the question. The campaign began to look as though it was going to go the same way as the Peninsula Campaign. This time, though, people knew, or suspected, too much about McClellan to believe an excuse that flimsy. "There has been a disposition, now that General McClellan had taken a fresh start, to judge him most charitably," wrote a skeptical Whitelaw Reid, but no charity could "explain away that terrible, fateful delay that after claiming a glorious victory failed to make the slightest step toward improving it." The greatest skeptic was Lincoln. He sent no congratulatory telegram after Antietam; in fact, he sent nothing to McClellan at all for almost a month after the battle, and when he did write, it was to scold him for being content "merely to drive" the rebels "away." McClellan tried to defend himself, explaining to Lincoln that his cavalry had conducted two major reconnaissances south of the Potomac while "picketing and scouting one hundred and fifty miles of river front" and were seriously fatigued by this "most laborious service." Lincoln's answer bordered on a taunt:

"Will you pardon me for asking what the horses of your army have done since the battle of Antietam that fatigue anything?" [9]

What made McClellan's listlessness even more infuriating was renewed evidence that he was once again politically in play. The dead at Antietam had hardly been buried before the general was back to abusing Lincoln. "There never was a truer epithet applied to a certain individual," McClellan wrote to his wife, "than that of the 'Gorilla.' " When the Proclamation was released on September 22, McClellan began talking about how "the Presdt's late Proclamation" (along with "the continuation of Stanton & Halleck in office") was making it "almost impossible for me to retain my commission & self respect at the same time. I cannot make up my mind to fight for such an accursed doctrine as that of a servile insurrection." Since the Proclamation was, after all, a military order, McClellan was responsible for communicating it to the army in some form. He paused first to ask New York Democrat William Aspinwall what Aspinwall "and men like you" made of the "recent Proclamation of the Presdt inaugurating servile war, emancipating the slaves, & at one stroke of the pen changing our free institutions into a despotism," then turned to his own senior officers "for the purpose of asking our opinions and advice with regard to the course he should pursue respecting the Proclamation." [10]

Talk of that sort loosened the tongues of McClellan's staffers. Riding up from Washington to the Soldiers' Home at the end of the day on September 25, Lincoln told John Hay that "he had heard of an officer who said that they did not mean to gain any decisive victory but to keep things running on so that they the army might manage things to suit themselves." An investigation was on foot, "and if any such language had been used, his head should go off." Hay anxiously wondered whether Lincoln ought to be paying more attention to "the McClellan conspiracy," but Lincoln waved it off. "He merely said that McC. was doing nothing to make himself either respected or feared." [11]

But the investigation did pick up a suspect. On the morning of September 27, Major John J. Key—an "Additional Aide de Camp" of Halleck's staff rather than McClellan's, but the brother of McClellan's judge advocate general, who was "a most intimate and confidential adviser of General McClellan"—was hauled onto Lincoln's own office carpet and subjected to the kind of examination that a lawyer like Lincoln knew how to conduct. Was it true that Key had told a War Department lawyer that the reason "McClellan had not followed up the victory last week" was that that "is not the policy" in the Army of the Potomac? Was it true that Key had explained that "it would have been impolitic and injudicious to have destroyed the Rebel army, for that would have ended the contest without any compromise, and it was the army policy at the right time to compel the opposing forces to adopt a compromise"?

Brazenly, Key made no effort "to controvert the statement." Instead, he tried to shift the questioning in the direction of proving "that he was true to the Union" and that the preservation of the Union required the protection of slavery. Lincoln was not amused. "If there was a 'game' ever among Union men, to have our army not take an advantage of the enemy when it could, it was his object to break up that game." In the end, Lincoln concluded that Key's "silly treasonable talk" amounted to little more than small fish who wanted to be thought big stuff and that Key's crime lay mostly in the folly of repeating such trash than in any real act of "disloyalty." Besides, there was no way to draw a line from Key to anyone else, much less McClellan. But Lincoln "wanted an example" made all the same. He cashiered Key on the spot. When Key appealed to Lincoln for reinstatement in November, Lincoln turned him down.[12]

For all the endless rumors about McClellan over the past year, it was still disturbing for Lincoln to get so distinct a whiff of genuine treason. T. J. Barnett, an Interior Department clerk and soon-to-be federal judge, advised Samuel Barlow that "dread of the army" and "fear of a revolution in the North" pervaded the administration. Four days after closing the book on Major Key, Lincoln boarded a special armed train from Washington, heading through Baltimore to Harpers Ferry. Publicly, he was going to visit McClellan to "see if in a personal interview he could not inspire him with some sense of the necessity of action"; privately, to his old Illinois friend Ozias Hatch, he confided that he was going "up there to satisfy himself personally without the intervention of anybody, of the purposes intentions and fidelity of McClellan, his officers, and the army."[13]

Over the course of three days, Lincoln "reviewed the troops respectively at Loudon Heights and Maryland Heights" and rode over the Antietam and South Mountain battlefields with McClellan. Lincoln was fully prepared to find the army hailing McClellan as a new Caesar. Pausing at "an eminence which overlooked the camps" of the army, Lincoln stopped, spread out his arms, and asked Hatch what he thought he saw. "Why," replied Hatch, "I suppose it to be part of the grand army." No, Lincoln replied sardonically, *that is General McClellan's body guard.* But in this case, Lincoln was wrong. No matter what McClellan's staffers promised him about the Army of the Potomac's unshakeable fidelity, that army was beginning to have its doubts about its commandant. Few of the men in the ranks could understand any better than Lincoln McClellan's strange inactivity after Antietam. "It is not for me to attempt any criticism of military measures or military men," Captain George Freeman Noyes wrote several months after the battle, "but only to delineate truly the bitter feelings of disappointment shared by so many in our army that day."

Now, riding beside McClellan, Lincoln "seemed to tower as a giant" to the army. John McClernand, who accompanied Lincoln to Harpers Ferry, had orders to watch "closely to see if, in any division, or regiment, I could find symptoms of dissatisfaction, or could hear an allusion to the proclamation. I found none. I heard only words of praise." One soldier in the Twenty-second Massachusetts thought that Lincoln's "kindly smile," stretched as it was across a "careworn and anxious face . . . touched the hearts of the bronzed, rough-looking men more than one can express. It was like an electric shock. It flew from elbow to elbow; and with one loud cheer which made the air ring, the suppressed feeling gave vent, conveying to the good president that his smile had gone home and found a ready response." For the first time, soldiers of the Army of the Potomac began to refer to Lincoln as "Father Abraham." [14]

McClellan saw none of this. "People had assured him that the army was so devoted to him that they would as one man enforce any decision he should make," an assurance that inclined him to treat Lincoln as though he were some kind of interloper rather than the commander in chief. Lincoln's "ostensible purpose is to see the troops & the battle fields," McClellan wrote, but under that cover he believed that Lincoln was really aiming "to push me into a premature advance into Virginia," which the president and the Radicals would then use to embarrass him. He told General William F. Smith that he was prepared to present the president with "a protest against" the Proclamation. But instead of agreeing, Smith recoiled in horror: "General, do you not see that looks like treason: & that it will ruin you and all of us." And the Army of the Potomac's officers were not the only ones less certain about following McClellan in October than they had been in July. As McClellan saw Lincoln off, he "was quite surprised to meet Mr. [William] Aspinwall en route to my camp," and Aspinwall frankly counseled McClellan to "submit to the Presdt's proclamation & quietly continue doing my duty as a soldier." [15]

Two days later, McClellan grudgingly issued a General Order to the Army of the Potomac, "publishing to the Army the Presdnts proclamation of Sept 22nd." Unwilling to let the Proclamation be read to the Army as though it deserved no objections, McClellan tacked onto the Order an appendix, to be read out afterwards, which was almost as insolent in its implications as the Harrison's Landing letter. It was true, McClellan acknowledged, that "the Constitution confides to the Civil Authorities legislative judicial and executive"—and not to soldiers— "the power and duty of making expounding & executing the federal laws." That did not mean that the army did not have the right, as citizens, to "temperate and respectful expressions of opinion." But "the remedy for political error if any are committed is to be found only in the action of the people at the polls." It was a strange commentary—more than provocative in its suggestion that there was anything in a presidential proclamation that would make soldiers unhappy in obeying it, but falling far short of actually provoking any resistance from those soldiers.[16]

So, once back in Washington, Lincoln decided to make no move against McClellan. For one thing, the general had made promises about crossing the Potomac; Lincoln wanted to see if he would keep them. "After the battle of Antietam," he explained to John Hay, "I went up to the field to try to get him to move & came back thinking he would move at once." For another, there was the continuing problem of who was available to put in McClellan's place: "I had great fears I should not find successors . . . who would do better," he explained wearily to Carl Schurz. But the most important restraint on Lincoln's dealings with Mc-Clellan right now was political. October of 1862 would bring the first round of off-year Congressional elections to Indiana, Ohio, and Pennsylvania, followed in November by Congressional, legislative, and governors' elections in eight other Northern states. Dismissing the victor of the war's most important battle was exactly the sort of gesture that would sprinkle oil all over an electorate already inflamed by the Proclamation. For now, McClellan could remain in place.[17]

No one had any doubt that the Proclamation would make more than enough trouble for Lincoln at the polls, without making McClellan into another issue. "We shall now be assailed front, flank and rear by our enemies," John W. Forney predicted to Lincoln, "and if we would save the next national House of Representatives the power of the Administration must be strongly felt in every Congressional district in the free states." Indiana governor Oliver P. Morton, the Cassandra among the North's governors, "spoke very earnestly" to Salmon Chase on October 5, sure of "State defeat on the 14th, and loss of all the Congressional Districts except [George] Julian's, [Schuyler] Colfax's, and perhaps [John P. C.] Shanks'." Morton was right about one thing: The Proclamation had breathed new and toxic life back into the Northern Democrats. In New York, Republicans ran the upstate abolitionist General James Wadsworth for governor; the Democrats ran Horatio Seymour, and Seymour's speech to the Democratic nominating convention amounted to a declaration of political war on emancipation. The Emancipation Proclamation was a "scheme for an immediate emancipation and general arming of the slaves . . . [which] is a proposal for the butchery of women and children, for scenes of lust and rapine, of arson and murder unparalleled in the history of the world."[18]

"The Democrats are organizing for a party contest this fall," Lyman Trumbull warned. "They have called a state convention [in Trumbull's Illinois] and are calling congressional and county conventions of a purely party character throughout the State." Even in Massachusetts, "the old Democracy (more than half of which is now in armed Rebellion) are rallying against the Proclamation." More than organizing, the Democrats were positively relishing the prospect of using the Proclamation to retake control of Congress. "The Emancipation Proclamation is the knell of the Republican party of the north and gives all the border states to the South," Samuel Butterworth boasted to Samuel Barlow. The Iowa Republican Josiah Grinnell was actually on the campaign trail, "crossing the country together in a carriage" with his Democratic opponent, "when a stage driver brought out a telegram with a message" about the Proclamation. The Democrat whooped with joy. The Proclamation proved "as strong as proofs of Holy Writ" that Lincoln had sacrificed the Constitution to abolition, " 'all of which,' said he, 'assures my election.' " Mark my words, John Sherman warned Salmon Chase: In "the next Congress—the Admin. will be in the minority in the House." [19]

It is one measure of Lincoln's reverence for constitutional process that it seems never to have entered his head to use his war powers to declare a national emergency and suspend the elections. He certainly did not refrain out of misplaced confidence. When Hannibal Hamlin returned from campaigning in Maine in October, he found Lincoln "greatly worried over the military situation and the development of the McClellan problem as a political issue." He had good reason. The October elections in Pennsylvania, Ohio, and Indiana cost the Republicans "almost everything," according to John Nicolay. In Pennsylvania, where Lincoln had enjoyed a 60,000-vote majority in 1860, Democratic candidates for Congress collected 4,000 votes more than all the Republican candidates combined, and the Pennsylvania Congressional delegation would number thirteen Democrats and eleven Republicans. Ohio, where Democrats outpolled Republicans by 5,500 votes, would send a Congressional delegation of fourteen Democrats and only three Republicans to the next Congress. "We are all blue . . . on account of the election news," Nicolay wrote. "We have not yet heard from Iowa, but expect that that too will be swallowed up by the general drift." [20]

Worse was yet to come. New York and New Jersey cast their votes for governor, the House of Representatives, and the state legislature on November 4. The results were as close to disaster for Lincoln as one could get without actual loss of life. Horatio Seymour coasted to victory over James Wadsworth by 10,700 votes in the New York governor's race, while the Congressional delegation shifted to seventeen Democrats (including the violently antiadministration mayor of New York City, Fernando Wood) and fourteen Republicans. "It looks like a great, sweeping revolution of public sentiment," wailed George Templeton Strong. "All is up. . . . The Historical Society should secure an American flag at once for its museum of antiquities." New Jersey elected a Democratic governor, Joel Parker, by 14,000 votes, and sent a new Congressional delegation of four Democrats and only one Republican, James Scovel (himself a conservative ex-Democrat), while Illinois would send eleven Democrats and only three Republicans and surrender the state legislature to a twenty-eight-seat Democratic majority. (And in Illinois, the Republicans who lost, like Leonard Swett in the Eighth district, were precisely those who had vigorously supported emancipation.)

All told, the 1862 Congressional elections cut down thirty-one Republicans, and across the North, voting for Republican candidates declined by 16 percent from 1860. While Republicans still retained majorities in both the House and the Senate for the Thirty-eighth Congress, there was no guarantee that there would be a majority willing to endorse emancipation. "Seldom has the personnel of a House been so completely changed with a change of parties," admitted Albert Gallatin Riddle. "Indeed there were well grounded apprehensions that in the uncertainty of party lines in some States and districts the House might not be organized by an unquestioned Republican majority." [21]

But what this reveals is of how adamant Lincoln was about emancipation, and his "vow," that he would take the chance of these touch-and-go elections, in the midst of an unwon war, and issue an Emancipation Proclamation only weeks before the voting began. Looked at coldly, the timing of the Proclamation amounted to political suicide: Lincoln was putting the most highly charged issue of the war before the voters, and the voters into the hands of the opposition, without any time for the shock to wear off. "Three main causes told the whole story" of the election, Lincoln wrote to Carl Schurz on November 10: The soldiers went off to war, leaving only the grumblers and disaffected at home; the Democrats saw the Proclamation as an opportunity to sow political havoc; and the newspapers "furnished them with all the weapons to do so." Still, when a delegation of "unconditional Union Kentuckians" waited on him at the White House on November 21 to discuss "at length the question of Emancipation," Lincoln stated as plainly as he knew how that "he would rather die than take back a word of the Proclamation of Freedom." Instead of complaining about the Proclamation, he recommended that the Kentuckians go back home and reconsider "his scheme for the gradual abolishment of Slavery." William Owner, Washington's unrepentant Southern sympathizer, saw (to his dismay) that "the Presdt is grieved at the result of the elections, but if any believe that he will change his course or policy because of the result they are woefully mistaken. He will not retreat from the Proclamation . . . or anything else because of an election, State or Congressional." [22]

Now that the storm had broken, Lincoln had no more need to dally over George McClellan. The day after the New York and New Jersey elections, Lincoln wrote out the order relieving him of command of the Army of the Potomac and turning it over to General Ambrose Burnside; for good measure, he also relieved McClellan's chief lieutenant, Fitz-John Porter, whom Pope had accused as the chief culprit in losing the second Bull Run battle. To the Army of the Potomac, it "was almost as great a shock to the men as if the general commanding had been assassinated." All through the army's camps, "discussions and acrimonious bitter debates ran high," and in Washington, Benjamin French feared "disaffection in the Army, and disaster everywhere."

When McClellan reviewed the army two days later to take his farewell of them, the old loyalties quickened to the point of eruption. "As he rode along the lines, electric magnetism was as nothing to the wild and boundless enthusiasm which greeted its relieved commander," wrote one soldier. "It surged and raged; cheer upon cheer rolled along the fronts of the command." Soldiers "crowded around him to shake his hand & eager for some parting words & when his receding form made them realize they were losing their beloved commander they ran after him with tears & lamentations crying, 'Come back to us McClellan!

Come back to us McClellan!' " Inevitably, there came the plea that had hung on the horizon ever since Harrison's Landing: *Lead us to Washington, General, we'll follow you.*

But the moment when McClellan could have taken that cry as the will of God had already passed, fading and dying somewhere over the bloodied waters of Antietam Creek. And whatever else George McClellan was, he was not a traitor, to his country or to his oath. He rode down the lines of the army he had built and quietly boarded the special train that would bear him out of military life forever. Once he was gone, a quiet purge of McClellanite officers began, and William Owner noticed that two members "of Genl McClellan's staff were arrested at Trenton on Friday and sent to this city. Charges as usual unknown to outsiders." Having outmaneuvered Robert E. Lee, McClellan had now been outmaneuvered by Abraham Lincoln.[23]

THE ARMY of the Potomac provided the first test of the Proclamation; Congress would provide the second. When the lame-duck session of the Thirty-seventh Congress convened on the first day of December 1862, it was hard to guess whether Lincoln faced more danger from the Proclamation's friends or from its foes. The Democratic minority saw no point to waiting until next December (when the newly elected Thirty-eighth Congress and its swollen Democratic ranks would be sworn in) and set out eagerly to "attack the proclamation & do every thing possible to prevent a vigourous prosecution of the war." At the same time, the prospect of a rejuvenated Democratic opposition in the next Congress inspired Radical Republicans with the energy of despair, and that energy turned for its target partly on Lincoln (to prevent any backsliding from the preliminary Proclamation) but mostly on the halfhearted in Lincoln's cabinet. "I fear nothing will ever serve us," Zachariah Chandler warned Lyman Trumbull, "but . . . that a change of policy & men shall *instantly* be made," and that meant getting rid of the halfhearted emancipators in the cabinet—Montgomery Blair, Edward Bates, and above all the unreliable William Henry Seward. "For God and the country's sake, send someone to *stay* with the President who will control and hold him." Not surprisingly, no one on either side of the aisle in Congress was happy with the Annual Message Lincoln sent to Capitol Hill on December 1.[24]

The message ran to almost 8,500 words—one of Lincoln's longest official papers—and it must have taken John W. Forney, as secretary of the Senate, at least an hour and a half to read it aloud to the assembled members. It was not until halfway through the message, after a dreary recitation of the year's foreign policy and budget, the reports of cabinet officers, a Sioux uprising in Minnesota, and the projected transcontinental railroad, that Lincoln finally turned everyone's attention to the issue of the hour. "On the twenty-second day of September last a proclamation was issued by the Executive," at which point, Lincoln promptly skipped over any explanation, defense, or other discussion of the Proclamation to explain why the best conclusion anyone should draw from reading it was a decision to adopt "what may be called 'compensated emancipation.'"

Consider, Lincoln asked, the folly of this war. Did anyone really believe that, even if the Confederacy should be successful in its bid for independence, the North American continent could be, in any practical way, divided between two republics? "There is no line, straight or crooked, suitable for a national boundary, upon which to divide" the existing states, and any effort to manufacture one would set geography at war with economics. "Separate our common country into two nations, as designed by the present rebellion," and everyone west of the Appalachians "is thereby cut off" from transportation and ocean commerce "not, perhaps, by a physical barrier, but by embarrassing and onerous trade regulations." The Southern states had no future apart from the common future all the American states shared together. "In all its adaptations and aptitudes," the continent "demands union, and abhors separation." The rebels might win the war today, but tomorrow, or a year after, someone among them would inevitably be talking about reunion. "In fact, it would, ere long, force re-union, however much of blood and treasure the separation might have cost." And at that moment, Southerners would have to come to grips all over again with the fact that the rest of the nation would not allow them to spread slavery anywhere outside its present domains. The same geography that made nonsense of the notion of an independent Confederacy would, sooner or later, make nonsense of the continuation of slavery. Was it not time, after viewing the wreckage piled upon wreckage of the last twenty months, to see that the war was a merry-go-round that would always bring Southerners back to the same problem they had started with?

The means of stopping the merry-go-round, however, lay easily at hand, so for the last time, Lincoln held out to the slave states the olive branch of compensated emancipation. What he offered was little more than an amplification of the March 6 resolution he had written for Congress, although this time, to underscore the seriousness of the offer, he cast it in the form of three proposed amendments to the Constitution: Any "State, wherein slavery now exists, which shall abolish the same" outright at any point before 1900 "shall receive compensation from the United States"; any state whose slaves had been freed already "by the chances of the war" will also be compensated retroactively, but only for slaveowners "who shall not have been disloyal"; and, to answer the invariable question of *what will we do with them?* Lincoln recommended an amendment authorizing Congress to "appropriate money, and otherwise provide, for colonizing free colored persons, with their own consent, at any place or places without the United States."

For anyone in Congress who hoped that the Emancipation Proclamation signaled the end of Lincoln's buyout offers to slaveowners, as well as for those who simply hoped that the president would stop nagging them about it, these proposals must have sounded like a joke told one too many times. But Lincoln was entirely in earnest. "Mr. Lincoln's whole soul is absorbed in his plan of remunerative emancipation," David Davis wrote to Leonard Swett. "He believes that . . . if Congress will pass a Law authorizing the issuance of bonds for the payment of the emancipated negroes in the border states that Delaware, Maryland, Kentucky & Mo. will accept the terms." What his renewal of the buyout offer illustrated, however, was not second thoughts about emancipation: Charles Sumner saw clearly that the point of the message was "declaring & vindicating Emancipation." Rather, it pointed to an ongoing worry in Lincoln's mind about the status of a war powers proclamation in law, or at least its prospects for survival in the federal courts. He had no intention himself of retreating from the Proclamation. "I cannot recall my proclamations," Lincoln told the Kentuckian Duff Green, but "whether they are binding or not will be a question for the courts." (As late as 1865, he would tell Confederate vice-president Alexander Stephens that "his own opinion was that as the proclamation was a war measure and would have effect only from its being an exercise of the war power," the question of how it might be appealed after the end of the war had no obvious answer.) For his own part, Lincoln "never would change or modify the terms of the proclamation in the slightest particular." He told General Stephen A. Hurlbut in July that "I think [the Proclamation] is valid in law, and will be so held by the courts." Even if not, "I think I shall not retract or repudiate it. Those who shall have tasted actual freedom I believe can never be slaves, or quasi slaves again." But presidential bluster might, however, exert little sway over federal judges, especially since "the Executive power itself would be greatly diminished by the cessation of actual war." The only path to emancipation that would be free from federal judicial tampering lay through the legislatures, and it was to the legislatures he would continue to appeal.[25]

Lincoln was not the only one who worried about the courts. "There is a chance," warned the abolitionist Robert Dale Owen, "that the Supreme Court, if still in the hands of the Slave Power, when peace supervenes, may declare it inoperative." That worry received an added boost in November when the prominent Kentucky jurist George Robertson filed suit in state court against Colonel William L. Utley of the Twenty-second Wisconsin on the grounds that Utley and his regiment had refused to deliver up a runaway slave whom Robertson had demanded. Lincoln could see exactly where Robertson intended to go: Robertson would undoubtedly win his suit in Kentucky, Utley would appeal to the federal courts for protection, and the entire question of Lincoln's powers to emancipate anyone would become fair game for an unfriendly federal judiciary.

Lincoln tried to head Robertson off with a private note on November 26 begging him in the name of "the life of the nation" to "convey" title to the slave to Utley "so that he can make him free." For this resolution, Lincoln offered Robertson "any sum not exceeding five hundred dollars." This offer may have been the closest Abraham Lincoln ever came to bribery, and it did not work. Robertson knew very well what the game was, and he tartly informed Lincoln, after a personal visit to the White House, that if the president thought that all he was concerned about was money, he could not be more mistaken. "My object in that suit was far from mercenary—it was solely to try the question whether the civil or the military power is Constitutionally supreme in Kentucky." (As it turned out, Lincoln's anxiety was not misplaced: Robertson pursued the case into the federal circuit courts and finally won a judgment against Utley in 1871; it would hardly have boded well for the Proclamation, if it were to be eventually dragged into the same courts.)[26]

Lincoln was quite aware that dredging up plans for compensated emancipation "will be unsatisfactory to the advocates of perpetual slavery." So, lest they think that by stolidly folding their arms as they had done in months past they could extort more compromises from him, he went on to warn them that neither "the war, nor proceedings under the proclamation of September 22, 1862, [would] be stayed because of the recommendation of this plan." Only its "timely [*i.e.*, before January 1] adoption, I doubt not, would bring restoration and thereby stay both." Once that deadline passed, there would be no "return to bondage" of "the class of persons therein contemplated."

Nor would there be any talk about compulsory deportation as a sort of consolation prize for slaveholders who couldn't tolerate the thought of blacks in America in any condition other than slavery. His recommendation of an amendment funding colonization "does not oblige, but merely authorizes, Congress to aid in colonizing such as may consent," and "it comes to nothing, unless by the mutual consent of the people to be deported, and the American voters, through their representatives in Congress." Much as he admitted that "I strongly favor colonization," Lincoln proceeded to reel off a series of arguments against it. Most of the reasons "urged against free colored persons remaining in the country" are "largely imaginary, if not sometimes malicious." White laborers who hated and feared blacks as competitors for jobs were seeing ghosts for bedsheets. Is it "dreaded that the freed people will swarm forth, and cover the whole land? Are they not already in the land? Will liberation make them any more numerous?"

One thing was certain: If the slave states signed on to compensated emancipation now, then "this assurance would end the struggle now, and save the Union forever." Take the chance: "As our case is new, so we must think anew, and act anew." At the very least slaveholders should accept compensation for the sake of lessening an "expenditure of money and of blood" that would leave the fundamental problems of the future still unsolved. "We must disenthrall our selves," Lincoln pleaded, and only then "we shall save our country." If we do not, he added darkly, the future will not hold us guiltless. "We know how to save the Union. The world knows we do know how to save it. We—even we here—hold the power, and bear the responsibility."[27]

There is little evidence that Lincoln's appeal won over anyone in Congress. Lincoln "has urged in his message a most impracticable scheme of compensated emancipation [which] nobody likes," Ohio congressman William Parker Cutler scribbled in his diary. "Nobody will give it a cordial support & yet he has loaded his friends down with its odium while probably nothing will be done with it." The Republican majority, led by New Hampshire senator Daniel Clark and Maine senator William Pitt Fessenden, engineered a joint resolution "approving the policy of the President in setting slaves free in insurrectionary districts" on December 15. But the vote in the House was only seventy-eight to fifty-one in favor. In both houses of Congress, the Radicals were restless and unsatisfied, wondering why the Proclamation "was not made universal" and "immediate." Some of them, fearful that Lincoln "would recoil from his Emancipation proclamation," were already talking about taking "the extreme step in Congress of withholding supplies for carrying on the war—leaving the whole land in anarchy," and Lincoln was wary of "a conspiracy among the Radical members of Congress to stop the supplies & end the war in that way, making him have the responsibility."[28]

Then, two weeks into the session, General Burnside led the Army of the Potomac into a doomed attempt to cross the Rappahannock River at Fredericksburg and assault Lee's comfortably entrenched Confederates on the hills west of the city. In one day, Burnside's incompetence as a commanding general cost the Union over 12,000 dead, wounded, and missing, and the federals withdrew back across the Rappahannock to settle into a demoralized and desertion-riddled winter encampment. George Templeton Strong shuddered at the "universal bitter wrath" in New York City over Fredericksburg. "The most thorough Republicans, the most loyal administration men, express it most fiercely." Yet none were as fierce as the Radicals in the Senate Republican caucus. Furious at the Fredericksburg debacle, the Radicals were determined that it was now or never for a reshuffling of the cabinet. "Common sense, if not common honesty, has fled from the cabinet," William Pitt Fessenden complained. Seward would be the first into the tumbril according to the Washington rumor mill, and Frémont would be called out of storage "to displace Burnside." Fessenden prophesied, "I very much fear there will be an outbreak in Congress," and indeed there was. On December 17, a senatorial delegation headed by Vermont senator Jacob Collamer presented Lincoln with the demand that he rid himself of Seward as secretary of state. Lincoln outmaneuvered them as gracefully as he had outmaneuvered McClellan, and Seward stayed in place. But Lincoln now had the additional worry, as he explained to Orville Hickman Browning, that "if he should refuse to issue his proclamation there would be a rebellion in the north, and that a dictator would be placed over his head within the week." [29]

This outrage was only what Lincoln heard from his own party. The fury of the Democrats over the Proclamation knew no bounds. Thaddeus Stevens retorted in disgust that the Proclamation, when read "on the floor of Congress, was received with a howl by Secession democrats, by border state slaveholders, and was condemned by very many timid republicans, who deemed it injurious to their party." The Proclamation "counselled the slaves to insurrection," announced a parade of Democrats at the podium; more than that, it was "palpably unconstitutional, and shocking to the civilization of the age." Clement Vallandigham, who had been gerrymandered out of his Ohio seat and was sitting in his last session in Congress, wanted Lincoln indicted "of a high crime against the Constitution and the States," and Kentucky representative

George Yeaman demanded a resolution declaring that "the proclamation of the President of the United States, of date the 22nd of September, is not warranted by the Constitution" and "is an assumption of power dangerous to the rights of citizens and"—with unconscious irony—"to the perpetuity of a free people.".

Without a majority, there were few real obstructions the opposition in Congress could throw in the Proclamation's path. It remained for John Crisfield, the Maryland Democrat who had once defended Lincoln as a moderate on the floor of the House, to launch one final and impotent missile on December 19. "The professed motive" for the war "was to suppress the rebellion," and for months, said Crisfield, Lincoln had kept the government, "with hopeful spirit and strong arm," marching firmly on that path. But "the president at last gave way," and "as the thunderbolt from a cloudless sky, the PROCLAMATION fell upon the country." With indignation, Crisfield stripped each sentence out of the Proclamation, one after the other, and held them up to blistering denunciation. Of them all, none fired Crisfield's indignation more than the promise that the United States will *recognize and maintain the freedom of such persons, and will do no act or acts to repress such persons, or any of them, in any efforts they may make for their actual freedom.* The slave "may cruelly slay his master, apply the torch to his dwelling, consign his family to indiscriminate butchery, or commit any enormity he judges necessary for his 'actual freedom.' " Lincoln was not just weak, not just treasonous: He was mad, since Crisfield found it "hard to see how a sane mind can, in view of all the circumstances, arrive at such a conclusion." [30]

Congress adjourned for the Christmas holidays on December 23 without having done anything more than talk about the Proclamation. "It is as well," Gideon Welles grumbled into his diary, "the few real business men, of honest intentions, will dispatch matters about as well and fast without as with them." With only a week remaining before emancipation became military law, not a single murmur of interest had been heard from the Confederacy about heeling over toward Lincoln's ultimatum, which was not surprising. However, there had been some motion from Missouri's representatives in Congress about taking advantage of the compensation provisions offered in Lincoln's Annual Message. Even more encouraging, the western Virginia statehood movement had lined up squarely behind the compensated emancipation scheme Lincoln had recommended to Delaware in 1861, to the Border states in 1862, and to the entire nation in the Annual Message.

Virginia's mountainous western counties had never displayed the interest in slaveholding that the Tidewater and central Virginia developed. Western Virginians had been at the forefront of the discussions in the Virginia House of Delegates about emancipation in 1831, and they were the most resistant to secession thirty years later. When Virginia finally voted to secede and join the Confederacy in May 1861, the Old Dominion's westernmost counties refused to join and set themselves up as the "Restored" government of Virginia. Congress was only too happy to welcome a rebellion against the rebellion, and in July, two senators and five representatives of the "Restored" government, speaking for forty-eight western Virginia counties, were seated in Washington. The Restorers did not abolish slavery and rejected even a proposal for gradual emancipation in December 1861. But they did forbid further importation of slaves, and when the Restored government petitioned for recognition as an entirely new state in May 1862, the Senate Committee on Territories made gradual emancipation a requirement.

The West Virginia statehood bill passed through both houses of Congress only after bitter debate and a good deal of heart searching among even the Radicals. Dividing a state—in this case, Virginia—violated the Constitution's ban on the division of states without their consent, not to mention having the appearance of legitimizing secession (even if it was a secession from secession itself). There was some salve to constitutional consciences in the argument that the "Restored" government had given all the assent Virginia could give at that moment to a division, or that the same military necessity that justified emancipation justified the recognition of West Virginia without the state of Virginia's permission.[31]

But Democrats reaped a harvest of argument from the "utter and flagrant unconstitutionality of this scheme," and the arguments troubled Lincoln enough that he asked "for opinions from each of his Cabinet" on December 23 about signing the West Virginia statehood bill. They trooped into the regular cabinet meeting on December 26 with prepared papers, led by Montgomery Blair and Edward Bates counseling postponement or veto. Lincoln heard them out, but much as he refused to regard secession as having any legal or constitutional standing, he balked at the implication that rebel states still possessed all the constitutional powers they had always possessed. "It is said that the admission of West-Virginia, is secession, and tolerated only because it is our secession," Lincoln admitted. "Well, if we call it by that name, there is still difference enough between secession against the constitution, and secession in favor of the constitution" to justify signing the statehood bill. Behind this reasoning was Lincoln's reluctance to cold-shoulder the one and only Southern government that had actually embraced the legislative solution to slavery. "It is said, the devil takes care of his own," Lincoln quipped. "Much more should a good spirit—the spirit of the Constitution and the Union—take care of its own. I think it can not do less, and live." The bill was signed.[32]

Lincoln said nothing about the Proclamation, and a few people dared to wonder whether he would actually put it into effect on January 1. A suspicious Moncure Conway could not understand how Lincoln could reconcile the Proclamation with the Annual Message. "If the President means to carry out his edict of freedom on the New Year, what is all this stuff about gradual emancipation." One Illinois politician warned Lincoln that "some of his personal friends in Illinois were inclined to look upon the Proclamation as a sort of scarecrow to the rebels, or a tub thrown to the whale." This "greatly mortified" Lincoln, but the question was being widely asked all the same. "Will Abe Lincoln stand firm and issue his promised proclamation on the first of January, 1863?" George Templeton Strong wondered. "Nobody knows, but I think he will."

In the last week of December, Z. C. Robbins, a patent lawyer and old Washington hand, paid a call on John Nicolay and took the chance to say to Lincoln, "I hope there will be no backing out on your part" from the Proclamation. "Well, I don't know," Lincoln replied. "Peter denied his Master. He thought he wouldn't, but he did." A committee of New York abolitionists headed by the old-line abolitionist parsons George Cheever and William Goodell waited on Lincoln on December 31 to press him for some confirmation about the Proclamation. Lincoln would only say, "To-morrow at noon, you shall know—and the country shall know—my decision." [33]

The cabinet already knew. At the regular Monday cabinet meeting on December 29, Lincoln "read the draft of his Emancipation Proclamation, invited criticism, and finally directed that copies should be furnished to each." The time had come for the last revisions to be suggested, and Lincoln had made some revisions of his own to the preliminary Proclamation of September 22. No manuscript of this final draft survives in Lincoln's hand, but four of the printed copies belonging to Attorney General Bates, Montgomery Blair, Salmon Chase, and William Seward, together with their comments, do. The comments do not make particularly instructive reading. Bates tweaked a word here, a word there, and Chase wrote an entirely new preamble that was longer than Lincoln's entire proclamation, but the bulk of the comments touched on only two issues.

The first was the precise identification of which states and parts of states were exempt from the Proclamation, now that they were under Union occupation. Here Lincoln had to be precise, since any piece of Southern territory behind Union lines had some ground for insisting that federal civil law had now been restored there, and that war-powers proclamations, like martial law, no longer had force in those districts. (Lincoln would, in fact, wait until the next morning to receive a final and accurate list of the occupied districts, so that he could identify, in some cases county by county, where the Proclamation was intended to apply. Otherwise, some slaveholder from those districts would be sure to file suit in the same federal courts whose authority, a few weeks before, he might have been defying.) Chase and Welles opposed this precise discrimination, although only on the ground that it would create a jurisdictional muddle "in freeing parts of States, and not freeing others." [34]

The second target of the cabinet's comments was Lincoln's controversial promise that the federal government *will recognize and maintain the freedom of said persons and will do no act, or acts to repress said per-*

sons, or any of them, in any suitable efforts they may make for their actual freedom. Lincoln thought he had softened the inflammatory implications of that promise by inserting the modifier *suitable* before *efforts* and adding, in this final draft, an additional *appeal to the people so declared to be free, to abstain from all disorder, tumult, and violence, unless in necessary self defence.* But Bates, Seward, Blair, and even Chase all urged him to strike it out entirely, and two days later, when the cabinet met to review the final draft, both Chase and Seward proposed a rewriting "enjoining upon, instead of appealing to, those emancipated, to forbear from tumult." Montgomery Blair was even more schoolmasterish. He wanted Lincoln to wag his finger at the slaves and "appeal to them to show themselves worthy of freedom by fidelity & diligence in the employments which may be given to them by the observance of order & by abstaining from all violence not required by duty or for self-defence." In the end, Lincoln would concede to the objections. The *military and naval authorities* would simply *recognize and maintain the freedom of said persons.* The Proclamation would then *enjoin upon the people so declared to be free to abstain from all violence, unless in necessary self-defence; and I recommend to them that, in all cases when allowed, they labor faithfully for reasonable wages.*[35]

Otherwise, the final draft simply executed the threat contained in the preliminary Emancipation Proclamation. *Whereas, on the twenty second day of September, in the year of our Lord one thousand, eight hundred and sixty-two, a proclamation was issued by the President of the United States,* Lincoln began, it was now time to implement the provisions of that proclamation. Except in those parts of the Confederacy back under federal control—and the listing was left blank until Lincoln had the final tally from the War Department—*I do order, and declare, that all persons held as slaves within said designated States, and parts of States, are, and henceforward forever shall be free.* There was a slight shift in wording at this crucial point from the first draft and the preliminary Proclamation. Both of them had spoken of emancipation dramatically, but only prospectively, as making the slaves *then, thenceforward, and forever* free. In the final draft, the time had come to make the prospect a present reality: The slaves *are, and henceforward forever shall be* free.[36]

There were, however, two other peculiar changes made at the last minute. The cabinet came together one more time to review the Proclamation on December 31, and at that meeting, Salmon Chase "proposed a felicitous closing sentence": *Upon this act, sincerely believed to be an act of justice, warranted by the Constitution, upon military necessity, I invoke the considerate judgement of mankind, and the gracious favor of Almighty God.* It was, in effect, the offering of a quadruple warrant for the Proclamation—*military necessity,* of course, but also a claim to constitutional sanction, an appeal to heaven, and an abstract resort to *justice.* Abstractions were just what Lincoln had hoped to keep out of the Proclamation, since even the slightest attempt to justify the Proclamation on any other grounds than the war powers might put the whole document in legal peril. But Sumner had earlier urged him "that there must be something about 'justice' & 'God' " in the Proclamation, and in the end, Lincoln agreed. In a document so spare of rhetorical invention, Lincoln could not resist, at the end, words which would make it memorable.[37]

It was not just the handsome flourish of the words, though, that pleased Lincoln. Chase's suggestion evoked two elements that touched directly on Lincoln's deepest faiths. One was the *Almighty God,* the sovereign and predestinating Calvinistic God to whom he had made the vow that brought forth the Proclamation in the first place. He always carefully left aside any implication that he knew what or who this Almighty God was, but the war had brought home to him, in the most savage way possible, the realization that God had purposes in this war that were surprising everyone. "If I had been allowed my way this war would have been ended before this, but we find it still continues," he had written to the English Quaker Eliza P. Gurney that October. No matter what the rest of the world assumed the meaning of the war to be, "we must believe that He permits it for some wise purpose of his own, mysterious and unknown to us," and it was fitting that the Proclamation should embody that.

The other faith Chase's suggestion called up was the Declaration of Independence. Even hedged about as it was with invocations of constitutionality and military necessity, the echo of the Declaration—*the con-*

siderate judgement of mankind reminding readers of Jefferson's concern for a "decent Respect to the Opinions of Mankind," and *the gracious favor of Almighty God* paralleling the invocation of "Nature and Nature's God"—was unmistakable in Chase's wording. It would make the Proclamation virtually a second Declaration. Lincoln was still, like Jefferson, leaving carefully aside any implication that he was endorsing any particular church's creed in this God. But he was also making abundantly clear that he was no longer able to speak of the war or its purposes without some deference to a supernatural will that dwarfed the operations of mere progress.

Lincoln made one other change to the final draft which is less easy to explain. As he was shifting the specific wording that proclaimed freedom into the present tense, he also deleted the word *forever* from the announcement that *all persons held as slaves* were now freed. *Forever* had appeared in all three previous versions of the Proclamation. But the final draft now simply declared that those "persons" *are, and henceforward shall be free.* He had never believed that a military proclamation could guarantee freedom *forever,* beyond the time of the war emergency that called for it. Rather than give the judges even one spike to hang the Proclamation on, at the last minute Lincoln withdrew what he knew he could not actually promise.

THE NEXT DAY, New Year's Day, dawned with "scarce a cloud . . . to obscure the brilliant rays of light emitted from the great alchemist." Lincoln had "never retired that night," and early in the morning, he walked down the corridor from the family quarters of the White House to his office and wrote out his final revision with Chase's closing.

He covered three long sheets of paper, saving himself the trouble of writing in one instance by pasting two paragraphs from a previously printed circular onto the first page as an insertion. But he would wait for an official copy to be made before signing it, as he only did on state documents, with his full name—*Abraham Lincoln.* A clerk was summoned to take the written draft over to the State Department for it to be engrossed, and in the meantime Lincoln ate his usual meager breakfast ("an egg, a piece of toast coffee & c," according to John Hay). Mary Lincoln (who, according to her son Robert "was very much opposed to the signing of the Emancipation Proclamation") appeared in the doorway, "inquiring in her quick sharp way, 'Well, what do you intend doing?' " Lincoln only looked upwards, "as to heaven," and replied, "I am a man under orders, I cannot do otherwise." [38]

Secretary of State Seward arrived with the engrossed copy for Lincoln's signature just after midmorning. But here matters stalled. With his lawyer's eye, Lincoln noticed that the closing subscription in the engrossed copy contained an error. It read: "In testimony whereof I have hereunto set my name and caused the seal of the United States to be affixed." The draft had omitted the usual subscription form, leaving that technicality to be supplied by the State Department's copyist, who dutifully wrote it out in what he thought was the desired form. But it was not. Setting his *name* to a document *in testimony* was what he did in the subscription of treaties; setting his *hand* was what he did *in witness whereof* to presidential proclamations—calling out the first troops, announcing the blockade, setting aside days of fasting and prayer—and that was what he wanted here.[39] He could not let this error pass, not with this Proclamation, which would be scrutinized down to the last syllable like no other document he had written in his life. And so Seward and the botched copy were sent back to the State Department for a corrected one.

There would not be time to wait for Seward to return with a re-copied version. Although New Year's Day was a holiday in official Washington, presidential custom obliged Lincoln to preside at a New Year's levee at a quarter after eleven, downstairs in the White House. He had only enough time left to get ready and then proceed down the broad White House staircase with his wife, still dressed in her mourning black for the death of their son Willie ten months before. The well-wishers' line began with the diplomatic corps, "arrayed in gold lace, feathers and other trappings, not to mention very good clothes," followed by the justices of the Supreme Court, the stoop-shouldered Roger Taney at their head, and by the resident judges of the federal circuit court and the lower courts; then those members of the cabinet like Gideon Welles who were not holding their own levees; then a procession of generals and admirals; and even a delegation of veterans of the War of 1812. At noon, the doors of the White House were opened to the general public. "The Press was tremendous," wrote Noah Brooks for the *Sacramento Union*, and "the jam most excessive; all persons, high or low, civil, uncivil, or otherwise, were obliged to fall into an immense line . . . all forcing their way along the stately portico of the White House to the main entrance." Through it all, "the President appeared to be in fine spirits and cracked an occasional joke with some of his more intimate friends." [40]

The doors were finally closed at two o'clock, and Lincoln went back upstairs. Some time that afternoon, the two Sewards reappeared with a corrected version of the Proclamation and the handwritten draft Lincoln had finished earlier that day. By that time, Lincoln was thoroughly exhausted. "I was tired that day," he admitted later to New Jersey congressman James Scovel, but his determination to finish this work was as high as heaven. With the engrossed copy spread out before him, Lincoln picked up a pen he had already promised to Charles Sumner as a keepsake and, after dipping it in his inkwell, moved to sign it. His hand and forearm were trembling, and he put down the pen.

After a moment he tried again, and again the shaking in his enormous, bony hand made him set the pen on the desk. "I could not for a moment, control my arm," Lincoln later told his loyal Congressional ally Isaac Arnold. "I paused and a superstitious feeling came over me which made me hesitate." Was this all a mistake? Was the trembling a sign, yet another divine warning, this time that he had gone too far, had overreached himself, had taken a step which would end only in disaster? Then he remembered "that I had been shaking hands for hours, with several hundred people." As much to assure himself as the Sewards, Lincoln declared that "I never in my life felt more certain that I was doing right than I do in signing this paper." The tremor in his hand was not because of doubt or hesitation over the Proclamation, but merely because "I have been receiving calls and shaking hands till my arm is stiff and numb." But if that explained the meaning of the tremors to his own satisfaction, it might not convince others if the shakiness caused his signature on the Proclamation to waver. "They will say, 'he had some compunctions.'" But then the iron again came back into him. "Anyway, it is going to be done." And he signed "slowly and carefully," slightly cramping the final *m* in his first name and the loop of the *L* at the beginning of *Lincoln*. There it was, as clear as it needed to be: *Abraham Lincoln*. He looked up with a smile, "and a laugh followed at his apprehension," and he remarked quietly, "That will do." [41]

"The signature looks a little tremulous," Lincoln admitted to Speaker of the House Schuyler Colfax "and other friends that night," but "not because of any uncertainty or hesitation on my part." It was rather exhaustion: "Three hours' hand-shaking is not calculated to improve a man's chirography." Whatever the state of his hand, "my resolution was firm. . . . Not one word of it will I ever recall." Secretary Seward then signed it also, and Lincoln called in Nicolay to copy the formal superscription ("By the President of the United States. A Proclamation") and subscription onto the written draft, which he and Seward then signed again. Lincoln would keep the draft for himself; Seward took the engrossed copy and left for the State Department, where the Great Seal of the United States would be embossed on the Proclamation. By evening, the Government Printing Office would begin printing a two-page broadsheet, which for the first time gave the document the title by which it would always thereafter be known: "Emancipation Proclamation." For all of Lincoln's attempts to embargo the final text of the Proclamation, someone in the State Department had leaked the text of the first, uncorrected engrossed copy to a reporter, so by nightfall, Gideon Welles was able to read a bootlegged version of the Proclamation on the pages of the *Evening Star*. [42]

Anticipation, mingled with anxiety that Lincoln might at the last minute lose heart, drew together enormous crowds in every major Northern city on New Year's Day. In New York, an enormous "grand jubilee" was organized at the "colored" Shiloh Presbyterian Church for the evening of December 31. "By 9 o'clock in the evening the church was filled to overflowing, nearly one-third of the audience being white." Speaker after speaker hailed the dawn of emancipation, and when the clock struck twelve, "the Chairman read a dispatch from Washington, saying that President Lincoln would issue the Emancipation proclamation at 12 o'clock M., to-day." The crowd went up in "tumultuous cheers, which lasted for some minutes, and were followed by three cheers for

ABRAHAM LINCOLN, three cheers for freedom, &c. &c." The next day, Henry Raymond editorialized in the *New York Times* that "President Lincoln's proclamation, which we publish this morning, marks an era in the history, not only of this war, but of his country and the world."[43]

In Philadelphia, prayer meetings were held in both morning and afternoon on New Year's Day. "Our Chief Magistrate is now putting to his lips the trumpet of Providence," announced one speaker at the Broad Street Baptist Church, while another, Henry Augustus Boardman of the Tenth Presbyterian Church, rejoiced that "slavery might pass away, through the baptism of blood and fire" and "thanked God that might no more should make right." One Treasury official, making a circuit of Philadelphia's twenty black churches on New Year's Day, wrote to Lincoln, "During thirty years of active Anti-Slavery life, I have never witnessed, such intense, intelligent and devout 'Thanksgiving.' . . . The Black people all trust you" and "thought there must be some design of God in having your name 'Abraham' that if you were not the 'Father' You were to be the 'Liberator' of a People." There were even demands that the Liberty Bell in Independence Hall be rung. In city after city—Buffalo, New York; Haverhill, Massachusetts; Pittsburgh; Chicago—salutes of one hundred cannon were fired.[44]

In Boston, the epicenter of abolitionism, two great meetings were organized at Music Hall and at Tremont Temple, the first largely for whites and the second for Boston's black community. Tremont Temple hosted the elite of black abolitionism—Frederick Douglass, Charles Lenox Redmond, William Wells Brown, John S. Rock. Ascending the rostrum, Douglass thanked God that he was alive to see the end of slavery. Thirty years ago, he reminded the crowd of 3,000, white Bostonians "deemed it a duty that they owed to God" to break up abolitionist meetings and destroy abolitionist presses. Now, Douglass quipped, "Things was a-workin." It was not until Douglass was finished, however, that the news of the Proclamation was rushed into the church, and it was not until another seven speakers had taken their turn at the rostrum that the full text of the Proclamation was hurried in to be read. "The joyous enthusiasm manifested was beyond description. Cheers were proposed for the President and for the proclamation, the whole audience rising to their feet and shouting at the tops of their voices, throwing up their hats and indicating the gratification in every conceivable manner." "It was a day & an occasion never to be forgotten," wrote Eliza Quincy to Mary Todd Lincoln. "I wish you & the President could have enjoyed it with us, here." [45]

In Norfolk, Virginia, 2,000 blacks ignored the exception the Proclamation made to "the cities of Norfolk & Portsmouth" and paraded in celebration, while another 10,000 looked on and cheered. Northwards, white Philadelphians found that "nearly all the places of business occupied by colored people were closed . . . in honor of the emancipation of the slaves of the South," and in New York City, Henry Highland Garnet presided over a daylong "jubilee" which "was kept up to late hour in the evening . . . shouting, praying and rejoicing." The same evening, slaves in federally occupied Corinth, Mississippi, "assembled at that place and officers attended, making lectures and stating that they were free," and afterward "the negroes" were issued "each a pistol" and told to seek out their masters and "act as *missionaries*" to liberate others. (In later years, ex-slaves would recount stories that described Lincoln personally appearing at the plantation gates at the head of a column of black soldiers, announcing, "You ain't got no more master and no more missus," or opening the smokehouse and telling the newly freed slaves, "Help yourselves; take what you need; cook yourselves a good meal!" The contrabands at Port Royal could only "with some difficulty" be "made to believe he was not a Colored man, who went around, begging for jobs of rails to split, till he was made president.")[46]

On January 3, the Government Printing Office produced the official State Department edition of the Proclamation for distribution to the diplomatic corps, followed by a 15,000-copy version distributed through the Adjutant General's office. Governor John Andrew was so ardent in his enthusiasm for the Proclamation that he printed a separate edition "in tiny book form" for Massachusetts regiments to hand out "to let the darkies know that they are free." [47]

Lincoln finished out the day of January 1 with a note to the secretary of war about the plea of "an old lady of genteel appearance" who had protested government appropriation of her boardinghouse and another note to General Halleck. Paying a brief visit to the War Department telegraph office to see if there was news of the war from Tennessee, he showed so little excitement that "no one would have supposed from Lincoln's perfectly composed manner at the time that he had that day given to the world a document of imperishable human interest, which meant so much to the country, and especially to four millions of slaves, whose shackles were forever loosed." He had dinner and entertained Colfax and some Congressional friends in the evening, until "great processions" of whites and blacks (numbers of them clutching the leaked version of the Proclamation in the *Evening Star*) came by the White House and called for him to come out and speak to them. He only came to the window and bowed as the throng cheered and promised that "they would hug him to death."

Lincoln needed no celebrations. He had told Charles Sumner more than a year before, "I know very well that the name which is connected with this act will never be forgotten." He was satisfied, he said to James Scovel, that it was "my greatest and most enduring contribution to the history of the war." Later he would tell the artist Francis Carpenter that "as affairs have turned, *it is the central act of my administration, and the great event of the nineteenth century.*"[48]

JOHN NICOLAY wrote the lead editorial for John W. Forney's *Daily Morning Chronicle* on January 2, 1863, sparing nothing in heaping praise onto the Proclamation and his boss. But from almost the first sentence, the principal note was defensive. Celebration was mixed heavily with the urge to justify the Proclamation and the war powers. "Slavery caused the war: it is with the sword of his war power under the Constitution that President Lincoln now destroys the right arm of the rebellion—African slavery." The editorial was also weighed down with another defensive posture, the assurance that the emancipation would be followed posthaste by colonization. "This day," declared Nicolay, "is the initial point of the separation of the black from the white race." America was destined "to be the theater of the white man's achievements," not those of the "black race," who could be more suitably shuffled off to "the equatorial regions of Central and South America." The *National Republican* was more hopeful—"The President's proclamation of yesterday is the great event of the day and of the century"—and the *Chicago Tribune* prophesied that Lincoln could now "claim a proud place among the benefactors of human kind." New York lawyer Edward Bullard hailed "the PROCLAMATION of January 1, 1863," as "the greatest event within the last eighteen hundred years." The abolitionist Moncure Conway thought that "a victorious sun appeared about to rise upon the New World of free and equal men." Even William Lloyd Garrison finally had something from Lincoln he could praise. The Proclamation, wrote Garrison in *The Liberator*, was "a great historic event, sublime in its magnitude, momentous and beneficient in its far-reaching consequences." [49]

But most of the newspaper pundits and politicos showed no more enthusiasm for the Proclamation, now that it was law, than they had in September when it was only a threat. Thomas Ewing, a veteran Ohio politician and two-time cabinet secretary, told Orville Hickman Browning that "he thought it not improbable many of our officers would resign, and a 100,000 of our men lay down their arms"; another of Browning's visitors thought "that scarcely one of the 200,000 whose term of service is soon to expire will re-enlist." Then there were the legal questions: "We do not deny that the President, as commander-in-chief of the army and navy, may, in time of armed rebellion . . . rightfully liberate slaves," argued the editorial lead of the *National Intelligencer*. "But it is denied . . . that the executive . . . has the right to 'order and declare' that slaves now held to service by certain State laws shall . . . be then thenceforward and forever free."

Farther afield, the inaugurals of the new Democratic governors in New York and New Jersey became anti-Proclamation carnivals. New Jersey governor Joel Parker used his inaugural to predict a slave insurrection and a general massacre of all blacks; New York governor Horatio Seymour described the Proclamation as a "bloody, barbarous, revolutionary, and unconstitutional scheme." The New Jersey legislature outdid the new governor and passed a series of peace resolutions. And in Illinois, John McClernand warned Republican governor Richard Yates that "from all I see and hear a revolution is brewing in the Northwest."[50]

The weapons for such a revolution were already in the hands of Northern soldiers, and some of them were talking wildly enough to make their comrades wonder if they planned on using them. A federal general confided to Missourian Wirt Adams that "the people of the West had engaged in this contest solely for the preservation of the Union and the unrestricted navigation of the Mississippi River," but "Lincoln's emancipation proclamation of 1st of January had converted the war into an abolition crusade, which would not be approved by the people of the West, and would entirely estrange them from the Lincoln Government." A lieutenant in the Eighty-sixth Illinois surveyed his company and found to his shock that "only 8 men in Co. K. approve the policy and proclamation of Mr. Lincoln."

One relative of an Illinois cavalryman confidently promised that "every man that has got the sand will throw off on the Lincoln Government now after the proclamation setting the nigger free. Ill[inois]'s is bound to go with the Southland." In the 106th Pennsylvania (part of the Army of the Potomac's Philadelphia Brigade), opinion about the proclamation was running strongly against, with "many . . . boldly stating that they would not have entered the army had they thought such would have been the action of the Government." It was worse still in the Fifty-first Pennsylvania—a regiment which had lost a third of its men at Antietam—where "officers and men swore that they would neither draw a sword or fire a shot in support of such a proclamation." Rather than risk armed resistance, many soldiers decided the path of protest lay to the rear. One Vermont infantryman reported in late January that "20 deserted out of one battery that went with us in one night." The soldiers "are getting disgusted . . . and it is nothing uncommon for a Capt. to get up in the morning and find half his company gone." Of the more than 13,000 desertions Illinois regiments suffered during the war, the single largest number occurred immediately after the Proclamation was issued; one regiment, the 109th Illinois, had to be disbanded for disloyalty.[51]

Nobody liked the Proclamation less than the Border, if only because the bombshell of emancipation had fallen so close to them. Hamilton

Gray put the fears of the Border states in the bluntest terms: "If the Negroes be freed in any of the Southern States, which are in rebellion, they will at once, make their way to the loyal or 'border States,' and there become a pest to Society." Little more than a week after Lincoln signed the Proclamation, the Tennessee Unionist William G. "Parson" Brownlow warned Montgomery Blair that "things are not working . . . in Kentucky. I fear the Legislature will take strong action against the proclamation, and even against the Administration." James A. Garfield, who had just been elected to Congress, thought that "all the men who are worth talking to are in favor of it, now that it has been promulgated," but he was sure that "it can only have an adverse effect in Ky. and Tenn."

And that was the reaction from Lincoln's friends. The Democratic opposition in the Border states was far less self-contained. "The President's proclamation has come to hand at last," wrote the *Louisville Daily Democrat.* "We scarcely know how to express our indignation at this flagrant outrage of all constitutional law, all human justice, all Christian feeling." William Owner was delighted when the news reached Washington that "the Gov of [Kentucky] in his recent message to the Legislature recommends that Ky reject the emancipation Proclamation, and protests against any interference with her State policy, as unwarranted by the Constitution." Kentucky Democrats, sniffing the opportunity to overturn the Unionist majorities in the Kentucky legislature, called a state convention in February for the purpose of "preparing the Kentucky Mind for revolt against the Union" and had to be forcibly dispersed by federal troops. Even in Pennsylvania, Democratic newspapers like the Harrisburg *Patriot and Union* assured the party faithful that the Proclamation, by declaring that "this Government will do no act or acts to repress rebellion," was nothing else but a "cold-blooded invitation to insurrection and butchery." [52]

In Illinois, where the lower half of the state was practically part of the Border, the new Democratic legislature convened with political murder in its heart, seasoned with a touch of sexual paranoia. "Our country is becoming almost a nation of widows and orphans," one Democratic representative luridly asserted, "who, if the President's emancipation proclamation be carried into effect, will become prey to the lusts

of freed negroes who will overrun our country." Others raged at the
Proclamation as "unconstitutional, contrary to the rules and usages of
civilized warfare, calculated to bring shame, disgrace and eternal infamy upon the hitherto unsullied flag of the Republic, and Illinois . . .
will protest against any war which has for its object the execution or enforcement of said proclamation." On February 4, shortly before the session ended, one last resolution announced "that we believe the further
prosecution of the present war cannot result in the restoration of the
Union and the preservation of the Constitution as our fathers made it,
unless the President's emancipation proclamation be withdrawn" and
(like a similar resolution in New Jersey) asked for the naming of five
commissioners to go to Washington and urge Congress to issue an
armistice and arrange for a peace convention. "All the democratic members of the legislature are open secessionists," wrote one anxious observer. "They talked about going to Washington, hurling Mr Lincoln
from the presidential chair, and inaugurating civil war north." [53]

But the battle over the Proclamation would not be won by the newspapers or by the state legislatures or even, in the constitutional sense, by
the soldiers. It would be won by the lawyers and the judges, and they con-
stituted the third, and most technical, challenge to Lincoln and emancipation. "When Mr. Lincoln entered upon his official duties," recalled
James G. Blaine, "the Judicial Department of the Government differ-
enced in every conceivable way from his construction of the Constitution
in so far as the question of slavery was involved." The Democratic press
clapped its hands in glee at "the possibility of a review of Mr. Lincoln's
proceedings by the Supreme Court," and even a paper as friendly to the
administration as Henry Raymond's *New York Times* thought that "it is
a matter of utmost importance to the President, to the slaves, and to the
country, that it should come in a form to be sustained." [54]

This form Lincoln had struggled to achieve, even to the point of par-
ing the Proclamation's language down to the barest legalese. Yet even
with the most careful crafting, the Proclamation was vulnerable to legal
objection on at least three counts. First, what was the exact nature of the
war powers which Lincoln exercised as a *"military necessity"*? Did they
really exist? Second, assuming that the war powers were constitutional,

had Lincoln used them in a constitutional way? And third, what was the reasoning that led Lincoln to emancipate through the use of a proclamation rather than an executive order or a general military order? What force would a proclamation have as the means of declaring slaves emancipated?

The courts had always been the ghost at the emancipation banquet, a ghost that could pose a real menace if it materialized in the shape of jurists such as Benjamin Robbins Curtis. Born the same year as Lincoln, Curtis was second in his class at Harvard, rose to associate justice of the Supreme Court, and was one of the two dissenters from Roger Taney's dictum in *Dred Scott* in 1857, after which he resigned from the Court. Curtis stood second to none as an enemy of the extension of slavery, but he was convinced to his stony New England marrow that any possible good that might come from the Emancipation Proclamation was more than outweighed by the manner in which Lincoln had issued it. Curtis hurried a pamphlet, *Executive Power*, into print before the end of 1862; in it, he offered exactly the arguments Lincoln had flinched from.

Curtis wanted it understood that he had no problem with the war itself—"The war in which we are engaged is a just and necessary war"— but he argued that the North had no right to feign horror at secession if it proceeded to do even worse damage to the Constitution by "an executive decree" that "proposes to repeal and annul valid State laws which regulate the domestic relations of their people." Lincoln's attempt to justify the Proclamation as a "fit and necessary war measure" meant nothing to Curtis. He was, in the first place, not sure that there were any such things as war powers in the Constitution, or at least not "any express grant of power." True, the Constitution made the president commander in chief of the army and navy, but all this meant was that Lincoln enjoyed the rank of "general-in-chief" and had no more martial-law powers on the field than any other general. He might be able to confiscate slaves, as property, but he had no right to nullify state statutes concerning slavery and declare any of them free. "He cannot make a law. He cannot repeal one." The powers Lincoln was claiming as the authority for issuing the Emancipation Proclamation were not the powers of a president; they were the powers of a "usurper." If a president could "disregard any one positive prohibition of the Constitution, or . . . exercise any one power not delegated . . . by the Constitution," merely because there was a war on, what would keep him from using the war "to disregard each and every provision of the Constitution"?[55]

Curtis's attack on the Proclamation had a double sting for the president. Lincoln had every right to expect a cascade of hot criticism from Democrats, but it was galling to find the Proclamation under fire from friends who now turned out in as much howling force as Democrats. In the lead of this troop were Joel Parker, the Massachusetts Republican judge and law professor who had tried to lead the People's Party insurrection; Robert C. Winthrop, the former Speaker of the House of Representatives; and Samuel Osgood, the Unitarian minister and Transcendentalist editor.[56] These were the New England moderates, "the old Whigs," Lincoln thought of as men of like character and principles with himself: He was now about to discover that they were not.

Parker had even less patience than Curtis with the notion of presidential war powers. "There is no sound foundation on which to rest such extreme 'War Powers' as are claimed . . . for the President," Parker declared, "nothing in the language of the Constitution" and, unbelievably, "nothing in the situation of the country." To find a "power of emancipation" attached to the "power to make war" was to find nothing less than "a power to change Constitutional rights . . . at the pleasure of the President in time of war." Robert Winthrop was even less circumspect in his estimate of the war powers. As a war-powers measure, the Proclamation was "undoubtedly one of the most startling exercises of the one-man power—which the history of human government, free or despotic, has ever witnessed." [57]

Suppose, however, that the Constitution did confer some sort of war powers on the president. This still made no difference to Parker, since the Proclamation reached far beyond what could even remotely be considered a war power. Whatever "war powers" were, it was certain they could only apply to specific geography and specific people. They were limited to the actual combatants and were not to cast themselves at civilian targets; they were to apply in war zones where actual fighting took place, not across the southern half of an entire continent. But the

Proclamation, by freeing slaves everywhere in the Confederacy, made no "distinction between the places and persons involved in the war, and those not within the limits of military occupation and actual hostilities." Violating the rules of both geography and people, it nullified itself. It also violated the rule of time: "Martial law . . . only suspends the municipal law for the time being. It does not subvert it permanently." Neither should the war powers. And if only the Proclamation had stuck to that rule and allowed the army to emancipate "by force" the "slaves who came within their lines," Parker promised that he "should have no controversy with any one who supported it." But constitutional nicety was something "President Lincoln and his supporters" plainly did not understand. They had been blinded by what Robert Winthrop called "schemes of philanthropy," and if the blindness persisted and the proclamations kept on coming, "we shall find ourselves plunged irretrievably into the fearful and fathomless abyss." Either that, Samuel Osgood agreed, or Lincoln would make himself "liable to impeachment or running the risk of strengthening rebellion by revolution." [58]

Lincoln would find that these risks would be to no purpose. "The Constitution still recognizes the rights of the inhabitants" of the Confederacy "so far as they have not committed crimes against the United States which cause a forfeiture," Joel Parker asserted, and their rights included those of property. Lincoln could proclaim as he liked. It would be only "a paper attempt at emancipation," because no court in the United States would uphold it. The "right of all persons who held slaves under the State laws . . . exists as before, and will continue to exist after the first of January." By the same logic, "the President may notify Queen Victoria that . . . he will proclaim in what part of her Indian dominions the sepoys shall be emancipated . . . but would Her Majesty be very much alarmed?" Not any more than if his "dog might bark at the moon." The best Lincoln could hope for, once the war was over, was that the courts would recognize the freedom of whichever slaves had managed to achieve "actual freedom" for themselves. But Samuel Osgood was more worried that, even at best, the Proclamation would cause the injection "of despotic principles" into the "national life," which would doom the republic "to certain destruction." Or it might trigger that fantasy of every white generation, the slave insurrection, and that would "unite" the rebels "in a determination to fight to the uttermost." [59] Why jeopardize the war and the future of the nation by running such risks? Did Lincoln seriously believe that the Proclamation would be more than a paper bugle?

The passion and urgency with which Parker, Curtis, Winthrop, and the other Brahmin critics of the Proclamation presented their case sat strangely beside the unreality and detachment of the case itself. Perhaps State Street was sufficiently far removed from the front lines that none of the Brahmins noticed the impossibility of waging civil wars under rules written for peace, or the lunacy of the notion that constitutions grant equal standing to the people who are trying to protect them and the people who are trying to destroy them. Pointing out these holes was therefore the first task of the lawyers who linked arms behind the Proclamation—Solicitor General William Whiting; the New Yorkers Grosvenor Porter Lowrey, Charles Kirkland, and Daniel Gardner; the New Haven minister Leonard Bacon; and the Bostonians Charles Mayo Ellis and Joel Prentiss Bishop.

"The Commander-in-chief, in time of war, is authorized and bound to use any and all accessible means not forbidden by the laws of war, which in his judgment may be useful or necessary to subdue the enemy," Grosvenor Lowrey patiently explained, and if emancipating slaves subdued the enemy, then proclamations emancipating them were fully consistent with the president's power as commander in chief. The problem was pinpointing just where the Constitution granted such war powers. Some of the pro-Proclamation jurists wondered why this was a problem at all. Charles Kirkland was reminded of Diogenes searching with his lamp at midday: The war powers, he argued, arose from the simple need for national self-preservation. No one needed to go hunting through the Constitution to see that, and it was no part of a commander in chief's responsibility to dicker over the fine points of constitutional navigation while a storm was howling around his ears. Lincoln possessed war powers simply by "the law of self-preservation." In like manner, William Whiting located the war powers in the law of nations and argued that "the laws of war give the President full belligerent rights; and when the army and navy are once lawfully called out, there are no limits to the war-making power of the President."

But for those who preferred to find the war powers inside the letter of the Constitution, there were several ways of teasing out evidence for them. One possibility was to appeal to Lincoln's constitutional oath of office—"to preserve, protect and defend"—for all the justification the Proclamation or the war powers needed. If emancipating slaves was necessary—and *necessary* was Lincoln's favorite word in this situation—to preserving, protecting, and defending the Constitution, then the oath gives the president "power equal to the demands of his duty." If "a proclamation of freedom to the slaves, is necessary as a means of crushing the enemy," wrote the New Haven minister Leonard Bacon, "then that is just the thing which he must do, or violate his oath." Joel Bishop, on the other hand, believed that the war powers lurked behind the Constitution's guarantee of a "republican form of government" to the states. "A republican government implies the voluntary suffrage of the people," he reasoned. In South Carolina, "the blacks . . . who are within our lines, are as loyal to the government of the United States as any persons within our territorial limits." Therefore, it was allowable—it was even demanded—that Lincoln fulfill the obligation to guarantee "a republican form of government" to them by emancipating them, arming them, and giving them the vote.[60]

New York lawyer Daniel Gardner had no doubt, either, that the Proclamation was exactly in accord with those "demands." It was the "slaveholders and their allies" who had "gotten up" this war, and there was nothing unfitting about seizing their slave property as punishment—if not punishment to the slaveholders themselves, then at least as punishment to the rebel cause that depended on "the agricultural and domestic labor of the slaves" to release "tens of thousands of whites" for service "in the rebel army." What, asked Charles Kirkland, "in reason, in common-sense, in national law, in the law of civilized warfare" could possibly constitute an objection to a Proclamation that deprived "our enemy of his means of warfare?" Slaves, argued Grosvenor Lowrey, "are forcibly held" to serve the enemy; so, in "the interest of the nation, and for the purpose of weakening the enemy, the Commander-in-chief proposes to invite the persons so held, to . . . cease to serve it. What is the objection to this?" Nor did it make any sense to Charles Mayo Ellis to clip the Proclamation's wings on the ground that any war power the president might have could extend no further than the usual limited scope of martial law. This was a civil war, and a civil war with "no parallel in history." On those terms, the so-called "field of this dire war is the whole Union, and the ocean, too," and it was "altogether too technical" to croak that Lincoln's "Proclamation cannot go beyond his army in any such sense. Indeed, it is simply absurd." If, in the process, the Proclamation stripped Southerners of their property rights, that was simply too bad. Grosvenor Lowrey brushed away any bleating about the Constitution conferring the same rights in war as in peace. "Rebels in arms against the Constitution, must not be spoken of, as men having constitutional rights." [61]

Lowrey shared none of Joel Parker's skepticism about the legal force of the Proclamation. So what if emancipation violated the slaveholder's rights to "property"? It could be said (with some help from the same legalistic detachment that clouded the reasoning of Winthrop, Parker, and Osgood) that the Proclamation actually interfered with no slaveowner's rights *directly;* it was merely the occasion for the slaves themselves to cast the slaveowners' property rights into oblivion. "Whenever the slave has, under Mr. Lincoln's proclamation, done one voluntary act inconsistent with his master's assumed right to full control over him, he has, as our agent and ally, taken possession of himself."

This self-seizure, they predicted, would involve no threat of violence or racial insurrection. Charles Kirkland dismissed any fears that the Proclamation would signal more Nat Turners. "I am not an abolitionist," Kirkland claimed. "I am even called by some a pro-slavery man." Yet he saw no likelihood of "scenes of bloodshed, no 'servile war,' in the event of the practical carrying out of this proclamation." To the contrary: "Its effect will be to take eight hundred thousand fighting and working men from the rebels . . . instead of [their] working rebel plantations, raising corn, wheat, cotton, and building rebel fortifications." If the freed slaves could then also be armed and enlisted in the Union Army, wouldn't that "spare our white citizens" from getting shot and allow "colored emancipated soldiers, burning to conquer the masters who have reduced them to the condition of brutes," to do all the dying necessary to restore the Union? But even if there was a slave insurrection, why should the lovers of the Union complain? "What is there about a black insurrection," asked Lowrey, "so much more obnoxious to the laws of nations than a white insurrection?" The ultimate appeal was simply to the fait accompli of the Proclamation itself. What did Curtis and Parker expect Lincoln to do—rescind it? "Are there any who would annul the proclamation," asked Montgomery Blair, speaking before the Maryland legislature, and pull down on themselves responsibility for reinvigorating "the institution so skilfully plied to instigate war, and so essential to provide the means for its prosecution?" The milk of emancipation was spilled; who wanted to take responsibility for putting it back into the bottle?[62]

The shield Kirkland, Lowrey, and the others tried to hold over the Proclamation gratified Lincoln. (Kirkland, in fact, got a personal note of thanks from the president). But the president was lawyer enough himself to understand that the defenders of the Proclamation often overshot the constitutional mark as much as the critics. It might be true in general, as Daniel Gardner had argued, that the "slaveholders and their allies" had "gotten up the war" and therefore deserved to lose their slaves as just and appropriate punishment. But not all slaveholders were actual rebels, in any sense that a court of law would recognize, and yet their slaves were being emancipated along with everyone else's. It might also be true in general, as Charles Kirkland insisted, that the "agricultural and domestic labor of slaves" was the sine qua non of the Confederate war effort. But taken one by one, not every slave was contributing directly or tangibly to clothing, feeding, or arming the Confederate military; yet all the slaves of the Confederacy were being emancipated. And was not Grosvenor Lowrey being too clever by half in suggesting that the Proclamation was only providing the slaves with incentives to seize freedom for themselves? The Proclamation did not just invite slaves to resist or to run away; it declared them free, and it made no effort to slough onto the shoulders of the slaves a responsibility that Lincoln clearly articulated as his own.

No scorecard tallied up the points made by each debater, but taking the debate as a whole, it is hard to see the Proclamation's defense counsel as anything but marginally successful in making a direct constitutional case for it. Grosvenor Lowrey admitted that the war powers he spent so much time applauding as "the faithful friends and servants of the Constitution . . . are not constitutional powers; and I am compelled to call them extra-constitutional for want of a better name." Parker and Curtis believed they already knew what that name was—*illegal*—and Lowrey's admission can only have brought dry smiles to the Boston jurists' faces. Alexander Twining, writing in the *New Englander and Yale Review*, struggled to justify the war powers as "none the less potent" for being constitutionally invisible, or for having "slumbered in our history, unfamiliar to political logicians and to the popular apprehension." But the very fact of slumber and invisibility was the best argument one could make *against* the Proclamation. If Curtis and Parker, in their animus toward the Proclamation, remind us of strict-constructionist Southern judges from the 1950s, using the letter of the Constitution to shield segregation from federal interference, Bishop, Kirkland, and Lowrey are bound to remind us of the postmodern penchant for finding law within concepts of justice rather than the Constitution.[63]

Curiously, no one rose to defend the Emancipation Proclamation *as* a proclamation. Both Lowrey and Henry J. Raymond (in the latter's double capacity as editor of the *New York Times* and chair of the Republican National Committee) were concerned that "to have been technically correct," Lincoln should have decreed emancipation by a military order, distributed through the War Department down the chain of army command, rather than as a civil proclamation handled through the State Department. But until 1873, no rules governed what presidents might use as the means for a presidential pronouncement. *Military orders*, of course, sprang from the president's role as commander in chief, but they operated only within the circumscribed world of the American military. *Executive orders* were civil directives the president issued to parts of the executive branch, but up until Lincoln's presidency, they were often nothing more than an endorsement on a legal brief. And *proclamations* were, if anything, even more humble in stature. The majority of

Lincoln's presidential proclamations were either ceremonial, like Thanksgiving Day proclamations, or routine matters of wartime procedure. (Of the fourteen proclamations Lincoln made before January 1, 1863, six were issued in the first weeks of the war, calling out the militia and the volunteers and scheduling the special session of the Thirty-seventh Congress; two others proclaimed days of "humiliation" and "thanksgiving"; another revoked Hunter's recruitment proclamation; and the rest identified which Southern ports were closed and which ones were now opened under federal occupation.) From time to time, Congress would require a presidential proclamation as the signal for implementing new legislation, as it did with the Second Confiscation Act. But even then, it was the legislation they proclaimed, not the proclamations themselves, that had real importance.[64]

Still, presidential proclamations could on occasion have teeth, especially when they emerged from the few constitutional areas where presidents were granted authority of their own by the Constitution, such as the conduct of foreign policy. (Washington had used a proclamation to announce American neutrality in the French revolutionary wars; James Buchanan, Lincoln's predecessor, had used a presidential proclamation in 1858 to direct the suppression of the "Mormon War" in Utah.)[65] Clearly, Lincoln believed that the Emancipation Proclamation emerged from another of those areas of presidential authority—in this case, the role of commander in chief—and he was correct in understanding that there was some precedent for presidents to issue proclamations in that capacity. (Again, Washington had resorted to a proclamation to deal with the Whiskey Rebellion in 1795, an instance that served as the model for Lincoln's calling out of the states' militia in 1861.) But the long gestation of the Emancipation Proclamation managed to blur the distinctions among the various legislative authorities that stood behind the different kinds of proclamation. The first draft began as an enabling proclamation for the Second Confiscation Act, yet the final sentence, which announced Lincoln's intention to emancipate, made no reference to Congress or the Confiscation Act at all. The preliminary Proclamation of September 22 actually contained a military order within it. Not until the Proclamation appeared in the form of the final draft did Lincoln un-

ambiguously make it an exercise of an exclusively presidential preroga-
tive, based entirely on the war powers.

And what were the war powers? Lincoln insisted that the Constitution's provision for suspending the writ of habeas corpus in times of rebellion or invasion was a recognition on the part of the Founders that
rebellion and invasion created a new constitutional sphere, and within
that sphere, the president's designation as commander in chief granted
him all of the war powers necessary to deal with the emergency. "He
thinks that he will be able to make it clear that he usurps no power by
the Proclamation," T. J. Barnett diligently informed Samuel Barlow. But
Lincoln just as stubbornly contended, against friends of the Proclamation like Lowrey, that the war powers were not a blank check to do anything he liked, including "a great many things otherwise unlawful." For
all that Lincoln knew, those might include the emancipation of slaves,
or, what was closer to the truth, the courts might take the first opportunity the end of the war presented to strike down the Proclamation as a
wholly unwarranted use of the war powers. (They might, for that matter, strike down the entire war-powers doctrine; there simply was no
body of American jurisprudence on the subject to offer any certainty.)
When Charles Tuckerman, a New York financier, argued that Lincoln's
signature alone carried all the authority any measure required, Lincoln
retorted, "Oh, I know that, and so it would be very easy for me to open
that window and shout down Pennsylvania Avenue." Later in 1863,
when Salmon Chase pressed Lincoln to expand the Proclamation to the
rest of occupied Virginia and Louisiana, on the simple strength of an executive order, Lincoln reminded him that "the original proclamation
has no constitutional or legal justification, except as a military measure," and "military necessity did not apply to the exempted areas." For
a president of the United States to fling legal prudence to the wind on
the grounds that he considered something "morally right" would not
give the nation morality, but despotism. "Would I not thus give up all
footing upon Constitution or law? Would I not thus be in the boundless
field of absolutism?" [66]

It is one of the greatest of American historical oddities that the document Lincoln labored so studiously to keep within the bounds of the

Constitution should be the very document his critics exhibit as proof that Lincoln had no regard for the Constitution or else regarded it as somehow spiritually inferior to the Declaration of Independence. True, Lincoln's most famous speeches—starting with the most famous of them all, at Gettysburg—put the Declaration of Independence, not the Constitution, at the center of his political faith. "I have never had a feeling politically that did not spring from the sentiments embodied in the Declaration of Independence," Lincoln said in 1861, and "if this country cannot be saved without giving up that principle . . . I would rather be assassinated on this spot." But it is a far leap to jump from there to the Proclamation and interpret Lincoln—as George Fletcher, Charles Black, Mark Tushnet, and Garry Wills have—as a sort of egalitarian revolutionary, tossing aside the Constitution's concern with preserving individual liberty in favor of the Declaration's pursuit of equality. The mere absence of references to the Constitution in the Gettysburg Address or the Second Inaugural are a poor argument on which to rest a theory about Lincoln's politics (there are, for instance, no references to the Declaration in the Second Inaugural; what case should be made from *that*?), especially when Lincoln had much more to say about the virtues of the Constitution than the legal pundits like to think. "To those . . . who in the plenitude of their assumed powers, are disposed to disregard the Constitution, law, good faith, moral right, and every thing else," Lincoln declared in one of his earliest speeches to the Illinois legislature, "I have nothing to say." His earliest extended political statement, the Springfield Young Men's Lyceum address on "The Perpetuation of Our Political Institutions," from January 1838, closes with a ringing denunciation of the role of "passion" in politics and a call for "general intelligence, [sound] morality" and, in particular, "a reverence for the constitution and laws." In 1838, as a congressman advocating programs of tax-supported "internal Improvements," Lincoln attacked proposals to amend the Constitution as a mistake leading to ruin:

> No slight occasion should tempt us to touch it. Better not take
> the first step, which may lead to a habit of altering it. Better,

rather, habituate ourselves to think of it, as unalterable. It can scarcely be made better than it is. New provisions, would introduce new difficulties, and thus create, and increase appetite for still further change. No sir, let it stand as it is. New hands have never touched it. The men who made it, have done their work, and have passed away. Who shall improve, on what *they* did?

The absolutism that drove William Lloyd Garrison and Wendell Phillips to attack the Constitution as an "infamous bargain" which "shields none but those who wield the cowskin, or who consent with the thief, the adulterer, and the oppressor" was precisely what alienated Lincoln from the abolitionists. "Those who would shiver into fragments the union of these States; tear to tatters its now venerated constitution; and even burn the last copy of the Bible, rather than slavery should continue a single hour," Lincoln said in 1852, "together with all their more halting sympathizers, have received and are receiving their just execration." [67]

Even when Chief Justice Taney's *Dred Scott* decision seemed to suggest that the Constitution actually did protect the extension of slavery into the territories, Lincoln refused to see Taney's opinion as any reason to surrender confidence in the ultimate justice of the Constitution. In his mind, *Dred Scott* was not an interpretation of the Constitution but a perversion of it.

If this important decision had been made by the unanimous concurrence of the judges, and without any apparent partisan bias . . . it then might be, perhaps would be, factious, even revolutionary, to not acquiesce in it as a precedent. But when, as it is true we find it wanting in all these claims to the public confidence, it is not resistance, it is not factious, it is not even disrespectful, to treat it as not having yet quite established a settled doctrine for the country.

Lincoln would call not for defiance of the Court but rather for patience in awaiting a new decision. "We do not propose that when Dred Scott is decided to be a slave, that we will raise a mob to make him free," Lincoln warned his own party during the Lincoln-Douglas debates. "If . . . there be any man in the republican party who is impatient of . . . the constitutional obligations bound around it, he is misplaced, and ought to find a place somewhere else." [68]

Much as he appealed to "this great principle of equality" as the heavy artillery to be used against slavery, Lincoln also added, "Don't interfere with anything in the Constitution. That must be maintained, for it is the only safeguard of our liberties." Nor was he exaggerating for political effect when, en route to his inauguration in 1861, he remarked, "When I shall speak authoritatively, I hope to say nothing inconsistent with the Constitution, the union, the rights of all the States, of each State, and of each section of the country." To do otherwise would be a monstrous instance of precisely the bad faith he had always shrunk from: "I have never understood that the Presidency conferred upon me an unrestricted right to act officially upon" his own "primary abstract judgment on the moral question of slavery." As he explained to the Kentucky editor Albert G. Hodges, his presidential oath bound him to "preserve, protect, and defend the Constitution of the United States" as he found it, not as he wished it to be. Even for the sake of ending slavery, he would not permit himself the flimsy excuse that "I might take an oath to get power, and break the oath in using the power." The outbreak of the war, however, had made necessary the use of certain "indispensable means"—chiefly, emancipation—which might not, under normal circumstances, be constitutional. But he would resort to those means only because they were "indispensable to the preservation of the constitution," and because he could not turn aside from using them without risking "the wreck of government, country, and Constitution all together." And even in his description of the war powers, he rigidly segregated decisions which he believed as commander in chief he needed to take to "best subdue the enemy" in time of rebellion from meddling in "the permanent legislative functions of the government." [69]

Lincoln did "not doubt either" the justice of emancipation or "that it will come in due time." In 1858, he had spoken of his pride "in my passing speck of time, to contribute an humble mite to that glorious consummation, which my own poor eyes may not last to see." But he could not agree with Henry David Thoreau's dictum that "there is no such thing as accomplishing a righteous reform by the use of 'expediency.' " [70] What Thoreau sneered at as "expediency" was for Lincoln prudence, and the kind of prudence that regarded constitutional means as being fully as sacred as abolitionist ends. Prudence drove Lincoln to seek emancipation, not through a righteous imposition that ignored the Constitution as "a covenant with hell" but through a legislative solution; it was precisely his constitutionalism that never allowed any rest to his anxieties that a presidential proclamation based on the concept of war powers might not survive a postwar challenge in the civil courts.

Grateful as he was for the loyalty of Lowrey, Kirkland, and the other lawyers who rose to the Proclamation's defense, Lincoln rarely invoked their arguments himself. Of them all, Lincoln found only the appeal to his presidential oath in any way convincing. In fact, if Lincoln had been as convinced as they were that emancipation really was part of the arsenal of war powers, he would have had no reason not to issue a war-powers emancipation decree at the very outbreak of the war. Certainly, the hostility emancipation faced in Congress and in Northern public opinion had hardly been less in April of 1861 than it was eighteen months later. But Lincoln could not pretend that the Constitution gave presidents plenary powers, even to do good deeds. Even if he embraced with true faith Lowrey's and Bishop's arguments that the Constitution really did equip him with far-reaching war powers, he was nagged by the fear that the courts and the lawyers just might, in the end, decide that issuing proclamations of emancipation was not among them.

If Lincoln had any hope of turning the American legal mind in favor of the Emancipation Proclamation, it would have to be by arguments he fashioned himself, and he would have to be his own best apologist for the Proclamation. And that was the task to which he now turned his no-longer-trembling hand.

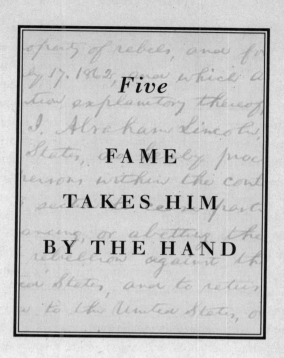

Five

FAME
TAKES HIM
BY THE HAND

*T*HE PUBLIC LETTER—a personal commentary on policy or events, cast in the private form of a letter but intended for official or newspaper publication—had a long history in early American politics, largely because it satisfied two highly contradictory expectations people had of politicians before the Civil War. In a republic, impartial and public-spirited virtue—rather than connections, power, or noble birth—was supposed to govern the character of the elected leaders of the people. Virtue, unhappily, required that those who aspired to that leadership behave as though they didn't, since anyone who wanted so badly to be elected that he would openly campaign for it was probably more interested in power than virtue. The model, held forth in every schoolbook, was George Washington, selflessly laying aside command of the Revolutionary army once the war was done to devote himself to the private life of a farmer and waiting for the call of the people to assume office. But even in Washington's time, the American political landscape quickly developed into a cockpit of conflicting ideologies and parties, and the American public increasingly wanted to know whether a candidate would be a good representative of their ideological or party interests rather than whether he was virtuous. A public letter published in a newspaper or journal allowed a politician to state his interests where everyone could read them. But by masquerading as a letter written to a friend or constituent, it preserved the fiction that the candidate was modestly engaged in a personal conversation, not braying for votes from the housetops. Presidential candidacies had been made and unmade by the skill with which politicians used the public letter, so it comes as no surprise that Lincoln's skill with public letters was second only to his gifts as a public speaker and debater. His reply to Horace Greeley's "The Prayer of Twenty Millions" was a particularly telling example of that skill, since it allowed Lincoln to speak publicly for himself on the pages of the *National Intelligencer*, but as if in a private note expressing only a personal opinion rather than national policy.

Lincoln wrote four public letters in the eight months after the final issue of the Emancipation Proclamation. The first was a brief reply to a series of resolutions passed by a workingmen's convention in Manchester, England, on January 19, 1863. The second was written on June 12, 1863, in response to Erastus Corning and a convention of New York Democrats. A third followed two weeks later, critiquing the resolutions of the Ohio Democratic State Convention. Finally, he wrote the letter of August 26, 1863, to James Cook Conkling and the "mass Union meeting" Conkling had organized in Lincoln's hometown of Springfield. Like the Greeley letter, these four letters were intended to lead independent lives: The Corning letter was republished as a Union League pamphlet to the tune of 50,000 copies under the title *Truth from an Honest Man: The Letter of the President*, while the others were published by Benjamin B. Russell under the title *The Letters of President Lincoln on Questions of National Policy*. New York secretary of state Chauncey M. Depew remembered reading them all with unabashed admiration: Lincoln's "series of letters were remarkable documents. He had the ear of the public; he commanded the front page of the press, and he defended his administration and its acts and replied to his enemies with skill, tact, and extreme moderation." And as one modern Lincoln biographer observes, the public letter became Lincoln's most perfect vehicle "to explain his views, counter criticism, and manifest his humanity." [1]

All four of these letters made at least some arguments in favor of emancipation in some fashion. The Manchester letter was chiefly devoted to wooing the favor of the British working classes, but it nevertheless managed to touch the emancipation base by presenting emancipation as a kind of moral compensation for the sufferings of British millworkers, thousands of whom had been laid off while the U.S. Navy's blockade of the South choked off supplies of raw cotton to British mills. The British ruling classes had no love for the American republic, and it became a point of obsession with abolitionists such as Charles Grandison Finney that the British aristocracy "wish to see our Republick broken up" and would strike hands with disgruntled workers to "take advantage of this great rebellion to try to secure our overthrow" by intervening in American affairs and imposing a negotiated settlement to the war. Even in the face of economic ruin, however, British workers could not be persuaded to make cause with Southern slaveholding; and between January and March 1863, a series of mass demonstrations in Manchester and London cheered Lincoln and his Proclamation. One set of resolutions from a meeting in Manchester dismissed the notion that the Union's war was the workingman's enemy and hailed Lincoln instead for showing that "the victory of the free north . . . will strike off the fetters of the slave."

This was just the view Lincoln wanted to encourage, and when Charles Francis Adams, the American minister to Great Britain, forwarded the resolutions to Lincoln, the president took the trouble to write out a reply for publication in England. The war, he acknowledged, had subjected "the workingmen of Europe" to "a severe trial." It was also true that, in technical terms, the formal cause of the war was a domestic political question—whether "a free and constitutional election" ought to be allowed "to preside in the government of the United States" without interference from the losers—and of no interest to English millworkers with families to feed. But the Proclamation now made it clear that the war was also an attempt by the rebels to overthrow a "government, which was built upon the foundation of human rights, and to substitute for it one which should rest exclusively on the basis of human slavery." For recognizing that, and suffering for it, Lincoln promised the Manchester workingmen that they would have the "admiration, esteem, and the most reciprocal feelings of friendship among the American people."[2]

The Corning and Ohio Democratic Committee letters, which Lincoln published in Greeley's *New York Tribune*, did not actually mention the Proclamation, but they did offer a vigorous defense of the legal principle of war powers on which the Proclamation was issued, and no one who read them would have had any trouble seeing them at least parenthetically as a justification of the Proclamation. The immediate cause for those letters, however, was the arrest of Clement Vallandigham, in May 1863, for preaching disobedience to "King Lincoln" at a political rally at Mount Vernon, Ohio. Vallandigham's seizure was the doing of the hapless Ambrose Burnside, who had been reassigned after Fredericksburg to the more sedate regions of the Department of the Ohio. Spoiling for a chance to redeem himself, Burnside took calculated umbrage at Vallandigham's antiwar rabble-rousing and finally ordered a company of infantry to break down Vallandigham's door in the middle of the night and haul the voluble Democrat before a tribunal of eight Union officers. Vallandigham promptly filed a writ of habeas corpus for himself and was just as promptly waved away by a federal judge in Cincinnati, who pointed out that Lincoln had suspended the writ in the Department of the Ohio and that all determinations about habeas corpus were up to the department commander.[3]

Lincoln found out about the arrest after the fact. But since it was his war powers which the judge invoked against Vallandigham, it was Lincoln who became the focus of Democratic outrage across the North. Both the New York and Ohio State Democratic Committees sent public protest letters, and even Oliver Morton, the Republican governor of Indiana, expressed fears about the wisdom of the seizure. Privately, Lincoln rebuked Burnside, "doubting there was a real necessity for" Vallandigham's arrest; publicly, he realized that he could not undercut

Burnside without undercutting his own appeals to the war powers. So, on June 12, 1863, Lincoln replied to the New York letter, addressing himself to the committee's president, Erastus Corning (the head of the New York Central Railroad, who, it was said, had once offered Lincoln a job as chief counsel for the railroad), and the nineteen "others" who had signed the letter. Two weeks later, he wrote to the nineteen members of the Ohio State Democratic Committee, defending the constitutional legitimacy of war-powers actions.

Lincoln began his argument by making a distinction that he thought was crucial to the understanding of any type of war powers: The writ of habeas corpus was indeed "the great means through which the guarantees of personal liberty are conserved," but the writ was intended by the Constitution only to operate in times of peace. The Constitution made a separate provision for times "of rebellion or invasion," and in those times, a different rule had to prevail, which included "certain military arrests, and proceedings following from them." This situation, Lincoln insisted, "is precisely our present case—a case of rebellion, wherein the public safety does require the suspension" of the writ and perhaps a few other things too.

Of course, it could be argued that Vallandigham's words were nothing more than a political speech—a speech that broke no one's arm or robbed his purse—uttered to a civilian audience far away from any battlefield. But that, Lincoln replied, was not exactly true. To the extent that Vallandigham persuaded "a father, or a brother, or a friend" to convince a "soldier boy that he is fighting in a bad cause" and should desert, he really *was* "damaging the military power of the country" and jeopardizing the "public safety." Arresting Vallandigham—"not for punishment" of his opinions but for the "prevention" of military harm—should therefore lie squarely within the design of the Constitution in providing a separate legal sphere for "a case of rebellion." [4]

It was possible, Lincoln conceded (as he always liked to do), that he was wrong, but that was a matter of opinion that only the end of the war would allow the courts to settle. The New York committee thinks the war powers are "unconstitutional. I think they are not." Even if he *is* wrong, and it turns out the president was not really "the man who holds the power and bears the responsibility" in time of rebellion, then the people have it within their power to deal with him "by all the modes they have reserved to themselves in the Constitution"—namely, a presidential election—and Lincoln declared himself quite willing to abide by their judgment at that time. For now, he asked only three questions of the Ohio Democrats: first, is there "now a rebellion in the United States"? If so—and not even the Ohio Democrats could dispute that— would they agree to do nothing that "will tend to hinder the increase or favor the decrease or lessen the efficiency of the army and navy"? Then, would "each of you" agree to "do all he can" to support "the effort to suppress the rebellion?" Lincoln had them boxed in, because not even the most unconvinced Democrat was prepared to argue that Vallandigham was an asset to the Union war effort. By extension, anything that *could* be shown to be an asset under the rubric of the presidential war powers ought at least to be allowed to pass without hindrance for the time being.

This was an argument about civil liberties, not the emancipation of slaves, but the logic behind Lincoln's dealing with both was identical, especially if the Emancipation Proclamation could be seen as a military asset too. This was, of course, precisely how he had closed the Proclamation—"warranted by the Constitution upon military necessity"—and in his notes for the Corning letter, he originally intended to use the Proclamation explicitly as an example of the kind of "military necessity" that the Constitution permitted under the circumstances of "rebellion." (A preliminary draft of the Corning letter in the Library of Congress has on its cover sheet a note from Lincoln: "Albany letter Manuscript & something about Proclamation.") In the end, the Corning letter was lengthy enough just in its consideration of the Vallandigham incident without adding the complexities of emancipation. Those would have to wait for a public letter devoted entirely to the subject of emancipation and "military necessity."

Lincoln did not have to wait long. The political demonstrations staged by anti-emancipation Democrats in the Illinois legislature that spring put the Illinois state Republican committee to work planning a statewide counterdemonstration of its own, a "Mass Meeting" in

Springfield of Republicans and prowar Democrats who would redeem the reputation of the president's home state for the war effort. The chair of the state Republican convention, James Cook Conkling, was prepared to bring in the biggest Republican artillery he could find as speakers— Radical senators Zachariah Chandler and James R. Doolittle, Union generals Richard J. Oglesby and John McClernand, Governor Richard Yates of Illinois, and former Harvard president and Massachusetts governor Edward Everett. But the attraction Conkling hoped would secure "hundreds of delegates" from "every county" in the state was Lincoln himself. "We intend to make the most imposing demonstration that has ever been held in the Northwest," Conkling wrote to Lincoln on August 14, 1863, six weeks after Lincoln sent off the letter to the Ohio Democrats. "It would be gratifying to the many thousands who will be present on that occasion if you would also meet with them." Lincoln, who ventured out of Washington only on rare occasions during the war, toyed with the idea and then decided instead to send yet another public letter, which he asked Conkling to read aloud to the meeting in his stead.

Much as Conkling was disappointed at Lincoln's decision, the promise of a public letter for the meeting touched off wild speculation that Lincoln was about to make a major policy announcement about emancipation. "President Lincoln has written a letter to the Mass Convention to meet in this city," wrote the proadministration *Chicago Tribune*'s Springfield correspondent. "Its perusal will gladden the heart of every true Union man in the country, vindicate the President's fame and character, and be the keynote of the next Presidential campaign." Or it might, observed the anti-Lincoln *Chicago Times*, include a repudiation of the Emancipation Proclamation and "a statement" of "an amnesty to the great mass of the Southern people."[5] The *Tribune*'s prophecy was actually a political guess, since Lincoln strictly embargoed release of the letter until the day of the Springfield meeting. But it was a better guess than the *Times*'s, because the letter turned out to be Lincoln's most extensive and forthright defense of emancipation since the issuance of the Proclamation itself.

The Conkling letter, 1,662 words long, falls logically into six sections. The first was a simple salutation to Conkling and to the organizers

of the meeting, "my old political friends." It also made an opening political gesture of recognition to loyal Democrats, "those other noble
men, whom no partizan malice, or partizan hope, can make false to the
nation's life." But the ears Lincoln really wanted to fill were those of the
critics of emancipation and especially the legion of complainers who
grumbled that they had supported the war to restore the Union, not to
see it decoyed into a crusade to free black slaves.

"There are those who are dissatisfied with me," Lincoln said simply,
and their dissatisfaction came down to one thing: "You desire peace; and
you blame me that we do not have it." What he asked the dissatisfied to
do at that point was to reflect on how peace could be obtained. "There
are but three conceivable ways." First was to keep on with the war and
"suppress the rebellion by force of arms. This I am trying to do." Could
there be any disagreement with that? "Are you for it?" he asked rhetorically. Lincoln presumed so, but he accepted for the moment that they
weren't, and moved on to suggest a second way to bring peace: "give up
the Union." Were there any takers for that? "Are you for it?" This time,
he presumed not. In that case, "If you are not for *force,* nor yet for *dissolution,* there only remains some imaginable compromise." But could
anyone really imagine from where such a Union-saving compromise
would come? Not from anyone in the South. "The strength of the rebellion, is its military—its army," The president explained, and the rebel
military showed no inclination at all to compromise.[6]

Meeting and dismissing these objections laid open the path to what
Lincoln understood to be the real grounds for "dissatisfaction." He
began the third section of the letter with an accusation: "But, to be
plain, you are dissatisfied with me about the negro." Indeed they were,
and he knew that this "difference of opinion between you and myself
upon that subject" was the issue before which all the other dissatisfac-
tions were little more than smoke screens. Lincoln's gambit at that moment was to turn the debate from a vicious argument about race to a
more imposing argument about the Union. "I certainly wish that all
men could be free," Lincoln wrote, an assertion so disarming that no one
could easily object; knowing that, Lincoln turned the knife deftly on his
critics by adding, "while I suppose you do not." Having cast the emanci-

pation-haters neatly to the disadvantage, Lincoln still protested that he did not propose to make even that an issue: "Yet I have neither adopted, nor proposed any measure, which is not consistent with even your view"—he then added the crucial proviso—"provided you are for the Union."

The strategy of the letter was now becoming apparent: make emancipation a "military necessity" for the restoration of the Union, then let the opposition's professed love for restoring the Union force them into recognizing, or at least acquiescing in, the "necessity" for the Proclamation. Had any of his emancipation policies been anything except services to the cause of the Union? He had not, he reminded them, acted wildly or irresponsibly on the subject of emancipation. "I suggested compensated emancipation; to which you replied you wished not to be taxed to buy negroes." True, federal compensation would have meant using tax dollars to "buy negroes." But this expenditure was only "to save you from greater taxation to save the Union" by means of war. (Corollary: If *you are for the Union*, there was no reason to oppose compensated emancipation, especially when taxation for compensation promised to be far less expensive than taxation for war.) There was, Lincoln knew, a counterargument lurking here, that the Proclamation was *so* radical a gesture that it was itself the principal reason the Union was becoming impossible to restore. "Some of you profess to think its retraction would operate favorably for the Union." But practically speaking, the truth was that "the war has certainly progressed as favorably for us, since the issue of the proclamation as before." (Corollary: If *you are for the Union*, there is no reason to retract the Emancipation Proclamation.) The irony of these protests, Lincoln pointed out, was that all the while "you say you will not fight to free negroes," there were large numbers of emancipated blacks who "seem willing to fight for you." [7]

But for the jurists, like Parker or Curtis, the real question was not whether emancipation was a legitimate "military necessity" but whether the Constitution gave Lincoln the power to resort to military necessities in the first place. "You dislike the emancipation proclamation; and, perhaps, would have it retracted. You say it is unconstitutional." But this, as he had already warned both the New York and Ohio

Democrats, was a matter of interpretation, not constitutional fact. If the Constitution designates the president as commander in chief in time of war, "rebellion or invasion," emancipations of an opponent's slaves should be perfectly within the legal category of military actions allowable to weaken the enemy. "The most that can be said, is, that slaves are property. Is there—has there ever been—any question that by the law of war, property, both of enemies and friends, may be taken when needed? And is it not needed whenever taking it, helps us, or hurts the enemy?" Of course, it was possible to quibble whether such a war-powers dictum as the Emancipation Proclamation should be considered "valid . . . as law." But if it wasn't, there was no use calling for the Proclamation's retraction now, because litigation would find out whatever defects it had in the law's own good time; if, on the other hand, the Proclamation was valid, then what point would be served by retracting it? "If it is valid, it needs no retraction. If it is valid, it can not be retracted, any more than the dead can be brought back to life." [8]

Lincoln would grant this much to his political critics: if they wished "exclusively to save the Union" and not to emancipate slaves, their love for the Union (if really *you are for the Union*) was quite acceptable to Lincoln and should carry them forward with him to the goal of saving it. "Fight you, then, exclusively to save the Union." If he should ask them to fight after that for emancipation, then "it will be an apt time, then, for you to declare you will not fight to free negroes." The joke was that by the time the critics had fought and saved the Union, the war for black freedom would also be over. But while the war was still on, there was no other way to get black help to save the Union than through guaranteeing that freedom. "Negroes, like other people, act upon motives." If, for the sake of saving the Union, "they stake their lives for us, they must be prompted by the strongest motive—even the promise of freedom." Here, Lincoln added ominously, "the promise being made, must be kept." [9] There would, in other words, be no taking back of the Emancipation Proclamation. A pledge of life had to be balanced with a pledge of freedom.

Lincoln was particularly anxious that his declarations about the permanence of emancipation had been clearly heard, so he quizzed Illinoisan Anson Miller about it when Miller reported to the White House later that month. Miller, who had attended the meeting, told Lincoln, "that the passage in the latter which was most vehemently cheered was the one about the colored men; and I quoted it to him: 'We have promised the colored men their rights; and, by the help of God, that promise shall be kept.' When I told him this, he replied, very earnestly, 'Well God helping me, that promise shall be fulfilled.' " [10] The newspapers, like the crowd, also understood what Lincoln was getting at. The *Chicago Tribune* hailed the letter for its reaffirmation of the permanence of emancipation. "It has been feared that even he looked upon his Proclamation as a temporary expedient, born of the necessities of the situation, to be adhered to or retracted as a short-sighted or time-serving policy dictated; and that when the moment for attempting compromise might come, he would put it aside," the *Tribune* editorialized. "The Springfield letter dispels all doubts and silences all croakers. In a few plain sentences, than which none more important were ever uttered in this country, Mr. Lincoln . . . gives the world assurance that that great measure of policy and justice, which . . . guarantees freedom to three millions of slaves, is to remain the law of the republic. . . . God bless Old Abe!"

WAS EMANCIPATION really a military asset? The answer had to be *yes*, if Lincoln's argument for including emancipation among the military necessities was to have any staying power. In the summer of 1863, the jury on that question was still out. For more than a year and a half, a slow leakage of contrabands and fugitives had been trickling northwards into the Union Army's lines, then into refugee camps, and, for a favored few, into freedom in the North. They were drawn mostly from the upper South and the Border, and the agitation they raised among both Northerners and Southerners was greatly out of proportion to their actual numbers. All told, there may have been as few as 60,000 contrabands and other runaways in Union hands by September of 1862, and probably not more than 200,000—in other words, not more than 5 percent of the total number of enslaved blacks in the Confederacy and the Border. Many slaves seized the opportunity of the war's confusion to grab at whatever freedom the circumstances offered, but the halfheartedness of Union generals, the ineffectiveness of the Confiscation Acts, and the simple risks involved kept the numbers of those fugitives few. "Every time a bunch of No'thern sojers would come through they would tell us we was free and we'd begin celebratin'," remembered Ambrose Douglass, a slave in North Carolina. But "before we would get through somebody else would tell us to go back to work, and we would go. Some of us wanted to jine up with the army, but we didn't know who was goin' to win and didn't take no chances."

Soon enough, the fugitives learned that running away might get a slave out of the master's control, but that this was not the same thing as emancipation. Escape from bondage was temporary and could disappear the moment a master showed up with paperwork in his hand, demonstrating loyalty to the federal government and ownership of a slave. Even where white soldiers displayed the best of intentions, blacks knew that they were only passing through and could not always be counted on to come to the aid of slave rebels. "I spose dat you'se true," commented one Georgia slave dryly as Sherman marched to the sea, "but, massa, you'se 'll go way to-morrow, and anudder white man'll come."[11]

The Emancipation Proclamation radically altered this situation. Union soldiers now had the power to declare emancipation, and not just to encourage flight, to slaves across the Confederacy. A column of soldiers passed John McCline's home north of Nashville in December 1862 and urged him to "come on, Johnny, and go with us . . . and we will set you free." Victoria Perry watched "a Yankee come by the house" and call the slaves together so that a Union officer could announce "all we were free. My mother shouted, 'The Lord be praised.' " It scarcely mattered how word of the Proclamation arrived, whether informally along the slave grapevine or more openly, as in the case of James Simms of Savannah, who brought copies of the Proclamation from Virginia to distribute among Savannah's blacks. The superintendent of contrabands at Fortress Monroe was surprised to find "some men who came here from North Carolina" already "knew all about the Proclamation." A rebel prisoner at Fortress Monroe told him "that one of his negroes had told him of the proclamation five days before he heard it in any other way," while others claimed that "their negroes gave them their first information" of the proclamation. One Union soldier believed that "intelligence of 'Massa' Linkum's emancipation proclamation had doubtless reached every Negro household from Mason and Dixon's line to the Gulf of Mexico."

In many instances, slaveowners tried to suppress news of the Proclamation, and some were successful enough that their slaves learned nothing about emancipation until the arrival of Union soldiers or even after the conclusion of the war. When Clara Barton arrived at Andersonville, Georgia, in June 1865, to undertake identification of the Union prisoner-of-war dead, she was surrounded by blacks, "asking me their little questions in their own way, which was to the effect, if they were free." But even the most stringent censorship could not entirely block out rumors and suspicions. In Alabama, Louis Hughes's master tried to suppress news of the proclamation, but word spread from whisperer to whisperer in the quarters. "We knew it was our right to be free," Hughes recalled, "for the proclamation had long been issued." The Proclamation "is well-known by the negroes," warned a Georgia planter, "and is causing some trouble by the bad ones." Slaves on Louisiana plantations staged parties in anticipation of "emancipation day," and one of them told a Union soldier, "We gwine to be Massa Linckum's children new year's morning'!" [12]

Such reports offered at least one proof of the "military necessity" for an Emancipation Proclamation: the social havoc it was bound to wreak all across the Confederate heartland. The *Weekly Anglo-African* tried to measure the impact of Lincoln's decree when it described the Proclamation as "beckoning" the slaves to run for "the dreamed promise of freedom! Bidding them leap from chattel-hood to manhood, from slavery to freedom." And leap they did, as the presidential mandate for freedom triggered a cascade of running away in 1863 that began sweeping off the underpinnings of slavery. "The hopes of freedom, kindled by the emancipation proclamation, paralyzed the industrial power of the rebellion," wrote Secretary of War Stanton in evaluating the causes of Southern defeat. "Slaves seized their chances to escape; discontent and distrust were engendered; the hopes of the slave and the fears of the master . . . shook each day more and more the fabric built on human slavery." Rebel prisoners at Fortress Monroe told the contraband superintendent that the Proclamation "had played hell with them" since the first of January. In the Mississippi River valley, as many as 20,000 slaves took French leave of their masters after the Proclamation was issued, clogging contraband camps in Baton Rouge, New Orleans, Natchez, and Union-occupied Vicksburg. William Seward estimated at the beginning of 1865 that the Proclamation had directly freed 200,000 slaves, and the final total may have reached as high as 400,000.[15]

Even in the areas that were technically exempt, the Proclamation made "the condition of things . . . unsettled, revolutionary, with nothing clearly defined, neither slave nor slaveholder having any rights which they felt bound mutually to respect." Once the Proclamation was issued, the former slave H. C. Bruce noticed that "slave property in the state of Missouri was almost a dead weight to the owner; he could not sell because there were no buyers." Although Missouri was exempt from emancipation, the Proclamation still managed to destabilize slavery even where it remained legal. "All the negroes in this country will run off," predicted a Missouri secessionist at the end of October 1862, "they go in droves every night." In Unionist Tennessee, which was also exempt from the Proclamation, General William S. Smith complained in March 1863 that "whole families . . . are stampeding and leaving their masters." The exasperated general thought that "something should be done to shield our service from the charge of furnishing an Asylum to the Servants of loyal men living in districts not affected by the emancipation proclamation." But Smith had not been able, all through the fall and winter of 1862, to keep "abolition officers from Michigan and other northern states" from telling Kentucky slaves "that on the first day of January next, they are all to be free, and will have a right even to kill their masters who may attempt to restrain them."

Major General Lovell Rousseau wrote to the adjutant general of the Department of the Cumberland in January 1864 that "slavery is virtually dead in Tennessee, although the State is excepted from the emancipation proclamation. Negroes leave their homes and stroll over the country uncontrolled." The commandant of the military district around

Norfolk, Virginia, "told the Negroes in the contraband camp" at Craney Island, "before the issuing of the President's Proclamation, that they were free." He was embarrassed to discover, after the Proclamation was published, that the Norfolk district had been exempted. But when the contrabands appealed to the army surgeon at Craney's Island "to ask him if there was no hope for them," he pointed across Hampton Roads toward Fortress Monroe and asked, "What should you do if you knew that you could become free by going to yonder point." Three hundred "took the hint . . . and went to Fortress Monroe." [14]

The Proclamation would have accomplished enough in wartime terms just by conveying to the slaves a new legal status that banished all obligation to their rebel masters. But the damage wrought by the Proclamation went deeper, like a stake in the heart of slavery's collective psyche, and the dread grew in white Southerners as they beheld around them people who would not consent any longer to be *things*. Black war correspondent Thomas Morris Chester described the Proclamation as a renovation of black humanity. It "protects the sanctity of the marriage relationship . . . justifies the natural right of the mother over the disposition of her daughters, and gives to the father the only claim which Almighty God intended should be exercised by man over his son" and "ends the days of oppression, cruelty and outrage, founded on complexion, and introduces an era of emancipation, humanity and virtue, founded upon the principles of unerring justice."

Whether the Proclamation acted upon someone at once or not until 1865, the word of its coming upset not only the law of slavery but the personal humiliations it fastened on its victims. For male slaves, emancipation meant an emergence into a manhood that slavery had denied them. Freedom was yearned for by some simply "because the treatment was so bad," wrote Louis Hughes, but those who "had looked into the matter" and understood the personal dynamic of slavery looked for a more substantial transformation. They "longed to stand out in true manhood." Aaron Ford, called together with his brothers to hear about "freedom" from his father, remembered feeling a peculiar kind of rejuvenation: "Please me, I felt like a new man." A soldier in the Thirty-ninth Illinois wanted to "try the effect of the President's proclamation" on any slave he met by telling him "to go where he pleased, as he was now a free man." He particularly remembered "one man who very deferentially raised his miserable excuse of a hat and said, 'I'se massa. I feel like a man now.' "[15]

Manhood might be representational, as ex-slaves adopted new names or added on to old ones to achieve a sense of self-respect. "After freedom, when us was told we had to have names," Peter Clifton's father took the last name of his master, Ben Clifton, "and him took dat titlement, and I's been a Clifton ever since." New surnames allowed slaves to copy the way free people identified themselves and so become "clean of slavery." Or manhood might be political: emancipated slaves would be "allowed to express their opinions as were white men." For others, manhood was about claiming gender authority. "As soon as they get free from slavery," one slave remembered, black men rushed to claim families and marriage. "They go before some antislavery clergyman, and have the solemn ceremony of marriage performed according to the laws of the country." Women too saw the reconstruction of family as integral to emancipation. "After we were set free," remembered Victoria Perry, "my mother always wanted to go back to her home at Bradford, Virginia," and because "she had no way to go back except to walk," walk she did, and "we had to pick up just what we could get." Black men and women alike "desired freedom, thinking they could reclaim a wife, or husband, or children."[16]

To experience emancipation was also to experience a liberation from place, whether a plantation or a factory, and that liberation also removed some key underpinnings of Southern resistance. Emancipated slaves flocked to cities, whether Northern cities, beyond the Union lines, or Southern cities once the war was over. One disgruntled Virginian complained at the end of 1862 that "the slaves, seduced from their homes, have flocked in[to] town," and "idle, impudent and thievish," they were "dreaming of freedom by the first of January, and liable to be led to acts of disorder and violence by rabid abolitionists." The slaves' motivation had less to do with finding dimly imagined opportunities or retaliation elsewhere, and more with putting behind them the scenes of bondage. Emancipated slaves "usually speak kindly of their masters and mistresses," but they did not want to be near them. "By no slyness or innuendo, can they be led to say they want to see them." Emancipation meant the ability to move, and to move away. "I's want to be a free man," one ex-slave explained to Whitelaw Reid. "Cum when I please, and nobody say nuffin to me, nor order me roun'." Ultimately, however, mobility came to mean moving to land of one's own. The Port Royal experiment took the first halting steps at carving up the plantations owned by slaveowners and, at the hopeful prompting of Rufus Saxton, selling them off to the slaves who had once worked them. On January 16, 1865, General William T. Sherman issued Special Field Order No. 15, claiming a thirty-mile-wide strip of coastal land from Charleston to the St. Johns River and offering "possessory title" of parcels up to forty acres to 40,000 former slaves.[17]

Nothing, however, would better prove the point of the Proclamation's "military necessity" than an idea Lincoln had at first resisted for fear of its effect on the North and then embraced for the effect it would have on the South. It was spelled out in the Proclamation itself, in Lincoln's promise *to recruit freed slaves into the armed service of the United States to garrison forts, positions, stations, and other vessels, and to man vessels of all sorts in said service.* In July, the Second Confiscation Act had provided Lincoln with the authority to set aside federal and state black recruitment, and seeing that revision as justification enough, Rufus Saxton lunged ahead in August with the project of reviving David Hunter's aborted attempt to enlist ex-slaves as soldiers. As a result, by the time the Proclamation was read on New Year's Day at Port Royal, the first regiment of these volunteers, serving under Boston abolitionist Thomas Wentworth Higginson, was on hand and ready to receive the regiment's colors. There, the first of January was celebrated as a "day of Jubilee." Black soldiers from Saxton's newly organized First Regiment of South Carolina Volunteers threw open their camp to "thousands of the colored people," and the ceremonies were climaxed by a reading of the Proclamation and the presentation of regimental flags to Sergeant Prince Rivers and Corporal Thomas Jordan. "Prince said he would die before surrendering" the regiment's flag, "& that he wanted to show it to all the old masters."

Once the Proclamation was a public fact, Massachusetts and Connecticut opened recruitment for all-black volunteer regiments with white officers, followed by, in May, the establishment by the War Department of a bureau to muster directly into federal service the 138 infantry regiments of what became known as the United States Colored Troops. (The USCT also recruited six regiments of cavalry, fourteen of heavy artillery, and ten batteries of field artillery.) In Louisiana, three regiments of "Native Guards," which had been organized in 1862 as all-black militia units for the rebel state government, turned and offered their services to the Union occupation of New Orleans. The First Kansas Colored Volunteers, recruited privately from Missouri runaways by Kansas senator James Lane, were mustered into federal service two weeks after the Emancipation Proclamation became law.[18]

As Lincoln had feared, Northern whites were no happier at the prospect of armed blacks than they were at the prospect of emancipated blacks. In November 1863, the Second USCT was mobbed in the streets of Philadelphia as it attempted to board a troop train for New York, and on the way northward, the troop cars were stoned. In New York, the Union League offered to raise a regiment of black soldiers. But Governor Horatio Seymour "was . . . opposed to the whole system of using negro regiments." The League was as persistent, though, as Seymour was stubborn, and the governor finally compromised by telling the League to get whatever authorization it wanted from the War Department. The league paid the costs of creating the Twentieth USCT. But its organizers "found pretty soon that our recruits . . . were abused worse than any negroes had been on the plantations, and they were abused by men who wore the uniform of the Army of the United States."

Still, as the casualty lists of 1863 lengthened with the weight of battles at Chancellorsville, Gettysburg, and Chickamauga, white prejudice against black enlistment began to yield to the pragmatic realization that black men were as good at stopping bullets or digging sanitation trenches as whites. "I did not think Mr. Lincoln wise in issuing his proclamation," declared John Brough, stumping Ohio in July 1863 as the Union candidate for governor against Clement Vallandigham. But if "we whip these men down South . . . with their slaves, I had rather do it, than to send any more of our sons and brothers down there." An officer in the Fifth Rhode Island Artillery advised his governor, William Sprague, that if Rhode Island would "offer all possible inducements for the Col. people to enlist," it will turn out to be "an Exceedingly popular thing," because "we can thus build up our Army to any extent & press this war to a speedy conclusion." [19]

What the pragmatists like Brough or the resisters like Seymour dreaded about black enlistment was not merely the mixing of the races in uniform; they feared the political conclusions that inevitably followed the first sight of black men in Union blue. First, black enlistment made the Emancipation Proclamation irrevocable. No one in their right mind could seriously recommend canceling the Proclamation after ordering black soldiers into the nightmare of war. "Every negro regiment of a thousand men presents just one thousand unanswerable arguments against the revocation of the President's proclamation," rejoiced Zachariah Chandler, and "every fight wherein a negro regiment distinguishes itself by desperate valour . . . adds fourfold to their number and weight." Lincoln himself had said as much in the closing paragraph of the Conkling letter: When the war was finally over, "there will be some black men who can remember that, with silent tongue, and clenched teeth, and steady eye, and well-poised bayonet, they have helped mankind on to this great consummation." What, then, would the critics have to say to such men, who had helped them make their own case for the Union and democracy? By the same token, he added, "I fear there will be some white ones, unable to forget that, with malignant heart, and deceitful speech, they have strove to hinder it." [20]

The second conclusion was linked to the first: the sacrifice that earned manhood also earned citizenship. "Once let the black man get upon his person the brass letters U.S.," said Frederick Douglass at a recruiting rally in Philadelphia, "let him get an eagle on his button, and a musket on his shoulder, and bullets in his pocket, and there is no power on the earth or under the earth which can deny that he has earned the right of citizenship in the United States." But that was only the argument Douglass wanted to impress upon whites. For the ex-slaves, Douglass preached enlistment as a necessary part of the emancipation project of reclaiming black manhood. "You will stand more erect, walk more assured, feel more at ease, and be less liable to insult than you were ever before," Douglass wrote that spring. "In defending your country now against rebels and traitors you are defending your own liberty, honor, manhood and self-respect." A Missouri slave, Samuel Cable, enlisted in the Fifty-fifth Massachusetts, and since "I am a soldier now," he wrote his wife that he would henceforward be able to "strike at the heart of this system that so long has kept us in chains." Elijah Marrs caught the contagion of emancipated manhood when he "formed into line" for the first time in the Twelfth U.S. Colored Artillery. "The Orderly Sergeant called the roll, and when he called 'Marrs, Elijah' . . . I felt freedom in my bones. . . . Then all fear vanished." [21]

Indeed it had. "Three colored regiments"—the three regiments of what had been the Louisiana Native Guards—"already organized, have petitioned Gen. Banks to be put in the front rank at Port Hudson, that they may have a chance of removing the stigma of alleged cowardice from their race, & vindicate their rights & abilities as soldiers," George Denison, a Treasury official, reported with amazed satisfaction to Salmon Chase. Nathaniel Banks obliged, so the former Louisiana black militia led six furious assaults on the Confederate entrenchments at Port Hudson on May 27, 1863. Little more than a week later, four under-strength black regiments held a federal fort at Milliken's Bend, Louisiana, with such stubbornness that even the commander of the Confederate attackers had to admit that "this charge was resisted by the negro portion of the enemy's force with considerable obstinacy."

The most dramatic proof of emancipated manhood came in July, when the Fifty-fourth Massachusetts—the premier black volunteer regiment, with two of Frederick Douglass's sons on the muster rolls and the son of Boston Brahmins, Robert Gould Shaw, in command—spearheaded the ill-starred assault on Battery Wagner, which guarded the approaches to Charleston Harbor. "There is a fiery energy about them beyond any thing of which I have ever read," Thomas Wentworth Higginson testified about his men, and even Ulysses S. Grant—a onetime slaveholder—complimented their discipline and their record for having "fought bravely." In time, white soldiers in the ranks joined in the compliments. "I have often herd of men say that they would not fight beside a negro soldier," wrote a private in the Eighty-ninth Illinois after the battle of Nashville in December 1864, "but . . . the whites and blacks charged together and they fell just as well as wee did."

The conclusion he drew was just what Douglass, and Lincoln, wanted all his comrades to draw: "I have seen a great meny fighting for our country. Then why should they not be free." [22]

FRANCIS CARPENTER first had the idea of painting "a historical picture of the first reading of the Proclamation of Emancipation" late in 1863. Wheedling endorsement from House Speaker Schuyler Colfax and from Owen Lovejoy, as well as financial backing from "an old friend who has made a large fortune," Carpenter persuaded Lincoln to sit for the picture, and the artist moved to Washington in February 1864 to begin work, gradually taking over the state dining room in the White House as a studio for an enormous canvas (nine feet by fourteen and a half). He cajoled Lincoln and the cabinet to allow one of Mathew Brady's assistants to photograph them in the postures Carpenter planned to paint them in, then took up a chair in Lincoln's office so that he could sketch the president "listening to the various petitioners." Callers wondered whether Lincoln was wise to conduct presidential business in front of someone who, for all they knew, was a live wire to the newspapers. But Lincoln waved them in: "Oh, you need not mind him; he is but a painter." [23]

From the very beginning, Carpenter was determined to keep the "conventional trappings" of allegorical symbols and classical allusions to an absolute minimum and paint the reading of the first draft in all its "republican simplicity." The only "mingling of fact and allegory" he permitted himself was in the arrangement of the cabinet members around Lincoln. The president sat by himself, slightly to the left of center, and at his right hand, Carpenter placed Chase and Stanton—the most ardent advocates of emancipation. On Lincoln's left appeared Welles and Seward, then Montgomery Blair and Caleb Blood Smith, and finally, the furthest removed, Attorney General Bates—a spectrum of opinion on the proclamation running from the most radical to the most unwilling. There were, Carpenter knew, "two elements in the Cabinet, the radical and the conservative," and Lincoln sat between them, "nearest that representing the radical, but the uniting point of both."[24]

The political message of the painting was subtle, and its impact was muted compared to the acclaim Carpenter's realistic detail earned for him when the painting was finally exhibited in July at the White House. "The Great sensation of the city during the past few days has been Carpenter's picture of 'The Emancipation Proclamation before the Cabinet,' " wrote Lois Bryan Adams, who joined "the hundreds of comers and goers listening to the criticisms of this great work of art." "In your great picture you have succeeded in bringing out and making the faces show their thoughts," Montgomery Blair complimented Carpenter. "You have not sunk the natural in the heroic, a fault so common that it must be difficult for an artist to avoid it." Seward, however, caught the political message all too clearly. Far from the Proclamation's being "the great feature of the Administration," the real work of emancipation was accomplished through the preservation of the Union, Seward objected, and if Carpenter wanted to capture *that* on canvas, he would have done better to have painted Lincoln suspending the writ of habeas corpus.[25]

It was a curious, half-envious comment, and it may well stand for us as the first attempt to interpret the Proclamation for history. Of course, Seward, the raconteur, was notorious for dropping outrageous opinions into discussions to watch how far the ripples spread. Seward smirked to Chase that Lincoln might as well "issue a Proclamation, on the invasion of Pennsylvania, freeing all the Apprentices of that State, or with some similar object." On the day after the final version of the Proclamation was published, Seward told Orville Hickman Browning (who agreed that the Proclamation was "useless" and "mischievous") that the Emancipation Proclamation was purely symbolic. Like the Revolutionary War veteran who "could not rest until he had a liberty pole raised in his village" (despite the fact that he was "as free without it as with it"), wars require proclamations, even though they do their work just as well without them. "What is liberty without a pole?" the old veteran said. "And what," said Seward, "is war without a proclamation?" He flippantly described the Proclamation to Donn Piatt as "a puff of wind over an accomplished fact. . . . The emancipation proclamation was uttered in the first gun fired at Sumter and we have been the last to hear it. As it is, we show our sympathy with slavery by emancipating slaves where we cannot reach them and holding them in bondage where we can set them free." Yet, earlier in the day, wearing his business hat as secretary of state, Seward had also said that "the Proclamation of the President adds a new and important element to the war. Assuming, as I believe, its policy to be an unchangeable one, it is not to be doubted that, sooner or later, it will find and reach a weakness in every nook and corner of the insurrectionary region." In the end, the truth was not so much one or the other of Seward's opinions, or even a midpoint between, but a matter of both at the same time.[26]

Much of what lay behind Seward's apparent sarcasm was his appreciation that many of the Proclamation's principal accomplishments would lie in what it did *not* do. One very big thing it did *not* do was to set off an uprising within the Union armies. Halleck warned Lincoln, Stanton, and Chase that the Proclamation and emancipation "were very distasteful to the Army of the West, and . . . also to the Army of the Potomac," but neither triggered mass mutiny after all. If anything, the Proclamation forced officers and generals who had originally been indifferent to slavery and emancipation to get off their fences and embrace both emancipation and black enlistment. Ulysses S. Grant had been a Douglas Democrat before the war and, through his wife's family, a slaveowner. When he took command of the Twenty-first Illinois in 1861, he was determined to observe all the niceties of Southern property rights and evenhandedly enforced Halleck's General Order No. 3 expelling fugitives and slave hunters alike from his camps around Ft. Donelson. But as Southern military resistance stiffened, so did Grant's inclination toward emancipation, and by the summer of 1863, Grant wrote personally to Lincoln to pledge his support for both emancipation and "arming the negro." William Tecumseh Sherman, too, was an unapologetic racist who, despite the Second Confiscation Act, was still instructing federal troops occupying Memphis in the summer of 1862 to have "nothing to do with confiscation." But by 1863, like Grant, Sherman had become reconciled to the need to "destroy every obstacle, if need be, take every life, every acre of land, every particle of property" to win the war. In 1864, in a dramatic letter published in the Northern newspapers, he announced himself "in favor of universal emancipation," although he never could agree to black enlistment and took only one black regiment with him on his famous March to the Sea.

Union soldiers alternately praised and abused soldiers in the black regiments. George Tillotson, a sergeant in the Eighty-ninth New York, was willing to agree that "the negro is a human being," but in Tillotson's eyes, that only granted blacks "a right to stay on the footstool." Tillotson was amazed when the regimental quartermaster "said he had rather his daughter marry a negro than a white man. For my part sooner than come to that I would see the whole black rase exterminated." But by the end of the war, Union soldiers had come to the point of admitting that "prejudice against color is fast going away, and the negroes . . . will soon prove to the white race that they are not such an inferior race as they have been represented to be." J. C. Williams, an officer in the Fourteenth Vermont, had heard "much . . . about the negro being stamped with the marks of physical and intellectual inferiority," but by November 1862, "what little I have seen of them" around the Army of the Potomac's camps in Virginia "disproves the statement. I find them possessed with intelligence beyond my expectations." One Maine soldier admitted to his sister that "instead of thinking less of a negro, I have sadly learned to think them better than many white men that hold responsible positions." [27]

Another thing the Proclamation avoided doing was forcing the moral and physical catastrophe of mass deportations to African or Central American colonies. "There are some, and the President is among them," complained Radical congressman Henry Winter Davis in October 1862, "who labor under the delusion that you can free the Negroes and send them off at once to a foreign land." But Lincoln had always "objected unequivocally to compulsion." Colonization was to be "liberal" and "not in any sense compulsory." And even though Lincoln went so far as to appoint a commissioner for colonization, James Mitchell, and to circulate a proposal to the English, French, Dutch, and Danes for the use of their West Indian islands as freedmen's colonies, the only plan that actually produced a colony was a harebrained scheme for using Haiti's Île de Vaches, hatched by a speculator named Bernard Kock.

Kock was an entrepreneur who had leased Île de Vaches for twenty years from the Haitian government, and his plan looked to plant 5,000 freedmen there (at the cost to the government of fifty dollars a head) "for the cultivation of cotton, it producing, he says, the best Sea Island in great perfection, two crops per annum, and continuing to produce for ten years from one planting." The most that could be recruited for Île de Vaches were 453 contrabands from Fortress Monroe, who were shipped to the island in April of 1863 and dumped there, under Kock's banana-republic governorship, without shelter, tools, or food. Smallpox had broken out among the contrabands at sea, and by September, rumors of conditions had grown so poisonous that Lincoln sent an investigator, who reported that the contrabands wanted nothing so badly as a chance to escape Kock's petty tyranny and return to the United States. Lincoln sent a steamer to evacuate the Île de Vaches colony in March of 1864, and that was the last anyone heard on the subject from him. "The President has sloughed off that idea of colonization," John Hay wrote with relief, and Congress withdrew any further funding for colonization experiments.[28]

A much more important consequence of the Proclamation that, like colonization, never managed to materialize in the way the pessimists had predicted was foreign intervention. "European intervention—and from England especially—was, at the time when the Proclamation was issued, our most anxious liability," wrote Alexander Twining in 1865, and Lincoln himself was constantly alive to the possibility that "foreign countries might acknowledge the Confederacy" and use the war as an excuse to break up the American experiment in republicanism. That anxiety had been turned by the Chicago ministers' delegation in September 1862 into an argument in favor of an emancipation proclamation, since they reasoned with Lincoln that "to proclaim emancipation would secure the sympathy of Europe and the whole civilized world, which now saw no other reason for the strife than national pride and ambition, an unwillingness to abridge our domain and power. No other step would be so potent to prevent foreign intervention."

Lincoln conceded that there was some truth in the notion that converting the war for the Union into a war against slavery would recruit so much moral sympathy that Europe would never dare to intervene: "emancipation would help us in Europe, and convince them that we are incited by something more than ambition." A major part of his gratitude for the Manchester workingmen's resolutions was their recognition that the war had assumed the outline of a crusade for freedom. But the idea that the Proclamation would work as a kind of talisman to ward off the unwelcome attentions of the British and the French had far less importance for Lincoln than is often assumed. "It would help somewhat," he admitted to the Chicago clergymen, "though not so much, I fear, as you and those you represent imagine." If anything, Lincoln had to fear more that the British would intervene *because* of an emancipation proclamation than that they would without one. So long as emancipation was seen as a "direct encouragement to servile Insurrections," the British government was eager to head off anything that might awaken memories of the racial carnage of the Indian Mutiny. It was, in fact, two weeks *after* Lincoln issued the preliminary Proclamation that William Ewart Gladstone predicted Southern victory to an enthusiastic crowd in Newcastle, while the foreign secretary, Lord John Russell, was so appalled at the appearance of the Proclamation that he pressed for a diplomatic intervention to head off the "acts of plunder, of incendiarism, and of revenge" he was sure would follow emancipation. But the costs of such an intervention, and the possibility that it might give an opening to French adventurism in Mexico, pulled the British back from the brink; it was only over the following year that emancipation gradually became the government's principal rationale for *not* intervening.[29]

Surely the biggest surprise was that the much-predicted race war never occurred, and no one may have been more surprised than Lincoln himself. When Chaplain John Eaton was called to consult with Lincoln about the organization of the contraband camps, he found the president "considering every possible means by which the Negro could be secured in his freedom," and in the context of emancipation, "every possible means" was usually a euphemism for slave insurrection. And there is at least some evidence that Lincoln was privately willing to turn a blind eye to an insurrection that he could not overtly encourage. James R. Gilmore, Lincoln's back stairs to Horace Greeley and the editorial page of the *New York Tribune,* forwarded to Lincoln in May 1863 the proposal of a Tennessee Unionist, Augustus Montgomery, to "induce the blacks to make a concerted and simultaneous rising . . . to arm themselves with any and every kind of weapon that may come to hand." Lincoln was initially inclined to regard the plan as "a hoax," but he also signaled to Gilmore that he "had no objection whatever to your publishing what you propose concerning the negro insurrection," so long as Gilmore did not cite Lincoln as personally authorizing the insurrection. In the end, nothing came of it but some sporadic "outbreaks among the blacks in Georgia and Alabama" in August of 1863. But in February of 1865, Lincoln encouraged Martin Delany to raise a black legion "commanded entirely by black officers . . . to penetrate through the heart of the South" in the fashion of Sherman's March to the Sea and "make conquests, with the banner of emancipation unfurled, proclaiming freedom as they go." This plan, Lincoln assured Delany, was something he had had "in contemplation" from the moment "when I issued my Emancipation Proclamation" and was the reason why the preliminary Proclamation contained the peculiar wording "prohibiting any interference on the part of the army" to any efforts by blacks to achieve their actual freedom.[30]

Even without an armed uprising, Lincoln certainly hoped that the Proclamation would provoke more defections by slaves to the Union lines than had as yet occurred. By the summer of 1864, with George McClellan the Democratic candidate for the presidency, Lincoln was sufficiently disappointed by the numbers of runaways that he proposed to Frederick Douglass a movement "outside the army to induce the slaves in the rebel states to come within the federal lines." As it had been after the Harrison's Landing letter, Lincoln's motive was anxiety over McClellan. Lincoln "thought now was their time," because if McClellan won the election, *"only such of them as succeeded in getting within our lines would be free after the war was over."* Douglass, meeting Lincoln for the second time, was taken aback to discover that Lincoln had "a deeper moral conviction against slavery than I had ever seen before in any thing spoken or written by him." He agreed to "undertake the organization of a band of scouts, composed of colored men, whose business should be somewhat after the original plan of John Brown." But the sudden upswing in Lincoln's military and political fortunes, and his reelection that fall, rendered the plan moot.[31]

Despite the hopes of unappeased abolitionists that "insurrection may spring up in the South against the insurrection there, and in aid of our arms," there was no San Domingue and no Nat Turner. Ohio congressman William Holman thought it was odd, to put it mildly, that "three and a half or four millions of Africans remain right in the very hotbed of this rebellion, with your proclamations cast broadcast over the South inviting them to freedom; nay, your policy urged them to assert their freedom and pledges the nation to maintain it." Yet, "they have remained perfectly indifferent and passive until your Army has reached them, idle spectators of the war." Even Lincoln was a little surprised by black quiescence, "and he frankly stated that he had been disappointed in the blacks, who had not rallied as he supposed they would when the proclamation was issued." [32]

On the other hand, by the end of 1864, the failure of the emancipated slaves to revolt was actually becoming an argument in favor of emancipation, since it demonstrated the restraint and self-control the slaves possessed, even in the face of easy and bloody opportunity. "Nine-tenths of the able-bodied Southern population have been in arms for more than two years" and "the President's Emancipation Proclamation was made public nearly a year ago," concluded Francis Wayland in the *Atlantic Monthly*, and yet none of "the old men, women, and children remaining at home" had been slaughtered, massacred, or brutalized.

What Wayland did not understand was that the slaves failed to rise up not because of some mysterious superabundance of mercy but because the Proclamation had given them what they needed, and they were more than content to let the white armies, along with their black regiments, do the bleeding. "When the negroes can gain nothing by rising against their masters," Joel Prentiss Bishop remarked, "but everything by keeping quiet, they will not rise." This unlooked-for quiescence was, in some measure, helped by centuries of mistrust. Blacks saw no more reason, in the end, to trust Northern whites than they did Southern whites. Thomas Morris Chester explained that "the terrible recollection that fugitive slaves were returned by Union officers, and were made to pass through the severest torture, and the impression which this engendered, that the Yankees would sell them to Cuba," persuaded many slaves that it was better to "suffer the evils they have than fly to others they know not of." [33] But its fundamental root was in the Proclamation itself. Even if the Brahmin lawyers professed an inability to see freedom in the Proclamation, the slaves most certainly had.

THAT SO FEW of the dire things promised for the Proclamation ever came true is a measure of Lincoln's skill as a legal draftsman and his determination to make the Proclamation proof against the political hounds that surrounded it. That feat, real as it is, has tended to overshadow the things that the Proclamation really did accomplish. Lincoln's critics were quick to take William Seward's sarcasm one step further and claim that the Proclamation had never freed anyone at all. "Where he has no power Mr. Lincoln will set the negroes free; where he retains power he will consider them as slaves," said the London *Times*. The Proclamation was mere political gesture, with no real force, "like a Chinaman beating his two swords together to frighten his enemy." But sound and fury were not Lincoln's style, and whatever his personal uncertainties about the legal standing of the Proclamation after the war, no one below the Mason-Dixon Line had any doubts about its efficacy. In time, it would become clear even to the nay-sayers that the Proclamation closed and locked the door on any possibility that slavery could be tiptoed around, or that the war could be fought as though slavery had nothing to do with it. In practical terms alone, Lincoln explained in 1864, trying to adopt "a different policy in regard to the colored man, deprives us of his help, and this is more than we can bear. . . . Throw it away, and the Union goes with it." But it was also a matter of principle with Lincoln. It was bad faith of the worst imaginable sort to "retain the service of these people with the express or implied understanding that upon the first convenient occasion, they are to be re-inslaved. It *can* not be," and what was more important, "it *ought* not to be." But if, by some incredible circumstance, Congress did agree to negotiate an end to the war by backtracking on the Proclamation, they would have to do so without him as president. To abandon the Proclamation, he told Congress in his annual message in December 1863, "would be not only to relinquish a lever of power, but would also be a cruel and an astounding breach of faith. I may add at this point, that while I remain in my present position I shall not attempt to retract or modify the emancipation proclamation; nor shall I return to slavery any person who is free by the terms of that proclamation, or by any of the acts of Congress." He repeated that promise a year later, adding for sharper effect, "If the people should, by whatever mode or means, make it an Executive duty to re-enslave such persons, another, and not I, must be their instrument to perform it." Emancipation was now securely wedged into the war's equation as a sine qua non of victory.

This was not just bluff. Slave runaways from the Confederacy now had a legal claim on freedom and could not be arrested as fugitives or interned as contrabands; every rebel county, every rebel city, and every rebel state the Union armies overran became free territory for at least the duration of the war; prosecutions for violations of the Proclamation went forward in at least two documented cases while the war was in progress. "I hold that this Proclamation did, in law, free every slave in all the region it covered," declared Charles Drake, the antislavery Missouri Radical, and "on the very day it was issued." No one should "for a moment imagine that the Emancipation Proclamation had no force in law," warned the abolitionist Robert Dale Owen. "By that instrument three millions of slaves were legally set free." Their owners across the Confederacy might prevent them from exercising that freedom at that moment. But since when had laws lacked force simply for being prospective? Or for being obstructed by rebels? "It is true," Owen admitted, "that many of these people are working as slaves still; but in the eye of the law, they are freedmen. Our own right to freedom is not better than theirs." Even Montgomery Blair agreed, however reluctantly, that "the proclamation of the President . . . has announced the extinction of slavery." [34]

The slaves certainly had no doubts about the power of the Proclamation. It was from the Proclamation that blacks over and over again dated a conclusive sense of liberation from slavery, even if in practice they remained slaves. "On January 1, 1863," recalled William Henry Singleton, Lincoln "signed the Emancipation Proclamation," and though Singleton himself had to wait until May to find a way to the Union Army, it was still the Proclamation "which made me and all the rest of my race free." Captain Charles B. Wilder, the superintendent of the contraband camp at Fortress Monroe, noticed runaways from as far as North Carolina crowding into the camp who "knew all about the Proclamation and they started on the belief in it." When Richard Hill, interviewed by a Congressional committee on reconstruction in 1866, was asked when he became free, he replied, "When the proclamation was issued"; it was then that he decided to run away from his master in Richmond. Edmund Parsons testified before the same committee that "I have been a slave from my childhood up to the time I was set free by the emancipation proclamation." Daniel Pettis ran away from his master in Huntsville, Alabama, in January 1865 because "under the Proclamation of the President of the United States, I consider myself a Free Man." Even William Thornton, a black Baptist minister in one of the Virginia counties exempted from the Proclamation, still dated his freedom from the Proclamation and considered himself "made free under the proclamation." Whatever the fine print of exemptions, "the negroes [now have] altogether different feelings from those of former times," wrote a federal provost marshal in the summer of 1863, "a spirit of independence—a feeling they are no longer slaves." [35]

Feelings, however, are not admissible as evidence in a court of law. Lincoln did not mean (as John Nicolay remarked) "to rely merely upon" the Proclamation's "sentimental effect," and he never shook off his anxiety that "what the courts might ultimately decide was beyond his knowledge as well as beyond his control." George Julian knew firsthand that Lincoln "doubted his right to emancipate under the war power." For all of his determination not to retract or amend the Proclamation, Lincoln would have no choice but to "abide the decisions of judicial tribunals," even if it meant a protest resignation, and he continued throughout the war to press for a legislative solution in the states, based on compensation and gradualism. "Why can't you make the border State members see it?" Lincoln pressed Missouri senator John B. Henderson. "Why don't you turn in and take pay for your slaves from the Government? Then . . . we can go ahead with emancipation of slaves in the other States by proclamation and end the trouble."

West Virginia, rather than Delaware (as Lincoln had originally anticipated), became the first model for court-proof emancipation, and despite the truculence of the Border staters in 1862, both Missouri and Maryland finally followed the path to emancipation by 1865—a fact that underscores how much Lincoln had to gain by *not* issuing an Emancipation Proclamation and simply letting the war and the lure of compensation wear out Border state resistance. The new Unionist governments of Louisiana, Arkansas, and Tennessee followed suit by February 1865. On the other hand, Kentucky and Delaware remained obdurate. So, with the shadow of the 1864 elections coming over him, Lincoln once again reached for an alternative weapon that might move emancipation forward, despite whatever happened to him politically. When the Thirty-eighth Congress, with its new load of Democrats aboard, met in December 1863, Ohio representative James Ashley proposed both a comprehensive reconstruction plan for the defeated South and an amendment to the Constitution that would universally abolish slavery throughout the Union. Ashley was followed in the Senate by John B. Henderson and Charles Sumner with abolition amendments. In the House, where Democrats had made the greatest gains in the disastrous 1862 elections, the amendment proposal failed on June 15, 1864, rhetorically stomped to death by Fernando Wood of New York, Robert Mallory of Kentucky, and George Pendleton of Ohio, who declared that it was "better for our country, better for man, that negro slavery exist a thousand years, than that American white men lose their constitutional liberty in the extinction of the constitutional sovereignty of the Federal States of this Union." It was yet another reminder of just how far out on the political limb the Proclamation rested.[36]

The failure of the amendment that summer came on top of the descent of the Union armies into bloody stalemates outside Richmond and Atlanta and the nomination by the Democrats of McClellan on a peace platform. Lincoln grew so apprehensive of defeat in the general election in November that, in addition to calling in Frederick Douglass to formulate a secret operation to accelerate slave runaways, Lincoln asked the cabinet to endorse a pledge to "save the Union between the election and the inauguration" by whatever means, since McClellan "will have secured his election on such ground that he can not possibly save it afterwards." But at the end of the summer, a string of Union victories pulled Northern voters back behind Lincoln, and the election instead turned into a landslide referendum for his administration and for emancipation—perhaps not for emancipation as a nonnegotiable requirement for peace, but certainly for it as a legitimate object of legislation and policy. In October, Roger Taney died (killed, as Nathaniel Banks told John Hay, by the prospect of Lincoln's reelection) and Lincoln appointed Salmon Chase as chief justice, simultaneously removing a political thorn from his flesh and securing a majority for the "emancipation policy of the Government" on the Supreme Court.[37]

Lincoln was now ready to twist whatever Congressional arms remained hanging at their sides for the abolition amendment. "Mr. Lincoln had strong hopes, that the constitutional amendment abolishing and prohibiting slavery throughout the Republic" could be resurrected, and he insisted to Edwin Morgan, the new chairman of the Republican National Committee, that such an amendment be included in the Republican election platform for 1864. After his reelection, Lincoln used his Annual Message to Congress on December 6, 1864, to remind the Senate and the House that the "proposed amendment of the Constitution abolishing slavery" had already "passed the Senate" and only "failed for lack of the requisite two-thirds vote in the House of Representatives." The "intervening election" had shown what the opinion of the people was on the amendment, and if the Thirty-eighth Congress did not dredge it up again for reconsideration, then "the next Congress will pass the measure if this does not." If it was simply a matter of time, why wait? "The voice of the people now, for the first time," has been "heard upon the question," and the people's representatives needed to reflect on whether they should follow that directive. On that cue, Ashley went to work, lobbying queasy Republicans and nervous Democrats, backed by Lincoln's promise that "whatever Ashley had promised should be performed." Ashley reintroduced the amendment to the lame-duck session of the Thirty-eighth Congress at the beginning of January 1865. Lincoln himself "left no means unapplied"; he promised judgeships, collectorships, and customs houses to every weak brother in the antiamendment ranks. The disheartened Democratic opposition crumbled. "The wish or order of the President is very potent," one Democrat grumbled; "he can punish and reward," and he did.[38]

When the vote came on January 31, the abolition amendment barely achieved the two-thirds vote constitutional amendments require, but barely was good enough. Nothing in the Constitution requires the approval of the president for a constitutional amendment to be sent out to the states for ratification, but Lincoln signed it anyway, using, as he so rarely did, his full name. He also took the opportunity to sum up in a few sentences his strategy, from 1861 onwards, for blotting out slavery. Lincoln "thought all would bear him witness that he had never shrunk from doing all that he could to eradicate Slavery," he said to a crowd of jubilant serenaders at the White House, and especially "by issuing an emancipation proclamation." All along, he had been fearful that "a question might be raised whether the proclamation was legally valid" or whether the Proclamation alone "would have no effect upon the children of the slaves born hereafter." But a constitutional amendment "is a King's cure for all the evils." It was the ultimate legislative solution. "It winds the whole thing up."[39]

And so it seemed. "I wish you could have been here the day that the constitutional amendment was passed forever abolishing slavery from the United States," Charles Douglass wrote to his father. "Such rejoicing I never before witnessed, cannons firing, people hugging and shaking hands, white people I mean, flags flying. I tell you, things are progressing finely." Looking backward over four years, Robert Dale Owen was sure that racial enmity was passing away: "The whites have changed, and are still rapidly changing, their opinion of the negro." John Forney rejoiced that "social life at the nation's capital has itself been revolutionized . . . In 1857–58 a white man could not safely advocate ordinary justice to a black man." But now, "How wonderful is the decay of prejudices that seemed to be eternal!" In New England, racial segregation in public schools was being abolished; the black lawyer John S. Rock was admitted to practice law before the Supreme Court; Henry Highland Garnet was invited to address the House of Representatives on February 2, 1865, making Lois Bryan Adams marvel, "What less than a revolution could have brought about what has now been witnessed by all Washington— the spectacle of a black man preaching against slavery from the Speaker's desk in the House of Representatives at the Capitol?" [40]

In Philadelphia, Washington, and New York City, racial segregation in streetcars was abolished; civil rights in the form of government hiring, jury duty, and offering testimony equally with whites in court were established by Congress. Illinois, so notorious for antiblack racism before the war and anti-emancipation legislature during the war, repealed its "Black Laws" in 1865 and was the first state to ratify the new Thirteenth Amendment. Even a special homestead act, designed by George Julian to divide up "the plantations of rebels" into "small farms for the enjoyment of the freed-men, who have earned their right to the soil by generations of oppression," was adopted by the House in 1864 and almost made it into the Republicans' "National Union" platform for the 1864 election. In 1865, the bill establishing a Freedmen's Bureau to oversee and protect the interests of the newly freed slaves provided for the sale of confiscated rebel lands to blacks in forty-acre lots. [41]

There remained only the vote. "It seems perfectly clear," wrote one of Lincoln's Illinois acquaintances, Julian Sturtevant, in 1863, "that the universal emancipation of the negro carries with it by inevitable necessity his admission to the full enjoyment of all equality, political and social." For some, this was simply a matter of justice. "Are not these people, then, as fit in all respects to enjoy and exercise the rights civil and political of citizenship, as they whose only qualification is a shade of whiter skin?" asked James McKaye, a War Department inspector, after a tour of the South. "Men born on our soil are Americans, be they black or white," agreed New York lawyer W. W. Broom in *Great and Grave Questions for American Politicians* in 1865, "and are to be endowed with political power, that is permanent." George Boutwell argued that in "a popular government," where political life is based on universal human rights rather than on aristocratic status, it was illogical "to exclude any portion of our citizens from the enjoyment of the elective franchise." No one could speak about equal possession of rights and then practice unequal distribution of them without admitting that "our theory of government is wrong." Besides, the more Boutwell thought about it, the more it appeared that arming the former slave with a ballot was a very effective way of creating a Republican constituency in the Democratic South once the war was over. "The colored people are loyal, and in many States they are almost the only loyal people who are trustworthy supporters of the Union," Boutwell said in a speech in the House in mid-1864. "Will you reject them?" Blacks themselves saw voting rights as the next logical stage of emancipation. "If we fight to maintain a Republican Government," wrote one soldier of the Fifty-fourth Massachusetts, "all we ask is the proper enjoyment of the rights of citizenship." John Mercer Langston warned, "The colored man is not content when given simple emancipation. . . . There is one thing more . . . the free and untrammelled use of the ballot." [42]

So, once the notion of colonization was buried, Lincoln also began toying with the idea of extending voting rights to at least some of the freed slaves. The wall of separation between federal and state jurisdictions still meant that neither he nor Congress had the power of extending voting rights on their own; that was still something the states defined. But as with gradual emancipation, there was nothing to prevent Lincoln from setting out federal bait. In August 1863, he instructed the military governor of Louisiana, George F. Shepley, to begin the process for writing a new antislavery state constitution by creating a roll of "all the loyal citizens of the United States" in the occupied parishes of Louisiana. Based on a lengthy opinion written by Attorney General Bates the previous November, this directive was intended to include, under the heading of *citizens,* "all free persons . . . of whatever color." In a general reconstruction plan Lincoln issued in December 1863, the president required only that new state constitutions include an explicit affirmation of emancipation and loyalty oaths that included the Proclamation, rather than black voting rights. When preliminary elections in Louisiana chose Michael Hahn, a moderate with no eagerness to endorse black voting, as the new free-state governor, Lincoln wrote him a letter, less for the pur-pose of congratulation than to "barely suggest for your private consider-ation, whether some of the colored people may not be let in—as, for instance, the very intelligent, and especially those who have fought gal-lantly in our ranks." Hahn did not take the hint; the state constitutional convention that followed in April obediently eliminated slavery but lim-ited voting rights and public-office holding to whites; all that it left open was a vague possibility that black voting rights might be considered at a future time.[43] Of course, from Lincoln's perspective, in striking out slav-ery and eliminating racial categories in almost every other aspect of pub-lic life, the Louisiana constitution was "better for the poor black man than" the one "we have in Illinois," and Lincoln was willing to live with that for now. Still, he regarded the Louisiana constitution as an inferior article at best. If the so-called Wadsworth Letter of January 1864 can be credited, Lincoln wrote General James Wadsworth (the onetime mili-tary governor of the District) that "I cannot see . . . how, under the cir-cumstances, I can avoid exacting . . . universal suffrage" as the price of the South's readmission to the Union, "or, at least, suffrage on the basis of intelligence and military service," since the black soldiers, at least, have "demonstrated in blood their right to the ballot."

In September 1864, Lincoln commissioned one of his secretaries, William Stoddard, as federal marshal for eastern Arkansas and sent him off with the urging "to get the ballot into the hands of the freedmen . . . in any way and every way you can." To Charles Adolphe Pineton (a French nobleman who traveled with Lincoln during the president's tri-umphal visit to Richmond in April 1865), Lincoln remarked that "the restoration of the Rebel States to the union must rest upon the principle of civil, and political equality of both races." Isaac Arnold hinted at pos-sessing evidence "which I cannot now make public" that Lincoln's "pol-icy would have embraced general, [but] not universal amnesty" for the rebels and "negro suffrage."

John Hay remembered Lincoln saying to him in the spring of 1865 that "a man who denies to other men equality of rights is hardly worthy of freedom." In his last public speech, on April 11, 1865, Lincoln freely admitted that it was "unsatisfactory to some that the elective franchise is not given to the colored man" in Louisiana, and the *some* included himself. "I would myself prefer that it were now conferred on the very intelligent, and on those who serve our cause as soldiers." [44]

The question was not whether Louisiana's constitution was perfect but whether it contained the potential to be made perfect. Rejecting the Louisiana constitution would do nothing but discourage the ex-slaves, as if to say, " 'This cup of liberty which these, your old masters, hold to your lips, we will dash from you, and leave you to the chances of gathering the spilled and scattered contents in some vague and undefined when, where, and how.' " By accepting the progress Louisiana has already made, Lincoln reasoned, "the colored man . . . in seeing all united for him, is inspired with vigilance, and energy, and daring . . . Grant that he desires the elective franchise, will he not attain it sooner by saving the already advanced steps toward it, than by running backward over them?"

Yes, and entirely too soon, in the estimate of one of the crowd who gathered that night at the White House to hear Lincoln's speech. "That means nigger citizenship," the man growled. "Now, by God, I will put him through. That will be the last speech he will ever make." It was the actor, negrophobe, and Confederate agent John Wilkes Booth. [45]

WE KNOW ALREADY where the road beyond this crossing leads. "Reconstruction" is the guilty secret of our history, an immense and shattered promise for which we compensated over almost a century with a determined and energetic forgetting. Virtually from the moment of Lincoln's death on the morning of April 15, 1865, all the possibilities bound up in the Emancipation Proclamation began rapidly to unravel, and within a dozen years, the freed slaves of the South had been recaptured by the ex-Confederate ruling class in a weir of economic dependency, political intimidation, and racial terror.

The regression began with the problem of land, which in turn began with the problem of Lincoln's vice-president and unplanned-for successor, Andrew Johnson. Johnson was a Tennessee Unionist who, as military governor of Tennessee, had managed Tennessee's transition to a free-state constitution; he had gotten the nod to replace Hannibal Hamlin on

Lincoln's reelection ticket as a symbol of Lincoln's willingness to reach out to Southern Unionists in reuniting the divided nation. No one had ever seriously dreamt of seeing him sit in Lincoln's chair, especially after Johnson turned up drunk for the inaugural ceremonies at the Capitol on March 4. Within five weeks of taking the oath, Johnson was reaching out entirely too far to the South, and not just to Southern Unionists.

On May 29, Johnson issued two proclamations of his own, the first of which granted "amnesty and pardon, with restoration of all rights of property, except as to slaves" to all rebels, including the highest Confederate officials, who had only to make "special application" to Johnson to receive "clemency . . . liberally extended." The Sherman Reservation, the confiscated plantations at Port Royal that had been sold off for taxes, the Southern homestead legislation—all were shoved by Johnson's amnesty into the political abyss, and along with them, most of the hope of the ex-slaves to own the land they had worked in bondage for generations. (A Southern Homestead Act would finally be passed by Congress in 1866, but it offered not confiscated rebel property, but poor-quality federally owned land in Alabama, Arkansas, Mississippi, and Florida; in 1876, the act was repealed.)

Although Johnson was the sort of populist not unwilling "to plunder the rich for the benefit of the poor," the *Saturday Review* observed that "his system of redistribution never included the negroes." Likewise, Johnson offered no particular objections to black voting rights, but he offered no particular encouragement for them, either. In the simplest terms, the former slaves were not Johnson's concern. His war had been fought to bring down the slaveowning aristocrats and free the nonslaveholding white yeomanry from their domination, not to emancipate the blacks. "He was, at heart," George Julian bitterly reflected, "as decided a hater of the negro and of everything savoring of abolitionism, as the rebels from whom he had separated." [46]

Johnson's amnesty ignited a political war with the Radical Republicans in Congress that made Lincoln's conflicts with them look like friendly scrimmages. Johnson had precious little of Lincoln's political skills, and it is no wonder he lost as badly and as frequently as he did. But it was no cakewalk for the Radicals, either. With the end of the war, the

Radicals no longer had the wartime atmosphere of crisis and improvisation as their tool for rallying reluctant moderate Republicans into line. "The Republicans were everywhere divided on the question" of Reconstruction, George Julian said, "while the current of opinion was strongly against the introduction of . . . the suffrage question." The moderates now emerged as a restraining influence on both Johnson and the Radicals, punishing Johnson with endorsements of black civil rights in the Fourteenth and Fifteenth Amendments and a celebrated impeachment, but refusing to challenge Johnson's return of rebel property or to convict him after the impeachment.

Wartime moderates carried over into Reconstruction the kind of uneasy agnosticism about the future of the ex-slaves that Samuel Osgood articulated in *Harper's Monthly* when he wrote: "Precisely what is to be done with the negro we do not profess to say . . . How can the nation be one again, with such a barrier as those millions of blacks between the two sections?" Charles Drake, who had risked even more than his neck to promote abolition in Missouri, wanted the ex-slaves to "pass through an apprenticeship" like that of the British West Indies before talking about "the instant right of uncontrolled freedom." William Kimball, writing in what had until recently been a pulpit for emancipation enthusiasm, the *Continental Monthly*, could not bring himself to think even in terms of apprenticeship. "They are simply minors, subjects of the Government, but not a part of the Government," and so "they are necessarily excluded from the highest prerogatives of citizenship." [47]

Against Johnson and the moderates, the Radicals railed in fury. Twenty months after his amnesty proclamation, Johnson's haphazard administration had alienated so many members of Congress that the Radicals were able to seize control of the Reconstruction process from the president's hands and pass two Reconstruction acts, which imposed military oversight over the Southern states and set out procedures for registering voters. In this brief moment of opportunity, pleaded Charles Wilder (who had once been the superintendent of contrabands at Fortress Monroe), the next step should be land redistribution from the rebels to their onetime slaves. "The promises of the Government that land would be set apart for them" were the motives that "cheered and encouraged them in their struggle with destitution." Land ownership guaranteed economic independence, and economic independence alone could guarantee that the ex-slaves could withstand the political pressures that their former masters would try to use to return them to de facto slavery. James McKaye thought it axiomatic that "no such thing as free, democratic society can exist in any country where all the lands are owned by one class of men and are cultivated by another."

But standing firmly to block the goal of land distribution was the Supreme Court, fully as determined to preserve prewar property rights in land (if no longer in slaves) as President Johnson. Beginning with *ex parte Milligan* and *ex parte McCardle* in 1866 and 1867, the Supreme Court began chipping away at the war-powers doctrine. In *Slaughterhouse Cases* in 1873 and *Civil Rights Cases* in 1883 it threw stark restraints around the federal government's ability to protect the freedpeople. Finally, it gave legal sanction to outright segregation in *Plessy v. Ferguson* in 1896. Even though Lincoln had filled Roger Taney's place as chief justice with Salmon Chase, the Court nevertheless managed to do to Reconstruction exactly what he had always feared it might do to the Emancipation Proclamation. He had been right about the legislative solution, after all.[48]

The defeated Confederates made no secret of their surprise or their pleasure. The Radical Republican Carl Schurz, who was journeying through the South to survey Southern conditions, reported that at first the defeated Confederates had been "so despondent that if readmission [to the Union] at some future time under whatever conditions had been promised, it would have been looked upon as a favor." But with the publication of Johnson's amnesty, "new hopes" rekindled in Southern hearts. "I am told by all Union men that after the surrender of the rebel armies, the men returned perfectly quiet," one Union officer wrote to Lyman Trumbull. As soon as Johnson's amnesty put "the control of everything" in the South back into their hands, "at once they became insolent, abused the Government openly . . . drunk with power, ruling and abusing every loyal man, white and black." One Rhode Island officer who leased an abandoned North Carolina plantation and put the plantation's former slaves to work as free laborers was impressed by how "they work well, are obedient, and inclined to learn," but the whites were as "hostile to the Yankees as ever they were."

The ex-Confederates quickly organized new civil governments that conceded the end of slavery, but refused to ratify the Thirteenth Amendment; others passed "black codes" which fastened de facto slavery back onto blacks, and with every passing year, a new weight would be added to the balance—lynching, beating, poll taxes, literacy tests. As one former Confederate treasury secretary wrote, Johnson's plan "held up before us the hope of a 'white man's government,' and this led us to set aside negro suffrage . . . It was natural that we should yield to our old prejudices." [49]

The pardoned rebels, as the sarcastic Southern humorist "Bill Arp" put it, considered themselves "conquered, but not convinced," and among the unconvinced were many who seriously hoped that the death of Lincoln and the end of the war would work a suspension of emancipation. "There seems to be," wrote one Marylander, "an ill-defined belief, a vague hope that, in the revolution of affairs, slavery will . . . be resurrected." Some slaveowners tried to qualify or discount the news of emancipation. "You have been told by the Yankees and others that you are free," warned one planter. "This may be so! . . . But the terms and time of your ultimate freedom is not yet fully and definitely settled." In South Carolina, Johnson's amnesty left Henry William Ravenal "in doubt as to the emancipation policy," and he hoped that if emancipation had to be accepted once and for all, Congress would see that "policy & humanity would dictate" that the Emancipation Proclamation and the Thirteenth Amendment be set aside as the means for it. Still, others tried to conceal the news of emancipation entirely. "We did not hear about President Lincoln's freedom proclamation in 1863," recalled black South Carolinian James H. Johnson. It was not until "General Lee surrendered" that "we learned we were free." [50]

Those Southerners who understood that emancipation was not going to disappear were encouraged by the Johnson amnesty to create forms of labor peonage that would keep blacks in what would remain practical slavery. James Gilmore interviewed a planter in Nashville, "a singularly self-possessed, gentlemanly-looking man, of about fifty," who told Gilmore that he would probably convert his slaves into free wage earners, "set them at work, and pay them." But that did not mean he would regard them as his "social and political equal," or allow them to make any contract they liked with him, or go and work anywhere else. "Freedom of itself, Sir, will not make the black my equal." The best evidence of that was the North. "At the North he is not politically or socially on a par with the white, and there he has had fifty years of freedom."

In Maryland, slavery was abolished in 1864, but it was replaced with restrictions on blacks' freedom to contract with any employer they chose and by the seizing of the children of unemployed blacks and binding them as "apprentices" without the consent of their parents. "Slavery is abolished," wrote William Grosvenor, "but peonage, or some other plan of forced labor, hardly less unjust or dangerous to the nation than slavery itself, is the natural result of the present condition of affairs at the South." The "old master," James McKaye learned, is "still enthralled by his old infatuation" with slavery. Even when former slaveowners "consent to hire them," their attitude toward "their old slaves . . . is by no means friendly . . . Many of them admit that the old form of slavery is for the present broken up . . . but they scoff at the idea of freedom for the negro"; they hoped for the reestablishment of "some form of the slave system" once the Union armies were gone.[51]

The more Reconstruction was turned into an empty gift box, the more blacks protested in confusion and anger. "I wonder if our white fellow men realize the true sense of brotherhood?" asked Susie King Taylor, who had once been a slave at Port Royal. "We thought our race was forever free from bondage, and that the two races could live in unity with each other." But the first principle did not lead naturally into the second, and as she "read almost every day what is being done to my race in the South," Taylor was driven to cry, "Was the war in vain? Has it brought freedom, in the full sense of the word, or has it not made our condition more hopeless?" H. C. Bruce, another ex-slave, thought that simple justice "seems to demand one year's support" for the freed slaves to get an honest start as independent farmers, along with "forty acres and a mule to each." Instead, "four million people" were "turned loose without a dollar and told to 'Root hog or die!' " Black workers in the cities began to organize to resist the imposition of white work rules, and in August 1865, labor conflicts in Charleston broke out into "serious and bloody riots, between white and colored citizens and troops." Savannah dockworkers staged a strike against low wages, and in late 1865, farmworkers in the old Sherman Reservation staged work stoppages to protest the reclamation of plantation land by their former masters. Outside the cities, black laborers who were cheated on farm labor rose in protest against white landowners, "seizing and holding property upon some of the places." [52]

The aid Congress and the Union soldiers offered to the freedpeople was uneven and halfhearted. "Tired, after four years of energetic war, the people (as a people) are not only in a state of torpor, but are rapidly becoming politically too oblivious," sighed New Yorker W. W. Broom. In the South, Unionists and Republican converts played to the votes of newly enfranchised slaves, but all too often their primary interest was in "gaining political power, not social change," and for all the talk of building an interracial Republican coalition in the defeated South, most white Republicans "found the freedmen embarrassing." In Lynchburg, Virginia, federal agents helped local farmers force blacks into signing unfair labor contracts, and across the South, federal military commanders preferred to keep their noses clean by deferring to Southern white advice. As Frederick Douglass sardonically remarked, Northern whites were better at benevolence than justice. The legislation authorizing the Freedmen's Bureau was allowed to lapse in 1872, and one by one other Northern aid agencies ran out of funds or out of energy.

While Congress mandated voting rights for over 700,000 blacks in the occupied South, Northern white legislatures slammed the door on voting for free blacks. A referendum on black voting in Connecticut in 1865 went down to defeat; even in the District of Columbia, white voters decided to restrict voting to whites only. In Philadelphia, whites "were not in favor of anything approaching fellowship with the Negro," recalled Alexander McClure. "It was not uncommon to see both men and women waiting at the corner for a street car and refusing to enter it because they saw a colored passenger within, and the conductors . . . made it a special point not to notice a negro who waited at the street corner for admission." When the Union League of Philadelphia proposed to celebrate the Fourteenth and Fifteenth Amendments with a parade of Philadelphia's African-Americans through the city, white Democrats responded with a race riot that left numerous blacks wounded and four of them, including the black educator Octavius Catto, murdered. The 180,000 blacks who had served in the United States Colored Troops as soldiers were written off as having "fought no battles; or if engaged at all in such, they were trifling affairs." Squeezed out of Memorial Day parades, segregated out of Union veterans' organizations, the black veterans of the Civil War were made to watch the meaning of the war for emancipation erased in favor of celebrations of national reconciliation between Northern and Southern whites. Years later, one former slave bitterly described emancipation as being "turned loose like a bunch of stray dogs . . . No sir, we was not given a thing but freedom." [53]

Yet racism was not universally at fault for the failure of Reconstruction to carry emancipation beyond what John Mercer Langston decried as "the enjoyment of the simplest and merest human ownership." A good deal of that failure arose from a simple inability to anticipate all that emancipation might involve. The "age of emancipation" was the offspring of ideology, not practice, and the result was that none of the great emancipations that took place in the nineteenth century had more than the dimmest idea that emancipation was a process rather than a simple event. Lacking a template for predicting the needs or the outcomes of emancipation, abolitionists across the Euro-American world floundered into the same postemancipation morasses.

Serf emancipation in Russia followed the same painful trajectory as American emancipation by failing to undertake serious land reform, a failure that sowed the seeds for the revolutionary unrest that eventually brought down the tsarist regime in 1917. Slave emancipation in the British West Indies, so carefully planned out in gradual stages of apprenticeship, compensation, and free labor, steadily unraveled as the freed slaves refused to play by the imperial script and turn themselves into productive wage laborers on the sugar plantations.

By the mid-1840s, not even the most loyal of British abolitionists could conceal their disappointment at the economic damage done by the failure of emancipation to live up to the promises of free-labor profitability, and beginning in the 1850s, the British increasingly turned to imported labor from India to produce sugar. In France, the initial enthusiasm of French abolitionists, inspired by the example of the West Indies emancipation, for the abolition of slavery in their own colonies was chilled by the subsequent example of British failure. The Dutch, finding that slave-produced sugar in Suriname was actually 30 percent cheaper than free-labor sugar in the Dutch East Indies, sanctioned the introduction of slave labor to Java; the Spanish in Cuba actually watched the value of slaves climb as mechanization made Cuban sugar production more efficient.[54]

EVEN THOUGH there would be no "forty acres and a mule," it is not clear even from our vantage point that land redistribution would have staved off the failures of Reconstruction. The national Homestead Act of 1862 opened up over three million acres of federally owned land for little more than the cost of staking a claim and paying a registration fee. But the lands the Act put up for settlement in the High Plains were some of the most unpromising agricultural soils in the world, and became the seedbed for political instability, range warfare, and rural poverty for the next seventy years. By contrast, the New Deal did almost nothing to redistribute property; yet, the New Deal is by far the most successful national social strategy of modern times. Unless we are prepared to insist that political rights are mere bourgeois illusions apart from economic power, then Lincoln and his Proclamation actually pushed the boundaries of emancipation further than any other similar emancipation effort in that century. The ex-slaves certainly saw political rights rather than economic justice as their primary goal, and as the historian Eric Foner has written, "uniquely in post-emancipation societies, the former slaves during Reconstruction enjoyed universal manhood suffrage and a real measure of political power." Even in the pit of Reconstruction's failures, over 2,000 black men eventually held public offices, ranging from Hiram Revels (a former slave who was elected to the Mississippi Senate seat once held by Jefferson Davis) and P. B. S. Pinchback (briefly governor of Louisiana) to state legislators, federal marshals, and justices of the peace. Even without confiscation and redistribution of land, black families still managed to increase their share of farm ownership in the South from only 2 percent in 1870 to 21 percent in 1890.[55]

"While it is true that the White people brought our forefathers here and sold them into slavery," wrote Alexander Heritage Newton, "the Colored race has an endless debt to pay their White friends who bought their liberty with their own blood." And among those "White friends," first place invariably went to Abraham Lincoln. "There are four millions of people in this country who now regard Abraham Lincoln as their deliverer from bondage, and whose prosperity, through all the coming centuries, will render tribute of praise to his name and memory," declared George Boutwell four days after Lincoln's death. Even Charles Sumner, who had chided Lincoln without end over emancipation, admitted that a good deal of his chiding was a matter of calculated excess. "I knew him well," Sumner wrote to Lot Morrill two months after Lincoln's assassination, "& saw much of him."

> I think his delays tended to prolong the war. . . . But the victory was won at last, & Emancipation secured. History dwells on results rather than the means employed. . . . the late Presdt. put his name to Emancipation—made speeches that nobody else could have made—& early dedicated himself to the support of Human Rights as announced in the Decltn. of Indep. Therefore, we honor him, & Fame takes him by the hand.[56]

Booker T. Washington, who came the closest of any African-American to being a sort of national spokesman for American blacks in the Jim Crow era, lauded Lincoln in 1891 as "that great man, the 'first American,' " and in his autobiography, he claimed, "I think I do not go too far when I say that I have read nearly every book and magazine article that has been written about Abraham Lincoln. In literature he has been my patron saint." In the 1918 poster *Welcome Home*, a black soldier returning from the First World War greets his family underneath a portrait of Lincoln; the 1919 print *The Emancipation Proclamation* surrounds a central oval of Lincoln with vignettes of black accomplishment. The first African-American biography of Lincoln, William Lilly's *Set My People Free* in 1932, reaches only as far as his inauguration as president in 1861, but all the same, it portrays Lincoln as a lifelong enemy of slavery.[57]

For more than half a century after the Proclamation, African-Americans turned the anniversary of the Proclamation into an emancipation holiday. There was no uniformity in the exact date, since there had been no uniformity to when news of the Proclamation reached the ears of slaves. In the North, April 6, July 4, August 1, September 22, and November 1 were all celebrated for their connections with some aspect of emancipation; in Texas, blacks choose June 19—"Juneteenth"—as their Emancipation Day since the news of the Proclamation was not officially read to Texas slaves until June 19, 1865. What was probably the first of these jubilees occurred on New Year's Day in 1866, when over 10,000 blacks crowded the Charleston racecourse to hear speeches from white Union army generals and African-American ministers. Over the years, Emancipation festivals included parades, barbecues, prayer meetings, sermons, speeches, and invariably, readings of the Emancipation Proclamation. (As late as the 1970s, William Wiggins found that the Atlanta Emancipation celebrations still eagerly recruited readers of the Proclamation. One of the organizers explained that they wanted a "reading of the Emancipation Proclamation so that it is a burning fire for the audience," and "whenever they found a person who would really do it with understanding, it was a great and glorious thing.")[58]

In 1913, the fiftieth anniversary of the Proclamation brought on a rush of black celebrations. A bill to fund a national emancipation exhibition died in Congress after lengthy hearings, but states and cities sponsored a full calendar of events to mark the anniversary. In North Carolina, the Negro Ex-Slaves Association organized a reunion of former slaves; in Richmond, a National Negro Exposition debuted in the summer of 1915; in Chicago, 135,000 people turned out for exhibitions that memorialized Lincoln and the progress of American blacks since the proclamation. James Weldon Johnson composed an ode for the front page of the *New York Times* on New Year's Day, 1913, entitled, "Fifty Years," hailing the Proclamation as the beginning of black freedom:

> *O brothers mine, to-day we stand*
> *Where half a century sweeps our ken,*
> *Since God, through Lincoln's ready hand,*
> *Struck off our bonds and made us men.*[59]

FOR AT LEAST another generation, the image of Lincoln and the Proclamation still exerted a powerful pull on black loyalties. The rise of "Jim Crow" segregation in the South occurred hand in hand with the efforts of Southerners to downplay the significance of slavery, both for the war and for Lincoln, and blacks battled back by keeping slavery, and Lincoln's image as the Great Emancipator, at the forefront of the nation's memory of the war. "There is a belated but persisting view of this great character as a sort of sublimated politician, concerned only with saving the Union," warned Albert E. Pillsbury at Howard University, but this was only the tactic of Southern white racists who wanted to deprive blacks of Lincoln's mantle. "They have studied Abraham Lincoln to little purpose who see in the supreme act of his life any motive less lofty than the act itself." Even the great singer Paul Robeson, at the opposite end of the political spectrum from any latter-day Republican, still invoked the name of Lincoln, in his case as a sort of honorary socialist. In 1951, speaking at the funeral of Mother Bloor, Robeson grouped Bloor "in the tradition of Sojourner Truth, Harriet Tubman, John Brown, Lincoln, Douglass and Thaddeus Stevens," thereby creating one of the most jumbled versions of filiopietism yet seen in America. Little more than a decade later, Martin Luther King Jr., stood on the steps of the Lincoln Memorial to tell of his "dream" of racial harmony and call upon Americans to fulfill the promise of Lincoln's "momentous decree." [60]

But even as King spoke, the disenchantment provoked by the failures of Reconstruction began to bleed into a disenchantment with Lincoln and the Proclamation. No one traced the arc of this disenchantment with greater accuracy than W. E. B. Du Bois. Born five years after the Proclamation in Massachusetts and having earned a Ph.D. from Harvard in 1895, Du Bois felt little need to drape himself in the protective imagery of Lincoln. In 1922, as editor of the NAACP's magazine, *The Crisis,* Du Bois shocked black and white readers equally by describing Lincoln as "a poor Southern white, of illegitimate birth, poorly educated and unusually ugly, awkward, ill-dressed." That he should also be the author of black freedom only showed Du Bois that "he was big enough to be inconsistent—cruel, merciful; peace-loving, a fighter; despising Negroes and letting them fight and vote; protecting slavery and freeing slaves." The subsequent outcry forced Du Bois to recant on the pages of *The Crisis,* but he could not surrender his criticism entirely and warned blacks not to be so naive as to forget that the same Lincoln who wrote the Proclamation had also uttered a string of racist and derogatory comments about blacks.[61]

Once he left *The Crisis* in 1934, Du Bois issued no more qualifications. In a lecture in 1936 on "The Negro and Social Reconstruction," Du Bois mentioned Lincoln as the champion of colonization, not emancipation. In 1952, as Du Bois plunged further into Marxism and pan-Africanism, he mocked the naïveté of believing that Lincoln had any interest in the slaves for their own sake. "The Civil War resulted in emancipation for the slaves, not because the North or Abraham Lincoln fought for this, but because freedom for the slaves whose labor supported the South was the only way to win the war." The only good thing he could say about the Proclamation at the end of his life was that "the task was left unfinished," and that comment he never published.[62]

Du Bois died, an expatriate in Ghana, in 1963, the year of the Proclamation's centennial. This time, unlike 1913, the anniversary arrived under a cloud of bitterness and denial. The long, dry decades of Jim Crow had rendered the Emancipation Proclamation remote, almost impotent, to black minds. The organizer of a symposium on the Proclamation at the University of Chicago wondered sardonically why "there was not a grand and official national celebration of the hundredth anniversary of the Emancipation Proclamation," and answered his own question with another question: "What is there to celebrate?" James Baldwin, in *The Fire Next Time,* advised his nephew that "the country is celebrating one hundred years of freedom one hundred years too soon." The Emancipation Proclamation was only "a technical emancipation" in Baldwin's eyes, so long as the African-American remained "the most despised creature in his country." Martin Duberman's play *In White America* rehearsed the history of black freedom in just the fashion of the 1913 Emancipation pageants, but this time it was a drama of bitterness and unslaked thirst, with no mention at all of Abraham Lincoln.[63]

From time to time, the civil rights movement would still invoke the name of Lincoln. (Roy Wilkins admitted in his autobiography to rubbing the head of a bust of Lincoln that Attorney General Ramsey Clark kept in his office, "as I often did when we were squeezed into an awful corner.") But the leadership of the movement clearly owed its inspiration to other sources. Martin Luther King, Jr., made occasional references to Lincoln and the Proclamation, but his practical ideal was Gandhi. Echoing Du Bois, King described Lincoln the night before his own assassination in Memphis as "a vacillating president" who "finally" decided that he had no choice but "to sign the Emancipation Proclamation." Black historian John Hope Franklin issued a short history of the Proclamation for the centennial that still stubbornly cast Lincoln in the role of Great Emancipator. But Franklin's voice was lost in the fracturing of the civil rights crusade and the breaking away of a Black Power movement that wanted nothing to do with Lincoln, the Proclamation, or anything else white liberals had to offer. As Julius Lester wrote in *Look Out, Whitey! Black Power's Gon' Get Your Mama!* (1968), "Blacks have no reason to feel grateful to Abraham Lincoln. How come it took him two whole years to free the slaves? His pen was sitting on his desk the whole time." Disenchantment now turned into outright denunciation, marked vividly in February 1968, when Lerone Bennett posed the wickedly provocative question, "Was Abe Lincoln a White Supremacist?" on the pages of the black cultural magazine *Ebony*. Student protesters at Howard University at once took up the cry, denouncing "Abraham Lincoln . . . as a reactionary white supremacist" and repudiating any civil rights strategy based on "molding the black student into a strange and pathetic hybrid acceptable to whites." [64]

Bennett spent the next thirty years refining and enlarging his case against Lincoln and the Proclamation, and when it emerged in its fullest form in 1999 as *Forced into Glory: Abraham Lincoln's White Dream*, Bennett indicted Lincoln as a white supremacist who issued the Emancipation Proclamation precisely to head off the real emancipation that abolitionists and blacks were pressing for. Although Bennett's book was scorned and sometimes caricatured by white reviewers, it awakened its readers to what is surely one of the most dramatic transformations in American historical self-understanding in the past century: the slow, almost unnoticed withdrawal of African-Americans from what was once the great consensus of blacks' admiration for Abraham Lincoln. When, a year after *Forced into Glory* was published, Bennett was invited to lecture in Harlem at the Schomburg Center for Research in Black Culture, white participants in the program were visibly shaken, not only by Bennett's violent harangue against Lincoln but by the enthusiastic applause (laced with anti-Semitic comments) of the black audience.

BENNETT'S ACID SKEPTICISM scorches more than just the historical standing of Abraham Lincoln and the Emancipation Proclamation. The withdrawal from Lincoln by African-Americans has moved in step with the emergence of a profound nihilism in the minds of many Americans who see no meaning in American freedom and no hope for real racial progress. At just the moment when the engagement of blacks and whites as Americans has never been more necessary, simply (as William Julius Wilson argues) for the sake of economic survival in the face of devastating economic globalization, and even at the moment when (as Orlando Patterson has reminded us) blacks have never been closer to the goal of economic and civil integration into the American mainstream, the levels of resentment, despair, and alienation over America's racial future have never been higher. Bennett's book was an uncomfortable marker of the depth of that bitterness, funneled at the single largest popular symbol of racial reconciliation in American history.[65]

For all of Bennett's occasional gestures toward "rainbow" politics, the full effect of *Forced into Glory* was contempt—for the American experiment as it has been lived out, and for Lincoln as its badge of hope. Bennett, after all, had no desire to diminish Lincoln's historical stature. "Lincoln is a key, perhaps the key, to the American personality, and . . . what we invest in him, and *hide* in him, is who we are," Bennett acknowledged, and he cheerfully admitted that any book about Lincoln and emancipation is a book "about race, heroes, leadership, political morality, scholarship, and the American Dream." [66] The difference was that Bennett was dubious, if not simply hopeless, about them all, and he saw Lincoln's importance at the vortex of America's racial struggle as a sign of how overwhelming the odds against equality and reconciliation were. If the Emancipation Proclamation was the empty and faint-hearted gesture of an unrepentant racist, then of course the whole history of American racial politics that flows downstream from the Proclamation becomes tainted.

But there was once a time when Lincoln and his Proclamation enjoyed a far more golden importance in the minds of black and white Americans alike. George Boutwell, reminiscing for Allen Thorndike Rice twenty years after Lincoln's death, thought that "Lincoln's fame" would "be carried along the ages" by his writings, and especially the "three great papers . . . the proclamation of emancipation, his oration at Gettysburg, and his second inaugural address." Placing the Proclamation first was not just a slip of Boutwell's pen, since Boutwell was convinced that the Proclamation was Lincoln's greatest document.

If all that Lincoln said and was should fail to carry his name and character to future ages, the emancipation of four million human beings by his single official act is a passport to all of immortality that earth can give. There is no other individual act performed by any person on this continent that can be compared with it. The Declaration of Independence, the Constitution, were each the work of bodies of men. The Proclamation of Emancipation in this respect stands alone. The responsibility was wholly upon Lincoln; the glory is chiefly his. No one can now say whether the Declaration of Independence, or the Constitution of the United States, or the Proclamation of Emancipation was the highest, best gift to the country and to mankind.[67]

The Proclamation, wrote Robert Dale Owen, "forms an era in our national history. It severed the past from the future." It was, according to Isaac Arnold, "of almost divine inspiration," and "indeed the *magna charta of the negro race."* When Lincoln's Tomb was dedicated in 1874, the figure of Lincoln standing before the tomb's obelisk held a copy of the Emancipation Proclamation in its left hand. The first Lincoln statue in Washington, the *Freedman's Monument* of Thomas Ball, captures Lincoln in the act of freeing a slave as he rises from a kneeling position, and eight of the eleven outdoor statues of Lincoln installed in public squares and parks before the end of the century depicted him in various poses with the Proclamation.[68]

One does not have to make the Emancipation Proclamation scripture, or Lincoln a saint, for it to regain the place Boutwell, Johnson, Washington, Owen, and Arnold awarded it. Speaking at the dedication of Ball's statue, Frederick Douglass described Lincoln as "a white man [who] shared the prejudices common to his countrymen toward the colored race." While it was true that "in his heart of hearts he loathed and hated slavery," that was not the same thing as feeling sympathy with the victims of it. "We are at best only his stepchildren," Douglass cautioned; Lincoln "was not, in the fullest sense of the word, either our man or our model." Yet Douglass felt compelled to admit that the Emancipation Proclamation was an act of spectacular political daring, with every promise of being only the first in a series of such acts from Lincoln. In that last public speech on April 11, 1865, Lincoln praised the fledgling Reconstruction government of Louisiana for "giving the benefit of public schools equally to black and white, and empowering the Legislature to confer the elective franchise upon the colored man." By the time of his last cabinet meeting, on the day of his assassination, Lincoln's "expressions in favor of the liberality toward negro citizens in the reorganization" of the defeated Confederacy "were" (according to Whitelaw Reid) "fuller and more emphatic than" at any earlier time. Schuyler Colfax recalled, that on that morning, Lincoln had spoken "with great impressiveness of his determination to secure liberty and justice to all, with full protection for the humblest, and to re-establish on a sure foundation the unity of the Republic after the sacrifices made for its preservation." In the end, his death at the hands of Booth grew directly from that "determination."[69]

Douglass, after all, had come to praise Lincoln, not to bury him. "I have said that President Lincoln was . . . pre-eminently the white man's president, entirely devoted to the welfare of white men." And sure enough, when Lincoln was "viewed from the genuine abolition ground," he naturally seemed "tardy, cold, dull, and indifferent." But this was not the only yardstick Douglass wanted to apply to Lincoln. "Measuring him by the sentiment of his country, a sentiment he was bound to consult, he was swift, zealous, radical, and determined." And so, whatever the failures of Reconstruction, whatever the personal failures of foresight, and whatever the rage of unappeased racial justice, for Douglass at least, Lincoln "is doubly dear to us, and his memory will be precious forever." [70]

So said Frederick Douglass in 1876; true as it was then, I feel sure it will yet be true again for all Americans, black as well as white, for as long as the republic—and the Emancipation Proclamation—stands.

Postscript

FATHER ABRAHAM

HEN HE, HICKMAN was looking up through the calm and peaceful light toward the great brooding face; he, Hickman, standing motionless before the quiet, less-and-more-than-human eyes which seemed to gaze from beneath their shadowed lids toward some vista of perpetual dawn which lay beyond infinity . . . *Yes, with all I know about him and his contradictions, yes. And with all I know about men and the world, yes. And with all I know about white men and politicians of all colors and guises, yes. And with all I know about the things you had to do to be and stay yourself—yes! She's right, she's cut through the knot and said it plain; you are and you're one of the few who ever earned the right to be called "Father." George didn't do it, though he had the chance, but you did. So yes, it's all right with me; yes. Yes, and though I'm a man who despises all foolish pomp and circumstance and all the bending of the knee that some still try to force us to do before false values, yes, and yes again. And though I'm against all the unearned tribute which the weak and lowly are forced to yield up based on force and false differences and false values, yes, for you "Father" is all right with me. Yes . . .*

Ralph Ellison, *Juneteenth*,
edited by J. F. Callahan (1999)

Appendix

THE TEXTS

OF THE EMANCIPATION

PROCLAMATION

1. FIRST DRAFT: JULY 22, 1862

Lincoln's original manuscript is in the Abraham Lincoln Papers, Library of Congress. It is reproduced on pp. 402–4 of Nicolay and Hay, *Abraham Lincoln: A History,* volume six, and can be accessed as an electronic image at the Library of Congress's website, at http://lcweb2.loc.gov/ammem/al-html/almgall.html.

In pursuance of the sixth section of the act of congress entitled "An act to suppress insurrection and to punish treason and rebellion, to seize and confiscate property of rebels, and for other purposes" Approved July 17, 1862, and which act, and the Joint Resolution explanatory thereof, are herewith published, I, Abraham Lincoln, President of the United States, do hereby proclaim to, and warn all persons within the contemplation of said sixth section to cease participating in, aiding, countenancing, or abetting the existing rebellion, or any rebellion against the government of the United States, and to return to their proper allegiance to the United States, on pain of the forfeitures and seizures, as within and by said sixth section provided.

And I hereby make known that it is my purpose, upon the next meeting of congress, to again recommend the adoption of a practical measure for tendering pecuniary aid to the free choice or rejection, of any and all States which may then be recognizing and practically sustaining the authority of the United States, and which may then have voluntarily adopted, or thereafter may voluntarily adopt, gradual abolishment of slavery within such State or States—that the object is to practically restore, thenceforward to be maintain[ed], the constitutional relation between the general government, and each, and all the states, wherein that relation is now suspended, or disturbed; and that, for this object, the war, as it has been, will be, prossecuted. And, as a fit and necessary military measure for effecting this object, I, as Commander-in-Chief of the Army and Navy of the United States, do order and declare that on the first day of January in the year of Our Lord one thousand, eight hundred and sixtythree, all persons held as slaves within any state or states, wherein the constitutional authority of the United States shall not then be practically recognized, submitted to, and maintained, shall then, thenceforward, and forever, be free.

2. PRELIMINARY EMANCIPATION PROCLAMATION: SEPTEMBER 22, 1862

Lincoln's original manuscript was donated for sale as a fundraising premium at the Albany Army Relief Bazaar in 1864 and purchased by the abolitionist Gerrit Smith; in 1865, it was acquired by the New York State Library. It is reproduced on pp. 406–7 of Nicolay and Hay, *Abraham Lincoln: A History*, volume six.

By the President of the
United States of America
A Proclamation

I Abraham Lincoln, President of the United States of America, and Commander-in-chief of the Army and Navy thereof, do hereby proclaim and declare that hereafter, as heretofore, the war will be prossecuted for the object of practically restoring the constitutional relation between the United States, and each of the states, and the people thereof, in which states that relation is, or may be suspended, or disturbed.

That it is my purpose, upon the next meeting of Congress to again recommend the adoption of a practical measure tendering pecuniary aid to the free acceptance or rejection of all slave-states, so called, the people whereof may not then be in rebellion against the United States, and which states, may then have voluntarily adopted, or thereafter may voluntarily adopt, immediate, or gradual abolishment of slavery within their respective limits; and that the effort to colonize persons of African descent with their consent upon this continent, or elsewhere, with the previously obtained consent of the Governments existing there, will be continued.

That on the first day of January in the year of our Lord, one thousand eight hundred and sixty-three, all persons held as slaves within any state, or designated part of a state, the people whereof shall then be in rebellion against the United States shall be then, thenceforward, and forever free; and the executive government of the United States, will, including the military and naval authority thereof, recognize and maintain the freedom of such persons, and will do no act or acts to repress such persons, or any of them, in any efforts they may make for their actual freedom.

That the executive will, on the first day of January aforesaid, by proclamation, designate the States, and parts of states, if any, in which the people thereof respectively, shall then be in rebellion against the United States; and the fact that any state, or the people thereof shall, on that day be, in good faith represented in the Congress of the United States, by members chosen thereto, at elections wherein a majority of the qualified voters of such state shall have participated, shall, in the absence of strong countervailing testimony, be deemed conclusive evidence that such state and the people thereof, are not then in rebellion against the United States.

That attention is hereby called to an act of Congress entitled "An act to make an additional Article of War" approved March 13, 1862, and which act is in the words and figure following:

Be it enacted by the Senate and House of Representatives of the United States of America in Congress assembled, That hereafter the following shall be promulgated as an additional article of war for the government of the army of the United States, and shall be obeyed and observed as such:

Article——. All officers or persons in the military or naval service of the United States are prohibited from employing any of the forces under their respective commands for the purpose of returning fugitives from service or labor, who may have escaped from any persons to whom such service or labor is claimed to be due, and any officer who shall be found guilty by a court-martial of violating this article shall be dismissed from the service.

SEC. 2. *And be it further enacted,* That this act shall take effect from and after its passage.

Also to the ninth and tenth sections of an act entitled "An Act to suppress Insurrection, to punish Treason and Rebellion, to seize and confiscate property of rebels, and for other purposes," approved July 17, 1862, and which sections are in the words and figures following:

SEC. 9. *And be it further enacted,* That all slaves of persons who shall hereafter be engaged in rebellion against the government of the United States, or who shall in any way give aid or comfort thereto, escaping from such persons and taking refuge within the lines of the army; and all slaves captured from such persons or deserted by them and coming under the control of the government of the United States; and all slaves of such persons found on [or] being within any place occupied by rebel forces and afterwards occupied by the forces of the United States, shall be deemed captives of war, and shall be forever free of their servitude and not again held as slaves.

SEC. 10. *And be it further enacted,* That no slave escaping into any

State, Territory, or the District of Columbia, from any other State, shall be delivered up, or in any way impeded or hindered of his liberty, except for crime, or some offence against the laws, unless the person claiming said fugitive shall first make oath that the person to whom the labor or service of such fugitive is alleged to be due is his lawful owner, and has not borne arms against the United States in the present rebellion, nor in any way given aid and comfort thereto; and no person engaged in the military or naval service of the United States shall, under any pretence whatever, assume to decide on the validity of the claim of any person to the service or labor of any other person, or surrender up any such person to the claimant, on pain of being dismissed from the service.

And I do hereby enjoin upon and order all persons engaged in the military and naval service of the United States to observe, obey, and enforce, within their respective spheres of service, the act, and sections above recited.

And the executive will in due time recommend that all citizens of the United States who shall have remained loyal thereto throughout the rebellion, shall (upon the restoration of the constitutional relation between the United States, and their respective states, and people, if that relation shall have been suspended or disturbed) be compensated for all losses by acts of the United States, including the loss of slaves.

In witness whereof, I have hereunto set my hand, and caused the seal of the United States to be affixed.

Done at the City of Washington, this twenty second day of September, in the year of our Lord, one thousand eight hundred and sixty two, and of the Independence of the United States, the eighty seventh.

Abraham Lincoln

By the President
William H. Seward,
Secretary of State

3. FINAL DRAFT: DECEMBER 29–31, 1862

Whereas, on the twenty second day of September, in the year of our Lord one thousand, eight hundred and sixty-two, a proclamation was issued by the President of the United States, containing among other things the following, to wit: [blank space for insertion]

Now therefore I, Abraham Lincoln, President of the United States, by virtue of the power in me vested, as Commander-in-Chief, of the Army, and Navy of the United States in time of actual armed rebellion against the authority and government of the United States, and as a proper and necessary war measure for suppressing said rebellion, do, on this first day of January in the year of our Lord one thousand eight hundred and sixty three, and in accordance with my intention so to do, publicly proclaimed for one hundred days as aforesaid, order and designate as the States and parts of States in which the people thereof respectively are this day in rebellion against the United States, the following to wit: Arkansas, Texas, Louisiana, except the Parishes of [blank space for insertion], Mississippi, Alabama, Florida, Georgia, South Carolina, North Carolina, and Virginia, except the forty-eight counties designated as West Virginia, and also the counties of [blank space for insertion].

And by virtue of the power, and for the purpose aforesaid, I do order, and declare, that all persons held as slaves within said designated States, and parts of States, are, and henceforward forever shall be free; and that the Executive government of the United States, including the military and naval authorities thereof, will recognize and maintain the freedom of said persons and will do no act, or acts to repress said persons, or any of them, in any suitable efforts they may make for their actual freedom. And I hereby appeal to the people so declared to be free, to abstain from all disorder, tumult, and violence, unless in necessary self defence; and in all cases, when allowed, to labor faithfully, for wages.

And I further declare, and make known, that such persons of suitable condition, will be received into the armed service of the United States to garrison and defend forts, positions, stations, and other places, and to man vessels of all sorts in said service.

4. EMANCIPATION PROCLAMATION: JANUARY 1, 1863

Lincoln's original manuscript was donated in October 1863 for sale as a fund-raising premium at the United States Sanitary Commission's fair in Chicago. It was bought by the Chicago Historical Society and destroyed in the Great Chicago Fire of 1871. A reproduction, however, had been made by Benton Lossing for his *Pictorial History of the Civil War* (1868) and is reproduced on pp. 422–28 of Nicolay and Hay, *Abraham Lincoln: A History,* volume six, and can be accessed as an electronic image at the Library of Congress's website, at http://lcweb2.loc.gov/ammem/alhtml/almgall.html. The State Department's printed authorization form, signed by Lincoln and directing the secretary of state "to affix the Great Seal of the United States" to "my Proclamation," was obtained by the Chicago Historical Society in May 2001.

By the President of the
United States of America:
A Proclamation.

Whereas, on the twentysecond day of September, in the year of our Lord one thousand eight hundred and sixty two, a proclamation was issued by the President of the United States, containing, among other things, the following, towit:

That on the first day of January, in the year of our Lord one thousand eight hundred and sixty-three, all persons held as slaves within any State or designated part of a State, the people whereof shall then be in rebellion against the United States, shall be then, thenceforward, and forever free; and the Executive Government of the United States, including the military and naval authority thereof, will recognize and maintain the freedom of such persons, and will do no act or acts to repress such persons, or any of them, in any efforts they may make for their actual freedom.

That the Executive will, on the first day of January aforesaid, by proclamation, designate the States and parts of States, if any, in which the people thereof, respectively, shall then be in rebellion against the United States; and the fact that any State, or the people thereof, shall on that day be, in good faith, represented in the Congress of the United States by members chosen thereto at elections wherein a majority of the qualified voters of such State shall have participated, shall, in the absence of strong countervailing testimony, be deemed conclusive evidence that such State, and the people thereof, are not then in rebellion against the United States.

Now, therefore I, Abraham Lincoln, President of the United States, by virtue of the power in me vested as Commander-in-Chief, of the Army and Navy of the United States in time of actual armed rebellion against [the] authority and government of the United States, and as a fit and necessary war measure for suppressing said rebellion, do, on this first day of January, in the year of our Lord one thousand eight hundred and sixty three, and in accordance with my purpose so to do publicly proclaimed for the full period of one hundred days, from the day first above mentioned, order and designate as the States and parts of States wherein the people thereof respectively, are this day in rebellion against the United States, the following, towit:

Arkansas, Texas, Louisiana, (except the Parishes of St. Bernard, Plaquemines, Jefferson, St. Johns, St. Charles, St. James[,] Ascension, Assumption, Terrebonne, Lafourche, St. Mary, St. Martin, and Orleans, including the City of New-Orleans) Mississippi, Alabama, Florida, Georgia, South-Carolina, North-Carolina, and Virginia, (except the fortyeight counties designated as West Virginia, and also the counties of Berkley, Accomac, Northampton, Elizabeth-City, York, Princess Ann, and Norfolk, including the cities of Norfolk & Portsmouth[)]; and which excepted parts are, for the present, left precisely as if this proclamation were not issued.

And by virtue of the power, and for the purpose aforesaid, I do order and declare that all persons held as slaves within said designated States, and parts of States, are, and henceforward shall be free; and that the Ex-

ecutive government of the United States, including the military and
naval authorities thereof, will recognize and maintain the freedom of
said persons.

And I hereby enjoin upon the people so declared to be free to abstain
from all violence, unless in necessary self-defence; and I recommend to
them that, in all cases when allowed, they labor faithfully for reasonable
wages.

And I further declare and make known, that such persons of suitable
condition, will be received into the armed service of the United States to
garrison forts, positions, stations, and other places, and to man vessels of
all sorts in said service.

And upon this act, sincerely believed to be an act of justice, warranted by the Constitution, upon military necessity, I invoke the considerate judgment of mankind, and the gracious favor of Almighty God.

In witness whereof, I have hereunto set my hand and caused the
seal of the United States to be affixed.

Done at the City of Washington, this first day of January, in the year
of our Lord one thousand eight hundred and sixty three, and of the
Independence of the United States of America the eighty-seventh.

                                                    Abraham Lincoln

By the President;
William H. Seward,
Secretary of State

Notes

INTRODUCTION

1. Marx in *Die Presse*, October 12, 1862, in *Europe Looks at the Civil War*, eds. B. B. Sideman and L. Friedman (New York: Collier, 1962), p. 160; Marx to Engels, October 20, 1862, in *The Civil War in the United States*, ed. Richard Enmale (New York: International Publishers, 1961), p. 258; Dodge, *Abraham Lincoln: Master of Words* (New York: D. Appleton & Co., 1924), pp. 130–31; Christopher A. Thomas, *The Lincoln Memorial and American Life* (Princeton, NJ: Princeton University Press, 2002), pp. 126–27.
2. Hofstadter, "Abraham Lincoln and the Self-Made Myth," in *The American Political Tradition and the Men Who Made It* (1948; rept. New York: Knopf, 1973), pp. 117, 129, 131. On Hofstadter, see Eric Foner, "The Education of Richard Hofstadter," in *Who Owns History? Re-Thinking the Past in a Changing World* (New York: Hill and Wang, 2002), pp. 25–46; John Patrick Diggins, *The Rise and Fall of the American Left* (New York: W. W. Norton, 1973, rev. ed., 1992), pp. 196–97, and *On Hallowed Ground: Abraham Lincoln and the Foundations of American History* (New Haven: Yale University Press, 2000), pp. 24–26.

3. One notable exception is Stephen B. Oates, who declared flatly in a 1976 essay on "Lincoln's Journey to Emancipation," that "I do not agree with Richard Hofstadter's view," even though it was "hugely popular both in and out of the academies." Oates, *Our Fiery Trial: Abraham Lincoln, John Brown and the Civil War Era* (Amherst: University of Massachusetts Press, 1979), p. 137. Another is William H. Freehling, who compares the opening of the Proclamation, where Lincoln "announced 'by virtue of the power in me vested as Commander-in-Chief of the Army and Navy of the United States'" as sounding "not like an entrepreneur's bill for past service but like a warrior's brandishing of a new weapon." See Freehling, *The South vs. the South: How Anti-Confederate Southerners Shaped the Course of the Civil War* (New York: Oxford University Press, 2001), pp. 118–19.

4. Michael Kammen, *Mystic Chords of Memory* (New York: Knopf, 1991), p. 599; Barry Schwartz, *Abraham Lincoln and the Forge of National Memory* (Chicago: University of Chicago Press, 2000), pp. 221–22.

5. Aristotle, *Nicomachean Ethics*, book six, chapters 11 and 12; Thomas Aquinas, *Summa Theologica*, II-I, Q. 57, 65; Emerson, "Prudence" [*Essays: First Series*, 1841] in *Selected Writings*, ed. Brooks Atkinson (New York: Modern Library, 1940), pp. 237–48; Montesquieu, "Considerations on the Causes of the Romans' Greatness and Decline," in *Selected Political Writings*, ed. Melvin Richter (Indianapolis, IN: Hackett Publishing, 1990), pp. 566, 104; Madison, No. 43, in *The Federalist*, ed. George W. Carey and James McClellan (Indianapolis, IN: Liberty Fund, 2001), p. 230; Harry Jaffa, *A New Birth of Freedom: Abraham Lincoln and the Coming of the Civil War* (Lanham, MD: Rowman & Littlefield, 2000), pp. 193–94, 384–85; Ethan Fishman, "Under the Circumstances: Abraham Lincoln and Classical Prudence," in *Abraham Lincoln: Sources and Style of Leadership*, eds. Frank J. Williams et al. (Westport, CT: Greenwood Press, 1994), pp. 3–15; AL, "Reply to Delegation of Baltimore Citizens," November 15, 1861, and "Annual Message to Congress," December 3, 1861, in *Collected Works of Abraham Lincoln*, ed. Roy P. Basler (New Brunswick, NJ: Rutgers University Press, 1953), volume five, pp. 24, 36, 49.

6. William Lee Miller, *Lincoln's Virtues: An Ethical Biography* (New York: Knopf, 2002), pp. 222–23; Thomas Sowell, *The Vision of the Anointed: Self-Congratulation as a Basis for Social Policy* (New York: Basic Books, 1995), p. 105.

7. McClure, *Lincoln and Men of War-Times: Some Personal Recollections of War and Politics during the Lincoln Administration* (Philadelphia: Times Publishing, 1892), pp. 101, 103.

8. Kant, "Fundamental Principles of the Metaphysic of Morals," in *Kant's Critique of Practical Reason and Other Works on the Theory of Ethics*, ed. T. K. Abbott (London: Longmans, 1873), pp. 20, 33; Peter J. Diamond, "The 'Enlightenment Project' Revisited: Common Sense as Prudence in the Philosophy of Thomas Reid," in *Prudence: Classical Virtue, Postmodern Practice*, ed. Robert Hariman (University Park, PA: Pennsylvania State University Press, 2003), pp. 101–103; John Rawls, *Lectures on the History of Moral Philosophy*, ed. Barbara Herman (Cambridge, MA: Harvard University Press, 2000), p. 156; Berlin, *Freedom and Its Betrayal: Six Enemies of Human Liberty*, ed. Henry Hardy (Princeton, NJ: Princeton University Press, 2002), pp. 59–60. The intrusion of the Kantian ethic has now grown into dominance through the work of the late John Rawls. The Rawlsian notion that we should (at least in imagination) divest ourselves of all the privileged experiences and unequal results of our personal history and assume an "original position" from which to determine social justice is not one that grows from "an actual historical state of affairs." In fact, "certain principles of justice are justified because they would be agreed to in an initial situation of equality," Rawls argued, in precisely the same spirit that Kant argued for the mandate of the categorical imperative, as a way of nullifying "the effects of specific contingencies." See Rawls, *A Theory of Justice* (New York: Oxford University Press, 1971), pp. 12, 21, 136, and *Political Liberalism* (New York: Columbia University Press, 1993), p. 23.

1. Four Ways to Freedom

1. David Detzer, *Allegiance: Fort Sumter, Charleston, and the Beginning of the Civil War* (New York: Harcourt, 2001), pp. 187–88; Foster to Joseph Totten, March 12, 1861, in *The War of the Rebellion: A Compilation of the Official Records of the Union and Confederate Armies* (Washington, DC: Government Printing Office, 1881–1906), Series One, volume one, p. 195.

2. Whittington B. Johnson, *Black Savannah, 1788–1864* (Fayetteville: University of Arkansas Press, 1996), p. 153; Clarence L. Mohr, *On the Threshold of Freedom: Masters and Slaves in Civil War Georgia* (Athens, GA: University of Georgia Press, 1986), p. 52; Tucker, "The Great Issue: Our Relations to It," *Southern Literary Messenger* 32 (March 1861), p. 162; "The Southern Confederacy," *DeBow's Review* 30 (March 1861), p. 355; *The South Alone, Should Govern the South and African Slavery should be Controlled by those only who are friendly to it* (Charleston: Evans & Cogswell, 1860), p. 41.

3. Cobb, "Letter . . . to the People of Georgia," in *Southern Pamphlets on Se-*

cession, November 1860–April 1861, ed. Jon L. Wakelyn (Chapel Hill, NC: University of North Carolina Press), p. 97; *The Political History of the United States of America during the Great Rebellion,* ed. Edward McPherson (Washington: Philip & Solomons, 1864), pp. 2–6.

4. Mohr, *On the Threshold of Freedom,* p. 41; Louis Hughes, *Thirty Years a Slave: From Bondage to Freedom* (Milwaukee: South Side Printing, 1897), p. 114; *Slavery in the Clover Bottoms: John McCline's Narrative of His Life during Slavery and the Civil War,* ed. Jan Furman (Knoxville: University of Tennessee Press, 1998), pp. 30, 37; William Wells Brown, *The Black Man, His Antecedents, His Genius, and His Achievements* (New York: Thomas Hamilton, 1863), pp. 175–76; Edmund Kirke [nom de plume for James R. Gilmore], *Among the Pines: or, South in Secession-Time* (New York: J. R. Gilmore, 1862), p. 19.

5. "Henry L. Benning's Secessionist Speech, Monday Evening, November 19," in *Secession Debated: Georgia's Showdown in 1860,* eds. William H. Freehling and Craig Simpson (New York: Oxford University Press, 1992), p. 120; Stephen V. Ash, *Middle Tennessee Society Transformed, 1860–1870: War and Peace in the Upper South* (Baton Rouge, LA: Louisiana State University Press, 1988), p. 66; *The Private Journal of Henry William Ravenal, 1859–1887,* ed. A. R. Childs (Columbia, SC: University of South Carolina Press, 1947), pp. 34, 78; David Brion Davis, *The Slave Power Conspiracy and the Paranoid Style* (Baton Rouge, LA: Louisiana State University Press, 1969), pp. 37–38; Mohr, *On the Threshold of Freedom,* p. 21.

6. Garrison, "Prospectus of the Liberator," *The Liberator,* December 15, 1837; Phillips, "Sims Anniversary," in *Speeches, Lectures, and Letters* (Boston: J. Redpath, 1863), p. 91; Blaine, *Twenty Years of Congress: From Lincoln to Garfield* (Norwich, CT: Henry Bill, 1884), volume one, p. 504.

7. Henry Greenleaf Pearson, *The Life of John A. Andrew, Governor of Massachusetts, 1861–1865* (Boston: Houghton Mifflin, 1904), volume one, pp. 148–49; "The War—How It Began and What Keeps It Up," *The Old Guard* 2 (January 1864), p. 4; *Autobiography of Thurlow Weed,* ed. Harriet A. Weed (Boston: Houghton Mifflin, 1883), p. 614; Forbes, in Dale Baum, *The Civil War Party System: The Case of Massachusetts, 1848–1876* (Chapel Hill, NC: University of North Carolina Press, 1984), p. 75; McClure, *Old Time Notes of Pennsylvania: A Connected and Chronological Record of the Commercial, Industrial and Educational Advancement of Pennsylvania* (Philadelphia: 1905), volume one, pp. 467–68; Cox, *Military Reminiscences of the Civil War* (New York: Charles Scribner's Sons, 1900), volume one, pp. 3–4; "I.N.F.," in H. Clay Reed, "Lincoln's Compensated Emancipation Plan

and Its Relation to Delaware," *Delaware Notes* 7 (1931), p. 41; Kenneth Scott, "Press Opposition to Lincoln in New Hampshire," *New England Quarterly* 21 (September 1948), pp. 326–41; Baker, *Slavery* (Philadelphia: John A. Norton, 1860), p. 15.

8. John Sherman, *Recollections of Forty Years in the House, Senate and Cabinet: An Autobiography* (Chicago: Werner, 1895), pp. 318–19; Albert Gallatin Riddle, *Recollections of War Times: Reminiscences of Men and Events in Washington, 1860–1865* (New York: G. P. Putnam's Sons, 1895), p. 7; Croffut, "Lincoln's Washington: Recollections of a Journalist Who Knew Everybody," *Atlantic Monthly* 145 (January 1930), p. 55.

9. Frederick W. Seward, *Reminiscences of a War-Time Statesman and Diplomat, 1830–1915* (New York: G. P. Putnam's Sons, 1916), p. 69; Conway, *Testimonies Concerning Slavery* (London: Chapman & Hall, 1865), p. 46; Stoddard, *Inside the White House in War Times: Memoirs and Reports of Lincoln's Secretary*, ed. Michael Burlingame (Lincoln, NE: University of Nebraska Press, 2000), p. 144; Robert Stanton, "Abraham Lincoln: Personal Memories of the Man," *Scribner's Magazine* 68 (July 1920), p. 34; French, *Witness to the Young Republic: A Yankee's Journal, 1828–1870*, eds. Cole and McDonough (Hanover, NH: University Press of New England, 1989), pp. 336–37.

10. McPherson, *Political History*, pp. 52–67; David M. Potter, *Lincoln and His Party in the Secession Crisis* (1942; Baton Rouge, LA: Louisiana State University Press, 1995), pp. 89–111.

11. Trumbull, "State of the Union," March 2, 1861, in *The Congressional Globe: The Official Proceedings of Congress, Published by John C. Rives, Washington, D.C.*, Thirty-Sixth Congress, 2nd Session, p. 1382; George Julian, *Political Recollections, 1840 to 1872* (1884; New York: Negro Universities Press, 1970), pp. 179–80, 185, 195; Boutwell, "Slavery the Enemy of the Free Laborer," in *Speeches and Papers Relating to the Rebellion and the Overthrow of Slavery* (Boston: Little, Brown, 1867), p. 59; W. H. Kingsley to J. R. Doolittle, January 26, 1860, in James Rood Doolittle Papers, New York Public Library; Chase to Whittier, November 23, 1860, in *The Salmon P. Chase Papers*, ed. John Niven et al. (Kent, OH: Kent State University Press, 1996), volume three, pp. 35–36; Chase to August Belmont, May 30, 1868, in *Letters, Speeches and Addresses of August Belmont* (New York: privately printed, 1890), p. 115.

12. Welles, *Lincoln and Seward: Remarks upon the Memorial Address of Chas. Francis Adams* (New York: Sheldon & Co., 1874), pp. 11–12; James M. Scovel, "Recollections of Lincoln and Seward," *Overland Monthly* 38 (October 1901), p. 266.

13. AL, "To Joshua F. Speed," August 24, 1855, and "Speech in Springfield," October 30, 1858, in *C.W.*, volume two, p. 323, and volume three, p. 334; AL, in *Inside Lincoln's White House: The Complete Civil War Diary of John Hay*, eds. Michael Burlingame and J. R. T. Ettlinger (Carbondale: Southern Illinois University Press, 1997), p. 218.

14. AL, "Protest in Illinois Legislature on Slavery," March 3, 1837, in *C.W.*, volume one, p. 75; Michael Burlingame, "The 1837 Lincoln-Stone Protest against Slavery Reconsidered," in *The Annual Lincoln Colloquium: Papers from the Thirteenth and Fourteenth Annual Lincoln Colloquia* (Springfield, IL: Lincoln National Home Historic Site, 2000), pp. 57–64; Roll and Taussig, in *Recollected Words of Abraham Lincoln*, eds. Don and Virginia Fehrenbacher (Stanford, CA: Stanford University Press, 1996), pp. 383, 433, 442, 443; Charles Maltby, *The Life and Public Services of Abraham Lincoln* (Los Angeles: Gilchrist Printing House, 1884), pp. 32–33; AL, "Speech at Peoria, Illinois," October 16, 1854, and "To Horace Greeley," March 24, 1862, in *C.W.*, volume two, p. 255, and volume five, p. 169.

15. *The Law Practice of Abraham Lincoln: Complete Documentary Edition*, ed. Martha Benner et al. (Urbana: University of Illinois Press, 2000); Mark E. Steiner, "Abraham Lincoln and the Antebellum Legal Profession," unpublished Ph.D. dissertation, University of Houston, 1993, chapter five; Daniel W. Stowell, "Abraham Lincoln and the Law of Slavery," unpublished paper, read at the Jefferson National Expansion Memorial, 2000; Albert Beveridge, *Abraham Lincoln, 1809–1858* (Boston: Houghton Mifflin, 1928), volume one, pp. 392–97.

16. AL, "Speech in Springfield," October 30, 1858, in *C.W.*, volume three, p. 334; J. L. M. Curry, "The Perils and Duty of the South," in *Southern Pamphlets on Secession*, p. 42; AL, in *Inside Lincoln's White House*, p. 218; Paul Verduin, "Partners for Emancipation: New Light on Lincoln, Joshua Giddings, and the Push to End Slavery in the District of Columbia, 1848–49," unpublished manuscript for the Lincoln Home National Historic Site, 1999, p. 4.

17. Douglass, "The Inaugural Address," *Frederick Douglass: Selected Speeches and Writings*, eds. P. Foner and Y. Taylor (Chicago, IL: Lawrence Hill Books, 1999), pp. 433, 435; Arnold, *The History of Abraham Lincoln and the Overthrow of Slavery* (Chicago: Clarke & Co., 1866), pp. 300, 685–86; Speed to Herndon, February 7, 1866, and Gillespie to Herndon, December 8, 1866, in *Herndon's Informants: Letters, Interviews, and Statements about Abraham Lincoln*, eds. Douglas L. Wilson and Rodney O. Davis (Urbana, IL: University of Illinois Press, 1998), pp. 197, 507; Boutwell, "Abraham Lincoln," in *Speeches and Papers Relating to the Rebellion*, p. 362.

18. George Anastaplo, "Slavery and the Federal Convention of 1787," in *Abraham Lincoln: A Constitutional Biography* (Lanham, MD: Rowman and Littlefield, 1999), pp. 61, 66; AL, "Speech at Elwood, Kansas," November 30, 1859, in *C.W.,* volume three, p. 496, and "Speech in Indianapolis," September 19, 1859, in *C.W.,* volume three, p. 465; AL, "First Joint Debate at Ottawa" in *The Lincoln-Douglas Debates,* ed. Harold Holzer (New York: Holt, 1993), pp. 76–77; Gilbert J. Greene, in *Recollected Words,* p. 183; Eric Foner, *Free Soil, Free Labor, Free Men: The Ideology of the Republican Party before the Civil War* (New York: Oxford University Press, 1970), pp. 75–76. Lincoln was echoed in his view of the Constitution as an antislavery document by Robert C. Winthrop, the Massachusetts Whig and onetime Speaker of the House; see "The Admission of California and the Adjustment of the Slavery Question" and "The Annexation of Texas" in *Addresses and Speeches on Various Occasions* (Boston: Little, Brown, 1852), pp. 450–51, 672–73.

19. Phillips, in Ralph Korngold, *Two Friends of Man: The Story of William Lloyd Garrison and Wendell Phillips and Their Relationship with Abraham Lincoln* (Boston: Little, Brown, 1950), p. 269; Thayer and Kelley, in *Inside Lincoln's White House,* p. 322; Browne, in *Recollected Words,* p. 61.

20. Julian, *Political Recollections,* p. 187; AL, "First Inaugural Address—Final Text," in *C.W.,* volume four, pp. 262, 263, 266, 268–69, 271.

21. Swett, in Herndon, *Herndon's Life of Lincoln: The History and Personal Recollections of Abraham Lincoln as Originally Written by William H. Herndon and Jesse W. Weik,* ed. Paul M. Angle (1942; New York: Da Capo Press, 1983), p. 270; see also Henry C. Whitney to Herndon, August 29, 1887, in *Herndon's Informants,* pp. 635–36.

22. Pelletan, *An Address to King Cotton* (New York: W. C. Bryant, 1863), p. 16; *Private Journal of Henry William Ravenal,* p. 55; Stowe, in Lyde Cullen Sizer, *The Political Work of Northern Women Writers and the Civil War, 1850–1872* (Chapel Hill, NC: University of North Carolina Press, 2000), p. 72; Wendy F. Hamand, " 'No Voice from England': Mrs. Stowe, Mr. Lincoln, and the British in the Civil War," *New England Quarterly* 61 (March 1988), pp. 5–6. From afar, John Stuart Mill made the same shrewd observation: Although Lincoln and the Republicans were not abolitionists, they were still "a Free-soil party." By forbidding the extension of slavery, the day of the Republican triumph was "the day of its doom. The slave-owners know this, and it is the cause of their fury." Mill, with startling prescience, predicted that if the war lasted longer than a few months, "it will have assumed a complete anti-slavery character," probably by the summer of 1862. See

Mill, "The Contest in America," *Harper's Monthly Magazine* 24 (April 1862), p. 680.

23. *O.R.*, Series One, volume two, p. 1007, volume five, pp. 339–40, volume forty-seven (part two), p. 184; and Series Four, volume one, p. 1139, volume two, pp. 222, 394, 841, and volume three, pp. 208, 1115; *Life and Public Services of Major-General Butler, the Hero of New Orleans* (Philadelphia: T. B. Peterson & Brothers, 1864), pp. 49–53.

24. "The Contrabands at Fortress Monroe," *Atlantic Monthly* 8 (November 1861), pp. 626–27; Robert F. Engs, *Freedom's First Generation: Black Hampton, Virginia, 1861–1890* (Philadelphia: University of Pennsylvania Press, 1979), pp. 18–22; Butler to Lt. Gen. Winfield Scott, May 27, 1861, in *O.R.*, Series Two, volume one, p. 754; Midori Takagi, *Rearing Wolves to Our Own Destruction: Slavery in Richmond, Virginia, 1782–1865* (Charlottesville, VA: University of Virginia Press, 1999), pp. 128–30; Johnson, *Black Savannah*, pp. 158–61; Freehling, *The South vs. the South*, p. 90; Mohr, *On the Threshold of Freedom*, pp. 140, 146, 151, 159; Alice Fahs, *The Imagined Civil War: Popular Literature of the North and South, 1861–1865* (Chapel Hill, NC: University of North Carolina Press, 2001), p. 152; Henry Wheaton, *Elements of International Law with a Sketch of the History of the Subject*, ed. Richard Henry Dana (1836; Buffalo, NY: William S. Hein, 1995), pp. 510–11; Herman Belz, "Protection of Personal Liberty in Republican Emancipation Legislation," in *Abraham Lincoln, Constitutionalism, and Equal Rights in the Civil War Era* (New York: Fordham University Press, 1998), pp. 103–104; Arnold, *Lincoln and the Overthrow of Slavery*, p. 212.

25. Louis S. Gerteis, *From Contraband to Freedman: Federal Policy toward Southern Blacks, 1861–1865* (Westport, CT: Greenwood Press, 1973), pp. 15–16.

26. Cameron to Butler, May 30, 1861, Gen. Robert Schenck to Col. James B. Fry, July 6, 1861, and Col. A. D. McCook to Capt. Donn Piatt, July 5, 1861, in *O.R.*, Series Two, volume one, pp. 754–59; Allan Johnston, *Surviving Freedom: The Black Community of Washington, D.C., 1860–1880* (New York: Garland Publishing, 1993), p. 115; Calvert to AL, August 3, 1861, in Abraham Lincoln Papers, Library of Congress.

27. Owner, diary entry for March 7, 1862, William Owner manuscript diary, Library of Congress; AL, "To Orville H. Browning," September 22, 1861, in *C.W.*, volume four, p. 532; Davis to George D. Prentice, April 28, 1861, in *Recollected Words*, pp. 133–34; Hay, diary entry, August 22, 1861, in *Inside Lincoln's White House*, p. 24.

28. Allan G. Bogue, *The Congressman's Civil War* (New York: Cambridge University Press, 1989), pp. xiv, 121–32; Allan G. Bogue, *The Earnest Men: Republicans of the Civil War Senate* (Ithaca, NY: Cornell University Press, 1981), pp. 49, 101, 109–110, 120; Leonard Curry, "Congressional Democrats, 1861–1863," in *Civil War History* 12 (September 1966), pp. 213–15; Morton Wilkinson interview with John G. Nicolay, May 23, 1876, in *An Oral History of Abraham Lincoln: John G. Nicolay's Interviews and Essays,* ed. Michael Burlingame (Carbondale, IL: Southern Illinois University Press, 1996), pp. 61–62; Edward L. Gambill, "Who Were the Senate Radicals?" *Civil War History* 11 (September 1965), pp. 237–44; Welles, "Administration of Abraham Lincoln, I," in *Lincoln's Administration: Selected Essays by Gideon Welles,* ed. Albert Mordell (New York: Twayne, 1960), p. 75.

29. David Turpie, *Sketches of My Own Time* (Indianapolis, IN: Bobbs-Merrill Co., 1903), pp. 201–202; Riddle, *Recollections of War Times,* pp. 31, 200–201; Stevens, "Speech on Republican Aims," January 25, 1860, in *The Selected Papers of Thaddeus Stevens,* ed. B. W. Palmer (Pittsburgh: University of Pittsburgh Press, 1997), volume one, p. 165; Lovejoy, in Mitchell Snay, "The Emergence of the Republican Party in Illinois," *Journal of the Abraham Lincoln Association* 22 (Winter 2001), pp. 94–95.

30. Christopher Dell, *Lincoln and the War Democrats: The Grand Erosion of Conser-vative Tradition* (Rutherford, NJ: Fairleigh Dickinson University Press, 1975), p. 41; Curry, "Congressional Democrats," pp. 215–23.

31. Frank L. Klement, *Lincoln's Critics: The Copperheads of the North* (Shippensburg, PA: White Mane Press, 1999), pp. 48, 54; Cox, *Military Reminiscences,* volume one, pp. 458–59; Horace White, *The Life of Lyman Trumbull* (New York: Houghton Mifflin, 1913), p. 203; Joseph Wright, "Slavery in the District," April 1, 1862, *Congressional Globe,* 37th Congress, 2nd Session, p. 1468.

32. Riddle, *Recollections of War Times,* p. 166; Heather Cox Richardson, *The Greatest Nation of the Earth: Republican Economic Policies during the Civil War* (Cambridge, MA: Harvard University Press, 1997), p. 68; Dell, *Lincoln and the War Democrats,* pp. 102–23; Harry V. Jaffa, "The Emancipation Proclamation," in *Equality and Liberty: Theory and Practice in American Politics* (New York: Oxford University Press, 1965), p. 153.

33. AL, "Message to Congress in Special Session," July 4, 1861, in *C.W.,* volume four, p. 426; Fouke, "The Civil War," July 8, 1861, Polk, "Approval of Presidential Acts," July 11/13, 1861, and Vallandigham, "National Loan," July 10, 1861, in *Congressional Globe,* 37th Congress, 1st Session, pp. 47–50, 25, 57, 64; McPherson, *Political History,* p. 286; Dell, *Lincoln and the War*

Democrats, pp. 76–80. Fouke had beaten Lincoln's old friend Joseph Gilles-pie in the Illinois Eighth District Congressional race in 1860.

34. E. D. Townsend, in Stephen B. Oates, *With Malice toward None: The Life of Abraham Lincoln* (New York: Harper & Row, 1977), p. 251; Owner, diary entry for July 22, 1861, in William Owner manuscript diary, Library of Congress; William C. Davis, *Battle at Bull Run: A History of the First Major Campaign of the Civil War* (Garden City, NY: Doubleday, 1977), pp. 92, 245, 253.

35. Throop, *The Future: A Political Essay* (New York: James G. Gregory, 1864), p. 80; Hendrick Wright, "Prosecution of the War," and Crittenden, "National Difficulties," July 22, 1861, in *Congressional Globe,* 37th Congress, 1st Session, pp. 222, 224; Greeley to AL, July 29, 1861, in Abraham Lincoln Papers, Library of Congress; Julian, *Political Recollections,* pp. 197–99; Sumner to Wendell Phillips, August 3, 1861, in *The Selected Letters of Charles Sumner,* ed. Beverly Wilson Palmer (Boston: Northeastern University Press, 1990), volume two, p. 74.

36. Chase, "Report of the Secretary of the Treasury," July 14, 1861, in *Congressional Globe,* 37th Congress, 1st Session, Appendix, p. 5.

37. Arthur Nussbaum, *A Concise History of the Law of Nations* (New York: Macmillan, 1954), pp. 113, 124, 147, 151, 156, 162, 186–87, 192, 198; Knud Haakonssen, *Natural Law and Moral Philosophy: From Grotius to the Scottish Enlightenment* (New York: Cambridge University Press, 1996), pp. 310–41; James Garfield Randall, *Constitutional Problems under Lincoln* (1926; revised edition, Urbana, IL: University of Illinois Press, 1951), pp. 297–300; David Armitage, "The Declaration of Independence and International Law," *William and Mary Quarterly* 59 (January 2002), p. 15.

38. Wheaton, *Elements of International Law,* pp. vii–viii; Mark E. Neely, *The Fate of Liberty: Abraham Lincoln and Civil Liberties* (New York: Oxford University Press, 1992), p. 146; Stewart Jay, "The Status of the Law of Nations in Early American Law," *Vanderbilt Law Review* 42 (1989), pp. 821–33; and Mark W. Janis, "American Versions of the International Law of Christendom: Kent, Wheaton and the Grotian Tradition," *Netherlands Law Review* 39 (1992), pp. 37–61.

39. Wheaton, *Elements of International Law,* p. 321; Trumbull, "Army Appropriations Bill," July 15, 1861, in *Congressional Globe,* 37th Congress, 1st Session, p. 120; John Syrett, "The Confiscation Acts: Efforts at Reconstruction during the Civil War," unpublished Ph.D. dissertation, University of Wisconsin, 1971, pp. 6–7.

40. Henry W. Halleck, *International Law; or, Rules Regulating the Intercourse*

of States in Peace and War (San Francisco: H. H. Bancroft, 1861), p. 577; Madeline Russell Robinton, "An Introduction to the Papers of the New York Prize Court, 1861–1865," unpublished Ph.D. dissertation, Columbia University, 1945, pp. 28–29.

41. Wheaton, *Elements of International Law,* pp. 362, 379. For this reason, Trumbull simultaneously began pressing for revision of the prize laws, in an effort to help the horse of "prize" catch up with the cart of confiscation (see Trumbull, "Prize Law," March 17 and March 18, 1862, in *Congressional Globe,* 37th Congress, 2nd Session, p. 1260).

42. McPherson, *Political History,* p. 149; O. H. Browning, diary entry for July 28, 1861, in *The Diary of Orville Hickman Browning,* eds. Theodore Calvin Pease and J. G. Randall (Springfield, IL: Illinois State Historical Library, 1925), volume one, p. 489; Stuart Anderson, "1861: Blockade vs. Closing the Confederate Ports," *Military Affairs* 41 (December 1977), pp. 190–94.

43. Trumbull and Pearce, "Confiscation of Property," July 22, 1861, in *Congressional Globe,* 37th Congress, 1st Session, p. 219; Halleck, *International Law,* p. 447.

44. Breckinridge, "Confiscation of Property," July 22, 1861, in *Congressional Globe,* 37th Congress, 1st Session, p. 219; Henry Wilson, *History of the Antislavery Measures of the Thirty-Seventh and Thirty-Eighth United-States Congresses, 1861– 1864* (Boston: Walker, Wise, 1864), pp. 4–5; Arnold, *Lincoln and the Overthrow of Slavery,* pp. 225, 228.

45. Wilson, *History of the Antislavery Measures in Congress,* pp. 10–11; Crittenden, "Confiscation Act—Again," August 2, 1861, in *Congressional Globe,* 37th Congress, 1st Session, p. 411.

46. Chase to Green Adams, September 5, 1861, in J. W. Schuckers, *The Life and Public Services of Salmon Portland Chase* (New York: Appleton, 1874), p. 428; "The Last of Congress," *New York Times,* August 7, 1861; Conway, *Autobiography, Memories and Experiences* (Boston: Houghton Mifflin, 1904), volume one, p. 386; Hay, "Washington Correspondence," *Missouri Republican,* November 29, 1861, in *Lincoln's Journalist: John Hay's Anonymous Writings for the Press, 1860–1864,* ed. Michael Burlingame (Carbondale, IL: Southern Illinois University Press, 1998), p. 151; Syrett, "The Confiscation Acts," pp. 93–98; Blaine, *Twenty Years of Congress,* volume one, p. 377. On the actual extent of confiscation litigation, see Randall, *Constitutional Problems under Lincoln,* pp. 288–92.

47. Sumner to John Jay, August 11, 1861, in *Selected Letters,* volume two, p. 76; Chandler to Mrs. Chandler, October 27, 1861, in Zachariah Chandler Papers, Bentley Historical Library, University of Michigan; Cameron to B. F.

Butler, August 8, 1861, *O.R.,* Series Two, volume one, pp. 761–62; Julian, *Political Recollections,* pp. 197–99.

48. William E. Gienapp, *The Origins of the Republican Party, 1852–1856* (New York: Oxford University Press, 1987), pp. 316–29.

49. AL, "To William H. Seward," December 29, 1860, March 11, 1861, and July 3, 1861, in *C.W.,* volume four, pp. 164, 281, 419.

50. Montgomery Meigs to F. P. Blair, August 28, 1861, in *O.R.,* Series One, volume three, p. 464; John Howe to Montgomery Blair, August 4, 1861, in Abraham Lincoln Papers, Library of Congress.

51. Frémont, "Proclamation," August 30, 1861, in *O.R.,* Series One, volume three, pp. 466–67; Frémont, "Emancipation Proclamation of Gen. Frémont," in McPherson, *Political History,* pp. 245–46.

52. Cushing, "Martial Law," in *Official Opinions of the Attorneys General of the United States* (Washington: R. Farnham, 1858), volume 8, pp. 368, 371; Levi Woodbury, "Martial Law in Rhode Island," in *Writings of Levi Woodbury, LL.D., Political, Judicial and Literary* (Boston: Little, Brown, 1852), volume two, pp. 70–105. Some constitutional lawyers, like S. S. Nicholas of Kentucky, found no authority whatsoever in the Constitution for martial-law proclamations. Nicholas believed, conveniently but implausibly, that "the patriotism and public spirit of a republic are more effective in calling forth . . . the utmost energies of a State, than all the coercive powers of the most absolute despotism." Nicholas, "Martial Law," *Conservative Essays, Legal and Political* (Philadelphia: J. B. Lippincott, 1863), p. 161.

53. Harold M. Hyman, *A More Perfect Union: The Impact of the Civil War and Reconstruction on the Constitution* (New York: Knopf, 1973), pp. 81–90; Joel Parker, "Habeas Corpus and Martial Law," *North American Review* 94 (April 1862), pp. 472–75; Philip S. Paludan, *A Covenant with Death: The Constitution, Law and Equality in the Civil War Era* (Urbana, IL: University of Illinois Press, 1975), pp. 130–33; Taney, "*Ex parte* John Merryman," in McPherson, *Political History,* pp. 155–58.

54. AL, "To Beriah Magoffin," August 24, 1861, in *C.W.,* volume four, p. 497; Speed to Lincoln, September 1 and September 3, 1861, in Abraham Lincoln Papers, Library of Congress; Speed to Chase, September 2, 1861, in Salmon P. Chase Papers, Historical Society of Pennsylvania, Philadelphia.

55. Holt to AL, September 12, 1861, Robert Anderson to AL, September 13, 1861, and J. F. Bullitt et al. to Joshua Speed, September 13, 1861, Abraham Lincoln Papers, Library of Congress; Davis to Chase, September 3, 1861, Salmon P. Chase Papers, Library of Congress; Chase to Jesse Stubbs, November 1, 1861, in *The Salmon P. Chase Papers,* volume three, p. 105.

56. N. H. Eggleston, "Emancipation," *New Englander and Yale Review* 21 (October 1862), p. 790; Speed to AL, September 1 and September 3, 1861, in Abraham Lincoln Papers, Library of Congress.

57. Louis Gerteis, *Civil War St. Louis* (Lawrence, KS: University Press of Kansas, 2001), p. 146; Montgomery Blair to AL, September 4, 1861, in Abraham Lincoln Papers, Library of Congress.

58. Nicolay, Memorandum, September 17, 1861, in *With Lincoln in the White House: Letters, Memoranda, and Other Writings of John G. Nicolay, 1860–1865,* ed. Michael Burlingame (Carbondale, IL: Southern Illinois University Press, 2000), p. 57; AL, "To John C. Frémont," September 2, 1861, in *C.W.,* volume four, p. 506, and *O.R.,* Series Three, volume one, pp. 766–67.

59. Welles, "Administration of Abraham Lincoln, I," in *Lincoln's Administration,* p. 70; Frémont to Lincoln, September 8, 1861, in *O.R.,* Series Three, volume one, pp. 767–68, and McPherson, *Political History,* pp. 246–47; Jessie Benton Frémont, "The Lincoln Interview: Excerpt from 'Great Events,' " in *The Letters of Jessie Benton Frémont,* eds. Pamela Herr and M. L. Spence (Urbana, IL: University of Illinois Press, 1993), pp. 264–67; AL, "To John C. Frémont," September 11, 1861, and "To Mrs. John C. Frémont," September 12, 1861, in *C.W.,* volume four, p. 519; "An Important Letter from the President to General Frémont," *Washington Sunday Morning Chronicle,* September 15, 1861. Amazingly, Frémont not only ignored Lincoln's first letter of September 2 but, without waiting to hear from his wife or Lincoln, issued his first "Deed of Manumission" to two slaves, Frank Lewis and Hiram Reed, owned by a St. Louis secessionist named Thomas Snead, and went on to emancipate twenty-one others. He later claimed never to have received Lincoln's order about confiscation, and to have only read about it in the newspapers. See Frémont, "Proclamation," in *O.R.,* Series Three, volume one, pp. 769–70; T. Harry Williams, "Frémont and the Politicians," *Journal of the American Military History Foundation* 2 (Winter 1938), pp. 181–84; and Vernon L. Volpe, "The Frémonts and Emancipation in Missouri," *Historian* 56 (Winter 1994), pp. 340–41.

60. Montgomery Blair to AL, February 18, 1863, in Blair Family Papers, Library of Congress; Francis P. Blair and Charles Zagonyi testimony, February 7 and 24, 1862, in *Report of the Joint Committee on the Conduct of the War* (Washington, DC: Government Printing Office, 1863), volume three, pp. 173, 190; Ida M. Tarbell, *The Life of Abraham Lincoln* (New York: McClure, Phillips, 1904), volume two, p. 61; John Hay, diary entry for December 9, 1863, in *Inside Lincoln's White House,* p. 123; Nicolay, Memorandum,

September 17, 1861, in *With Lincoln in the White House,* p. 58; Montgomery Blair to AL, September 14, 1861, and Leonard Swett to AL, November 9, 1861, in Abraham Lincoln Papers, Library of Congress; Edward Bates, diary entry for October 22, 1861, in *The Diary of Edward Bates, 1859–1866,* ed. Howard K. Beale (Washington, DC: Government Printing Office, 1933), p. 198.

61. Julian, *Political Recollections,* pp. 197–99; Conway, *Autobiography, Memories and Experiences,* volume one, p. 422; Pearson, *Life of John A. Andrew,* volume one, p. 250; Hans L. Trefousse, "Owen Lovejoy and Abraham Lincoln during the Civil War," *Journal of the Abraham Lincoln Association* 22 (Winter 2001), p. 22; Erastus Wright to AL, September 20, 1861, and Scripps to AL, September 23, 1861, Abraham Lincoln Papers, Library of Congress; Medill to Chase, September 15, 1861, in Salmon P. Chase Papers, Historical Society of Pennsylvania; Wade to Zachariah Chandler, September 23, 1861, in Zachariah Chandler Papers, Bentley Historical Library, University of Michigan; Sumner, in Charles Francis Adams, *Richard Henry Dana: A Biography* (Boston: Houghton Mifflin, 1891), volume two, p. 260; David Donald, *Charles Sumner and the Coming of the Civil War* (New York: Knopf, 1960), p. 388; Sumner, "The Hon. C. Sumner on a War for Emancipation" [October 1, 1861], in *The Anti-Slavery Reporter,* November 1, 1861, pp. 246–47; Sumner to Lieber, September 17, 1861, *Selected Letters,* volume two, p. 79; Frémont to Thomas Starr King, October 16, 1863, *Letters of Jessie Benton Frémont,* p. 356; Josiah Bushnell Grinnell, *Men and Events of Forty Years: Autobiographical Reminiscences of an Active Career from 1850 to 1890* (Boston: D. Lothrop Co., 1891), p. 174.

62. Browning to AL, September 17, 1861, in Abraham Lincoln Papers, Library of Congress.

63. AL, "To Orville H. Browning," September 22, 1861, in *C.W.,* volume four, pp. 531–32.

64. Browning to AL, September 30, 1861, in Abraham Lincoln Papers, Library of Congress; Hay, diary entry for December 9, 1863, in *Inside Lincoln's White House,* p. 123; AL, "To Orville H. Browning," September 22, 1861, in *C.W.,* volume four, p. 532; Lester, in *Recollected Words,* p. 295.

65. AL to Moncure Conway and Lester, in *Recollected Words,* pp. 120, 295.

66. Blaine, *Twenty Years of Congress,* volume one, p. 377.

67. Gillespie to Herndon, January 31, 1866, in *Herndon's Informants,* p. 183; AL, "Sixth Debate with Stephen A. Douglas," October 13, 1858, in *C.W.,* volume three, p. 255; Ward Hill Lamon and Dorothy Lamon Teillard, *Rec-*

ollections of Abraham Lincoln, 1847–1865, ed. James Rawley (1911; Lincoln, NE: University of Nebraska Press, 1994), pp. 67–68.

68. AL, "To Nathaniel P. Banks," August 5, 1863, "Message to Congress," March 6, 1862, "To Stephen A. Hurlbut," July 31, 1863, and "To John M. Schofield," June 22, 1863, in *C.W.,* volume five, p. 145, and volume six, pp. 291, 358, 365.

69. AL, "To George Robertson," August 15, 1855, and "Message to Congress," March 6, 1862, in *C.W.,* volume two, p. 318, and volume five, p. 145.

70. Nicolay, Memorandum, October 2, 1861, in *With Lincoln in the White House,* p. 59; AL to Joseph C. G. Kennedy, November 26, 1861, Abraham Lincoln Papers, Library of Congress.

71. William H. Williams, *Slavery and Freedom in Delaware, 1639–1865* (Wilmington, DE: Scholarly Resources, 1996), p. 175. On Fisher and other antislavery Delawareans, see J. Thomas Scharf, *History of Delaware, 1609–1888* (Philadelphia: L. J. Richards & Co., 1888), pp. 329, 585.

72. H. Clay Reed, "Lincoln's Compensated Emancipation Plan and Its Relation to Delaware," pp. 36–39; AL, "Drafts of a Bill for Compensated Emancipation in Delaware," *C.W.,* volume five, pp. 29–30. Fisher later adjusted the total federal offer upwards to $900,000, since federal bonds were trading well below par that winter.

73. Edward Everett Hale memorandum of a conversation with Charles Sumner, April 26, 1862, in *Memories of a Hundred Years* (New York: Macmillan, 1902), volume two, pp. 189–91; Browning, diary entry for December 1, 1861, in *Diary of Orville Hickman Browning,* volume one, p. 512; AL to Davis and to Gilbert Greene, in *Recollected Words,* pp. 132, 182.

2. THE PRESIDENT WILL RISE

1. Horatio Nelson Taft, diary entry for December 16, 1861, Taft Papers, Library of Congress; Fessenden, January 14, 1862, in *Life and Public Services of William Pitt Fessenden* (Boston: Houghton Mifflin, 1907), volume one, p. 259; Browning, diary entry for December 2, 1861, in *Diary of Orville Hickman Browning,* volume one, p. 513; *Washington Sunday Morning Chronicle,* December 8, 1861; John Hay, "Washington Correspondence, 3 December 1861," in *Lincoln's Journalist,* p. 156; Blaine, *Twenty Years of Congress,* volume one, p. 354; William Salter, *The Life of James W. Grimes: Governor of Iowa, 1854–1858, a Senator of the United States, 1859–1869* (New York: D. Appleton, 1876), pp. 187–88.

2. Cox, *Military Reminiscences,* volume one, p. 57.

3. Riddle, *Recollections of War-Times*, p. 63; Browning, diary entry for December 6, 1861, in *Diary of Orville Hickman Browning*, p. 516; Benjamin B. French, diary entry for November 3, 1861, in *Witness to the Young Republic*, p. 379; Thomas J. Rowland, *George B. McClellan and Civil War History: In the Shadow of Grant and Sherman* (Kent, OH: Kent State University press, 1998), p. 140.

4. Welles, "Administration of Abraham Lincoln, I," in *Lincoln's Administration*, p. 63; Hay, "Washington Correspondence, 27 January 1862," in *Lincoln's Journalist*, p. 203; Russel H. Beatie, *The Army of the Potomac: Birth of Command, November 1860–September 1861* (Cambridge, MA: Da Capo Press, 2002), p. 408; McClellan to Mary Ellen McClellan, October 11, 1861, to Samuel L. M. Barlow, November 8, 1861, and to Henry W. Halleck, November 11, 1861, in *The Civil War Papers of George B. McClellan: Selected Correspondence, 1860–1865*, ed. Stephen W. Sears (New York: Ticknor & Fields, 1989), pp. 106, 128, 130; George H. Gordon, *A War Diary of Events in the War of the Great Rebellion, 1863–1865* (Boston: James Osgood, 1882), p. 137; McClellan to Buell, November 7, 1861, and Halleck, "General Orders No. 3," in *O.R.*, Series Two, volume one, pp. 776–77, 778; Buell, "General Orders 13a," February 26, 1862, in *O.R.*, Series One, volume sixteen (part one), p. 497; Schuckers, *Life and Public Services of Salmon Portland Chase*, pp. 220–35; Chase, diary entry for December 25, 1861, in *Inside Lincoln's Cabinet: The Civil War Diaries of Salmon P. Chase*, ed. David H. Donald (New York: Longmans, Green, 1954), pp. 54–55; George Templeton Strong, diary entry for December 16, 1861, in *Diary of the Civil War, 1860–1865*, ed. Allan Nevins (New York: Macmillan, 1962), p. 196; Tarbell, *Life of Abraham Lincoln*, volume two, pp. 72–73; Edward Bates, diary entry for December 25, 1861, in *Diary of Edward Bates*, p. 215.

5. Julian, "The Cause and Cure of Our National Troubles," in *Speeches on Political Questions* (New York: Hurd & Houghton, 1872), pp. 154–80; Colfax, in O. J. Hollister, *Life of Schuyler Colfax* (New York: Funk & Wagnalls, 1886), p. 185; John A. Andrew to F. W. Bird, December 14, 1861, in Pearson, *Life of John A. Andrew*, volume two, p. 3; Stevens, "Abstract of Remarks at Republican Caucus, December 9, 1861, in Washington," *Selected Papers*, volume one, p. 230.

6. "Conduct of the War," December 3, 1861, and "War Powers," January 15, 1862, *Congressional Globe*, 37th Congress, 2nd Session, pp. 5–6, 347; Hans L. Trefousse, *Thaddeus Stevens: Nineteenth-Century Egalitarian* (Chapel Hill: University of North Carolina Press, 1997), pp. 116–17.

7. "Fugitive Slaves," December 4, 1861, "Return of Fugitive Slaves" and

"Confiscation of Rebel Property," December 5, 1861, and "Rendition of Fugitive Slaves," December 23, 1861, *Congressional Globe,* 37th Congress, 2nd Session, pp. 9, 16, 18, 159; Wilson, *History of the Anti-Slavery Measures,* pp. 18–21; Arnold, *Lincoln and the Overthrow of Slavery,* p. 252; Syrett, "The Confiscation Acts: Efforts at Reconstruction during the Civil War," pp. 23–25; Paludan, *A Covenant with Death,* pp. 36–38; Bruce Tap, *Over Lincoln's Shoulder: The Committee on the Conduct of the War* (Lawrence, KS: University Press of Kansas, 1998), pp. 21–30, 35; Philip S. Paludan, *"A People's Contest": The Union and the Civil War, 1861–1865* (New York: Harper & Row, 1988), pp. 64–65.

8. Arnold, *Lincoln and the Overthrow of Slavery,* p. 259; "The Administration and the Slavery Question," *Washington Sunday Morning Chronicle,* December 29, 1861; Sherman, *Recollections of Forty Years,* p. 316; "Confiscation of Property," April 7, 1862, in *Congressional Globe,* 37th Congress, 2nd Session, p. 1557; Syrett, "The Confiscation Acts: Efforts at Reconstruction during the Civil War," pp. 26–27.

9. "Object of the War," December 16, 1861, "Surrender of Fugitive Slaves," December 18, 1861, "Confiscation of Property," February 25, 1862, "Committee of the Whole," February 20, 1862, and Cox, "Emancipation and Its Results—Is Ohio to Be Africanized?" June 3, 1862, in *Congressional Globe,* 37th Congress, 2nd Session, pp. 88, 130, 903, 1049–54, and Appendix, pp. 242–49; Paludan, *"A People's Contest,"* pp. 95–96; *Life and Public Services of William Pitt Fessenden,* volume one, pp. 272–73; Browning, diary entries for March 10 and 14, 1862, in *Diary of Orville Hickman Browning,* pp. 533, 534.

10. Bingham, in Trefousse, *The Radical Republicans,* p. 217.

11. Ashley, "A Bold, Earnest, and Vigorous Policy Demanded," November 26, 1861, in *Washington Daily National Republican,* January 23, 1862; Wade to Zachariah Chandler, October 8, 1861, in Zachariah Chandler Papers, Bentley Historical Library, University of Michigan; Chandler, in Trefousse, *The Radical Republicans,* p. 180; Trumbull, in J. G. Randall, *Lincoln the President: Springfield to Bull Run* (New York: Dodd, Mead, 1945), p. 389; Bates, diary entry for December 31, 1861, in *Diary of Edward Bates,* p. 220; "Reminiscences of Julia Ward Howe," *Atlantic Monthly* 83 (May 1899), p. 706.

12. Sinclair Tousey, *The New Gospel of Peace According to St. Benjamin* (New York, 1863), p. 28; French, diary entry for January 8, 1862, in *Witness to the Young Republic,* p. 384; Fessenden, January 14, 1862, in *Life and Public Services of William Pitt Fessenden,* pp. 259–60; Stoddard, *Inside the White House in War Times,* p. 13; Hay, "Life in the White House in the Time of Lincoln," in *At Lincoln's Side: John Hay's Civil War Correspondence and Se-*

lected Writings, ed. Michael Burlingame (Carbondale, IL: Southern Illinois University Press, 2000), pp. 132, 136; Walter B. Stevens, *A Reporter's Lincoln*, ed. Michael Burlingame (Lincoln, NE: University of Nebraska Press, 1998), p. 171.

13. Turpie, *Sketches of My Own Time*, pp. 205–206; Sumner to Longfellow, April 7, 1861, in *Selected Letters*, volume two, p. 64; Titian J. Coffey, in *Reminiscences of Abraham Lincoln by Distinguished Men of His Time*, ed. A. T. Rice (New York: North American Publishing Co., 1886), p. 245; Borrett, "An Englishman in Washington in 1864," *Magazine of History* 38 (May 1929), p. 13.

14. Lamon, *The Life of Abraham Lincoln from His Birth to His Inauguration as President*, ed. Rodney O. Davis (Lincoln, NE: University of Nebraska Press, 1999), pp. 339–40; Welles, *Lincoln and Seward*, p. 32; Barbara J. Fields, *Slavery and Freedom on the Middle Ground: Maryland during the Nineteenth Century* (New Haven, CT: Yale University Press, 1985), pp. 110–11; AL, "Annual Message to Congress," December 3, 1861, in *C.W.*, volume five, pp. 48–49.

15. Phillips, in *Recollected Words*, p. 356.

16. William Henry Seward to George B. McClellan, December 4, 1861, in *O.R.*, Series Two, volume one, p. 783; McPherson, *Political History*, pp. 248–49; Hay, "Washington Correspondence, 24 November 1861," in *Lincoln's Journalist*, p. 151; Hollister, *Life of Schuyler Colfax*, p. 185; Edward Everett Hale, memorandum of conversation with Sumner, April 26, 1862, in "The War," *Memories of a Hundred Years*, volume two, pp. 191–92; Sumner, in *Recollected Words*, p. 433; Sumner to Cobden, December 31, 1861, in *Selected Letters*, volume two, p. 93.

17. Conway, "Personal Recollections of President Lincoln," *Fortnightly Review* 1 (May 1865), pp. 56–57; Chase, draft of message to Congress on compensated emancipation, February–March 1862, in Abraham Lincoln Papers, Library of Congress; Sumner to Orestes Brownson, February 2, 1862, in *Selected Letters*, volume two, p. 100.

18. AL, "Speech to the Springfield Scott Club," August 14, 1852, in *C.W.*, volume two, pp. 149–50; Charles G. Halpine, *Baked Meats of the Funeral: A Collection of Essays, Poems, Speeches, Histories and Banquets By Private Miles O'Reilly* (New York: Carleton, 1866), p. 105; John Seymour to Horatio Seymour, January 19, 1863, in Alexander J. Wall, *A Sketch of the Life of Horatio Seymour, 1810–1886* (New York: Lancaster Press, 1929), p. 30.

19. Harry J. Carman and Reinhard H. Luthin, *Lincoln and the Patronage* (New York: Columbia University Press, 1943), p. 27; Herndon, *Life of Lincoln*, p.

381; Lamon, *Life of Abraham Lincoln*, pp. 449, 460; James K. Moorhead interview with Nicolay, May 12/13, 1880, in *An Oral History of Abraham Lincoln*, p. 41; Weed, in *Recollected Words*, p. 462; Harry E. Pratt, "Simon Cameron's Fight for a Place in Lincoln's Cabinet," *Bulletin of the Abraham Lincoln Association* 49 (September 1937), pp. 5–6.

20. Randall, *Lincoln the President: Bull Run to Gettysburg*, pp. 54–55; McPherson, *Political History*, p. 249; Burton J. Hendrick, *Lincoln's War Cabinet* (1946; New York: Doubleday, 1961), pp. 65–76; Chase to John T. Trowbridge, March 31, 1864, in Schuckers, *Life and Services of Salmon Portland Chase*, pp. 418–20.

21. John D. Defrees to Josiah Gilbert Holland, August 8, 1865, in Holland Papers, New York Public Library; Francis Bicknell Carpenter, *Six Months at the White House with Abraham Lincoln* (New York: Hurd and Houghton, 1867), pp. 136–37; Browning, diary entry for December 12, 1862, in *Diary of Orville Hickman Browning*, volume one, p. 595; Helen Nicolay, *Personal Traits of Abraham Lincoln* (New York: Century, 1912), p. 238; Lamon, *Life of Abraham Lincoln*, p. 461; Nicolay, "Conversation with Gen. Cameron," February 20, 1875, in *An Oral History of Abraham Lincoln*, p. 43; AL, "To Simon Cameron," January 11, 1862, in *C.W.*, volume five, pp. 96–97; Benjamin P. Thomas and Harold M. Hyman, *Stanton: The Life and Times of Lincoln's Secretary of War* (New York: Knopf, 1962), pp. 133–42.

22. Phelps, in *Free At Last: A Documentary History of Slavery, Freedom, and the Civil War*, ed. Ira Berlin et al. (New York: New Press, 1992), pp. 22–25; "Report of Brigadier-General J. W. Phelps," December 5, 1861, in *O.R.*, Series One, volume six, pp. 465–68.

23. Daniel Ammen, "DuPont and the Port Royal Expedition," in *Battles and Leaders of the Civil War*, eds. Clarence Buel and Robert Underwood Johnson (1887; New York: Castle Books, 1956), volume one, p. 688; "Proclamation," November 8, 1861, in *O.R.*, Series One, volume six, pp. 604–605; Abraham J. Palmer, *The History of the Forty-Eighth Regiment New York State Volunteers* (Brooklyn, NY: Veteran Association of the Regiment, 1885), pp. 21–22.

24. Willie Lee Rose, *Rehearsal for Reconstruction: The Port Royal Experiment* (New York: Oxford University Press, 1964), pp. 144–45; Thomas and Hyman, *Stanton*, pp. 234–37; Edward A. Miller, *Lincoln's Abolitionist General: The Biography of David Hunter* (Columbia, SC: University of South Carolina Press, 1997), pp. 94–100; "General Orders No. 11," in *O.R.*, Series One, volume fourteen, p. 341; "Slavery Abolished in Three States," *Washington Daily National Republican*, May 17, 1862; Robert Schenk, "Major

General David Hunter," *Magazine of American History* 17 (January 1887), pp. 145–47.

25. Strong, diary entry for May 15, 1862, in *Diary of the Civil War*, p. 226; "Slavery Abolished in Three States," *Washington Daily National Republican*, May 17, 1862; Peter Sturtevant to AL, May 16, 1862, and Reverdy Johnson to AL, May 16, 1862, in Abraham Lincoln Papers, Library of Congress; Arnold, *Lincoln and the Overthrow of Slavery*, pp. 263–66; "General Hunter's Letter," July 5, 1862, in *Congressional Globe*, 37th Congress, 2nd Session, pp. 3121–24; Whitelaw Reid, "General Hunter's Negro Soldiers," July 6, 1862, in *A Radical View: The "Agate" Dispatches of Whitelaw Reid, 1861–1865*, ed. James G. Smart (Memphis, TN: Memphis State University Press, 1976), volume two, pp. 71–74.

26. Chase to David Hunter, May 20, 1862, and to Horace Greeley, May 21, 1862, in *Salmon P. Chase Papers*, volume three, pp. 202, 203; AL, "To Salmon P. Chase," May 17, 1862, and "Proclamation Revoking General Hunter's Order of Military Emancipation of May 9, 1862," in *C.W.*, volume five, pp. 219, 222; McPherson, *Political History*, pp. 250–51; Hay, "Washington Correspondence," May 19, 1862, in *Lincoln's Journalist*, p. 263.

27. AL, "Speech at Peoria, Illinois," October 16, 1854, in *C.W.*, volume two, pp. 249, 268; S. S. Cox, "Army Appropriations Bill," January 30, 1862, *Congressional Globe*, 37th Congress, 2nd Session, p. 573; Larry A. Greene, "The Emancipation Proclamation in New Jersey and the Paranoid Style," *New Jersey History* 91 (Summer 1973), p. 118; Lowell, "What Shall We Do with It?" *Continental Monthly* 1 (May 1862), p. 493.

28. William Seraile, *New York's Black Regiments during the Civil War* (New York: Routledge, 2001), p. 17; Dodson to Cameron, April 23, 1861, and Cameron's reply, April 29, 1861, in *O.R.*, Series Three, volume one, pp. 107, 133; Versalle F. Washington, *Eagles on Their Buttons: A Black Infantry Regiment in the Civil War* (Columbia, MO: University of Missouri Press, 1999), pp. 2–3; Benjamin Quarles, *Lincoln and the Negro* (New York: Oxford University Press, 1962), pp. 67–68; James M. McPherson, *The Struggle for Equality: Abolitionists and the Negro in the Civil War and Reconstruction* (Princeton: Princeton University Press, 1964), pp. 192–93.

29. George W. Julian, in V. Jacque Vogeli, *Free but Not Equal: The Midwest and the Negro during the Civil War* (Chicago: University of Chicago Press, 1967), p. 1; Walker, *Appeal to the Coloured Citizens of the World, but in Particular, and Very Expressly, to Those of the United States of America*, ed. Charles M. Wiltse (1829; New York: Hill & Wang, 1965), pp. 9, 16; Easton, "A Treatise on the Intellectual Character, and Civil and Political Condition

of the Colored People of the U. States" (1837), in *To Heal the Scourge of Prejudice: The Life and Writings of Hosea Easton*, ed. George P. Price and James Brewer Stewart (Amherst, MA: University of Massachusetts Press, 1999), pp. 72, 80. On the internalization of racial prejudice, see John Stauffer, *The Black Hearts of Men: Radical Abolitionists and the Transformation of Race* (Cambridge, MA: Harvard University Press, 2002), pp. 157–58; Delany, "The Origin and Objects of Ancient Freemasonry" and "The Condition, Elevation, Emigration and Destiny of the Colored Peoples of the United States," in *Martin R. Delany: A Documentary Reader*, ed. Robert S. Levine (Chapel Hill, NC: University of North Carolina Press, 2003), pp. 54, 192–93; Brown, *Clotelle; or, The Colored Heroine* (1867; Miami, FL: Mnemosyne Publishing, 1969), p. 21; Lovejoy's presentation of the "remonstrance" appeared in the *Alton* (Illinois) *Telegraph*, January 15, 1855. My particular thanks go to Michael Burlingame for sending me the text of Lovejoy's "remonstrance."

30. Mia Bay, *The White Image in the Black Mind: African-American Ideas about White People, 1830–1925* (New York: Oxford University Press, 2000), pp. 50, 53, 65–66; David L. Blight, *Frederick Douglass' Civil War: Keeping Faith in Jubilee* (Baton Rouge, LA: Louisiana State University Press, 1989), pp. 149–50; Washington, *Eagles on Their Buttons*, p. 6; Seraile, *New York's Black Regiments*, pp. 9–10.

31. Seward to C. F. Adams, in Frederick W. Seward, *Seward at Washington, Senator and Secretary of State: A Memoir of His Life* (New York: Derby & Miller, 1891), volume two, p. 94; Herbert W. Beecher, *History of the First Light Battery, Connecticut Volunteers, 1861–1865* (New York: A. T. De La Mare, 1901), p. 187; Lyman Jackman, *History of the Sixth New Hampshire Regiment in the War for the Union* (Concord, NH: Republican Press, 1891), p. 137.

32. Stephen V. Ash, *When the Yankees Came: Conflict and Chaos in the Occupied South, 1861–1865* (Chapel Hill, NC: University of North Carolina Press, 1995), pp. 31–32; McCline, *Slavery in the Clover Bottoms*, p. 39; Leon F. Litwack, *Been in the Storm So Long: The Aftermath of Slavery* (New York: Knopf, 1979), pp. 8, 29; Barbara J. Fields, *Slavery and Freedom on the Middle Ground*, p. 106; *The Union Must Stand: The Civil War Diary of John Quincy Adams Campbell, Fifth Iowa Volunteer Infantry*, eds. Mark Grimsley and Todd Miller (Knoxville, TN: University of Tennessee Press, 2000), p. 217.

33. Comm. Daniel Ammen to Capt. Thomas H. Stevens, April 2, 1862, in Abraham Lincoln Bookshop Catalog 149 (Fall 2001), no. 194; *By the Dim and*

Flaring Lamps: The Civil War Diary of Samuel McIlvaine, February through June 1862, ed. Clayton E. Cramer (Monroe, NY: Library Research Associates, 1990), p. 147.

34. Cox, *Military Reminiscences,* volume one, pp. 157–58; "The Negro as Viewed by a Michigan Civil War Soldier: Letters of John C. Buchanan," ed. George M. Blackburn, *Michigan History* 47 (April 1963), pp. 79–80; "Exciting Opposition to County Constables Attempt to 'Kidnap' a Free Colored Man from the Camp of the Seventh New York Cavalry," *Washington Daily National Republican,* April 7, 1862; Margaret Leech, *Reveille in Washington, 1861–1865* (New York: Harper & Brothers, 1941), p. 245.

35. John Eaton, *Grant, Lincoln and the Freedmen: Reminiscences of the Civil War* (New York: Longmans, Green, 1907), p. 2; *Private Elisha Stockwell, Jr. Sees the Civil War,* ed. Byron R. Abernethy (1958; Norman, OK: University of Oklahoma Press, 1985), p. 159; McCline, *Slavery in the Clover Bottoms,* p. 44; Homer B. Sprague, *History of the 13th Infantry Regiment of Connecticut Volunteers during the Great Rebellion* (Hartford, CT: Case, Lockwood & Co., 1867), pp. 79–80; "Swearing a Contraband," *Washington Sunday Morning Chronicle,* April 27, 1862; Alice Fahs, *The Imagined Civil War,* p. 214.

36. Peter Kolchin, *First Freedom: The Response of Alabama's Blacks to Emancipation and Reconstruction* (Westport, CT: Greenwood Press, 1972), p. 185; Conway, *Testimonies Concerning Slavery,* pp. 108–109; Vogeli, *Free but Not Equal,* p. 88.

37. Report of the American Freedmens Inquiry Commission to Edwin M. Stanton, June 30, 1863, in *O.R.,* Series Three, volume three, pp. 430–31; Colyer's report of May 25, 1863, and Eaton's April 1863 survey of conditions in the eight contraband camps under his supervision are in *Free at Last: A Documentary History,* pp. 175–78, 186–200; Gerteis, *From Contraband to Freedman,* pp. 30–31; William Child, *History of the Fifth Regiment New Hampshire Volunteers, in the American Civil War, 1861–1865* (Bristol, NH: R. W. Musgrove, 1893), p. 169.

38. Patricia C. Click, *Time Full of Trial: The Roanoke Island Freedmen's Colony, 1862–1867* (Chapel Hill, NC: University of North Carolina Press, 2001), pp. 2–3, 4, 5, 10–11, 36, 38; Eaton, *Grant, Lincoln and the Freedmen,* pp. 23–24, 204; Warren B. Armstrong, *For Courageous Fighting and Confident Dying: Union Chaplains in the Civil War* (Lawrence, KS: University Press of Kansas, 1998), pp. 86–93; Eric Foner, *Reconstruction: America's Unfinished Revolution, 1863–1877* (New York: Harper & Row, 1988), pp. 56–60; Ira Berlin et al., *Slaves No More: Three Essays on Emancipation and the*

Civil War (New York: Cambridge University Press, 1992), pp. 118–19; Lucy
Chase to Hannah E. Stephenson, December 9, 1864, in *Dear Ones at Home:
Letters from Contraband Camps,* ed. Henry L. Swint (Nashville, TN: Van-
derbilt University Press, 1966), p. 134.

39. Beecher, "Modes and Duties of Emancipation," November 26, 1861, in *Pa-
triotic Addresses in America and England, from 1850 to 1885, on Slavery, the
Civil War, and the Development of Civil Liberty in the United States,* ed. J. R.
Howard (Boston: Pilgrim Press, 1887), pp. 336–37.

40. Wilson, *History of the Rise and Fall of the Slave Power in America* (Boston:
James R. Osgood, 1873), volume one, pp. 302–306; Margaret Leech,
Reveille in Washington, pp. 235–36; Johnston, *Surviving Freedom,* pp.
75–78; Don E. Fehrenbacher, *The Slaveholding Republic: An Account of the
United States Government's Relations to Slavery* (New York: Oxford Univer-
sity Press, 2001), pp. 60–61; "An Act Concerning the District of Columbia,"
February 27, 1801, *The Debates and Proceedings of the . . . Sixth Congress*
(Washington: Gales & Seaton, 1851), pp. 1552–55.

41. "Colored People of the District of Columbia," *Washington Daily National
Republican,* March 29, 1862; Johnston, *Surviving Freedom,* 88–89; Henry
Greenleaf Pearson, *James S. Wadsworth of Geneseo* (New York: Charles
Scribner's Sons, 1913), p. 131.

42. Dickson, "Slavery in the District of Columbia," February 2, 1835, *Register
of Debates . . . of the Second Session of the Twenty-Third Congress* (Washington: Gales & Seaton, 1835), pp. 1131–40; Wilson, *History of the Rise and
Fall of the Slave Power,* volume one, p. 308; Fehrenbacher, *The Slaveholding Republic,* pp. 66–88.

43. William Henry Locke, *The Story of the Regiment* (New York: James Miller,
1872), pp. 69–70; "Contrabands," *Washington Sunday Morning Chronicle,*
March 23, 1862; "Great Influx of Contrabands," *Washington Daily National Republican,* March 12, 1862.

44. Leech, *Reveille in Washington,* pp. 141–42, 239–41; "Criminal Justice in the
District," *Congressional Globe,* 37th Congress, 2nd Session, January 10, 1862,
and January 14, 1862, pp. 264, 311–21; Weik, *The Real Lincoln: A Portrait*
(Boston: Houghton Mifflin, 1922), p. 218; Lamon, *Recollections of Abraham Lincoln,* pp. 258–59.

45. "Bills Introduced," December 16, 1861, "Reports from Committees," February 13, 1862, and "Slavery in the District," February 27, 1862, in *Congressional Globe,* 37th Congress, 2nd Session, pp. 89–90, 785; Senate Bill 108,
37th Congress (December 16, 1861); Wilson, *History of the Anti-Slavery
Measures,* pp. 40–41; McPherson, *Political History,* p. 212; Hans L. Tre-

fousse, *Benjamin Franklin Wade: Radical Republican from Ohio* (New York: Twayne Publishers, 1963), p. 33.

46. Wilson, *History of the Rise and Fall of the Slave Power*, volume three, pp. 272, 275–77; Arnold, *Lincoln and the Overthrow of Slavery*, p. 253; "Slavery in the District," in *Congressional Globe*, 37th Congress, 2nd Session, pp. 1191–92; Wilson, *History of the Anti-Slavery Measures*, pp. 42–45; Michael J. Kurz, "Emancipation in the Federal City," *Civil War History* 24 (September 1978), pp. 251–56; Ernest McKay, *Henry Wilson: Practical Radical* (Port Washington, NY: Kennikat Press, 1971), pp. 176–78.

47. "Slavery in the District," March 24, 1862, in *Congressional Globe*, 37th Congress, 2nd Session, pp. 1333–39; Wilson, *History of the Anti-Slavery Measures*, pp. 48–49.

48. Senate Bill 108, 37th Congress (April 9, 1862); Waitman T. Willey, "Slavery in the District," April 1, 1862, Sumner, "Slavery in the District," March 31, 1862, Saulsbury, "Slavery in the District," March 25, 1862, and Fessenden, "Slavery in the District," April 1, 1862, in *Congressional Globe*, 37th Congress, 2nd Session, pp. 1478, 1449, 1356–57, 1478; Wilson, *History of the Rise and Fall of the Slave Power*, volume three, pp. 274, 278.

49. Fessenden, "Slavery in the District," April 1, 1862, in *Congressional Globe*, 37th Congress, 2nd Session, pp. 1472, 1526; *The Statutes at Large, Treaties, and Proc-lamations of the United States of America, from December 5, 1859, to March 3, 1863* (Boston: Little, Brown, 1863), pp. 376–78; Wilson, *History of the Rise and Fall of the Slave Power*, volume three, p. 278; *Washington Sunday Daily Chronicle*, April 6, 1862.

50. Crittenden, "Emancipation in the District," in *Congressional Globe*, 37th Congress, 2nd Session, pp. 1634–37, 1648–49; Arnold, *Lincoln and the Overthrow of Slavery*, pp. 254–58; Wilson, *History of the Rise and Fall of the Slave Power*, volume three, pp. 279–83; "Emancipation in the District Is Triumphant," *Washington Daily National Republican*, April 12, 1862; Taft, diary entry for April 11, 1862, Horatio Nelson Taft manuscript diary, Library of Congress; Salmon P. Chase, diary entry for April 11, 1862, *Inside Lincoln's Cabinet*, pp. 70–71; Strong, diary entry for April 12, 1862, *Diary of the Civil War, 1860–1865*, p. 216.

51. AL, "Protest in the Illinois Legislature on Slavery," March 3, 1837, "Speech at Peoria, Illinois," October 16, 1854, "First Joint Debate with Stephen A. Douglas at Ottawa," August 21, 1858, and "Second Debate with Stephen A. Douglas at Freeport, Illinois," August 27, 1858, *C.W.*, volume one, p. 74, volume two, p. 259, and volume three, pp. 4, 41.

52. AL, "To John A. Gilmer," December 15, 1860, "To William H. Seward,"

February 1, 1861, and "To Horace Greeley," March 24, 1862, *C.W.*, volume four, pp. 152, 183, and volume five, p. 169; AL to Henry W. Blodgett, in *Recollected Words*, p. 34; AL, "Message to Congress," April 16, 1862, *C.W.*, volume five, p. 192. Some of them must have had a good season for questions, though, because Lincoln evidently communicated with a number of key congressmen during the debates over the District Emancipation bill. Orville Hickman Browning's diary shows Lincoln's old Illinois friend visiting the White House for extensive interviews with the president on March 28 and all through the week between April 4 and April 10; Ira Harris and Preston King of New York also had appointments with Lincoln, and Lincoln wrote at least one letter (to James McDougall of California) arguing for the District bill and another to *New York Times* editor Henry J. Raymond, who also served as the chair of the Republican National Committee. See Bogue, *Congressman's Civil War*, pp. 47–48, and *Lincoln Day-by-Day: A Chronology, 1809–1865*, ed. E. S. Miers (Dayton, OH: Morningside, 1991), volume three, pp. 101–105.

53. The District Emancipation bill passed the House on Friday, April 11, after the Senate had adjourned for the day; the bill then sat in limbo, waiting for the Senate to reconvene on Monday, April 14, and, in Sumner's account to John Andrew, was not actually brought over to the Senate chamber from the House "till Monday evng *after 5 o'clk* when it was promptly despatched to the president." Sumner to John Andrew, April 22, 1862, in *Selected Letters*, volume two, p. 109. See also AL, "Message to Congress," April 16, 1862, *C.W.*, volume five, p. 192; Browning, diary entry for April 14, 1862, in *Diary of Orville Hickman Browning*, volume one, p. 541.

54. Adams, *Letter from Washington, 1863–1865*, ed. Evelyn Leasher (Detroit, MI: Wayne State University Press, 1999), p. 33; Owner, diary entry for May 5, 1862, William Owner manuscript diary, Library of Congress; Edna Greene Medford, "Abraham Lincoln and Black Wartime Washington," in *Annual Lincoln Colloquium: Papers from the Thirteenth and Fourteenth Annual Lincoln Colloquia* (Springfield, IL: Lincoln National Home Historic Site, 2000), pp. 124–25.

55. Douglass to Charles Sumner, April 8, 1862, and *Douglass' Monthly*, May 1862, in *Frederick Douglass: Selected Speeches and Writings*, pp. 493–94; James M. McPherson, *The Negro's Civil War: How American Negroes Felt and Acted during the War for the Union* (New York: Pantheon, 1965), p. 45; "The Emancipation Bill Signed" and "Emancipation as Regarded by the Colored People," *Washington Daily National Republican*, April 17, 1862; McPherson, *Political History*, 212–13; Beecher, "The Success of American

Democracy," *Patriotic Addresses*, p. 354; Herman Belz, "The Protection of Personal Liberty in Republican Emancipation Legislation," in *Abraham Lincoln, Constitutionalism, and Equal Rights in the Civil War Era*, pp. 107–108; Bogue, *The Earnest Men*, pp. 152–59.

56. "Conflict between the Military and Civil Authorities," *Washington Daily National Republican*, May 24, 1862.

57. Leech, *Reveille in Washington*, pp. 246–47; Pearson, *James S. Wadsworth of Geneseo*, pp. 138–39; Lamon, *Recollections of Abraham Lincoln*, pp. 256–57; Owner, diary entry for May 24, 1862, William Owner manuscript diary, Library of Congress.

58. Owner, diary entry for May 17, 1862, William Owner manuscript diary, Library of Congress.

59. Click, *Time Full of Trial*, pp. 6–7; Pearson, *James S. Wadsworth of Geneseo*, pp. 132–33; Johnston, *Surviving Freedom*, pp. 121, 157, 159; "The Contrabands— Interesting Facts in Regard to Their Management, &c.," and "The Contrabands at 'Camp Barker,' " *Washington Daily National Republican*, July 21, 1862, and August 11, 1862; Stanley Harrold, *Subversives: Antislavery Community in Washington, D.C., 1828–1865* (Baton Rouge, LA: Louisiana State University Press, 2003), pp. 225–51.

60. Johnston, *Surviving Freedom*, pp. 122–23; Stoddard, *Inside the White House in War Times*, p. 122; Fahs, *The Imagined Civil War*, p. 117.

61. "The Emancipation Act," *Washington Sunday Morning Chronicle*, April 26, 1862.

62. Ray to Pierce, April 1860, Edward L. Pierce Papers, Houghton Library, Harvard University; AL, "Speech at Belleville, Illinois," October 18, 1856, in *C.W.*, volume two, p. 379; Robert Johannsen, *Lincoln, the South, and Slavery: The Political Dimension* (Baton Rouge, LA: Louisiana State University Press, 1991), pp. 1–5.

63. Reed, "Lincoln's Compensated Emancipation Plan and Its Relation to Delaware," pp. 39–45.

64. John B. Henderson, "Emancipation and Impeachment," *Century Magazine* 85 (1912), p. 198.

65. *Statutes at Large*, p. 617.

66. AL, "Message to Congress," March 6, 1862, and "To James A. McDougal," March 14, 1862, *C.W.*, volume five, pp. 144–46, 160; McPherson, *Political History*, p. 209; AL, "Emancipation," March 6, 1862, in *Congressional Globe*, 37th Congress, 2nd Session, pp. 1102–1103.

67. AL, "To William H. Seward," March 5, 1862, in *C.W.*, volume five, p. 144; Tarbell, *Life of Lincoln*, volume two, pp. 98–99; Edward Everett Hale

memorandum of conversation with Sumner, April 26, 1862, "The War," *Memories of a Hundred Years*, volume two, pp. 193–94.

68. Nicolay, journal entry for March 9, 1862, in *With Lincoln in the White House*, p. 73; McPherson, *Political History*, pp. 210–11.

69. J. W. Crisfield, in *Conversations with Lincoln*, Charles M. Segal, ed. (New York: G. P. Putnam's Sons, 1961), pp. 165–68; Perry, "Conduct of the War, Etc.," March 6, 1862, in *Congressional Globe*, 37th Congress, 2nd Session, pp. 1104–1105; Wilson, *History of the Anti-Slavery Measures*, pp. 81–85; Conway, *Autobiography, Memories and Experiences*, volume one, p. 346.

70. "The President's Emancipation Message," *Washington Daily National Republican*, March 10, 1862; Wilson, *History of the Anti-Slavery Measures*, p. 82; Blaine, "Confiscation of Rebel Property," *Political Discussions, Legislative, Diplomatic, and Popular, 1856–1886* (Norwich, CT: Henry Bill, 1887), p. 35; N. H. Eggleston, "Emancipation," *New Englander and Yale Review* 21 (October 1862), p. 783; Sumner to Francis W. Bird, March 12, 1862, in *Selected Letters*, volume two, p. 104.

71. "Aid to the States in Emancipation," in *Congressional Globe*, 37th Congress, 2nd Session, p. 1496; Wilson, *History of the Anti-Slavery Measures*, p. 91.

72. "Some Sense about the Nigger, at Last," *Vanity Fair* 5 (March 15, 1862), p. 130; AL, "To Horace Greeley," March 24, 1862, *C.W.*, volume five, p. 169; Schurz, in *Speeches, Correspondence and Political Papers of Carl Schurz*, ed. Frederic Bancroft (New York: 1912), volume two, pp. 328–29.

73. R. M. Kelly, "Holding Kentucky for the Union," *Battles and Leaders*, volume one, p. 391.

74. Hay, "Washington Correspondence," March 24, 1862, in *Lincoln's Journalist*, p. 235.

75. Kearny to Agnes Maxwell Kearny, March 17, 1862, and to Cortlandt Parker, June 22, 1862, in *Letters from the Peninsula: The Civil War Letters of General Philip Kearny* (Kearny, NJ: Belle Grove Press, 1988), pp. 34, 108; T. Harry Williams, *Lincoln and the Radicals* (Madison, WI: University of Wisconsin Press, 1941), p. 57; Bates, diary entry for December 31, 1861, in *Diary of Edward Bates*, p. 218; James F. Wilson, "Some Memories of Lincoln," *North American Review* 163 (December 1896), p. 667.

76. "General M. C. Meigs on the Conduct of the Civil War," *American Historical Review* 26 (1920–21), pp. 292–93; McClellan, in Segal, *Conversations with Lincoln*, pp. 154–55; Bruce Tap, *Over Lincoln's Shoulder*, pp. 107–108; McClellan, *Civil War Papers*, pp. 115, 135, 196, 269, 275.

77. Nicolay, conversation with Henry Wilson, November 16, 1875, in *Oral His-*

tory of Abraham Lincoln, p. 84; Hay, in *Inside Lincoln's White House*, p. 221–24.

78. Erasmus Keyes to Chase, June 17, 1862, *The Salmon P. Chase Papers*, volume three, pp. 212–13; Browning, diary entry for January 12, 1862, in *Diary of Orville Hickman Browning*, volume one, p. 523.

79. Allan Bogue, "William Parker Cutler's Congressional Diary of 1862–63," *Civil War History* 33 (December 1987), p. 323; Stoddard, "The Two Chieftains," *Inside the White House in War Times*, p. 61; Browning, diary entry for April 2, 1862, in *Diary of Orville Hickman Browning*, volume one, p. 537; Kearny, July 11, 1862, and July 24, 1862, in *Letters from the Peninsula*, pp. 133, 138.

80. Nicolay, journal entry for February 27, 1862, in *With Lincoln in the White House*, p. 72; Carpenter, *Six Months at the White House*, p. 130; AL, "President's General War Order No. 1," January 27, 1862, in *C.W.*, volume five, pp. 111–12; Hay, diary entry for March 1862, in *Inside Lincoln's White House*, p. 35.

81. Reid, July 16, 1862, in *A Radical View*, volume one, p. 209.

82. McClellan, "To Edwin M. Stanton," June 25, 1862, in *Civil War Papers*, p. 309.

83. McClellan, "To Edwin M. Stanton," June 28, 1862, in *Civil War Papers*, p. 323; David Homer Bates, *Lincoln in the Telegraph Office: Recollections of the United States Military Telegraph Corps during the Civil War*, ed. James A. Rawley (1907; Lincoln, NE: University of Nebraska Press, 1995), pp. 109–10; AL, "To George B. McClellan," June 28, 1862, in *C.W.*, volume five, p. 289.

84. Fisher, "Prohibition of Slavery," May 12, 1862, in *Congressional Globe*, 37th Congress, 2nd Session, pp. 2066–68; Reed, pp. 48–49; John H. Bayne to AL, March 17, 1862, in Abraham Lincoln Papers, Library of Congress; "Missouri's Rejection of the President's Emancipation Policy," *Washington Daily National Republican*, June 13, 1862; "Missouri State Convention," *Washington Evening Star*, June 17, 1862; Allan Nevins, *The War for the Union: The War Becomes Revolution, 1862–1863* (New York: Charles Scribner's Sons, 1960), pp. 115–16.

85. AL, "Proclamation Revoking General Hunter's Order of Military Emancipation of May 9, 1862," in *C.W.*, volume five, p. 223; McPherson, *Political History*, p. 250.

86. AL, "To George B. McClellan," July 2, 1862, in *C.W.*, volume five, pp. 301–302; Browning, diary entry for July 7, 1862, in *Diary of Orville Hickman Browning*, volume one, p. 552.

87. "The President's Visit to the Field," *Washington Evening Star*, July 11, 1862, and *Washington Sunday Morning Chronicle*, July 13, 1862; William C. Davis, *Lincoln's Men: How President Lincoln Became Father to an Army and a Nation* (New York: Free Press, 1999), pp. 66–70; *A Yankee at Arms: The Diary of Augustus D. Ayling, 29th Massachusetts Volunteers*, ed. Charles F. Herberger (Knoxville: University of Tennessee Press, 1999), p. 54. See also John Hay's account of the Harrison's Landing visit, in "Washington Correspondence," mid-July 1862, in *Lincoln's Journalist*, pp. 281–85, and Nicolay, "To Therena Bates," July 13, 1862, in *With Lincoln in the White House*, p. 85; a somewhat more garbled version of the Lincoln-McClellan meeting occurs in James C. Scovel, "Personal Recollections of Abraham Lincoln," *Overland Monthly* 18 (November 1891), pp. 505–506.

88. McClellan, "To Abraham Lincoln," June 20, 1862, in *Civil War Papers*, p. 304; George Ticknor Curtis, "McClellan's Last Service to the Republic," *North American Review* 130 (April 1880), pp. 312–16; Warren W. Hassler, *General George B. McClellan, Shield of the Union* (Baton Rouge: Louisiana State University Press, 1957), pp. 177–78; Stephen W. Sears, *George B. McClellan: The Young Napoleon* (New York: Ticknor & Fields, 1988), pp. 226–29.

89. McClellan, "To Abraham Lincoln," July 7, 1862, in *Civil War Papers*, p. 344, and in *O.R.*, Series One, volume eleven (part one), p. 73. The editor of McClellan's memoirs asserted that the Harrison's Landing letter was not made public until the end of 1862, after McClellan had been removed from command, but he believed Lincoln had discussed the letter with members of the cabinet, and that they in turn had leaked descriptions of it more broadly. McClellan did not release a version of the letter publicly until he published his official report on the Peninsula Campaign in August 1863. See *O.R.*, Series One, volume eleven (part one), pp. 73–74, and *McClellan's Own Story: The War for the Union, The Soldiers Who Fought It, the Civilians Who Directed It, and His Relations to It and to Them* (New York: Charles L. Webster, 1887), pp. 487–89. The letter was also printed in several campaign biographies for McClellan's unsuccessful bid for the presidency in 1864. See *The Life, Campaigns, and Public Services of General McClellan* (Philadelphia: T. B. Peterson & Bros., 1864), pp. 105–107; G. S. Hilliard, *Life and Campaigns of George B. McClellan, Major-General, U.S. Army* (Philadelphia: J. B. Lippincott, 1864), pp. 262–65; and William Henry Hulbert, *General McClellan and the Conduct of the War* (New York: Sheldon & Co., 1864), pp. 262–64.

90. McClellan, "To Abraham Lincoln," July 7, 1862, in *Civil War Papers*, p.

345. As T. Harry Williams commented acidly in 1962, "McClellan never grasped the political character of the war, he never accepted the civilian as a factor in the war. He did not even seem to comprehend that the political-civilian branch of the government was supposed to have a significant part in determining how the war should be conducted." See Williams, *McClellan, Sherman and Grant* (New Brunswick, NJ: Rutgers University Press, 1962), p. 29. Contrast this reading of the Harrison's Landing letter with the pro-McClellan versions in Porter S. Michie, *General McClellan* (New York: Appleton & Co., 1901), pp. 370–71; James Havelock Campbell, *McClellan: A Vindication of the Military Career of General George B. McClellan* (New York: Neale Publishing, 1916), pp. 261–67; William Starr Myers, *General George Brinton McClellan: A Study in Personality* (New York: Appleton-Century Crofts, 1934), pp. 307–11; Russell F. Weigley, "The American Military and the Principle of Civilian Control," *Journal of Military History* 57 (October 1993), pp. 34–35; and James G. Randall, *Lincoln the President: Bull Run to Gettysburg,* pp. 100–104. On previous military-civilian clashes, see Samuel P. Huntington, *The Soldier and the State: The Theory and Politics of Civil-Military Relations* (Cambridge, MA: Harvard University Press, 1957), p. 210.

91. John Bigelow, *Retrospections of an Active Life, 1817–1863* (New York: Baker and Taylor, 1909), p. 508; George Wilkes, *McClellan: From Ball's Bluff to Antietam* (New York: Sinclair Tousey, 1863), pp. 10, 23; Julian, "Indemnification Bill," February 18, 1863, in *Congressional Globe,* 37th Congress, 3rd Session, p. 1067; Meigs, in "General M. C. Meigs on the Conduct of the Civil War," p. 294; Key, in Nevins, *The War for the Union: The War Becomes Revolution, 1862–1863,* p. 231; McClellan, "To Mary Ellen McClellan," July 11, 1862, July 17, 1862, July 29, 1862, and August 10, 1862, in *Civil War Papers,* pp. 351, 362, 375, 390. Even contemporaries were unsure whether, in McClellan's mind, he was actually flirting with the idea of a coup d'etat or simply hopelessly clumsy in writing letters that, clumsy or not, he had no business writing in the first place. Jacob Dolson Cox believed that the Harrison's Landing letter was a bungled attempt by McClellan "to show Mr. Lincoln that they were not far apart in opinion, and to influence the President to take the more conservative course to which he thought him inclined when taking counsel only of his own judgment. . . . Under the guise of giving advice to the President, he was in fact assuring him that he did not look to the acknowledgment of the Confederacy as a conceivable outcome of the war; that the 'contraband' doctrine applied to slaves was consistent with compensated emancipation; that he favored the application of the principle

to the border States so as to make them free States." See Cox, *Military Reminiscences*, volume one, p. 357. In the White House, a different view prevailed. John Hay recorded in his diary the story that McClellan was repeatedly visited by Democratic politicians on the Peninsula who tried to convince him "to accept their propositions" that he announce himself as a candidate for the presidency, "& had written them a letter . . . giving his idea of the proper way of conducting the war, so as to conciliate and impress the people of the South with the idea that our armies were intended merely to execute the laws and protect their property &c. & pledging himself to conduct the war in that inefficient conciliatory style." Lincoln certainly believed the story, although he added, in 1864, that it spoke more of McClellan's "constitutional weakness and timidity" than "any such deeplaid scheme of treachery & ambition." Similarly, Salmon Chase would not "question his general loyalty to the country," but he did not "regard Genl. McClellan as loyal to the Administration." See Chase, diary entry for July 22, 1862, in *Inside Lincoln's Cabinet*, p. 98. Even so, in 1862, Lincoln suspected that McClellan "was playing false." See Hay, diary entry for September 25, 1864, in *Inside Lincoln's White House*, pp. 230–33. Even if McClellan was only playing politics, he was doing so with so little concern for discretion that one foreign observer, Frederick Miles Edge, who accompanied the Army of the Potomac on the Peninsula, asked whether McClellan was using "the Army of the Potomac as a weapon with which to crush the enemies of the union, or as a tool where with to build up a sectional political party?" See Edge, *Major-General McClellan and the Campaign on the Yorktown Peninsula* (London: Trubner & Co., 1865), p. 202.

92. Welles, "The History of Emancipation," p. 237; Joseph Smith to Andrew H. Foote, July 11, 1862, in The Gilder Lehrman Collection (GLC 5060), New-York Historical Society; Noah Brooks, *Washington in Lincoln's Time* (Washington, DC: Century Co., 1895), p. 16; Browning, diary entry for July 25, 1862, in *Diary of Orville Hickman Browning*, volume one, p. 553; Stephen W. Sears, *To the Gates of Richmond: The Peninsula Campaign* (New York: Ticknor & Fields, 1992), p. 351.

93. AL, "Appeal to Border State Representatives to Favor Compensated Emancipation," July 12, 1862, and "To the Senate and House of Representatives," July 14, 1862, in *C.W.*, volume five, pp. 317–19, 324; "An Important Consultation," *Washington Evening Star*, July 14, 1862; "The President's Appeal to the Border States," *Washington Daily National Intelligencer*, July 18, 1862.

94. The text of the majority report is in "The Border States and the President," *Washington Daily National Republican*, July 21, 1862, and in McPherson,

Political History, pp. 214–17; a seven-member minority composed their own letter, supporting Lincoln, and sent it to him the following day, in "Border State Congressmen to Abraham Lincoln," July 15, 1862, in Abraham Lincoln Papers, Library of Congress. Arnold, *Lincoln and the Overthrow of Slavery,* pp. 287–88; "The President and the Border States—A Message" and "The President and the Border State Congressmen," in *Washington Daily National Republican,* July 15 and July 16, 1862; "The President and the Border States," *Washington Sunday Morning Chronicle,* July 20, 1862; Hay to Mary Jay, July 20, 1862, in *At Lincoln's Side,* p. 23.

3. An Instrument in God's Hands

1. Carpenter, *Six Months at the White House,* p. 117.
2. Welles, *Diary of Gideon Welles: Secretary of the Navy under Lincoln and Johnson,* ed. John Torrey Morse (New York: Houghton Mifflin, 1911), volume one, pp. 70–71; Welles, "History of Emancipation," in *Selected Essays by Gideon Welles: Civil War and Reconstruction,* ed. Albert Mordell (New York: Twayne, 1959), pp. 237–40; Welles, *Lincoln and Seward,* p. 210.
3. *Statutes at Large,* pp. 589–92, 597–600; Saulsbury, "Term of Service of Militia," July 9, 1862, in *Congressional Globe,* 37th Congress, 2nd Session, p. 3198; Wilson, *History of the Anti-Slavery Measures,* pp. 204, 217; Arnold, *Lincoln and the Overthrow of Slavery,* pp. 266–70; Andrew to Francis P. Blair, Sr., July 5, 1862, in Pearson, *Life of John A. Andrew,* volume two, pp. 23–24, and Richard Yates to AL, July 11, 1862, Abraham Lincoln Papers, Library of Congress.
4. Hamilton, "No. 69," *The Federalist,* eds. George W. Carey and James McClellan (Indianapolis, IN: Liberty Fund, 2001), p. 357; Taney, in *Fleming v. Page,* Howard's Reports, volume 9, 50 U.S., p. 615. For modern commentary on the war powers, see Phillip J. Cooper, *By Order of the President: The Use and Abuse of Executive Direct Action* (Lawrence, KS: University of Kansas Press, 2002), pp. 16–17, 20–21, 117–19, 120–22, 124, 127, 130, 133, W. E. Binkley, *The Powers of the President: Problems of American Democracy* (New York: Russell & Russell, 1937), pp. 122–23, and Louis Fisher, *Constitutional Conflicts between Congress and the President* (Princeton, NJ: Princeton University Press, 1985), pp. 284–325.
5. Adams, "Indian Hostilities," in *Congressional Globe,* 24th Congress, 1st Session, Appendix, pp. 448, 450; *The Abolition of Slavery the Right of the Government from the War Power* (Boston: J. F. Wallcut, 1861), p. 4; Charles Francis Adams, "John Quincy Adams and Martial Law," *Proceedings of the*

Massachusetts Historical Society 15 (1901–02), pp. 437–78; James G. Blaine, "Confiscation of Rebel Property," March 7, 1862, in *Political Discussions*, p. 21; Sumner, in Adams, *Richard Henry Dana*, volume two, p. 260; Donald, *Charles Sumner and the Coming of the Civil War*, p. 388; Sumner, "The Hon. C. Sumner on a War for Emancipation" [October 1, 1861], in *The Anti-Slavery Reporter*, November 1, 1861, pp. 246–47; Sumner to Lieber, September 17, 1861, *Selected Letters*, volume two, p. 79; Beecher, "Modes and Duties of Emancipation," November 26, 1861, in *Patriotic Addresses*, p. 333.

6. "Senator Henderson's Reply to the President," July 21, 1862, in McPherson, *Political History*, pp. 218–20.

7. Browning, diary entries for July 14 and 15, 1862, in *Diary of Orville Hickman Browning*, volume one, pp. 558, 560; AL, "To Solomon Foot," July 15, 1862, and "To the Senate and House of Representatives," July 17, 1862, in *C.W.*, volume five, pp. 326, 328–31; Wade, "Confiscation of Rebel Property," July 16, 1862, "Confiscation and Emancipation," July 16, 1862, "Confiscation," July 17, 1862, in *Congressional Globe*, 37th Congress, 2nd Session, pp. 3375, 3400, 3406; McPherson, *Political History*, pp. 196–98; White, *Life of Lyman Trumbull*, pp. 173–17, 175; James G. Blaine, *Twenty Years of Congress*, volume one, pp. 376–77; "Address to the Loyal People of the United States," *Washington Daily National Republican*, July 17, 1862.

8. Chase, diary entry for July 21, 1862, in *Inside Lincoln's Cabinet*, p. 95; Schuckers, *Life and Public Services of Salmon P. Chase*, pp. 439–40.

9. Chase, diary entry for July 21, 1862, in *Inside Lincoln's Cabinet*, p. 96; AL, "To the Senate and House of Representatives," July 17, 1862, in *C.W.*, volume five, p. 329.

10. Nicolay and Hay, *Abraham Lincoln*, volume six, p. 124.

11. Chase to Richard C. Parsons, July 21, 1862, *The Salmon P. Chase Papers*, volume three, p. 231; AL, "Order concerning Subjects of Foreign Powers," July 21, 1862, in *C.W.*, volume five, pp. 334–35; "Grover's Theatre," *Washington Daily National Republican*, July 21, 1862.

12. Welles, "History of Emancipation," p. 241. Welles was explicit about the meeting occurring "in the library of the executive mansion, and not in the council chamber, where the regular sessions were usually convened." Chase makes no mention of the venue for the meeting in his diary, nor does Lincoln in the account he gave Francis Carpenter; nevertheless, Carpenter painted his "First Reading of the Emancipation Proclamation" with Lincoln's office as the meeting place.

13. "General Orders No. 154," in *O.R.*, Series One, volume eleven (part three), pp. 362–63.

14. Carpenter, *Six Months at the White House,* p. 21; Chase, diary entry for July 22, 1862, in *Inside Lincoln's Cabinet,* p. 99; Welles, "History of Emancipation," p. 243; Welles, *Lincoln and Seward,* p. 212; Nicolay and Hay, *Abraham Lincoln,* volume six, p. 128.

15. Welles, "History of Emancipation," p. 242; AL, "Emancipation Proclamation—First Draft," in *C.W.,* volume five, p. 336.

16. AL, "Emancipation Proclamation—First Draft," in *C.W.,* volume five, pp. 336– 337; Adams, in *The Abolition of Slavery the Right of the Government from the War Power,* p. 4.

17. Bates to B. Gratz Brown, March 17, 1860, in *Diary of Edward Bates,* p. 113; Welles, "History of Emancipation," p. 242.

18. Frederick J. Blue, "Friends of Freedom: Lincoln, Chase, and Wartime Racial Policy," *Ohio History* 102 (Summer/Autumn 1993), pp. 92–94; Schuckers, *Life and Services of Salmon P. Chase,* pp. 440–41; Chase, diary entry for July 22, 1862, in *Inside Lincoln's Cabinet,* p. 99; Chase to Benjamin Butler, July 31, 1862, *The Salmon P. Chase Papers,* volume three, pp. 236–37; Stanton, "The Cabinet on Emancipation, July 22, 1862," Edwin M. Stanton Papers, Container 8, Reel 3, Library of Congress. Oddly, Chase wrote to Francis Carpenter in 1866 to tell him that "so little important did any Cabinet meetings in July relating to the proclamation seem to me, that not the slightest trace of such meeting remain in my memory . . . for there was much talk which required no action and of which, I took no account." See Thomas F. Schwartz, "Salmon P. Chase Critiques 'First Reading of the Emancipation Proclamation of President Lincoln,' " *Civil War History* 33 (March 1987), p. 86.

19. Burton J. Hendrick, *Lincoln's War Cabinet* (1946; Garden City, NY: Doubleday & Co., 1961), p. 384; Carpenter, *Six Months at the White House,* pp. 72–73; Donn Piatt, *Memories of Men Who Saved the Union* (New York: Belford, Clarke, 1887), p. 150; White, *Life of Lyman Trumbull,* p. 222.

20. Carpenter, *Six Months at the White House,* p. 22; Howard Jones, *Abraham Lincoln and a New Birth of Freedom: The Union and Slavery in the Diplomacy of the Civil War* (Lincoln, NE: University of Nebraska Press, 1999), pp. 62, 83–115; Stanton, "The Cabinet on Emancipation, July 22, 1862," Edwin M. Stanton Papers, Library of Congress.

21. AL, "To Edwin M. Stanton," July 22, 1862, in *C.W.,* volume five, p. 338; Francis B. Cutting to Stanton, February 20, 1867, in Stanton Papers, Library of Congress; Benjamin Thomas and Harold Hyman, *Stanton: The Life and Times of Lincoln's Secretary of War* (New York: Knopf, 1962), p. 240; Chase, diary entry for July 22, 1862, in *Inside Lincoln's Cabinet,* p. 99,

and Schuckers, *Life and Public Services of Salmon Portland Chase*, p. 440; AL, "Proclamation of the Act to Suppress Insurrection," July 25, 1862, in *C.W.*, volume five, p. 341. See a directive concerning the employment of "persons of African descent," issued on August 16, 1862, in *O.R.*, Series Three, volume two, p. 397.

22. Browning, diary entry for July 21, 1862, in *Diary of Orville Hickman Browning*, volume one, p. 562; Joseph M. Wightman to AL, May 23, 1862, Abraham Lincoln Papers, Library of Congress, and *Washington Evening Star*, June 18, 1862. John Hay was amused by Wightman, "a fussy little Democrat with strong anti-abolition prejudices," and quipped that the mayor "thinks this is a Wight man's war." See Hay, diary entry for September 5, 1862, in *Inside Lincoln's White House*, p. 39; Baum, *The Civil War Party System*, pp. 63–65.

23. Conway, *Autobiography*, volume one, p. 388; Vogeli, *Free but Not Equal*, pp. 34–35; McPherson, *The Negro's Civil War*, pp. 69–70; "The Omnibus Riot," *Chicago Tribune*, July 17, 1862; "Riots of Laborers in Ohio," "Disturbances at Cincinnati," and "Anti-Negro Riot at Brooklyn (N.Y.)," *Washington Daily National Intelligencer*, July 22, 1862, and August 6, 1862; "Anti-Negroism in Illinois," *Washington National Republican*, June 26, 1862; "Negro Organizations in Washington," *Washington Evening Star*, August 4, 1862; Owner, diary entry for July 28, 1862, William Owner manuscript diary, Library of Congress; "The President's Visit to the Field," *Washington Evening Star*, July 11, 1862.

24. Carpenter, *Six Months at the White House*, pp. 21–23, 77; Gideon Welles, "History of Emancipation," p. 242; Stanton to Saxton, August 25, 1862, in *O.R.*, Series One, volume fourteen, p. 377.

25. Sumner to John Andrew, May 28, 1862, in *Selected Letters of Charles Sumner*, volume two, p. 115; Ryerson to Seward, May 23, 1862, William Henry Seward Papers, University of Rochester.

26. Hamlin, in "Senator Hamlin, of Maine," *New York Times*, September 8, 1879; Harry Draper Hunt, *Hannibal Hamlin of Maine: Lincoln's First Vice-President* (Syracuse, NY: Syracuse University Press, 1969), p. 198; Mark Scroggins, *Hannibal: The Life of Lincoln's First Vice President* (Lanham, MD: University Press of America, 1993), p. 217.

27. Whitney, *Life on the Circuit with Lincoln* (Boston: Estes & Lauriat, 1892), p. 536; Hamlin, in Charles Eugene Hamlin, *The Life and Times of Hannibal Hamlin* (Cambridge, MA: Riverside Press, 1899), pp. 428–29. On Hamlin's movements, see Hamlin's submission to John W. Forney on June 18 of his intention to be absent from the Senate the next day, in *Congressional Globe*,

37th Congress, 2nd Session, p. 2798, and *Bangor Daily Whig and Courier,* June 20, 1862.

28. Lovejoy, in McPherson, *Political History,* p. 233; Edward Magdol, *Owen Lovejoy: Abolitionist in Congress* (New Brunswick, NJ: Rutgers University Press, 1967), p. 339; Welles, "Administration of Abraham Lincoln, III," in *Lincoln's Administration,* p. 119; Lovejoy, in Browne, *Abraham Lincoln and the Men of His Time* (Chicago: Blakely-Oswald Printing, 1907), pp. 673–82; Colfax to Nicolay, August 26, 1875, in Nicolay-Hay Manuscripts, Illinois State Historical Library; Browning, diary entry for July 1, 1862, in *Diary of Orville Hickman Browning,* volume one, p. 558. Nicolay dismissed Colfax's story out of hand, but there remains some possibility that there may indeed have been a "lost" version of the Proclamation, since the daughter of Lincoln's valet, William Slade, remembered that her father "destroyed many old pieces of paper with notes upon them" for the Proclamation—so many, in fact, that by the time the Proclamation was published in September, Slade "already knew every word of it." Slade, in John E. Washington, *They Knew Lincoln* (New York: E. P. Dutton, 1942), p. 111.

29. Bates, *Lincoln in the Telegraph Office,* pp. 40, 42; Nicolay and Hay, *Abraham Lincoln,* volume six, pp. 141–42.

30. Bates, *Lincoln in the Telegraph Office,* pp. 138–41.

31. Thomas H. Sherman, *Twenty Years with James G. Blaine* (New York: Grafton Press, 1928), pp. 1–8; Wilson, *A Few Acts and Actors in the Tragedy of the Civil War in the United States* (Philadelphia: n.p., 1892), pp. 84–91. Stoddard, *Inside the White House in War Times,* p. 95.

32. "Reviews and Literary Notices," *Atlantic Monthly* 18 (November 1866), p. 645; Carpenter, *Six Months at the White House,* pp. 20, 86; Carpenter to Theodore Munger, February 22, 1864, in Munger Papers, Sterling Library, Yale University; Barrett to William Henry Herndon, October 1, 1866, and Joseph G. Monfort to Herndon, August 10, 1867, in *Herndon's Informants,* p. 364; Barrett, *Life, Speeches, and Public Services of Abraham Lincoln* (Cincinnati: Moore, Wilstach & Baldwin, 1865), p. 414; Blair, "The Republican Party as It Was and Is," *North American Review* 131 (November 1880), p. 426.

33. Welles, "History of Emancipation," p. 254; Duval, in *Recollected Words,* p. 146.

34. Hamilton to E. D. Morgan, August 4, 1862, in *Reminiscences of James A. Hamilton; or, Men and Events at Home and Abroad during Three Quarters of a Century* (New York: Charles Scribner & Co., 1869), p. 526; Speed to AL, July 28, 1862, Abraham Lincoln Papers, Library of Congress; "The Prosecu-

tion of the War," *Washington Evening Star*, August 4, 1862; Welles, "Admin-
istration of Abraham Lincoln, I," in *Lincoln's Administration*, p. 119; Robert
L. Kincaid, *Joshua Fry Speed: Lincoln's Most Intimate Friend* (Chicago:
Abraham Lincoln Bookshop, 1943), p. 27; Gilmore, *Personal Recollections of
Abraham Lincoln and the Civil War* (Boston: L. C. Page, 1898), pp. 75, 82–83;
"Emancipation Proposed by the President," *Chicago Tribune*, August 23,
1862. Gilmore, under the pen name of Edmund Kirke, had just published
his antislavery novel *Among the Pines: or, South in Secession-Time* in June,
which promised, "Free their Negroes by an act of emancipation, or confiscation, and the rebellion will crumble to pieces in a day," p. 172; Browning,
"Conversation with Hon. Leonard Swett," March 14, 1878, in *Oral History
of Abraham Lincoln*, pp. 58–59; Hay, "Washington Correspondence," September 7, 1862, in *Lincoln's Journalist*, p. 309; Barney to Gideon Welles, September 27, 1877, in Gideon Welles Papers, New York Public Library.
Barney's claim was confirmed in passing by Henry Wilson in *Rise and Fall of
the Slave Power*, volume three, p. 388.

35. Chase, diary entry for August 3, 1862, in *Inside Lincoln's Cabinet*, pp.
105–106; "The Grand War Demonstration a Brilliant Success," *Washington
National Republican*, August 7, 1862; Eggleston, "Emancipation," p. 814;
"Mrs. L. Maria Childs to the President of the United States," *Washington
National Republican*, August 22, 1862.

36. Bates, diary entry for December 26, 1863, in *Diary of Edward Bates*, p.
326; AL to Joseph E. McDonald, in *Recollected Words*, p. 322; Julian, in
Reminiscences of Abraham Lincoln by Distinguished Men of His Time,
ed. Allen Thorndike Rice (New York: North American Publishing, 1886),
p. 60; Herndon to Jesse Weik, December 23, 1885, in *The Hidden Lincoln,
from the Letters and Papers of William H. Herndon*, ed. Emmanuel Hertz
(New York: Viking, 1938), p. 114; Jesse Weik, *The Real Lincoln*, p. 298;
Gilmore, *Personal Recollections of Abraham Lincoln and the Civil War*,
p. 81.

37. Greeley, "The Prayer of Twenty Millions," in *Dear Mr. Lincoln: Letters to
the President*, ed. Harold Holzer (Reading, MA: Addison-Wesley, 1993), pp.
156–61; "Greeley's Estimate of Lincoln: An Unpublished Address by Horace Greeley," *Century Magazine* 42 (July 1891), pp. 379–80.

38. James Welling, in Rice, *Reminiscences of Abraham Lincoln*, pp. 525–26;
Leech, *Reveille in Washington*, p. 75; Josiah Gilbert Holland, *Life of Abraham Lincoln* (Springfield, MA: Gurdon Bill, 1866), p. 354; Arnold, *Lincoln
and the Overthrow of Slavery*, p. 289. On the *National Intelligencer*'s own
editorial comment on the letter, see "The President's Letter," in *Abraham*

Lincoln: A Press Portrait, ed. Herbert Mitgang (1971; Athens, GA: University of Georgia Press, 1989), pp. 301–302.

39. AL, "To Horace Greeley," August 22, 1862, in *C.W.*, volume five, pp. 388–89; McPherson, *Political History*, p. 211; Henry Hoyt Horner, "Lincoln Replies to Horace Greeley," *Lincoln Herald* 53 (Spring 1951), pp. 2–10, and (Summer 1951) pp. 14–25; Nicolay and Hay, *Abraham Lincoln*, volume six, pp. 152–53.

40. Pearson, *Life of John A. Andrew*, volume two, p. 48; Arnold, *Lincoln and the Overthrow of Slavery*, p. 289; this message was repeated almost verbatim in "The President's Letter to Mr. Greeley," *Chicago Tribune*, August 27, 1862. On the conflicting interpretations of the Greeley letter, see Don E. Fehrenbacher, "Only His Stepchildren," in *Lincoln in Text and Context: Collected Essays* (Stanford, CA: Stanford University Press, 1987), pp. 109, 283–84; Vogeli, *Free but Not Equal*, pp. 45–46; LaWanda Cox, *Lincoln and Black Freedom: A Study in Presidential Leadership* (Urbana, IL: University of Illinois Press, 1985), p. 12; and T. Harry Williams, *Lincoln and the Radicals*, pp. 172–73; Welles, "History of Emancipation," pp. 243–44.

41. Reid, "Lincoln and Greeley," August 24, 1862, in *A Radical View*, volume one, p. 215; "Letter of Horace Greeley to President Lincoln," *Baltimore Sun*, August 25, 1862; "A Letter from the President," *Washington Evening Star*, August 23, 1862; "The President to Editor Greeley," *Washington Morning Chronicle*, August 24, 1862; "The President's Reply to Horace Greeley," *Washington National Republican*, August 25, 1862; R. P. L. Baker to Francis Preston Blair, August 26, 1862, in Blair Family Papers, Library of Congress; Gay to AL, August 1862, Abraham Lincoln Papers, Library of Congress; James Parton, *Life of Horace Greeley, Editor of the "New-York Tribune," from His Birth to the Present Time* (Boston: Houghton, Mifflin, 1889), pp. 500–502; Williams, *Lincoln and the Radicals*, p. 173; Arnold, *The Life of Abraham Lincoln*, ed. James A. Rawley (1884; Lincoln, NE: University of Nebraska Press, 1994), pp. 255–56; Robert C. Winthrop, "A Star for Every State, and a State for Every Star," August 27, 1862, in *Addresses and Speeches on Various Occasions, from 1852 to 1867* (Boston: Little, Brown, 1867), p. 534.

42. Reid, "Lincoln and Greeley," ibid.; Gilmore, *Personal Recollections of Abraham Lincoln and the Civil War*, p. 84; "Greeley's Estimate of Lincoln," p. 380.

43. AL, "Order Constituting the Army of Virginia," June 26, 1862, in *C.W.*, volume five, p. 287; "Army Order," *Washington Evening Star*, August 16, 1862.

44. Herman Hattaway and Archer Jones, *How the North Won: A Military His-*

tory of the Civil War (Urbana, IL: University of Illinois Press, 1983), pp. 209–11; Thomas and Hyman, *Stanton: The Life and Times of Lincoln's Secretary of War*, pp. 215–17.

45. Peter Cozzens, *General John Pope: A Life for the Nation* (Urbana, IL: University of Illinois Press, 2000), pp. 8–28, 85; John J. Hennessy, *Return to Bull Run: The Campaign and Battle of Second Manassas* (New York: Simon and Schuster, 1993), pp. 4, 13; Chase to Pope, August 1, 1862, in Schuckers, *Life and Public Services of Salmon Portland Chase*, p. 378; "To the Officers and Soldiers of the Army of Virginia," July 14, 1862, in *O.R.*, Series One, volume 12, part three, pp. 473–74; "General Pope's Orders," *Washington Evening Star*, July 28, 1862.

46. McClellan, "To Samuel Barlow," July 30, 1862, to "Henry W. Halleck," August 1, 1862, August 4, 1862, and August 31, 1862, and "To Mary Ellen McClellan," August 10, 1862, August 17, 1862, and August 24, 1862, in *Civil War Papers of George B. McClellan*, pp. 377, 381, 389, 395, 404, 424; Halleck to McClellan, August 6, 1862, in *O.R.*, Series One, volume twelve (part two), p. 11.

47. John Hay, "Washington Correspondence," July 27, 1862, in *Lincoln's Journalist*, p. 287; "Gen. Pope's Address," *Washington Daily National Intelligencer*, July 16, 1862; "The President's Colonization Scheme. His Interview with a Committee of Colored Men," in *Daily National Republican*, August 15, 1862.

48. Forbes to Charles Sumner, September 15, 1862, in *Personal Reminiscences* (Boston: Little, Brown, 1878), p. 291; "Colonization Society," *North American Review* 18 (January 1824), p. 61; Seward, *Seward at Washington*, volume two, p. 227; Pearson, *James S. Wadsworth of Geneseo*, p. 244; Douglas R. Egerton, "Averting a Crisis: The Proslavery Critique of the American Colonization Society," *Civil War History* 43 (June 1997), pp. 142–56.

49. Boutwell, *Speeches and Papers Relating to the Rebellion*, pp. 177–78; Smith, *Considerations on the Slavery Question Addressed to the President of the United States* (New York: privately printed, December 24, 1862), p. 14; Montgomery Blair to James R. Doolittle, November 11, 1859, in J. R. Doolittle Papers, State Historical Society of Wisconsin; Eggelston, "Emancipation," p. 810; AL, "Speech at Springfield, Illinois," June 26, 1857, in *C.W.*, volume two, p. 409.

50. AL, "Annual Message to Congress," December 3, 1861, in *C.W.*, volume five, p. 48; on Guatemala, see Elisha O. Crosby to J. R. Doolittle, November 20, 1861, in James Rood Doolittle Papers, New York Public Library; on the Chiriqui proposal, see Thomas Francis Meagher, "The New Route through

Chiriqui," *Harper's Monthly Magazine* 22 (January 1861), p. 209; Ninian Edwards to AL, August 9, 1861, Francis P. Blair to AL, November 16, 1861, in Blair Family Papers, and James Mitchell to AL, December 13, 1861, in Abraham Lincoln Papers, Library of Congress; and Paul J. Shieps, "Lincoln and the Chiriqui Colonization Project," *Journal of Negro History* 37 (October 1952), pp. 418–53. See also Warren Beck, "Lincoln and Negro Colonization in Central America," *Abraham Lincoln Quarterly* 6 (September 1950), pp. 162–83; Quarles, *Lincoln and the Negro,* pp. 108–22; Gabor Boritt, "Did He Dream of a Lily-White America? The Voyage to Linconia," in *The Lincoln Enigma: The Changing Faces of an American Icon,* ed. Gabor Boritt (New York: Oxford University Press, 2001), pp. 1–19; Gary Planck, "Abraham Lincoln and Black Colonization: Theory and Practice," *Lincoln Herald* 72 (Summer 1970), pp. 61–77; and Janet L. Coryell, " 'The Lincoln Colony': Aaron Columbus Burr's Proposed Colonization of British Honduras," *Civil War History* 43 (March 1997), pp. 5–16.

51. Douglass, "Colonization," January 26, 1849, in *Frederick Douglass: Selected Speeches and Writings,* p. 126; Purvis, in William Wells Brown, *The Black Man, His Antecedents, His Genius, and His Achievements,* pp. 256, 258–59; "Interview between President Lincoln and a Committee of Colored Men," *Washington Evening Star,* August 15, 1862.

52. AL, "Address on Colonization to a Deputation of Negroes," in *C.W.,* volume five, pp. 370–75; "Colonisation," *Daily Morning Chronicle,* August 17, 1862. The curmudgeonly William Owner wrote in his diary that "Lincoln received a committee of nig deputies[. The] report says he gave them some advice, and told them he intended to ship them to Central America, didn't want their answer then, they must think over the matter and report their answer some future day. Dismissed them." Owner, diary entry for August 15, 1862, in William Owner manuscript diary, Library of Congress.

53. Douglass, "The President and His Speeches," September 1862, in *Frederick Douglass: Selected Speeches and Writings,* pp. 510–13; David W. Blight, *Frederick Douglass' Civil War: Keeping Faith in Jubilee* (Baton Rouge, LA: Louisiana State University Press, 1989), p. 139.

54. Randall, *Lincoln the President: Bull Run to Gettysburg,* pp. 137–38.

55. Theodore Gates, diary entry for August 29, 1862, in *The Civil War Diaries of Col. Theodore B. Gates, 20th New York State Militia,* ed. Seward R. Osborne (Hights-town, NJ: Longstreet House, 1991), p. 33; McPherson, *Battle Cry of Freedom: The Civil War Era* (New York: Oxford University Press, 1988), pp. 531–32; Nevins, *The War for the Union: The War Becomes Revo-*

lution, 1862–1863, p. 177; Hay, diary entry for September 1, 1862, in *Inside Lincoln's White House*, p. 38.

56. Pope to Halleck, September 1, 1862, in *O.R.*, Series One, volume twelve (part two), pp. 82–83; McClellan, "To Abraham Lincoln," August 29, 1862, in *Civil War Papers*, p. 416; Arnold, *Life of Abraham Lincoln*, pp. 291–93.

57. Browning, diary entry for November 12, 1862, in *Diary of Orville Hickman Browning*, volume one, pp. 584–85; Robert Todd Lincoln, in *Recollected Words*, p. 298; Hay, diary entries for September 1, 1862, and September 5, 1862, in *Inside the White House*, pp. 37, 39; Chandler to Trumbull, September 10, 1862, in Wilmer C. Harris, *Public Life of Zachariah Chandler, 1851–1875* (Lansing, MI: Michigan Historical Commission, 1917), p. 61; Welles, diary entry for September 10, 1862, in *Diary of Gideon Welles*, volume one, p. 119; Strong, diary entry for September 13, 1862, in *Diary of the Civil War*, p. 255.

58. McClellan, "To Mary Ellen McClellan," September 2, 1862, in *Civil War Papers of George B. McClellan*, p. 428; Chase, diary entry for September 1, 1862, in *Inside Lincoln's Cabinet*, p. 117. Welles, *Lincoln and Seward*, pp. 193, 195; Welles, diary entry for September 1, 1862, in *Diary of Gideon Welles*, volume one, pp. 102, 103–105.

59. Welles, diary entries for September 7, 1862, and September 2, 1862, in *Diary of Gideon Welles*, volume one, pp. 105, 113; Stoddard, *Inside the White House in War Times*, p. 91; "Political Astrology at Fault," *Washington Daily National Intelligencer*, August 22, 1862.

60. William D. Kelley, in *Recollected Words*, p. 276; Alexander Davenport, September 3, 1862, in *Soldiers' Letters, From Camp, Battle-field and Prison*, ed. Lydia Minturn Post (New York: Bunce Huntington, 1865), pp. 154–55; William H. Powell, in "The Second Battle of Bull Run," *Battles and Leaders*, volume two, p. 490; "From the Army," *Washington Evening Star*, September 4, 1862; Welles, diary entry for September 6, 1862, in *Diary of Gideon Welles*, volume one, p. 111.

61. Herndon interviews with David Davis, September 20, 1866, Sarah Bush Lincoln, September 8, 1865, and James H. Matheny, 1865–66, *Herndon's Informants*, pp. 107, 348, 472; Herndon to C. O. Poole, January 5, 1886, in Herndon-Weik Papers, Library of Congress.

62. Leonard Swett to Herndon, January 17, 1866, and Isaac Cogdal interview, 1865–66, in *Herndon's Informants*, pp. 167–68, 441; John B. Alley, in Rice, *Reminiscences of Abraham Lincoln*, pp. 590–91; Herndon to Jesse Weik, February 6, 1887, in Herndon-Weik Papers, Library of Congress.

63. Isaac Cogdal interview, 1865–66, in *Herndon's Informants*, p. 441; Herndon

to Jesse Weik, February 6, 1887, in Herndon-Weik Papers, Library of Congress; AL, "Speech at Springfield, Illinois," June 26, 1857, "First Lecture on Discoveries and Inventions," April 6, 1858, "Second Lecture on Discoveries and Inventions," February 11, 1859, "Fragment on Free Labor," September 17, 1859, and "Address before the Wisconsin State Agricultural Society," September 30, 1859, in *C.W.*, volume two, pp. 407, 437–42, and volume three, pp. 356–63, 462, 476.

64. AL, "Address at Cooper Institute, New York City," February 27, 1860, in *C.W.*, volume three, p. 534; Carpenter, *Six Months at the White House*, pp. 20, 22.

65. Browning interview with John G. Nicolay, June 17, 1875, in *Oral History of Abraham Lincoln*, p. 5; AL, "Remarks to a Delegation of Progressive Friends," June 20, 1862, in *C.W.*, volume five, pp. 278–79.

66. Nicolay and Hay, *Abraham Lincoln*, volume six, pp. 341–42; AL, "Meditation on the Divine Will," September 2, 1862, in *C.W.*, volume five, p. 404.

67. "The Christian War Meeting" and "Movement of the Churches," *Chicago Tribune*, September 5 and 9, 1862; the meeting, held in Bryan Hall on September 5, had featured a number of Lincoln's Illinois friends and acquaintances, including Owen Lovejoy, Grant Goodrich, and Julian Sturtevant. One of the clergymen, William Weston Patton, was a pioneer for black civil rights and later served as president of Howard University. AL, "Reply to Emancipation Memorial Presented by Chicago Christians of All Denominations," September 13, 1862, in *C.W.*, volume five, p. 419; McClure, *Lincoln and Men of War-Times*, p. 90; Welles, "History of Emancipation," p. 245; Patton, *President Lincoln and the Chicago Memorial on Emancipation* (Baltimore: Maryland Historical Society, 1888), pp. 11–16.

68. James V. Murfin, *The Gleam of Bayonets: The Battle of Antietam and Robert E. Lee's Maryland Campaign, September, 1862* (New York: Bonanza Books, 1965), pp. 98, 386; George Boutwell to Josiah G. Holland, June 10, 1865, in J. G. Holland Papers, New York Public Library; Carpenter, *Six Months at the White House*, p. 90; Welles, diary entry for September 22, 1862, in *Diary of Gideon Welles*, volume one, p. 143.

69. Murfin, *Gleam of Bayonets*, p. 132; McClellan, "To Abraham Lincoln," September 13, 1862, in *Civil War Papers*, p. 453.

70. Boutwell to Josiah G. Holland, June 10, 1865, in J. G. Holland Papers, New York Public Library; Carpenter, *Six Months at the White House*, p. 23; Hay, diary entry for September 24, 1862, in *Inside Lincoln's White House*, p. 40; Stoddard, *Inside the White House in War Times*, p. 95; Pierrepont, in *Recollected Words*, p. 360.

71. Chase, diary entry for September 22, in *Inside Lincoln's Cabinet*, p. 150; on Chase asking for the repeat of the "vow," see Arnold, *Lincoln and the Overthrow of Slavery*, pp. 295–96; Welles, diary entry for September 22, 1862, in *Diary of Gideon Welles*, volume one, p. 143; Welles, "History of Emancipation," p. 248.

72. Blair, "The Republican Party as It Was and Is," p. 426.

73. AL, "By the President of the United States of America: A Proclamation," in *Statutes at Large*, pp. 1267–68; AL, "Preliminary Emancipation Proclamation," September 22, 1862, in *C.W.*, volume five, p. 433.

74. Frederick Seward, *Seward at Washington, Senator and Secretary of State*, volume two, p. 133; Chase, diary entry for September 22, 1862, in *Inside Lincoln's Cabinet*, pp. 151–52; Welles, diary entry for September 22, 1862, in *Diary of Gideon Welles*, volume one, p. 143; Dana to Seward, September 23, 1862, Abraham Lincoln Papers, Library of Congress; Forney, in *Recollected Words*, p. 162; Barnett to Samuel Barlow, fall 1862, December 17, 1862, and December 30, 1862, in Samuel Barlow Papers, Huntington Library, San Marino, CA.

75. Stoddard, *Inside the White House in War Times*, p. 95; Hay diary entry for September 24, 1862, in *Inside Lincoln's White House*, p. 41.

4. The Mighty Act

1. "A Proclamation," *Washington Daily National Intelligencer*, September 23, 1862; "Proclamation by the President of the U. States," *Baltimore Sun*, September 23, 1862; "Emancipation of Slaves," *Chicago Tribune*, September 23, 1862; Hamlin to AL, September 25, 1862, in *Dear Mr. Lincoln*, p. 255, and Charles Eugene Hamlin, *Life and Times of Hannibal Hamlin*, p. 439; Evans, *Letter to the President of the United States* (Washington, DC; n.p., 1862), p. 3; William B. Hesseltine and Hazel C. Wolf, "The New England Governors vs. Lincoln: The Providence Conference," *Rhode Island History* 5 (January 1946), pp. 105–13; Hesseltine, "The Altoona Conference and the Emancipation Proclamation," *Pennsylvania Magazine of History and Biography* 71 (July 1947), pp. 201–205; Samuel J. Kirkwood, "The Loyal Governors at Altoona in 1862," *Iowa Historical Record* 7–9 (1891–93), pp. 210–14; "Address of Governors to the President," in McPherson, *Political History*, pp. 232–33; AL, "Reply to Delegation of Loyal Governors," September 26, 1862, in *C.W.*, volume five, p. 441; Harris to AL, October 2, 1862, and Jesse K. Dubois to AL, October 6, 1862, in Abraham Lincoln Papers, Library of Congress; "Republican Union State Convention," *Chicago Tribune*, September 25, 1862.

2. Stevens to Alanson J. Stevens, "Speech on Conquered Provinces," April 4, 1863, to the Union League of Lancaster, in *Selected Papers*, volume one, p. 397; Andrews, "The Great American Crisis," *Continental Monthly* 4 (December 1863), p. 664; Riddle, *Recollections of War Times*, p. 204; Sumner to Benjamin Perley Poore, September 23, 1862, in *Selected Letters*, volume two, p. 122; "Speech of Charles Sumner: The Necessity of the Emancipation Policy," *Washington Daily National Republican*, October 9, 1862; Parton, *The Life of Horace Greeley* (New York: Derby & Miller, 1868), p. 502; Strong, diary entry for September 28, 1862, in *Diary of the Civil War*, pp. 262–63; "A Serenade to President Lincoln," *Washington Daily National Republican*, September 25, 1862; Whitelaw Reid, September 25, 1862, *A Radical View*, volume one, p. 233; "Emancipation," S. J. Kirkwood, "The Loyal Governors at Altoona in 1862," *Iowa Historical Record* 8 (1892), p. 211.

3. Forbes to Sumner, October 16, 1862, in *Personal Reminiscences*, p. 294; "Proclamation of the President," *Washington Daily National Intelligencer*, September 23, 1862; "Spirit of the Morning Press," *Washington Evening Star*, September 23, 1862; Piatt, *Memories of Men Who Saved the Union*, p. 150; White, *Life of Lyman Trumbull*, p. 222.

4. B. S. DeForest, *Random Sketches and Wandering Thoughts; or, What I Saw in Camp* (Albany, NY: Avery Herrick, 1866), p. 196; James G. Blaine, *Twenty Years of Congress*, volume one, p. 488; Stoddard, *Inside the White House in War Times*, p. 97.

5. Owner, diary entries for September 24 and 30, 1862, William Owner manuscript diary, Library of Congress; Macon, *Letters to Chas. O'Conor: The Destruction of the Union Is Emancipation* (Philadelphia: John Campbell, 1862), p. 9; Bruce Tap, "Race, Rhetoric and Emancipation: The Election of 1862 in Illinois," *Civil War History* 39 (June 1993), pp. 108–10; "Civil War Letters of Brigadier-General William Ward Orme, 1865–1866," ed. Harry E. Pratt, *Journal of the Illinois State Historical Society* 23 (April 1930), pp. 254–55; Davis, "No Peace before Victory," in *Speeches and Addresses Delivered in the Congress of the United States and on Several Public Occasions* (New York: Harper & Bros., 1867), pp. 315–17; "The President's Proclamation," *Washington Sunday Morning Chronicle*, September 28, 1862.

6. Douglass, in Edna Greene Medford, "Beckoning Them to the Dreamed of Promise of Freedom: African-Americans and Lincoln's Proclamation of Emancipation," *The Lincoln Forum: Abraham Lincoln, Gettysburg, and the Civil War*, eds. John Y. Simon et al. (Mason City, IA: Savas Publishing, 1999), p. 49; Eggleston, "Emancipation," p. 818; Pearson, *Life of John A.*

Andrew, volume two, pp. 50–51; Benjamin Flanders to Salmon P. Chase, November 29, 1862, Abraham Lincoln Papers, Library of Congress.

7. Hay, diary entry for September 24, 1862, in *Inside Lincoln's White House*, p. 41; McClintock, in *Recollected Words*, p. 314; Arnold, *Lincoln and the Overthrow of Slavery*, p. 301; Lincoln made a similar comment about the "harpoon" to New York governor Edwin D. Morgan.

8. AL, "To Hannibal Hamlin," September 28, 1862, and "Reply to a Serenade in Honor of Emancipation Proclamation," in *C.W.,* volume five, pp. 444, 438; Boutwell, in Rice, *Reminiscences of Abraham Lincoln,* p. 127, and "Abraham Lincoln," in *Speeches and Papers Relating to the Rebellion,* p. 362; Sumner in *Recollected Words,* p. 435; Sumner to John Murray Forbes, December 28, 1862, *Selected Letters,* volume two, p. 136.

9. Murfin, *The Gleam of Bayonets,* p. 301; McClellan, "To Henry W. Halleck," September 22, 1862, *Civil War Papers,* pp. 478; Reid, "Antietam," September 25, 1862, *A Radical View,* volume one, p. 232; McClellan, "To Abraham Lincoln," October 25, 1862, *Civil War Papers,* p. 508; AL to George B. McClellan, October 25, 1862, in *C.W.,* volume five, p. 474.

10. McClellan, "To Mary Ellen McClellan," September 25, 1862, *Civil War Papers,* p. 481; Jacob Dolson Cox, *Military Reminiscences,* volume one, pp. 359–60.

11. Hay, diary entry for September 26, 1862, *Inside Lincoln's White House,* p. 41.

12. Welles, diary entry for September 24, 1862, *Diary of Gideon Welles,* volume one, p. 146; Hay, diary entry for September 25, 1864, in *Inside Lincoln's White House,* p. 232; "Record of Dismissal of John J. Key," September 26–27, 1862, and AL, "To John J. Key," November 24, 1862, in *C.W.,* volume five, pp. 442–43, 508; Hay, "Washington Correspondence," October 1, 1862, in *Lincoln's Journalist,* pp. 317–18; Michael Burlingame, *The Inner World of Abraham Lincoln* (Urbana, IL: University of Illinois Press, 1994), pp. 185–86; Key was still begging for reinstatement in December, as seen in Browning, diary entry for December 29, 1862, in *Diary of Orville Hickman Browning,* volume one, p. 605.

13. Barnett to Barlow, September 23, 1862, in Samuel Barlow Papers, Huntington Library, San Marino, CA; Nicolay, "Conversation with Hon. O. M. Hatch, Springfield, June 1875," *An Oral History of Abraham Lincoln,* p. 16; Lamon, *Recollections of Abraham Lincoln,* pp. 147–48.

14. Chase, diary entry for October 3, 1862, in *Inside Lincoln's Cabinet,* p. 166; Noyes, *The Bivouac and the Battlefield; or Campaign Sketches in Virginia and Maryland* (New York: Harper & Bros., 1863), pp. 211–13; Holland, *Life*

of *Abraham Lincoln*, p. 399; John L. Parker, *Henry Wilson's Regiment: History of the Twenty-Second Massachusetts Infantry* (Boston: Rand Avery, 1887), p. 205; William C. Davis, *Lincoln's Men*, p. 81.

15. Hay, diary entry for September 25, 1864, in *Inside Lincoln's White House*, p. 230; McClellan, "To Mary Ellen McClellan," October 5, 1862, in *Civil War Papers*, pp. 489–90.

16. Jacob Dolson Cox, *Military Reminiscences*, volume one, pp. 360–61; Nicolay and Hay, *Abraham Lincoln*, volume six, p. 180; "General Order No. 163," in *O.R.*, Series One, volume nineteen (part two), p. 395.

17. McClellan, "To Mary Ellen McClellan," October 29, 1862, in *Civil War Papers*, p. 515; Hay, diary entry for September 25, 1864, in *Inside Lincoln's White House*, p. 232; AL, "To Carl Schurz," November 24, 1862, in *C.W.*, volume five, p. 509.

18. Forney to AL, September 26, 1862, in Abraham Lincoln Papers, Library of Congress; Chase, diary entry for October 5, 1862, in *Inside Lincoln's Cabinet*, p. 167; William Seraile, *New York's Black Regiments during the Civil War*, pp. 22–23; Wall, *Sketch of the Life of Horatio Seymour*, p. 23.

19. Trumbull, in Mark E. Neely, Jr., *The Union Divided: Party Conflict in the Civil War North* (Cambridge, MA: Harvard University Press, 2002), pp. 20, 40; Charles Sumner to John Bright, October 28, 1862, in *Selected Letters*, volume two, p. 127; Grinnell, *Men and Events of Forty Years*, p. 126; Sherman to Chase, September 28, 1862, in *The Salmon P. Chase Papers*, volume three, p. 287.

20. Hamlin, *Life and Times of Hannibal Hamlin*, p. 442; Nicolay to Therena Bates, October 16, 1862, in *With Lincoln in the White House*, p. 89; McClure, *Lincoln and Men of War-Times*, pp. 101–102.

21. Strong, diary entry for November 5, 1862, in *Diary of the Civil War*, pp. 271–72; John Torrey Morse, *Abraham Lincoln* (Boston: Houghton Mifflin, 1899), volume two, pp. 121–25; Tap, "Election of 1862 in Illinois," p. 120; Riddle, *Recollections of War Times*, p. 249; Nevins, *The War for the Union*, pp. 325–34; "The New York Election," *Washington Daily Morning Chronicle*, November 16, 1862; "The Election of 1862," *Chicago Tribune*, January 3, 1863.

22. AL, "To Carl Schurz," November 10, 1862, and "Remarks to Union Kentuckians," November 21, 1862, in *C.W.*, volume five, p. 503; Owner, diary entry for November 8, 1862, in William Owner manuscript diary, Library of Congress.

23. *History of the Thirty-fifth Regiment Massachusetts Volunteers, 1862–1865* (Boston: Mills, Knight, 1884), p. 64; French, diary entry for November 23,

1862, in *Witness to the Young Republic*, p. 414; John L. Parker, *Henry Wilson's Regiment*, p. 214; Howard Thomson and William H. Rauch, *History of the "Bucktails": Kane Rifle Regiment of the Pennsylvania Reserve Corps* (Philadelphia: Electric Printing Company, 1906), p. 223; Mary Henry, diary entry for December 13, 1862, in Joseph Henry Papers, Smithsonian Institution; Bruce Catton, *Mr. Lincoln's Army* (Garden City, NY: Doubleday, 1951), p. 339; Owner, diary entry for November 13, 1862, in William Owner manuscript diary, Library of Congress.

24. "William Parker Cutler's Congressional Diary of 1862–63," p. 320; Chandler to Trumbull, September 10, 1862, in Harris, *Public Life of Zachariah Chandler*, pp. 60–61.

25. Davis to Swett, November 26, 1862, in *Concerning Mr. Lincoln, in Which Abraham Lincoln Is Pictured as He Appeared to Letter Writers of His Time*, ed. Harry E. Pratt (Springfield, IL: Abraham Lincoln Association, 1944), p. 95; Sumner to Wendell Phillips, December 4, 1862, in *Selected Letters*, volume two, p. 133; Green, in *Recollected Words*, p. 182; AL, "To Stephen A. Hurlbut," July 31, 1863, and "Annual Message to Congress," December 8, 1864, in *C.W.*, volume six, p. 358, and volume eight, pp. 151–52; Stephens, *A Constitutional View of the Late War between the States* (Philadelphia: National Publishing Co., 1870), volume two, pp. 610–11; William C. Harris, "The Hampton Roads Peace Conference: A Final Test of Lincoln's Presidential Leadership," *Journal of the Abraham Lincoln Association* 21 (Winter 2000), p. 50. Phillip S. Paludan has the most perceptive word to say about Lincoln's "abiding commitment to an orderly, gradual process of change" in the Annual Message; see *The Presidency of Abraham Lincoln* (Lawrence, KS: University of Kansas Press, 1994), pp. 165–66.

26. Owen, *Emancipation in Peace* (New York: Loyal Publication Society No. 22, 1863), p. 4; AL, "To George Robertson," November 26, 1862, in *C.W.*, volume five, p. 512; Lowell H. Harrison, *Lincoln of Kentucky* (Lexington, KY: University Press of Kentucky, 2000), pp. 233–35. Welles met Robertson coming out of Lincoln's office on December 20. Welles, diary entry for December 20, 1862, in *Diary of Gideon Welles*, volume one, p. 199.

27. AL, "Annual Message to Congress," December 1, 1862, in *C.W.*, volume five, pp. 527, 530–31, 534–35, 536, 537.

28. "William Parker Cutler's Congressional Diary of 1862–63," p. 320; James Welling, in Rice, *Reminiscences of Abraham Lincoln*, p. 533; "Liberation of Slaves," December 4, 1862, in *Congressional Globe*, 37th Congress, 3rd Session, p. 6; McPherson, *Political History*, p. 229; George B. Cheever to AL, November 22, 1862, and T. B. Thorpe and Benjamin Flanders to Salmon

Chase, November 29, 1862, Abraham Lincoln Papers, Library of Congress; T. J. Barnett to Samuel Barlow, November 18, 1862, in Samuel Barlow Papers, Huntington Library, San Marino, CA; Mark Krug, "The Republican Party and the Emancipation Proclamation," *Journal of Negro History* 48 (July 1963), pp. 108–11.

29. Strong, diary entry for December 18, 1862, in *Diary of the Civil War*, p. 281; W. H. Coleman to William Sprague, December 17, 1862, in Sprague Special Manuscript Collection, Rare Book and Manuscript Department, Columbia University; George W. Julian, *Political Recollections*, pp. 220, 221, 227. On the cabinet showdown, see Fessenden, December 7, 1862, in *Life and Public Services of William Pitt Fessenden*, volume one, p. 264; Welles, *Lincoln and Seward*, pp. 82–83; Burton J. Hendrick, *Lincoln's War Cabinet*, pp. 390–408; Browning, diary entries for December 16 and 30, 1862, in *Diary of Orville Hickman Browning*, volume one, pp. 596–97, 607; Bates, diary entry for December 19, 1862, in *Diary of Edward Bates*, p. 269.

30. Stevens, "Speech on the Conquered Provinces, April 4, 1863," in *Selected Papers*, volume one, p. 385; John Menzies, "President's Annual Message," December 11, 1862, Vallandigham, "Object of the War," December 16, 1862, Yeaman, "President's Proclamation," December 11, 1862, and Crisfield, "President's Annual Message," December 19, 1862, in *Congressional Globe*, 37th Congress, 3rd Session, pp. 15, 76, 80.

31. Richard O. Curry, *A House Divided: A Study of Statehood Politics and the Copperhead Movement in West Virginia* (Pittsburgh: University of Pittsburgh Press, 1964), pp. 90–91, 122–23; George Ellis Moore, *A Banner in the Hills: West Virginia's Statehood* (New York: Appleton-Century-Crofts, 1963), pp. 199–200.

32. John A. Bingham, "Admission of West Virginia," December 9, 1862, *Congressional Globe*, 37th Congress, 3rd Session, p. 37; Welles, diary entries for December 24 and 26, 1862, in *Diary of Gideon Welles*, volume one, pp. 206–207; Bates, diary entry for December 30, 1862, in *Diary of Edward Bates*, p. 271; AL, "To Members of the Cabinet," December 23, 1862, and "Opinion on the Admission of West Virginia into the Union," in *C.W.*, volume six, p. 17.

33. Conway, in McPherson, *The Struggle for Equality*, p. 120; Robbins, in "Personal," *New York Tribune*, July 26, 1895; Byron Sunderland, the Senate chaplain, told Ida Tarbell a similar story for her *Life of Abraham Lincoln*, volume two, p. 123–24; "Mr. Lincoln and the Proclamation," *Chicago Tribune*, November 26, 1863; Strong, diary entry for December 27, 1862, in *Diary of the Civil War*, p. 282; Goodell, in "The Old Liners," *Illinois State Journal*, in Emmanuel Hertz Scrapbooks, Library of Congress.

34. Welles, diary entry for December 29, 1862, in *Diary of Gideon Welles*, volume one, p. 209.

35. Chase to AL, December 31, 1862, in *Life and Public Services of Salmon Portland Chase*, p. 462.

36. AL, "By the President of the United States of America: A Proclamation," *Statutes at Large*, pp. 1268–69, and "Emancipation Proclamation," in *C.W.*, volume six, p. 28.

37. Welles, diary entry for December 31, 1862, in *Diary of Gideon Welles*, volume one, p. 211; Sumner to George Livermore, January 9, 1863, in *Selected Letters*, volume two, pp. 139–40; Blue, "Friends of Freedom: Lincoln, Chase, and Wartime Racial Policy," p. 95; Janet Chase Hunt, "Setting Free a Race. How the Emancipation Proclamation Was Made," *New York Tribune*, February 22, 1893.

38. "New Year's Day in Washington," *Washington Daily National Republican*, January 2, 1863; F. W. Stanley, "Emancipation Proclamation: Lincoln's Own Story Retold," *Christian Science Monitor*, September 22, 1937.

39. Hay to William Henry Herndon, September 5, 1866, in *Herndon's Informants*, p. 331; Charles Eberstadt, *Lincoln's Emancipation Proclamation* (New York: Duschnes Crawford, 1950), p. 15; James D. Richardson, *A Compilation of the Messages and Papers of the Presidents, 1789–1897* (Washington, DC: Government Printing Office), volume six, pp. 13–17, 36–38, 89–99.

40. Benjamin B. French, "At the President's Reception, January 1, 1863," Benjamin B. French Papers, John Hay Library, Brown University; Brooks, "How We Went a-Calling on New Year's Day," January 3, 1863, in *Lincoln Observed: Civil War Dispatches of Noah Brooks*, ed. Michael Burlingame (Baltimore: Johns Hopkins University Press), p. 17; "New Year's Day Reception," *Baltimore Sun*, January 2, 1863.

41. Scovel, in "Personal Recollections of Abraham Lincoln," *Overland Monthly* 18 (November 1891), p. 506; Seward, *Seward at Washington*, volume two, p. 151; John W. Forney, in Segal, *Conversations with Lincoln*, p. 235. Lincoln told Isaac Arnold that Sumner had stopped at the White House later that afternoon to retrieve the promised pen, and "out of the half a dozen on my table, I gave him the one I had most probably used." Arnold, *Lincoln and the Overthrow of Slavery*, p. 304.

42. Colfax, *Life and Principles of Abraham Lincoln, Delivered in the Court House Square, at South Bend, April 24, 1865* (Philadelphia: James B. Rodgers, 1865), pp. 16–17; Carpenter, *Six Months at the White House*, p. 87; Eberstadt, *Lincoln's Emancipation Proclamation*, pp. 15–16, 17; Welles,

diary entry for January 1, 1863, in *Diary of Gideon Welles*, volume one, p. 212. The uncorrected engrossed copy eventually made its way into the Oliver R. Barrett Collection, and the uncorrected subscription is reproduced in Carl Sandburg's history of the Barrett collection, *Lincoln Collector: The Story of Oliver R. Barrett's Great Private Collection* (New York: Bonanza Books, 1960), p. 176.

43. "Grand Emancipation Jubilee," *New York Times*, January 1, 1863; "The President's Proclamation," *New York Times*, January 2, 1863.

44. B. Rush Plumly to AL, January 1, 1863, in the Abraham Lincoln Papers, Library of Congress; "Religious Prayer for Our Country," in *Philadelphia Inquirer*, January 2, 1863; see also the reports in the *Philadelphia Daily North American*, January 5, 1863, the *Boston Evening Transcript*, January 2, 1863, and the *Philadelphia Inquirer*, January 3, 1863; Henry Mayer, *All on Fire: William Lloyd Garrison and the Abolition of Slavery* (New York: St. Martin's Press, 1998), pp. 545–46; "Celebration of New Year's Day. Jubilee Meetings in Music Hall and Tremont Temple," in *Boston Daily Advertiser*, January 2, 1863.

45. "The Emancipation Jubilee," *Boston Evening Transcript*, January 2, 1863; Frederick Douglass, *Life and Times of Frederick Douglass, Written By Himself*, ed. R. W. Logan (New York: Collier, 1962), pp. 351–53; Eliza S. Quincy to Mary Todd Lincoln, January 2, 1863, Abraham Lincoln Papers, Library of Congress.

46. Mansfield French to Salmon Chase, January 2, 1863, in *The Salmon P. Chase Papers*, volume three, p. 352; Susie King Taylor, *Reminiscences of My Life*, p. 18; Willie Lee Rose, *Rehearsal for Reconstruction*, pp. 196–97; Quarles, *Lincoln and the Negro*, p. 146; "The Emancipation," *Philadelphia Inquirer*, January 2, 1863; "The President's Proclamation," *New York Times*, January 2, 1863; C. R. Barteau [2nd Tennessee Cavalry], January 8, 1863, in *Free at Last: A Documentary History of Slavery, Freedom and the Civil War*, p. 97; William H. Wiggins, *O Freedom! Afro-American Emancipation Celebrations* (Knoxville: University of Tennessee Press, 1987), p. 71; Mrs. A. M. French, *Slavery in South Carolina and the Ex-Slaves; or, The Port Royal Mission* (New York: W. M. French, 1862), p. 143.

47. Eberstadt, *Lincoln's Emancipation Proclamation*, pp. 17–22; the Proclamation was issued as General Orders No. 1 for 1863 by the Adjutant General's Office and dated January 2 in *General Orders Affecting the Volunteer Force: Adjutant-General's Office, 1863* (Washington, DC: Government Printing Office, 1864), pp. 1–3.

48. Bates, *Lincoln in the Telegraph Office*, pp. 146–49; McPherson, *The Negro's*

Civil War, pp. 49–50; Edward Everett Hale memorandum of a conversation with Sumner, April 26, 1862, "The War," in *Memories of a Hundred Years,* volume 2, p. 189; Scovel, "Personal Recollections of Abraham Lincoln" (1891), p. 506; Carpenter, *Six Months at the White House,* p. 90.

49. Nicolay, "The Proclamation," in *With Lincoln in the White House,* pp. 99–102; "The Proclamation," *Washington Daily National Republican,* January 2, 1863; "The Proclamation!" *Chicago Tribune,* January 3, 1863; Bullard, *The Nation's Trial: The Proclamation: Dormant Powers of the Government: The Constitution a Charter of Freedom, and Not a "Covenant with Hell"* (New York: C. B. Richardson, 1863), pp. 2–3; Conway, *Autobiography,* volume one, p. 345; Garrison, in McPherson, *The Struggle for Equality,* p. 121; Lorraine A. Williams, "Northern Intellectual Reaction to the Policy of Emancipation," *Journal of Negro History* 46 (1961), p. 184.

50. Browning, diary entries for January 1 and 29, 1863, in *Diary of Orville Hickman Browning,* volume one, pp. 609, 671; "The Emancipation Edict," *Daily National Intelligencer,* January 3, 1863; "Inauguration of the Governor of New Jersey," *Daily National Republican,* January 21, 1863; Greene, "The Emancipation Proclamation in New Jersey and the Paranoid Style," pp. 108, 113; Hesseltine, *Lincoln and the War Governors* (New York: Knopf, 1948), p. 284; McClernand to Yates, February 16, 1863, Abraham Lincoln Papers, Library of Congress.

51. Adams, January 15, 1863, in *O.R.,* Series One, volume seventeen (part two), p. 836; D. Lieb Ambrose, *History of the Seventh Regiment, Illinois Volunteer Infantry* (Springfield, IL: Illinois Journal Co., 1868), pp. 126–27; Joseph R. C. Ward, *History of the One Hundred and Sixth Regiment Pennsylvania Volunteers* (Philadelphia: F. McManus, 1906), p. 152; Thomas V. Parker, *History of the 51st Regiment of P.V. and V.V.* (Philadelphia: King & Baird, 1869), p. 282; Sgt. Frederick Godfrey [Co. A, 4th Vermont], January 29, 1863, in *A War of the People: Vermont Civil War Letters,* ed. Jeffrey D. Marshall (Hanover, NH: University Press of New England, 1999), p. 133; Charles W. Wills, *Army Life of an Illinois Soldier, Including a Day by Day Record of Sherman's March to the Sea* (Washington, DC: Globe Printing, 1906), pp. 125–26; Joseph Miller to Pvt. William Wilmoth, January 25, 1863, in Lincoln Research Files ("Emancipation Proclamation"), Illinois State Historical Library; Victor Hicken, *Illinois in the Civil War* (Urbana, IL: University of Illinois Press, 1966), pp. 128–29, 139.

52. Gray to AL, January 7, 1863, and Truman Woodruff to AL, April 12, 1863, Abraham Lincoln Papers, Library of Congress; Brownlow to Montgomery Blair, January 9, 1863, in Blair Family Papers, Library of Congress;

Theodore Clarke Smith, *The Life and Letters of James Abram Garfield* (New Haven: Yale University Press, 1925), volume one, pp. 244–45; "The President's Proclamation," *Louisville Daily Democrat*, January 3, 1863; Owner, diary entry for January 10, 1863, in William Owner manuscript diary, Library of Congress; E. Merton Coulter, *The Civil War and Readjustment in Kentucky* (Chapel Hill, NC: University of North Carolina Press, 1926), pp. 173–79; Harrison, *Lincoln of Kentucky*, pp. 176–77, and "Lincoln and Compensated Emancipation in Kentucky," *Lincoln Herald* 84 (Spring 1982), p. 15; L. C. Turner to Edwin M. Stanton, September 30, 1862, in *O.R.*, Series Two, volume four, p. 585.

53. *Illinois State Register*, January 3, 1863; *Journal of the House of Representatives of the Twenty-Third General Assembly of the State of Illinois* (Springfield, IL: Baker & Phillips, 1865), pp. 66, 78, 83, 373; Mercy Levering Conkling to Clinton Conkling, January 11, 1863, in James C. & Clinton L. Conkling Papers, Illinois State Historical Library.

54. Blaine, *Twenty Years of Congress*, volume one, p. 504; David M. Silver, *Lincoln's Supreme Court* (Urbana, IL: University of Illinois Press, 1957), pp. 136–37.

55. Curtis, *Executive Power*, in *Union Pamphlets of the Civil War, 1861–1865*, ed. Frank Freidel (Cambridge, MA: Harvard University Press, 1967), volume one, pp. 456, 458–59, 465.

56. Parker, "Habeas Corpus and Martial Law," pp. 471–517.

57. Parker, *The War Powers of Congress, and of the President: An Address Delivered before the National Club of Salem*, March 13, 1863 (Cambridge, MA: H. O. Houghton, 1863), pp. 9–10; Parker, *Constitutional Law and Unconstitutional Divinity: Letters to Rev. Henry M. Dexter and to Rev. Leonard Bacon* (Cambridge, MA: H. O. Houghton, 1863), pp. 33–34; Winthrop, "The Presidential Election of 1864," in *Addresses and Speeches on Various Occasions, from 1852 to 1867*, pp. 620–21; "The War Power," *The Old Guard* 1 (July 1863), pp. 163, 164.

58. Parker, *Constitutional Law*, pp. 32, 34, 48; Parker, *War Powers*, p. 27; Winthrop, "The Nomination of McClellan," in *Addresses and Speeches*, pp. 593–94; Osgood, "The People and the Government," *Harper's Monthly* 25 (November 1862), p. 848. See also Montgomery Throop, *The Future: A Political Essay* (New York: James G. Gregory, 1864), pp. 96–98.

59. Parker, *Constitutional Law*, pp. 15, 42, 45; Parker, *War Powers*, p. 58; Throop, *The Future*, p. 333; Osgood, "The People and the Government," p. 846. See also S. S. Nicholas, "Confiscation and Attainder," *Conservative Essays*, p. 340.

60. Lowrey, *The Commander-in-Chief: A Defence upon Legal Grounds of the Proclamation of Emancipation; and an Answer to Ex-Judge Curtis' Pamphlet, Entitled "Executive Power"* (New York: G. P. Putnam, 1863), p. 12; Charles P. Kirkland, *A Letter to the Hon. Benjamin R. Curtis, Late Judge of the Supreme Court of the United States, in Review of His Recently Published Pamphlet on the "Emancipation Proclamation" of the President* (New York: Anson D. F. Randolph, 1863), pp. 9–10; Whiting, *War Powers Under the Constitution of the United States* (1864; Glorieta, NM: Rio Grande Press, 1971), p. 58; *Cause of the War—Proclamation—Arbitrary Arrests: Speech of the Hon. George I. Post, of Cayuga in the House of Assembly, March 3rd, 1863* (New York State Central Union Committee, 1863), p. 6; Daniel Agnew, *Our National Constitution: Its Adaptation to a State of War or Insurrection* (Philadelphia: C. Sherman, Son & Co., 1863), pp. 11, 15–16; Bacon, "Reply to Professor Parker," *New Englander and Yale Review* 22 (April 1863), p. 196; Bishop, *Thoughts for the Times* (Boston: Little, Brown, 1863), pp. 20–21, 24; "The Constitution as It Is—The Union as It Was," *Continental Monthly* 2 (October 1862), p. 379; W. E. Binkley, *The Powers of the President*, pp. 122–23.

61. Gardner, *A Treatise on the Law of the American Rebellion and Our True Policy, Domestic and Foreign* (New York: J. W. Amerman, 1862), p. 11; Kirkland, *Letter to the Hon. Benjamin R. Curtis*, pp. 8, 9, 13; Lowrey, *The Commander-in-Chief*, p. 20; Ellis, *The Power of the Commander-in-Chief to Declare Martial Law, and Decree Emancipation, as Shown from B. R. Curtis* (Boston: A. Williams & Co., 1862), pp. 12–13; Bishop, *Thoughts for the Times*, pp. 26–27.

62. Lowrey, *The Commander-in-Chief*, pp. 21, 22–23; Kirkland, *Letter to the Hon. Benjamin R. Curtis*, p. 15; Gardner, *Treatise on the Law of the American Rebellion*, pp. 14–15; Blair, *Speech of the Hon. Montgomery Blair, on the Causes of the Rebellion and in Support of the President's Plan of Pacification, Delivered before the Legislature of Maryland, at Annapolis* (Baltimore, MD: Sherwood & Co., 1864), p. 18. See also George S. Boutwell, "Our Danger and Its Cause," in *Speeches and Papers Relating to the Rebellion*, p. 173, and Charles D. Drake, who described the Proclamation as "irrevocable—as irrevocable as death," in "The Wrongs to Missouri's Loyal People," in *Union and Anti-Slavery Speeches, Delivered during the Rebellion* (1864; New York: Greenwood Press, 1969), p. 339.

63. Lowrey, *The Commander-in-Chief*, p. 21; Twining, "President Lincoln's Proclamation of Freedom to the Slaves," *New Englander and Yale Review* 24 (January 1865), pp. 183–84.

64. "The President's Proclamation," *New York Times*, January 6, 1863; Fisher, *Constitutional Conflicts*, p. 308; Cooper, *By Order of the President*, pp. 17, 124, 127, 130, 133. On Lincoln's other proclamations, see *Statutes at Large*, volume twelve, pp. 1258–67. Lincoln was not excessive, either, in the number of proclamations he had issued: the presidents of the 1850s (Fillmore, Pierce, and Buchanan) had issued twenty-seven proclamations during that decade.

65. Washington and Buchanan, in Richardson, *Messages and Papers of the Presidents*, volume one, pp. 156–57, 158–60, and volume five, pp. 493–95.

66. T. J. Barnett to Samuel Barlow, November 30, 1862, Samuel Barlow Papers, Huntington Library, San Marino, CA; Lowrey, *The Commander-in-Chief*, p. 15; Nicolay and Hay, *Abraham Lincoln*, volume six, pp. 434–35; Tuckerman, in *Recollected Words*, p. 449; Chase to AL, August 29, 1862, Abraham Lincoln Papers, Library of Congress; Chase had even drafted a sample executive order for Lincoln's use; AL, "To Salmon P. Chase," September 2, 1863, in *C.W.*, volume six, p. 428.

67. AL, "Speech in the Illinois Legislature," January 11, 1838, "On the Perpetuation of Our Political Institutions," and "Speech in United States House of Representatives on Internal Improvements," June 20, 1848, in *C.W.*, volume one, pp. 67, 115, 488; Garrison, "The Great Crisis!" December 29, 1832, and "Fourth of July in Providence," July 28, 1837, in *Documents of Upheaval: Selections from William Lloyd Garrison's* The Liberator, *1831–1835*, ed. Truman Nelson (New York: Hill & Wang, 1966), pp. 54, 120; AL, "Eulogy on Henry Clay," July 6, 1852, in *C.W.*, volume two, p. 130.

68. AL, "Speech at Springfield, Illinois," June 26, 1857, in *C.W.*, volume two, p. 401, and "Sixth Joint Debate at Quincy," in *The Lincoln-Douglas Debates: The First Complete, Unexpurgated Text*, ed. Harold Holzer (New York: HarperCollins, 1993), p. 291.

69. AL, "Speech at Kalamazoo, Michigan," August 27, 1856; "Speech in Buffalo, New York," February 18, 1861; "To Simon Cameron," July 17, 1861; "To Orville H. Browning," September 22, 1861; "To Edward Bates," June 15, 1862; "Reply to Emancipation Memorial Presented by Chicago Christians of All Denominations," September 13, 1862; and "To Albert G. Hodges," April 4, 1864, in *C.W.*, volume two, p. 366, volume four, pp. 221, 451, 532, volume five, pp. 271, 421, and volume eight, p. 281.

70. AL, "Fragment on the Struggle against Slavery," July 1858, in *C.W.*, volume two, p. 482; Thoreau, "Slavery in Massachusetts," in *Reform Papers*, ed. Wendell Glick (Princeton, NJ: Princeton University Press, 1973), p. 104.

5. Fame Takes Him by the Hand

1. AL, "To the Workingmen of Manchester, England," January 19, 1863, "To Erastus Corning and Others," May 28, 1863, "To Matthew Birchard and Others," June 29, 1863, and "To James C. Conkling," August 26, 1863, in *C.W.*, volume six, pp. 53–54, 260–69, 300–306, and 406–11; Chauncey M. Depew, *My Memories of Eighty Years* (New York: Charles Scribner's Sons, 1922), 30; James A. Rawley *Abraham Lincoln and a Nation Worth Fighting For* (Wheeling, IL: Harlan-Davidson, 1996), p. 53; David Bromwich, "Lincoln's Constitutional Necessity," *Raritan* 20 (Winter 2001), p. 23. The Conkling letter was reprinted as *The War Policy of the Administration: Letter of the President to Union Mass Convention at Springfield, Illinois* (Albany: Albany Journal, 1863), and in *The Letters of President Lincoln on Questions of National Policy* (New York: H. H. Lloyd, 1863), pp. 19–22.

2. Maltby, *Life and Public Services of Abraham Lincoln*, pp. 227–28; Randall, *Lincoln the President*, pp. 176–80; Jones, *Abraham Lincoln and New Birth of Freedom*, pp. 154–56; Finney to Alice Barlow, January 8, 1862, in Charles Grandison Finney Papers, Oberlin College Archives. Lincoln wrote a second, much briefer, acknowledgment on February 2 in reply to another mass meeting in London, this time describing the war (in language foreshadowing the Gettysburg Address) as a conflict which would "test whether a government, established on the principles of human freedom, can be maintained against an effort to build one upon the exclusive foundation of human bondage." "To the Working Men of London," in *C.W.*, volume six, p. 88.

3. McPherson, *Political History*, p. 162; Klement, *Lincoln's Critics*, pp. 124–27; Hesseltine, *Lincoln and the War Governors*, pp. 329–31; Roger Long, "Copperhead Clement Vallandigham," *Civil War Times Illustrated* 20 (December 1981), pp. 23–29.

4. McPherson, *Political History*, pp. 163–77; AL, "To Ambrose E. Burnside," May 29, 1863, in *C.W.*, volume six, p. 237.

5. "From Springfield," *Chicago Tribune*, September 1, 1863; "The News," *Chicago Times*, September 2, 1863.

6. AL, "To James C. Conkling," August 26, 1863, in *C.W.*, volume six, pp. 406–407.

7. AL, "To James C. Conkling," August 26, 1863, in *C.W.*, volume six, p. 408.

8. AL, "To James C. Conkling," August 26, 1863, in *C.W.*, volume six, p. 409; Wilson, *Rise and Fall of the Slave Power*, volume three, pp. 392–93.

9. AL, "To James C. Conkling," August 26, 1863, in *C.W.*, volume six, p. 409.

10. "EXTRA. Highly Important. Declaration of Principles by the President," *Washington National Republican*, September 3, 1863; "The 'Union' Mass Meeting," *Illinois State Register*, September 4, 1863; "The Springfield Mass Meeting," *Chicago Tribune*, September 4, 1863; Moses Coit Tyler, "One of Mr. Lincoln's Old Friends," *Journal of the Illinois State Historical Society* 29 (January 1936), pp. 256–57.

11. Douglass, in Litwack, *Been in the Storm So Long*, p. 187; Mohr, *On the Threshold of Freedom*, pp. 218–19.

12. Perry, in *The American Slave, Volume 3, Part 3, South Carolina Narratives*, ed. George P. Rawick (Westport, CT: Greenwood Press, 1972), p. 261; Ash, *When the Yankees Came*, pp. 154–56; Johnson, *Black Savannah*, pp. 170–71; Barton, in *Report of the Joint Committee on Reconstruction at the First Session, Thirty-ninth Congress* (1866; Westport CT: Negro Universities Press, 1969), p. 103; Hughes, *Thirty Years a Slave*, p. 172; Charles Wilder, in *Free at Last*, p. 109; Mohr, *On the Threshold of Freedom*, p. 217; *"Jottings from Dixie": The Civil War Dispatches of Sergeant Major Stephen F. Fleharty*, ed. P. J. Reyburn and T. L. Wilson (Baton Rouge, LA: Louisiana State University Press, 1999), pp. 90–91.

13. "The Great Event," *Weekly Anglo-African*, January 3, 1863; Stanton, November 22, 1865, in *O.R.*, Series Three, volume five, p. 534; Peter Cooper, *The Death of Slavery* (New York: Loyal Publication Society No. 28, 1863), p. 4; Eliot, *The Story of Archer Alexander*, p. 59. Capturing a precise reckoning for the total number of slaves freed by the Proclamation is a daunting task. The movement of slaves, runaways, contrabands, and freedmen in and out of contraband camps and through the Union armies defied the ability of nineteenth-century record keepers to record a precise total. Of the 180,000 blacks who served in the Union Army during the war, 110,000 were ex-slaves. These enlistees were the ones most obviously freed by the terms of the Proclamation, so we may certainly take that number as the minimum directly emancipated by the Proclamation between 1863 and 1865. Herbert Aptheker estimated in 1938 that approximately 500,000 slaves had escaped into freedom during the Civil War, a number accepted by both James McPherson and Edna Greene Medford. Louis Gerteis's table of "the number of blacks organized by freedmen superintendents" puts the number of slaves "under organized control" of the Union at 237,800, but the sources which Gerteis relies upon vary in their dates, from February 1864 to November 1865; Gerteis also estimates that another 1 million slaves were "within Union lines" before the end of the war. During the Hampton Roads conference in February 1865, Seward pegged the number of slaves

emancipated by the Proclamation at 200,000, but he cited no source for that number and may have been tempted to lowball his estimate in order to assure the Confederate commissioners at the conference that the actual impact of the Proclamation was containable. It is also not clear if Seward's figure included pre-Proclamation fugitives and contrabands. On the other hand, Union General John W. Geary claimed, by "my own Action" alone, to have liberated "over 25,000 slaves" under the terms of "the President's Proclamation" in Virginia alone, which suggests a much vaster net for the Proclamation than Seward's number implies. See McPherson, *Negro's Civil War*, p. 56; Gerteis, *From Contraband to Freedman*, pp. 193–94; Medford, "Lincoln's Emancipation Proclamation," p. 58, and for Seward, see John Goode, "The Peace Conference in Hampton Roads," *Southern Historical Society Papers* 29 (January-December 1901), p. 188; Geary to Edgar Cowan, August 4, 1863, The Gilder Lehrman Collection (GLC 673), New-York Historical Society.

14. Litwack, *Been in the Storm So Long*, p. 55; H. C. Bruce, *The New Man*, p. 102; Howard C. Westwood, "Grant's Role in Beginning Black Soldiery," *Journal of the Illinois Historical Society* 79 (1986), pp. 197–212; Willard Mendenhall, diary entry for October 30, 1862, in *Missouri Ordeal, 1862–1864: Diaries of Willard Hall Mendenhall*, ed. M. M. Frazier (Newhall, CA: Carl Boyer, 1985), p. 84; Marcellus Mundy to AL, November 27, 1862, in *Free at Last*, p. 83; Rousseau to Brig. Gen. H. Whipple, January 30, 1864, in *O.R.*, Series One, volume thirty-one (part two), p. 268; Lucy Chase, January 15, 1863, in *Dear Ones at Home*, p. 23.

15. "Speech of T. Morris Chester, Esq. of Liberia, in the Cooper Institute," *Weekly Anglo-African*, February 7, 1863; Hughes, *Thirty Years a Slave*, pp. 78–79; Ford, in *The American Slave, Volume 2, Part 2, South Carolina Narratives*, ed. Rawick, p. 79; Herbert Anthony diary, North Carolina, January 6, 1863, in "Negroes Rejoiced at Lincoln Manifesto," Jackson (MI) *Citizen Patriot*, February 10, 1935; Henry Bibb, *Narrative of the Life and Adventures of Henry Bibb* (Philadelphia: Rhistoric, 1970), p. 39.

16. Clifton, in *The American Slave, Volume 2, Part 1, South Carolina Narratives*, ed. Rawick, p. 207; Hughes, *Thirty Years a Slave*, pp. 78–79; *Narrative of the Life and Adventures of Henry Bibb*, p. 39; Perry, in *The American Slave, Volume 3, Part 3, South Carolina Narratives*, ed. Rawick, p. 261; Lucy Chase, July 1, 1864, in *Dear Ones at Home*, p. 121; Elizabeth Regosin, *Freedom's Promise: Ex-Slave Families and Citizenship in the Age of Emancipation* (Charlottesville, VA: University Press of Virginia, 2002), pp. 54–78.

17. Ash, *When the Yankees Came*, p. 158; Kolchin, *American Slavery*, p. 217;

French, *Slavery in South Carolina,* p. 275; Kolchin, *First Freedom,* p. 10; Mohr, *On the Threshold of Freedom,* pp. 95–96; Paul Cimbala, "The Freedmen's Bureau, the Freedmen, and Sherman's Grant in Reconstruction Georgia, 1865–1867," *Journal of Southern History* 55 (November 1989), p. 600; LaWanda Cox, "The Promise of Land for the Freedmen," *Mississippi Valley Historical Review* 45 (December 1958), pp. 428–30; Akiko Ochiai, "The Port Royal Experiment Revisited: Northern Visions of Reconstruction and the Land Question," *New England Quarterly* 74 (March 2001), pp. 97–99.

18. George S. Boutwell, "The Power of the Government to Suppress the Rebellion," in *Speeches and Papers Relating to the Rebellion,* p. 227; McPherson, *Political History,* p. 274; McPherson, *The Struggle for Equality,* pp. 196–97; William A. Gladstone, *United States Colored Troops, 1863–1867* (Gettysburg, PA: Thomas Publications, 1990), pp. 101–107; James G. Hollandsworth, *The Louisiana Native Guards: The Black Military Experience during the Civil War* (Baton Rouge, LA: Louisiana State University Press, 1995), pp. 2, 16–17.

19. Seraile, *New York's Black Regiments,* pp. 21, 22, 24–25; George Bliss, "Autobiography," George Bliss papers, New-York Historical Society; Brough, *Dayton Speech of Hon. John Brough* (Cincinnati: National Union Association of Ohio, 1863), p. 14; J. C. Jameson to William Sprague, March 14, 1864, Sprague Special Manuscript Collection, Rare Book and Manuscript Collection, Columbia University.

20. Chandler to Lyman Trumbull, August 6, 1863, in Harris, *Public Life of Zachariah Chandler,* p. 73; AL, "To James C. Conkling," August 26, 1863, in *C.W.,* volume six, p. 410.

21. Douglass, "Address for the Promotion of Colored Enlistments," July 6, 1863, and "Why Should a Colored Man Enlist?" in *Frederick Douglass: Selected Speeches and Writings,* pp. 530, 536; Cable, c. 1863, in 55th Massachusetts Infantry (Colored), Record Group 94, National Archives; Marrs, *Life and History of the Rev. Elijah P. Marrs,* p. 22; Gary Kynoch, "Terrible Dilemmas: Black Enlistment in the Union Army during the American Civil War," *Slavery and Abolition* 18 (August 1997), pp. 113–14.

22. Denison to Chase, January 8, 1863, in *The Salmon P. Chase Papers,* volume three, p. 362; Joseph P. Glatthaar, *Forged in Battle: The Civil War Alliance of Black Soldiers and White Officers* (New York: Free Press, 1990), pp. 123–30; "Report of Brigadier General Henry E. McCulloch," June 8, 1863, in *O.R.,* Series One, volume twenty-four (part two), p. 467; Higginson, in Alice Fahs, *The Imagined Civil War,* p. 166; Grant to Henry W. Halleck, July 24, 1863,

in *The Papers of Ulysses S. Grant,* ed. John Y. Simon (Carbondale, IL: Southern Illinois University Press, 1982), volume nine, p. 110; James M. McPherson, *For Cause and Comrades: Why Men Fought in the Civil War* (New York: Oxford University Press, 1997), p. 127.

23. Carpenter, *Six Months at the White House,* p. 30; Carpenter to Theodore Munger, February 22, 1864, Theodore T. Munger Manuscripts, Sterling Library, Yale University.

24. Carpenter, *Six Months at the White House,* pp. 26–27.

25. Adams, *Letter from Washington, 1863–1865,* pp. 179–80; Schwartz, "Salmon P. Chase Critiques 'First Reading of the Emancipation Proclamation of President Lincoln,'" pp. 84–87; Hendrick, *Lincoln's War Cabinet,* pp. 427–30; Harold Holzer et al., "Francis Bicknell Carpenter (1830–1900): Painter of Abraham Lincoln and His Circle," *American Art Journal* 16 (Spring 1984), pp. 67–69; Harold Holzer et al., *The Lincoln Image: Abraham Lincoln and the Popular Print* (1984; Urbana, IL: University of Illinois Press, 2001), pp. 110–26.

26. Chase, diary entry for September 12, 1862, in *Inside Lincoln's Cabinet,* p. 137; Seward in Browning, diary entry for January 2, 1863, in *Diary of Orville Hickman Browning,* volume one, p. 609; Seward, January 2, 1863, in Seward, *Seward at Washington,* volume two, p. 151.

27. Chase, diary entry for September 11, 1862, in *Inside Lincoln's Cabinet,* pp. 134–35; Brooks D. Simpson, "'The Doom of Slavery': Ulysses S. Grant, War Aims, and Emancipation, 1861–1863," *Civil War History* 36 (March 1990), pp. 36–56; Sherman, *Memoirs of General W. T. Sherman,* ed. Charles Royster (New York: Library of America, 1990), pp. 293–95, 365; Williams, *Life in Camp: A History of the Nine Months' Service of the Fourteenth Vermont Regiment, from October 21, 1862, When It was Mustered into the U.S. Service, to July 21, 1863, Including the Battle of Gettysburg* (Claremont, NH: Claremont Manufacturing Co., 1864), p. 29; George W. Tillotson to Elizabeth Tillotson, September 4, 1864, The Gilder Lehrman Collection (GLC 4558), New-York Historical Society; Lloyd Lewis, *Sherman: Fighting Prophet* (New York: Harcourt, Brace & Co., 1932), pp. 93, 119, 129, 134, 156, 245–46, 392–94, 411; Kathleen M. Cresto, "Sherman and Slavery," *Civil War Times Illustrated* 17 (November 1978), pp. 12–21; Joseph T. Glatthaar, *The March to the Sea and Beyond: Sherman's Troops in the Savannah and Carolinas Campaigns* (New York: New York University Press, 1985), p. 57; J. G. Nind [127th Illinois], in *Soldiers' Letters, From Camp, Battle-field and Prison,* p. 291; M. P. Larry, February 16, 1863, in *Yankee Correspondence: Civil War Letters between New England Soldiers and the Home Front,* eds. Nina Silber

and M. B. Sievens (Charlottesville, VA: University Press of Virginia, 1996), p. 98.

28. H. W. Davis, "The Democratic Hue and Cry a Sham," October 30, 1862, in *Speeches and Addresses*, pp. 305–306; Hay, "Washington Correspondence," September 22, 1862, in *Lincoln's Journalist*, p. 309; Browning, diary entry for January 11, 1863, in *Diary of Orville Hickman Browning*, volume one, p. 612; Nicolay and Hay, *Abraham Lincoln*, volume six, pp. 363–67; Hay, diary entry for July 1, 1864, in *Inside Lincoln's White House*, p. 217; Gary Gallagher, "The A'Vache Tragedy," *Civil War Times Illustrated* 18 (February 1980), pp. 5–10. Chaplain Eaton thought Lincoln's "distress" over the "mistakes" of the Île de Vache project was "as keen as it was sincere. . . . The spectacle of the President of the United States, conducting the affairs of the Nation in the midst of civil war," worrying over the fate of the contrabands he had dispatched there "was a spectacle that has stayed with me all my life." See Eaton, *Grant, Lincoln and the Freedmen*, pp. 91–92.

29. Twining, "President Lincoln's Proclamation of Freedom to the Slaves," *New Englander and Yale Review* 24 (January 1865), pp. 185–86; C. C. Hazewell, "The Beginning of the End," *Atlantic Monthly* 13 (January 1864), p. 122; Eaton, in *Recollected Words*, p. 148; AL, "Proclamation of Thanksgiving for Victories," April 10, 1862, and "Reply to Emancipation Memorial Presented by Chicago Christians of All Denominations," September 13, 1862, in *C.W.*, volume five, pp. 185, 422; Patton, *President Lincoln and the Chicago Memorial on Emancipation*, pp. 26–27; Adams to Seward, June 13, 1862, in Seward Papers; Jones, *Abraham Lincoln and a New Birth of Freedom*, pp. 115–55, and "History and Mythology: The Crisis over British Intervention in the Civil War," in *The Union, the Confederacy, and the Atlantic Rim*, ed. Robert E. May (West Lafayette, IN: Purdue University Press, 1995), pp. 42–51; Randall, *Lincoln the President*, pp. 176–80; Charles Francis Adams, "Queen Victoria and the Civil War," in *Studies Military and Diplomatic, 1775–1865* (New York: Macmillan, 1911), p. 410.

30. Eaton, *Grant, Lincoln and the Freedmen*, p. 173; Augustus Montgomery to William S. Rosecrans, May 17, 1863, in Abraham Lincoln Papers, Library of Congress; Gilmore, *Personal Recollections*, pp. 150–53, and Nicolay to Gilmore, June 14, 1863, in *With Lincoln in the White House*, p. 115; Delany, "The Council-Chamber.—President Lincoln," in *Martin R. Delany: A Documentary Reader*, pp. 386–87.

31. On the 1864 "John Brown plan," see Douglass, *Life and Times of Frederick Douglass*, pp. 357–59, and Douglass to Theodore Tilton, October 15, 1864,

in *Frederick Douglass: Selected Speeches and Writings*, p. 572. Chaplain Eaton claimed that Douglass had told him personally that "I have just come from Mr. Lincoln. . . . He treated me as a man; he did not let me feel for a moment that there was any difference in the color of our skins." But this is so similar to Douglass's own recollection in A. T. Rice's *Reminiscences* (p. 193) that it is more likely Eaton confected his account from Douglass's article. See Eaton, *Grant, Lincoln and the Freedmen*, p. 175.

32. Holman, "Homestead Law—Again," in *Congressional Globe*, 38th Congress, 1st Session, p. 1189; AL, in Segal, *Conversations with Lincoln*, p. 263.

33. Stephen Pearl Andrews, "The Great American Crisis," *Continental Monthly* 5 (January 1864), p. 96; Wayland, "Letter to a Peace Democrat," *Atlantic Monthly* 12 (December 1863), p. 777; Joel Prentiss Bishop, *Thoughts for the Times*, pp. 32–33; "Before Richmond, Feb. 3, 1865," in *Thomas Morris Chester, Black Civil War Correspondent*, ed. R. J. M. Blackett (Baton Rouge, LA: Louisiana State University Press, 1989), p. 249; Litwack, *Been in the Storm So Long*, p. 129.

34. Mitgang, *Abraham Lincoln: A Press Portrait*, pp. 320, 322; Nevins, *The War for the Union: War Becomes Revolution, 1862–1863*, pp. 235–36; Mark Neely, "Lincoln and the Theory of Self-Emancipation," in *The Continuing Civil War: Essays in Honor of the Civil War Round Table of Chicago*, eds. John Y. Simon and Barbara Hughett (Dayton, OH: Morningside Press, 1992), pp. 45–59; AL, "Annual Message to Congress," December 8, 1863, "Annual Message to Congress," December 6, 1864, and "To Isaac Schermerhorn," September 12, 1864, in *C.W.*, volume eight, pp. 1, 51, 152; Williams, *Life in Camp*, p. 64; Drake, "The Wrong to Missouri's Loyal People," in *Union and Anti-Slavery Speeches*, p. 339; Owen, *The Wrong of Slavery, the Right of Emancipation and the Future of the African Race in the United States* (Philadelphia: J. P. Lippincott, 1864), pp. 170–71; Owen, *The Conditions of Reconstruction: In a Letter from Robert Dale Owen to the Secretary of State* (New York: W. C. Bryant, 1863), p. 19; Blair, *Speech of the Hon. Montgomery Blair . . . at Annapolis*, p. 18.

35. Ash, *When the Yankees Came*, pp. 154–56; Singleton, *Recollections of My Slavery Days*, eds. K. M. Charron and D. S. Cecelski (Raleigh, NC: North Carolina Division of Archives and History, 1999), p. 49; Wilder, in *Free at Last*, eds. Berlin et al., p. 109; Pettis, Volunteer Enlistment Papers, 6th U.S. Colored Cavalry, Record Group No. 94, National Archives; McCline, *Slavery in the Clover Bottoms*, p. 51; Hill, Parsons, and Thornton in *Report of the Joint Committee on Reconstruction at the First Session, Thirty-Ninth Congress*, pp. 55, 59, 53.

36. Julian, *Political Recollections*, pp. 226–27; Nicolay and Hay, *Abraham Lincoln*, volume six, pp. 435, 440; Browning, diary entry for November 24, 1864, in *Diary of Orville Hickman Browning*, volume one, p. 694; Henderson, in Stevens, *A Reporter's Lincoln*, p. 172; Wilson, *History of the Anti-Slavery Measures*, p. 270; White, *Life of Lyman Trumbull*, pp. 223–24; Michael Vorenberg, "The Civil War, the Abolition of Slavery, and the Thirteenth Amendment," unpublished Ph.D. dissertation, Harvard University, 2000, pp. 64–78.

37. AL, "Memorandum concerning His Probable Failure of Re-election," August 23, 1864, in *C.W.*, volume seven, p. 514; Michael Vorenberg, " 'The Deformed Child': Slavery and the Election of 1864," in *Civil War History* 47 (September 2001), pp. 240–57; Hay, diary entry for October 13, 1864, in *Inside Lincoln's White House*, p. 241; Noah Brooks, "A Good Point Well Put," December 9, 1864, in *Lincoln Observed*, p. 154.

38. Tarbell, *Life of Lincoln*, volume two, p. 215; AL, "Annual Message to Congress," December 6, 1864, in *C.W.*, volume eight, p. 149; Vorenberg, "The Civil War, the Abolition of Slavery, and the Thirteenth Amendment," pp. 217–27, 242–45.

39. AL, "Response to a Serenade," February 1, 1865, in *C.W.*, volume eight, p. 254; Barrett, *Life of Abraham Lincoln*, pp. 684–86; Arnold, *Lincoln and the Overthrow of Slavery*, pp. 577, 588.

40. Blight, *Keeping Faith in Jubilee*, p. 186; Owen, *The Wrong of Slavery*, pp. 198–200; Forney, *Anecdotes of Public Men*, volume one, pp. 321, 322; Adams, February 27, 1865, *Letter from Washington, 1863–1865*, pp. 232–33; David Montgomery, *Beyond Equality: Labor and the Radical Republicans, 1862–1872* (New York: Knopf, 1967), p. 83.

41. Wilson, *Rise and Fall of the Slave Power*, volume three, pp. 507–15; George Julian, "Indemnification Bill," February 18, 1863, *Congressional Globe*, 37th Congress, 3rd Session, p. 1069; Julian, *Political Recollections*, p. 242; McPherson, *Struggle for Equality*, pp. 407–409; Foner, *Reconstruction: America's Unfinished Revolution*, p. 246; LaWanda Cox, "The Promise of Land for the Freedmen," pp. 431–32.

42. Sturtevant, "The Destiny of the African Race in the United States," *Continental Monthly* 2 (May 1863), p. 602; Boutwell, "Equal Suffrage" [December 1865] and "Rights of the Rebel States" [May 4, 1864], in *Speeches and Papers Relating to the Rebellion*, pp. 322–23, 417; McKaye, *The Mastership and Its Fruits: The Emancipated Slave Face to Face with His Old Master* (New York: W. C. Bryant & Co., 1864), pp. 14–15, 18; W. W. Broom, *Great and Grave Questions for American Politicians, with a Topic for America's*

Statesmen (New York: C. S. Westcott & Co., 1865), p. 42; McPherson, *For Cause and Comrades*, p. 128; Langston, "Citizenship and the Ballot," *Freedom and Citizenship*, pp. 99–100.

43. Edwin M. Stanton to George F. Shepley, August 24, 1863, in *O.R.*, Series One, volume twenty-six (part one), pp. 694–95; "Circumventing the Dred Scott Decision: Edward Bates, Salmon P. Chase, and the Citizenship of African-Americans," ed. J. P. McClure et al., *Civil War History* 43 (December 1997), pp. 279–80; AL, "To Michael Hahn," March 13, 1864, and "To Stephen A. Hurlbut," November 14, 1864 in *C.W.*, volume seven, p. 243, and volume eight, p. 107; Cox, *Lincoln and Black Freedom*, pp. 77–78, 94–95, 98.

44. AL, "To James Wadsworth," and "Last Public Address," April 11, 1865, in *C.W.*, volume seven, p. 101, and volume eight, pp. 403–404; Stoddard, in *Recollected Words*, p. 427; Chambrun, "Personal Recollections of Mr. Lincoln," *Scribners Magazine* 13 (January 1893), p. 36; Hay, "Recollection of a Remark by Lincoln," in *At Lincoln's Side*, p. 103. On the "Wadsworth Letter," see Arnold, *Lincoln and the Overthrow of Slavery*, pp. 656–57; Holland, *Life of Abraham Lincoln*, pp. 513–14; Ludwell H. Johnson, "Lincoln and Equal Rights: The Authenticity of the Wadsworth Letter," in *Journal of Southern History* 32 (February 1966), pp. 83–87; and Harold M. Hyman, "Lincoln and Equal Rights for Negroes: The Irrelevancy of the 'Wadsworth Letter,' " in *Civil War History* 12 (September 1966), pp. 258–66.

45. Edward Steers, *Blood on the Moon: The Assassination of Abraham Lincoln* (Lexington, KY: University Press of Kentucky, 2001), p. 91.

46. "By the President of the United States of America. A Proclamation," in *Radical Republicans and Reconstruction, 1861–1870*, ed. Harold Hyman (Indianapolis, IN: Bobbs-Merrill, 1967), pp. 249–52; Christine Bolt, *Victorian Attitudes to Race* (London: Routledge & Kegan Paul, 1971), p. 52; Julian, *Political Recollections*, p. 243.

47. Julian, *Political Recollections*, p. 263; Osgood, "Our Lessons in Statesmanship," *Harper's Monthly* 30 (March 1865), p. 477; Drake, "Immediate Emancipation in Missouri," June 16, 1863, in *Union and Anti-Slavery Speeches*, p. 290; Kimball, "Our Government and the Blacks," *Continental Monthly* 5 (April 1864), p. 435.

48. Wilder, in Engs, *Freedom's First Generation*, p. 106; Broom, *Great and Grave Questions*, p. 65; McKaye, *The Mastership and Its Fruits*, pp. 35, 37; Kenneth S. Greenberg, "The Civil War and the Redistribution of Land: Adams County, Mississippi, 1860–1870," *Agricultural History* 52 (April 1978), p. 303; Richard Paul Fuke, "A Reform Mentality: Federal Policy toward Black Marylanders, 1864–1868," *Civil War History* 22 (September

1976), p. 217; Harold Hyman, *A More Perfect Union*, pp. 503–505; James M. McPherson, *Ordeal by Fire: The Civil War and Reconstruction* (New York: Knopf, 1982), pp. 533–34; Foner, *Reconstruction*, p. 272. See the case summaries on *Slaughterhouse Cases* and *Civil Rights Cases* in *American Legal History: Causes and Materials*, eds. Kermit Hall, W. H. Wiecek, and Paul Finkelman (New York: Oxford University Press, 1991), pp. 236–42.

49. J. W. Shaffer to Trumbull, December 25, 1865, in White, *Life of Lyman Trumbull*, p. 242; B. J. Hubbard to William Sprague, February 10, 1866, in Sprague Special Manuscript Collection, Rare Book and Manuscript Collection, Columbia University; Pete Daniel, "The Metamorphosis of Slavery," *Journal of American History* 66 (June 1979), p. 90; Christopher Memminger to Schurz, April 26, 1871, in *Speeches, Correspondence and Political Papers*, volume two, p. 256.

50. Charles H. Smith, *Bill Arp So-Called: A Side Show of the Southern Side of the War* (New York: Metropolitan Record Office, 1866), p. 8; Fields, *Slavery and Freedom on the Middle Ground*, pp. 140–41; Ravenal, diary entry for May 25, 1865, in *Private Journal of Henry William Ravenal*, p. 238; Peter Kolchin, *First Freedom*, p. 30; Johnson, in *The American Slave, Volume 3, Part 3, South Carolina Narratives*, ed. Rawick, p. 45.

51. Edmund Kirke, *Down in Tennessee and Back by Way of Richmond* (New York: Carleton, 1864), pp. 26–27; Fields, *Slavery and Freedom on the Middle Ground*, pp. 138–39; W. M. Grosvenor, "The Rights of the Nation, and the Duty of Congress," *New Englander and Yale Review* 24 (October 1865), p. 756; McKaye, *The Mastership and Its Fruits*, pp. 22, 29.

52. Taylor, *Reminiscences of My Life*, p. 61; Bruce, *The New Man*, p. 117; Bernard E. Powers, *Black Charlestonians: A Social History, 1822–1885* (Fayetteville, AR: University of Arkansas Press, 1994), p. 76; Kolchin, *First Freedom*, p. 45.

53. Broom, *Great and Grave Questions*, pp. 51–52; Jacqueline Jones, *Soldiers of Light and Love: Northern Teachers and Georgia Blacks, 1865–1873* (Chapel Hill, NC: University of North Carolina Press, 1980), p. 53; Steven Elliott Tripp, *Yankee Town, Southern City: Race and Class Relations in Civil War Lynchburg* (New York: New York University Press, 1997), pp. 170, 179; Seraile, *New York's Black Regiments*, p. 102; McClure, *Old Time Notes of Pennsylvania*, volume one, pp. 595–96; Maxwell Whiteman, *Gentlemen in Crisis: The First Century of the Union League of Philadelphia, 1862–1962* (Philadelphia, 1975), p. 140; David Montgomery, "Radical Republicanism in Pennsylvania, 1866–1873," *Pennsylvania Magazine of History and Biography* 85 (October 1961), pp. 449–50; Herman Belz, "Equality and the Four-

teenth Amendment," in *Abraham Lincoln, Constitutionalism, and Equal Rights in the Civil War Era* (New York: Fordham University Press, 1998), pp. 184–86; Stuart McConnell, *Glorious Contentment: The Grand Army of the Republic, 1865–1900* (Chapel Hill, NC: University of North Carolina Press, 1992), pp. 213–14; Bay, *The White Image in the Black Mind*, p. 88.

54. Langston, "The Exodus" [1879], in *Freedom and Citizenship: Selected Speeches and Addresses* (Washington, 1883), pp. 233–34; Peter Kolchin, "Thoughts on Emancipation in Comparative Perspective: Russia and the United States South," *Slavery and Abolition* 11 (December 1990), pp. 360, 365; Dale E. Peterson, *Up from Bondage: The Literature of Russian and African American Soul* (Durham, NC: Duke University Press, 2000), p. 61; Seymour Drescher, *The Mighty Experiment: Free Labor versus Slavery in British Emancipation* (New York: Oxford University Press, 2002), pp. 168, 175, 193, 200; Eric Hobsbawm, *The Age of Capital, 1848–1875* (New York: Penguin/Meridian, 1984), pp. 202–207.

55. Foner, *Nothing but Freedom: Emancipation and Its Legacy* (Baton Rouge, LA: Louisiana State University Press, 1983), p. 3; Foner, "Introduction" to *Freedom's Lawmakers: A Directory of Black Officeholders during Reconstruction* (New York: Oxford University Press, 1993), pp. xiii–xxxi; Kolchin, *American Slavery*, p. 218; Foner, "The Ideology of the Republican Party," *The Birth of the Grand Old Party: The Republicans' First Generation* (Philadelphia: University of Pennsylvania Press, 2002), pp. 27–28; Herman Belz, "The New Orthodoxy in Reconstruction Historiography," in *Abraham Lincoln, Constitutionalism, and Equal Rights in the Civil War Era*, pp. 162–69.

56. Newton, *Out of the Briars: An Autobiography and Sketch of the Twenty-ninth Regiment Connecticut Volunteers* (1910; Miami: Mnemosyne Publishing, 1969), p. 76; Boutwell, "Abraham Lincoln," in *Speeches and Papers Relating to the Rebellion*, p. 368; Sumner to Lot M. Morrill, June 15, 1865, in *Selected Letters*, volume two, p. 306.

57. Washington, "A Sunday Evening Talk" [February 8, 1891], in *The Booker T. Washington Papers*, ed. Louis Harlan (Urbana, IL: University of Illinois Press, 1974), volume 3, p. 130; Washington, *Up from Slavery: An Autobiography* (New York: Doubleday, Page & Co., 1901), p. 309; Lorenzo J. Greene, diary entry for March 26, 1931, in *Selling Black History for Carter G. Woodson: A Diary, 1930–33*, ed. A. F. Strickland (Columbia, MO: University of Missouri Press, 1996), p. 333; Roy P. Basler, *The Lincoln Legend: A Study in Changing Conceptions* (New York: Houghton Mifflin, 1935), p. 220.

58. Michael Kammen, *Mystic Chords of Memory* (New York: Knopf, 1991), pp.

122, 123–24; Elizabeth Hyde Botume, *First Days amongst the Contrabands* (Boston: Lee & Shepard, 1893), pp. 203–205; William Wiggins, *O Freedom! Afro-American Emancipation Celebrations* (Knoxville: University of Tennessee Press, 1987), pp. 16–17.

59. David W. Blight, *Race and Reunion: The Civil War in American Memory* (Cambridge: Harvard University Press, 2001), pp. 370–74; Johnson, *Fifty Years & Other Poems* (Boston: Cornhill, 1917), pp. 1, 13.

60. Pillsbury, *Lincoln and Slavery* (Boston: Houghton, Mifflin, 1913), pp. 10–11; Henry W. Wilbur, *President Lincoln's Attitude towards Slavery and Emancipation, with a Review of Events before and since the Civil War* (Philadelphia: Walter H. Jenkins, 1914), p. 162; Robeson, *Paul Robeson Speaks: Writings, Speeches, Interviews,* ed. Philip S. Foner (New York: Brunner/Mazel, 1978), pp. 186, 283.

61. Du Bois, "Abraham Lincoln" [May 1922] and "Lincoln Again" [September 1922], in *W. E. B. Du Bois: Writings,* ed. Nathan Huggins (New York: Library of America, 1986), 1196, 1197–98.

62. Du Bois, "The Negro and Social Reconstruction" [1936], "Address at American Labor Party Election Rally," October 22, 1952, and "A Petition to the Honorable John F. Kennedy" [1961], in *Against Racism: Unpublished Essays, Papers, Addresses, 1887–1961,* by W. E. B. Du Bois, ed. Herbert Aptheker (Amherst, MA: University of Massachusetts Press, 1985), pp. 107, 284, 319.

63. Robert Goldwin, "Preface" to *100 Years of Emancipation* (Chicago: Rand Mc-Nally, 1964), n.p.; Baldwin, *The Fire Next Time* (New York: Dell Publishing, 1964), pp. 22, 115; Duberman, *In White America* (New York: New American Library, 1964).

64. Wilkins, "A Man's Life" (1982), in *The Eyes on the Prize Civil Rights Reader: Documents, Speeches, and Firsthand Accounts from the Black Freedom Struggle,* eds. Clayborne Carson et al. (New York: Viking Penguin, 1991), p. 324; King, "Call to a Prayer Pilgrimage for Freedom," April 5, 1957, and "Role of the Church in Facing the Nation's Chief Moral Dilemma" [1957], in *The Papers of Martin Luther King, Jr.,* ed. Clayborne Carson (Berkeley, CA: University of California Press, 2000), volume four, pp. 151, 191; *A Testament of Hope: The Essential Writings of Martin Luther King Jr.,* ed. James M. Washington (San Francisco: Harper & Row, 1986), p. 279; Bennett, "Was Abe Lincoln a White Supremacist?" *Ebony* 23 (February 1968), pp. 35–38, 40–42; Vivian Lyon Moore, "Was the Emancipation Proclamation Important?" *Michigan History* 46 (December 1962), pp. 333–34.

65. Michael Eric Dyson, "Black Youth, Pop Culture, and the Politics of Nostalgia," *Race Rules: Navigating the Color Line* (New York: Random House, 1996), pp. 135–40; Wilson, *The Bridge over the Racial Divide: Rising Inequality and Coalition Politics* (Berkeley, CA: University of California Press, 1999), p. 45; Patterson, *The Ordeal of Integration: Progress and Resentment in America's Racial Crisis* (Washington, DC: Civitas/Counterpoint, 1997), pp. 15–27.

66. Bennett, "Preface" to *Forced into Glory: Abraham Lincoln's White Dream* (Chicago: Johnson Publishing, 2000).

67. Raymond, *History of the Administration of President Lincoln* (New York: Derby & Miller, 1864), p. 479; Boutwell, in Rice, *Reminiscences of Abraham Lincoln*, pp. 133–34.

68. Owen, *The Conditions of Reconstruction*, p. 19; Holland, *Life of Abraham Lincoln*, pp. 70–71, 543; Arnold, *Lincoln and the Overthrow of Slavery*, pp. 295–96, and *Life of Abraham Lincoln*, pp. 253, 267; Welling, in Rice, *Reminiscences of Abraham Lincoln*, p. 517; Merrill D. Peterson, *Lincoln in American Memory* (New York: Oxford University Press, 1994), pp. 52–59; Joshua F. Speed, *Reminiscences of Abraham Lincoln and Notes of a Visit to California* (Louisville, KY: Bradley & Gilbert, 1896), p. 43; Barry Schwartz, *Abraham Lincoln and the Forge of National Memory* (Chicago: University of Chicago Press, 2000), p. 92; John Drinkwater, *Lincoln, The World Emancipator* (New York: Houghton, Mifflin, 1920), p. 16; Basler, "The Emancipator and Savior of the Union," in *The Lincoln Legend*, pp. 202–203.

69. Hollister, *Life of Schuyler Colfax*, p. 253; Reid, "Article on Lincoln and Negro Suffrage," July 23, 1865, in Hyman, *Radical Republicans and Reconstruction*, pp. 187–88.

70. Douglass, "Oration in Memory of Abraham Lincoln, Delivered at the Unveiling of the Freedman's Monument in Memory of Abraham Lincoln, in Lincoln Park, Washington, D.C., April 14, 1876," *Frederick Douglass: Selected Speeches and Writings*, pp. 621, 624.

Index

About the Author

ALLEN C. GUELZO is the Grace Ferguson Kea Professor of American History at Eastern University (St. Davids, Pennsylvania), where he also directs the Templeton Honors College. He is the author of five books, most recently the highly acclaimed *Abraham Lincoln: Redeemer President*, which won the Lincoln Prize for 2000.